REMOTENESS RECONSIDERED

REMOTENESS RECONSIDERED

The Atacama Desert and International Law

CHRISTOPHER R. ROSSI

University of Michigan Press
Ann Arbor

Published in the United States of America by
the University of Michigan Press
Printed and bound by CPI Group (UK) Ltd, Croydon, CR0 4YY

First published July 2021

A CIP catalog record for this book is available from the British Library.

ISBN 978-0-472-13257-7 (hardcover : alk. paper)

ISBN 978-0-472-12905-8 (ebook)

Cover photo: Iván A. Cortés Gómes. Mano Del Desierto sculpture by Mario Irarrázabal.

For Nicholas "Christian"

Contents

Digital materials related to this title can be found on the Fulcrum platform via the following citable URL https://doi.org/10.3998/mpub.11728155

Acknowledgments

I forever remain grateful to librarians for valuable assistance, including Don Ford, foreign, comparative, and international law librarian at the Iowa Law College; Ellen L. Jones, university reference librarian; Brett Cloyd, university research and government information librarian; Ryan Moore, information specialist at the Geography and Map Division of the Library of Congress; and once again, Arthur E. Bonfield, associate dean for research emeritus and Allan D. Vestal Chair and former head law librarian at the Iowa Law College. I am also grateful to John Reitz, Edward Carmody Professor of Law and director of graduate programs and visiting scholars, and Adrien Katherine Wing, associate dean for international and comparative law programs and Bessie Dutton Murray Professor of Law, for unhesitatingly encouraging and supporting my research. I also thank Jonathan C. Carlson, Victor and Carol Alvarez Fellow in Law, and Stella Burch Elias, professor and Chancellor William Gardiner Hammond Fellow in Law for comments on draft chapters. Iowa Law College students Thais Fernandes Pereira and Gada Al Herz helped to compile the bibliography, and Hsin-Yi "Sandy" Hsieh did a wonderful job tracking down errant or missing details and tending to bibliographic details.

I also extend particular thanks to Charles Jones, emeritus reader in international relations at Wolfson College, Cambridge, for insightful and pointed criticisms, and cartographic historian Chet Van Duzer, for clarifying some oddities associated with Martin Waldseemüller's amazing and curious early-sixteenth-century maps. I am grateful again to Arthur Bonfield for granting me access to his private collection of sixteenth- and seventeenth-century primary sources on the Age of Discovery, and for guiding me through the works of Samuel Purchas, Alexander Esquemelin, Amédée François Frezier, William Dampier, and other important recorders of the early modern age of exploration. University of Texas at Arlington professor emeritus Richard Francaviglia, currently associate scholar at Willamette University and the leading geographic authority on the Atacama Desert, provided careful and incisive comments about the history, geography, and cartography of the region that I think few others would ever have taken the time to detail. I am grateful to Richard for the time and energy he devoted to exploring connections between international law and geography. Claudio G. Hidalgo, a native of the Atacama and a longtime friend, provided perspective and backstories about the region. And once again, I thank Drake Nyemaster and Nick Onuf for helpful comments and suggestions.

University of Michigan Press editorial director Elizabeth Sherburn Demers saw immediate merit in this project and guided it along its way to publication. I am thankful to her for her editorial oversight, and to acquisitions assistant Haley Winkle for able day-to-day fixes. I am also particularly grateful to Daniel Otis for his exceptional review of the text, notes, and bibliographic material, and to managing editor Marcia LaBrenz.

Portions of this work were presented at the International Studies Association Midwest Conference in St. Louis in November 2019, at the American Society of International Law Midwest Works-in-Progress Interest Group Conference at John Marshall Law School in September 2019, and at the European Society of International Law Annual Convention at the National and Kapodistrian University of Athens in 2019. Portions of this work appeared or are reworked from articles published by the board of trustees of the Leland Stanford Junior University ("The Transboundary Dispute Over the Waters of the Silala/Siloli: Legal Vandalism and Goffmanian Metaphor," 53[1] *Stanford Journal of International Law* 55 [2017]; and the George Washington University ("The *Nomos* of Climate Change and the Sociological Refugee in a Sinking Century," 50[3] *George Washington International Law Review* 613 [2018]). I thank Robert Cronan of Lucidity Information Design for the cartographic depictions of the Atacama; the Geography and Map Division of the Library of Congress for the detailed images of Waldseemüller's 1507 *Universalis cosmographia* and 1516 *Carta marina*; and Iván Cortés, born to the Atacama, for the cover photo.

I am most grateful to my family for support and encouragement. This book is dedicated to my son, Nicholas Christian, who patiently waited his turn. I admire him and hope this effort lives up to his high standards.

ONE

Introduction

This book is about international law and international relations of the Americas. It attempts to reframe the understanding of their roles in the development of hemispheric relations by focusing on their encounter with the spatial dynamic of remoteness. Accordingly, this project rethinks the idea of boundaries. Boundaries frame and constrain our understanding about the practice and operation of international law, and boundaries also shape and frame our understanding of remoteness.

Remoteness depends on a combination of spatial factors. Temporality and geography inform spatial dynamics of remoteness. However, remoteness also can be understood by measurements other than time and space. Incongruities and discontinuities of historiography affect the idea of remoteness. So too do the inherent limitations of periodization and the hidden politics of cartography, along with the place-naming significance of toponyms. Doctrinal voices located within and removed from the power centers of academia also frame our understanding of remoteness, as does (not as obviously) the lingering significance of medieval travelogue literature, which importantly affected descriptions of the New World by European discoverers. This literature is interwoven with sentiments of the *mission civilisatrice* and dominant and historically informed international law frameworks, which continue to cast long shadows over the Americas.

These elements of remoteness help to orient the idea of remoteness. They provide a spatial compass to navigate problems of proximity that span the disciplines of international law and international relations. They also specifically apply to the turbulent history of the Americas. This story, in underexplored ways, has been constructed by dominant historiographic and doctrinal narratives. It has also been affected by cartographic presentation. Historians deal with remoteness when they periodize history, turning attention to seminal events such as Westphalia or the Grotian Moment while, by implication, casting shrouds around other places or subjects that then take on secondary significance. Cartographers also project viewpoints that they have a hand in creating. Each map they create presents a point of view, with preferences, skewings, and toponyms suggestive of the power of place-naming.

When untethered from the complexity of these broad navigational mooring lines, remoteness narrows its orientation and becomes an oblique measure of distance, in line with dominant Euclidean constructions. However, its contribution as a conceptual and explanatory tool in the international law and relations of the Americas connotes much more meaning than does the standard Euclidean formulation.

This point is artfully suggested by diplomats, who practice the "carefully calibrated ritual" of managing "social distances among states."[1] Diplomats articulate social rules and maintain relative distance among states. They attach a performative function to distance by invoking its name to buy time, check in with the home country, and develop or coordinate strategies to meet state objectives and new circumstances. Immanuel Kant (1724–1804) understood the nonlinear idea of distance as well. His *Third Definitive Article for a Perpetual Peace* located a right of universal hospitality (perhaps better understood as nonhostility) at the entrances of "foreign territory"—or across the "unappropriated regions" and "[u]ninhabitable portions of the [earth]," where people come into contact.[2] However, Kant projected a porosity to these buffer lands based on the ebb and flow of human interaction, not Euclidean logic. Even amid these distant or remote regions, his Enlightenment project extended to travelers a status-conferring membership in a burgeoning cosmopolitan world.

Critical orientations and methodologies, for instance Third World approaches to international law and postcolonial legal scholarship, also attempt to rework constructions of remoteness. They seek to express orientations that recalibrate dominant measurements of remoteness, although they often struggle to be heard. One wonders what crowding-out effects await critical perspectives as standard narrative treatments of international relations turn toward framing the relatively remote, unsecure, yet

---

1. Nicholas Onuf, *Relative Strangers: Reflections on Hospitality, Social Distance and Diplomacy*, *in* HOSPITALITY AND WORLD POLITICS 173, 186 ("carefully calibrated ritual"), 190 ("social distance") (Gideon Baker ed., 2013).

2. IMMANUEL KANT, PERPETUAL PEACE: A PHILOSOPHICAL ESSAY 137 ("foreign territory"), 138 ("[u]ninhabitable portions") (1917).

fast-changing landscapes of the High Arctic, the Amazon, Antarctica, the deep sea, outer space, unfolding extensions of continental shelves, High Himalayan glacial melt and its effects on transboundary basins and watercourses, and whatever else remains of the rapidly shrinking global commons. This study of remoteness has a hemispheric emphasis, although the conceptual adaptation of the idea of remoteness can certainly be applied to other and emerging contexts as well. Adding emphasis to international law's spatiality can yield insights about the problems and prospects of creating sustainable international legal futures.

State-centricity and Eurocentricity are often used as tropes to highlight dominant, perhaps transhistorical or timeless narratives of hemispheric relations. However, lessons can be learned about these narratives by looking at them from the edges of their well-trodden pathways, by uncovering muffled voices, or as this book attempts, by uncovering shrouded outposts and frontiers that provide subtle, regional coloration to the asserted timeless truths of international relations' grand analytical tools—sovereignty, anarchy, power, and the state.

Deserts provide convenient and powerful backdrops for perceptions of remoteness, even though popular stereotypes tend to diminish their complex characteristics. Saguaro cacti of the Sonora Desert attach to images of Mexican culture, cowboys, and almost an entire genre of western movies. The Kalahari Desert projects images of red-tinted sand, fantastic wildlife, and safaris. The clay pans of Sossusvlei and the Skeleton Coast in the Namib Desert frame commonplace images of desolation. And the film adaptation of T. E. Lawrence's *Seven Pillars of Wisdom* congers up lofty images of Arabian Desert sand dunes while projecting meta-images of romanticized nomadic life.

This book employs the Atacama Desert as a trope. It is often portrayed as a harsh and overlooked frontierland, casually described as a void despite harboring tremendous mineral wealth. Its emptiness nevertheless attracts intense attention and harbors much potential for conflict. Its consignment to the remote regions of international law abridges the spectrum of its human geography and arbitrarily masks the tensions of geographic space that conflict with environmental and human needs. The Atacama, reconceived from perspectives of extractivism, indigenous rights, water scarcity, and cross-border resource management, represents international law's interface with geospace. It provides an appropriately remote geospatial touchstone or mooring line to center our discussion of the remoteness concept.

Removed from the centrality of dominant international relations discourse, the Atacama naturally tends to drift away from standard retellings of hemispheric relations—why else would it be considered remote? The region is employed as a trope to assert the underappreciated perspective on how international law and relations have developed in the Americas. It is employed to refresh our general understanding about how spatial orientations frame, limit, and sometimes occlude our understanding of history. Remoteness, projected onto the concrete landscape of the Atacama, points to the structural difficulties and deficiencies of historical international law and contemporary international relations. Remoteness contributes to our understanding of international law's development in the Americas by providing focal points about the way hemispheric international relations have been framed. Remote vantage points reshape perspectives that have constructed and clouded hemispheric history and historiography. These perspectives are seldom seen and rarely considered. They can provide critical perspectives that better hone or perhaps recast the predominant storylines of international law and international relations.

More than a retrospective exercise, this book also argues that the construct of remoteness affects current issues confronting hemispheric relations. It contributes to an understanding of the contentious incorporation of neoliberal principles of international economic law across the hemisphere. It accounts for competing mineral resource policies that variously express sovereign concerns over natural resources within Latin American countries. It helps to explain the continuing abridgement of human rights and indigenous rights among the peoples of the Americas, casting them as resistance projects rather than progressive developments. And it provides an explanation for the paradox of a progressive rhetoric of hemispheric multiculturalism and yet its stagnant realization across the Americas. The perspective of remoteness highlights the relative relationship between Latin American polities and dominant themes of international law. This relationship can be interpreted in view of a reoriented perspective of Latin America's spatial encounter with post-Iberian international law. The idea of remoteness connects topical concerns of hemispheric relations to legacies of colonialism, which the Spanish conquest began to put into place 500 years ago.

Remoteness is a factor of spatial dynamics. It is an adjunct of international law's recent turn to history, which has invigorated theoretical discussions about problems of historiography, particularly about matters of coloniality. Although it is tempting to frame remoteness questions as outgrowths of international law's turn to history, spatial questions have long influenced the European engagement project with the New World.

The concept of remoteness is not as prosaic as it seems. It can be used as an analytical tool to uncoil the bound-up incongruities of international law's encounter in the Americas. This book incorporates temporal and geographic depictions of remoteness, using the Atacama Desert as a frame, to help situate the development of hemispheric international law and relations. However, it also employs other remote vantage points within the frame. It pays attention to historiographic usages of remoteness, implied by historians' never-ending discussions about what and when to periodize. Historians' penchant to periodize the history of the Americas naturally focuses on major turning points, which spotlight central events, areas, or time slots to understand hemispheric relations. The meaning of the year 1492 best illustrates this point. This is not the year that history began in the Americas, it is the year that it began in the European mindset.

Historiographic depictions spawn new generational imaginaries of spatiality, which perpetuate established iterations of temporality, geography—and remoteness. Periodization creates its own ideational and geographical constructs of remoteness, and it is under these constructs that many concepts of hemispheric international relations have been placed, almost by default. This point is particularly true when contemplating the Atacama Desert. Its historical relevance habitually attaches to the War of the Pacific (1879–1884), to the extent that it receives any historical attention. Its general history or importance as a means of understanding metropolitan engagement in the Americas and the continuing challenges associated with numerous topical problems of hemispheric relations are lost to its remote spatial placement in the mindset of international law and international relations.

Determining what to periodize necessarily embeds implied decisions about which markers fall on history's cutting-room floor. Preferencing certain voices to structure periodization and associated narratives mutes other voices and story lines. The ascension of central narratives produces by implication declinations of subaltern perspectives, as well as orientations compatible with dominant narratives that nevertheless find limited expression. These overlooked vantage points nevertheless form part of the fuller history of the Americas, a history that is uncovered by international law's turn to history and its recent reawakening turn to spatial dynamics.

This book most certainly picks up on international law's turn to history and informs that movement with revisitations of the age of metropolitan rule. However, attaching a spatial perspective to the pull of history uncovers nuances shaded by general abridgments of temporality, geography, and periodization. Generally, spatial problems of remoteness invite inappropriate or anachronistic shortcuts, which are taken to frame events in relation to temporal or calendrical distance. The shroud of remoteness tends to cover things that happened a long time ago. Spatial problems also reflect challenges of connecting or situating proximate or nearby events to objects or occurrences removed by geographic distance. Attenuations of geographic distance create associational problems of causation, rendering less certain the sequencing of historical events, the assignment of responsibility, and the explanation of what happened, what is happening, and conjectures about what is to come.

Certainly, remoteness as examined here in relation to the history of international law in the Americas reflects temporal and geographic problems of interpretation. Historical narratives of international law's encounter with the Americas preference European depictions of temporality, geography, and epochal turns of history's great wheel. Contemplating remoteness makes more visible the hidden politics and importance of cartography and exploration in shaping conceptions of the Americas. Reconstructing remoteness with a view toward cartographic presentation identifies important assumptions and characterizations about space in the Americas that carried over from the Age of Discovery. We shall see that the implications of medieval travelogue literature also informed the European construction of its idea of the Americas, interweaving assumptions about landscape with scientific curiosity, religious drive, and sentiments of the *mission civilisatrice.*

Hemispheric international relations history often has been connected to binary images of core and periphery, or metropolitan power and colonial subalternity, and more recently to neoliberalism and extractivism.[3] These dualities embed treatments of remoteness, too. They have been magnified by doctrinal perspectives of intellectual subordination and marginalization to European and North American information centers.[4] While no undertaking can canvass the significant amount of schol-

3. Many of the core-periphery distinctions trace to world systems theory. *See, e.g.*, IMMANUEL WALLERSTEIN, THE MODERN WORLD-SYSTEM, VOLUME I: CAPITALIST AGRICULTURE AND THE ORIGINS OF THE EUROPEAN WORLD-ECONOMY IN THE SIXTEENTH CENTURY (1974); SAMIR AMIN, UNEQUAL DEVELOPMENT: AN ESSAY ON THE SOCIAL FORMATIONS OF PERIPHERAL CAPITALISM (1976).

4. For various critiques of this dominant orientation, see Walter D. Mignolo, *The Making and Closing of Eurocentric International Law*, 36 COMP. STUD. S. ASIA, AFRICA AND THE MIDDLE EAST 182 (2016); SIBA GROVOGUI, BEYOND EUROCENTRISM AND ANARCHY, MEMO-

arship available, this study is sensitive to the architecture of information production and its orientation toward the Western academic polestar.

A sustaining interest in the historiography of international law is at the base of its so-called turn to history.[5] Equally grandiose in title and importance, albeit not as readily recognized, has been international law's spatial turn.[6] Philosophical treatments of this spatial turn have contrasted Newtonian and Cartesian conceptions of space, which view space as an objective and absolute phenomenon that

---

RIES OF INTERNATIONAL ORDER AND INSTITUTIONS (2006); WALTER D. MIGNOLO, LOCAL HISTORIES/GLOBAL DESIGNS: COLONIALITY, SUBALTERN KNOWLEDGES, AND BORDER THINKING (2000); SIBA GROVOGUI, SOVEREIGNS, QUASI SOVEREIGNS, AND AFRICANS: RACE AND SELF-DETERMINATION IN LAW (1996); Gyan Prakash, *Colonialism, Capitalism and the Discourse of Freedom*, 41 INT'L REV. SOC. HIST. 9 (1996).

5. *See generally* MARTTI KOSKENNIEMI, THE GENTLE CIVILIZER OF NATIONS: THE RISE AND FALL OF INTERNATIONAL LAW 1870–1960 (2001) (discussing the cultural context of international law and international lawyers in the development of international legal thought); Randall Lesaffer, *International Law and Its History: The Story of an Unrequited Love*, *in* TIME, HISTORY AND INTERNATIONAL LAW 27–42 (Matthew Craven, Malgosia Fitzmaurice, & Maria Vogiatzi eds., 2007) (discussing the troubled historiography of international law); Alexandra Kemmerer, *Turning Aside: On International Law and Its History*, *in* PROGRESS IN INTERNATIONAL LAW 69–93 (Russell A. Miller & Rebecca M. Bratspies eds., 2008) (discussing the need to respect intradisciplinary boundaries in the contextualization and study of international law's history); Thomas Skouteris, *Engaging History in International Law*, *in* NEW APPROACHES TO INTERNATIONAL LAW 99–122 (José María Beneyto & David Kennedy eds., 2012) (discussing the intimate relationship between international legal writing and history); INTERNATIONAL LAW AND ISLAM: HISTORICAL EXPLORATIONS (Ignacio de la Rasilla del Moral & Ayesha Shahid eds., 2018) (orienting international law's turn to history toward Islamic contributions).

6. On the grandiosity of the historical turn, see Matthew Craven, *Theorizing the Turn to History in International Law*, *in* THE OXFORD HANDBOOK OF THE THEORY OF INTERNATIONAL LAW 21 (Anne Orford & Florian Hoffmann eds., 2016). On international law's spatial turn, see CARL SCHMITT, NOMOS OF THE EARTH IN THE INTERNATIONAL LAW OF JUS PUBLICUM EUROPAEUM (G. L. Ulmen trans., 2006); Henry Jones, *Property, Territory, and Colonialism: An International Legal History of Enclosure*, 39 LEGAL STUD. 187–203 (2019); LAUREN BENTON, A SEARCH FOR SOVEREIGNTY: LAW AND GEOGRAPHY IN EUROPEAN EMPIRES, 1400–1900 (2010); Zoe Pearson, *Spaces of International Law*, 17 GRIFFITH L. REV. 489–514 (2008); Eliga H. Gould, *Entangled Histories, Entangled Worlds: The English-Speaking Atlantic as a Spanish Periphery*, 112 AM. HIST. REV. 764–86 (2007); Andrea Brighenti, *On Territory as Relationship and Law as Territory*, 21 CANADIAN J. LAW & SOCIETY 65–86 (2006). For contributions to invigorating the importance of spatial thinking, see JAMES C. SCOTT, THE ART OF NOT BEING GOVERNED: AN ANARCHIST HISTORY OF UPLAND SOUTHEAST ASIA (2009); Chris Butler, *Critical Legal Studies and the Politics of Space*, 18 SOC. & LEG. STUD. 313–32 (2009); Andreas Philippopoulos-Mihalopoulos, *Law's Spatial Turn: Geography, Justice and a Certain Fear of Space*, 7 LAW, CULTURE & THE HUMANITIES 187–202 (2010); DOREEN MASSEY, FOR SPACE (2005); DENIS COSGROVE, APOLLO'S EYE: A CARTOGRAPHIC GENEALOGY OF THE EARTH IN THE WESTERN IMAGINATION (2001); THE POWER OF PLACE: BRINGING TOGETHER GEOGRAPHICAL AND SOCIOLOGICAL IMAGINATIONS (John A. Agnew & James S. Duncan eds., 1989); YI-FU TUAN, SPACE AND PLACE: THE PERSPECTIVE OF EXPERIENCE (1977).

exists independently of the contents contained therein (and therefore may affect but not be affected by those same contents),[7] and Leibnizian projections of space, which regard space as a relational, processual surface on which social phenomena interact.[8] This book's spatial orientation is fundamentally Leibnizian. It joins modern geographic expositors of Leibniz's view, such as David Harvey, Henri Lefebvre, and Doreen Massey, who have attacked objectivity as a measure of spatial analysis and have discarded the idea of spatial hollowness along with geography's still-dominant Euclidean embrace of distance.[9] Instead, they favor a spatial justice theory (sometimes called justice-oriented geography), which envisions geography as a two-way interface between the subjects and the spatial container, the latter composed of temporal, processual, and normative constructs.[10] Lefebvre once helped formulate the *problématique* in terms of the need to bring geography up to speed with the Einsteinian revolution: if space is relative, then he agreed there was not simply a single given space, but a multiplicity of spaces—and times, too.[11] Michel Foucault

---

7. ISAAC NEWTON, PRINCIPIA 77 (Andrew Motte trans., 1846) ("Absolute space, in its own nature, without regard to anything external, remains always similar and immovable."); RENÉ DESCARTES, PRINCIPLES OF PHILOSOPHY 43–44 (Valentine Rodger Miller & Reese P. Miller trans., 1982) ("[W]e attribute a generic unity to the extension of the space, so that when the body which fills the space has been changed, the extension of the space itself is not considered to have been changed [or transported] but to remain one and the same.").

8. GOTTFRIED WILHELM FREIHERR VON LEIBNIZ, DISCOURSE ON METAPHYSICS AND THE MONODOLOGY 62 (George R. Montgomery trans., 2005) (". . . good actions will attain their rewards in a mechanical way through their relation to bodies, . . .").

9. *See generally* DAVID HARVEY, SOCIAL JUSTICE AND THE CITY (1973) (discussing the engagement and partiality of geography in view of urban crisis); HENRI LEFEBVRE, THE PRODUCTION OF SPACE (Donald Nicholson-Smith trans., 1991) (contesting the epithet of Euclidean space and discussing the concept of social space); MASSEY, *supra* note 6.

10. *See* Philippopoulos-Mihalopoulos, *supra* note 6, at 40 (affirming Lefebvre's view of "the possibility of space being much more than something pre-existing and empty of meaning, . . . [r]ather, space has been found to be both a product and producer of relations"); Isolde de Villiers, *Leibniz, Lefebvre and the Spatial Turn in Law*, 72 HTS TEOLOGIESE STUDIES/THEOLOGICAL STUDIES 1–6 (2016) (tracing the term "spatial justice" and looking at the underlying view of space that has influenced the spatial turn in law); Andrea Fischer-Tahir & Matthias Naumann, *Introduction: Peripheralization as the Social Production of Spatial Dependencies and Injustice*, *in* PERIPHERALIZATION: THE MAKING OF SPATIAL DEPENDENCIES AND SOCIAL INJUSTICE 9, 10 (Andrea Fischer-Tahir & Matthias Naumann eds., 2013) (noting that characterizations of spatial injustice frame the periphery as "a static entity" localized at natural margins, where the better interpretation denotes peripheries "as the outcome of complex processes of change").

11. *See* Gallia Burgel, Guy Burgel, & M. G. Dezes, *An Interview with Henri Lefebvre*, 5 ENVIRON & PLANNING 27, 34 (1987). *See also* MASSEY, *supra* note 6, at 9 ("[W]e recognize space as the product of interrelations . . . . [W]e understand space as the sphere of the possibility of the existence of multiplicity. . . . [W]e recognize space as always under construction.").

referred to this more deeply textured landscape of space (spaces) as *heterotopia*.[12]

Translated into international law, the optical characterization of empty space—objectified as *terra nullius*—created a spatial void that stimulated the simplistic economism of colonial drive and of conquest to fill the void. International law's spatial turn confronts problems of human geography, which historically have been placed beyond the ambit of international law's positivistic presentation as a state-centered creation. This project's turn to remoteness conceptualizes the derivative status of the person as an ongoing challenge for international law. It recognizes that international law's spatial turn also has attempted to confront anxieties over problems of fragmentation, or the deepening crevices between specialized international legal regimes and the presentation of international law as a unified field enhanced by multilateralism.[13] Remoteness, as much as it embeds spatial constructs, harbors psychological, social, and cultural constructs, as well.

* * *

The Atacama Desert is an appropriate trope to frame an inquiry into international law's engagement with the remote. Generally, perceptions of geographic and temporal remoteness pervade ideas about deserts, and this perception is particularly true of the Atacama. The Atacama's treatment as a remote area has been interrupted historically by attempts

---

12. Michel Foucault, *Of Other Spaces (1967), Heterotopias*, FOUCAULT.INFO, https://foucault.info/documents/heterotopia/foucault.heteroTopia.en/ (translated from ARCHITECTURE, MOUVEMENT, CONTINUITÉ no. 5 46–49 [1984]). Foucault elsewhere noted "[t]he use of spatial terms seems to have the air of anti-history[,]" where "[s]pace was treated as the dead, the fixed, the undialectical, the immobile." MICHEL FOUCAULT, POWER/KNOWLEDGE: SELECTED INTERVIEWS & OTHER WRITINGS, 1972–1977, at 70 (Colin Gordon ed., 1980).

13. On international law's fragmented spatial turn, see Harlan Grant Cohen, *Fragmentation*, *in* CONCEPTS FOR INTERNATIONAL LAW: CONTRIBUTIONS TO DISCIPLINARY THOUGHT 315 (Jean d'Aspremont, Sahib Singh, & G. C. McBain eds., 2019) (on spatial competitions between regimes such as trade law and the law of the sea, human rights law, and international humanitarian law); Nikolas M. Rajkovic, *On Fragments and Geometry: The International Legal Order as Metaphor and How It Matters*, 6 ERASMUS L. REV. 6, 7 (2013) (associating international law's fragmentation to cartography and the reduction of social space to background assumptions of planimetric maps, which need to be dug up); *see also* MARTTI KOSKENNIEMI, FRAGMENTATION OF INTERNATIONAL LAW: DIFFICULTIES ARISING FROM THE DIVERSIFICATION AND EXPANSION OF INTERNATIONAL LAW (2007), http://legal.un.org/ilc/documentation/english/a_cn4_1682.pdf (investigating the paradox of globalization as leading to increasing uniformity through multilateral treaties while also leading to the emergence of specialized and relatively autonomous legal regimes and spheres of legal practice).

to territorialize its emergent resources. As interests and abilities have aligned to extract these resources, perceptions of the Atacama's remoteness have changed. The Atacama Desert provides interesting and multiple perspectives to frame remoteness and its interplay with hemispheric history.

Adjectives such as *barren, bleak, lifeless,* and *empty* accompany geographic representations of the Atacama. It is a metaphoric wasteland, where one must look at the microbial level to detect any form of life capable of withstanding its punishing aridity. Scientists take advantage of the Atacama's pollution-free night sky and hyperarid climate to stargaze. NASA engineers use its topography to test-drive rovers intended for Martian landscapes. Astrobiologists drill into its soil chemistry to develop and calibrate detection devices that one day will search for life off this planet. The remoteness of the Atacama has made it a scientific means to a nonterrestrial end, an almost completely marginalized depiction of earthly landscape. Right-wing dictatorships, however, repurposed the landscape in the 1970s as a ready-made terminus for the Caravan of Death (*La caravan de la muerte*) and turned the Atacama into an unmarked gravesite for untold numbers of victims of extrajudicial killings.[14]

The Atacama's otherworldly geographic seclusion contributes to abridgments of its historical and human significance. No positive sense of place derives from a wasteland. Topophilia grows in gardens, not deserts. The Atacama and its history reveal a persistent entombment of alterity and subalternity for its peoples, conditions wrought not only by historical imaginaries of desert emptiness, but also by a colonial culture of temporal and spatial interlacement that diminishes such regions as distant and archaic.[15] This interplay between international law and

---

14. The Caravan of Death involved political prisoners executed and disappeared in the Atacama in the immediate aftermath of the Chilean military takeover in 1973. *See generally* GERVASIO SÁNCHEZ, LA CARAVAN DE LA MUERTE: LAS VÍCTIMAS DE PINOCHET (2001) (sharing the stories of family members of executed political prisoners). *See also* Patricio Guzman, *Nostalgia for the Light* (Atacama Productions 2012); PATRICIA VERDUGO, CHILE, PINOCHET, AND THE CARAVAN OF DEATH (2001); João de Caravalho Pina, *100 Words: On the Shadows of the Disappeared,* NPR (June 11, 2013), https://www.npr.org/sections/pictures how/2013/06/11/190329906/100-words-on-the-shadows-of-the-disappeared (including a photographic exposition of dissidents victimized by a coordinated surreptitious military action plan of murder, abduction, and suppression by six authoritarian regimes in Latin America [Operation Condor]).

15. Pietro Costa, *A "Spatial Turn" for Legal History: A Tentative Assessment, in* SPATIAL AND TEMPORAL DIMENSIONS FOR LEGAL HISTORY: RESEARCH EXPERIENCES AND ITINERARIES 27, 46 (Massimo Meccarelli & María Julia Solla Sastre eds., 2016).

human geography has created a subtext of marginality and the conditions for simmering conflict—a sublimated offshoot of remoteness that informs hemispheric relations today.

The Path of This Book

The path of this book continues in chapter 2 with a review of the desert trails of the Atacama and its geography and pre-Hispanic history. The trails themselves tell the story that peoples of the Atacama connected and engaged in commerce over the course of millennia. The trails provide evidence that the Atacama was never remote to the indigenous peoples who made the trails. The arrival of the Spanish and the commencement of their hemispheric conquest brought forth the beginnings of a new spatial design. This design not only built the basic grid of the viceroyalty system, but it created a stratified grid of servants, classes, and races to sustain and grow empire. When the empire collapsed in the early nineteenth century, the burgeoning republics looked to European international law to help craft the postimperial spatial order. A new spatial design arose, which was modeled from the Roman law principle of *uti possidetis.* An important part of chapter 2 investigates the lingering significance of *uti possidetis* as a spatial construct and as a support for today's system of state sovereignty.

Chapter 2 also introduces the qualities of remoteness used in this study to better understand the spatial complexity of international law's structure. These elements touch on the philosophical debate contrasting ideas of spatial construction. Newton construed the spatial interstice between objects as empty and hollow. Leibniz construed it as a plane of relational interaction. This chapter refreshes the Leibnizian view and borrows from social justice geographers who have developed and applied themes of human geography and place-based study to spatial interaction.

The chapter then explores other elements of remoteness that have influenced international law's construction in the Americas. These elements include the problem of historiography and the occluding significance of the epochal turns relating to the Spanish conquest, the Westphalian age of state sovereignty, and newer epochal arrivals, such as the onset of globalization and now the Anthropocene. The idea here is to point out the occluding significance of periodization in shaping main narratives of neoliberalism and climate change, ages that continue to shape our understanding of the Atacama.

The perspective from which international law's engagement in the Americas has been understood overwhelmingly reflects European emphases. This perspective renders remote other viewpoints that have been buried by the historiographic pull of standard narrations. The chapter also addresses how certain viewpoints are also diminished by the architecture of international legal knowledge creation and its centers of information distribution and publication, as well as by the *lingua franca* of international law, which tends to nominalize indigenous or outsider perspectives. The spatial construction of international law is not simply physical, it is ideologically crafted and sensitive to power arrangements.

The chapter also explores international law's spatial engagement with the Americas in relation to geographic remoteness, as expressed through the history of cartography and place-naming. Cartographic depictions of the New World again embedded assumptions and understandings of spatial arrangement. They were fortified by geography's development as a European discipline. The logs, charts, and spatial depictions of the New World by sixteenth- and seventeenth-century discoverers/plunderers—proto international lawyers and producers of the canon of primary texts on the age of exploration—facilitated the projection of the Atacama as a wasteland and the hemisphere as a terrain subject to illumination by the European Enlightenment project.

The chapter concludes with an investigation of the origins of the European mindset regarding deserts, which formed along with the literary development of the travelogue by medieval pilgrims to the Holy Land. Their imaginary involving the desert of the Exodus sustained for generations the idea of the desert as remote. The maturation of the literary form of the travelogue became enshrined in the canon of international law by the many explorers who provided these first-hand accounts of the New World, again sustaining the perspective of the hemisphere as a land of exoticized darkness in need of light.

Chapter 3 borrows from geographers' broad understanding of spatiality to interpret the Atacama Desert. The teachings of political geography and biogeography help to zoom in on this landscape, as does an additional focus on Carl Schmitt's idea of *nomos*, which was central to his theory of land appropriation. Schmitt articulated a bracketed theory of spatiality, which emphasized the spatial lines of amity drawn by Europe's *jus publicum*. Within the European lines of amity, competitions and violence could be contained by a common bond of Christian and spatial sensibility. Beyond the lines of amity, for instance in the New World and the Atacama, hegemonic power operated without such limitations.

The chapter spotlights the pre-Incan and Andean Cone kinship and community associations formed by the indigenous spatial design of the *ayllus*. Although partially respected and partially interrupted by the Spanish conquest, these associational and spatial networks influenced the development of the Andean Cone countries' political geography. The chapter investigates the imperial encounter with the Atacama, through harsh overland expeditionary penetrations from the Andean highlands, and from the sea-based extension of imperial control through the development of a Pacific-coast cabotage system. The cabotage system would increasingly connect the region to destabilizing imperial objectives, foreign labor migrations, and capital infusions. The spatial implications of silver mining played a critical role in the creation of the region's imperial power centers (*audiencias*), particularly the establishment of the Audencia of Charcas, which was taken from Perú to form what is now Bolivia. The motivation for this division related to the discovery and management of the silver lode at Potosí, and the consequences of this division materially affected the history of world trade and hemispheric relations.

Chapter 4 initiates a discussion of the Atacama's mineral resources and the successive competitions that ensued over their control. The initial interest in the Atacama's gold and silver holdings rapidly turned toward its mountains of guano, and then to its nitrate lodes. The demand for guano spurred Spanish revanchism, which resulted in Spain's war with Andean powers over the guano mounds off the Atacama's Peruvian coast. The discovery of Atacama nitrates fields stimulated another regional war that devastated Bolivia, humbled Perú, and secured for Chile its status as a regional power supported by foreign capital.

The foreign-capital infusions that penetrated the region during the Nitrate War established the basis for a continuing debate over the neoliberal implications of international law and their interface with transglobal capitalism in the twentieth century. This theme is developed more fully in the next two chapters, which deal with water allocation and scarcity issues, and extractivism and sovereign control over natural resources. Andean Cone countries are among the water-rich countries of the world. However, water scarcity presents existential concerns for indigenous peoples of the Atacama, who now compete for dwindling supplies based on legacies of neoliberal privatization policies and water-diversion practices that first developed in the Atacama to service the rise of the copper-mining interests. The most recent iteration of hemispheric international law's engagement with the remote Atacama now involves lithium extraction, which powers the rapidly expanding information-age and transportation industries. International law's interface with varying Andean Cone models of neoliberalism challenge hemispheric relations, implicate indigenous rights, reinforce patterns of subalternity, and harden structures that impede progressive developments in human rights while relegating such considerations to the periphery.

This book concludes with a consideration of international law's co-constitutive relationship with neoliberalism. This relationship is playing out in the remote region of the Atacama Desert, turning a language of international legal progressivity into a spatial arrangement that may more accurately reflect stasis. A consideration of international law's spatial configuration—its intellectual, academic, and neoliberal orientation—reinforces the structural impediments that diminish the fuller implications of international law's potential. Peripheralized voices of international law turn into resistance movements; the vocabulary of international law's spatial configuration inclines toward a rhetoric of progressivity that may not exist in practice, where human rights and multiculturalism become shibboleths for neoliberalism, rather than platforms for subjective natural rights. The concept of remoteness in the exoticized and marginalized Atacama Desert presents a dynamic platform to rethink international law's hemispheric gyre, where remoteness is a both a trope and an analytical tool of critique.

TWO

Remoteness Generally Reconsidered

Much international law has ripened at the remote and outer edges of our world, and these peripheries continue to challenge international law and its regulation of geospace. Entrepreneurs and their starships already blur the limits of outer space flight, historically more defined in science than in law. Rising sea levels and disappearing states suggest a coming age of climate refugees. Receding polar ice raises ice-entombed ownership questions over fabled passageways atop the world. The shrinking global commons presents numerous debates about resource extraction and the inequality of nations. Questions pertaining to the spatial and substantive periphery seem increasingly oriented as core points of discussion.

One area of the earth deemed remote is the Atacama Desert, situated on the western littoral of the South American continent. The irony is that the Atacama region is not as remote as it appears to be. It is one of the "unlikely places in which international law exists."[1] Although situated far from the epicenter of the Eurocentric Enlightenment project, shrouded by the Andes Mountains to the east and miniaturized by the Pacific Ocean expanse to the west, the Atacama Desert nevertheless occupies a central place in the hemispheric development of international relations.

Despite standard depictions, the Atacama Desert has never been empty. Human habitation in the Atacama Desert dates back thousands of years. The Chinchorros, Paracas, Chancay, and Nazca of the Atacama practiced mummification 2,000 years before the Egyptians.[2] The Atac-

1. Zoe Pearson, *Spaces of International Law*, 17 GRIFFITH L. REV. 489, 491 (2008).

2. *See Mummies: New Secrets from the Tombs*, a 2015 exhibition developed by the Field Museum in Chicago, *press release*, DENVER MUSEUM OF NATURE & SCIENCE (2019), https://

ama served first as a pre-Incan caravan route and exchange nexus for local peoples trading in prestige goods such as seashells, metal, beads, and ritualistic hallucinogens (cebil).[3] Anthropologically, there is "strong evidence" for the Atacama's use as an interethnic exchange circuit that connected both sides of the Andes Mountains to the Pacific Ocean from the first millennium.[4] These ancient routes later connected to the famous Inca Road, a series of pathways and nodal sites extending from Colombia to Central Chile, which Incan conquerors developed to fortify administrative objectives and secure imperial rule.[5] Iberian conquerors in the sixteenth century linked Mesoamerican routes to the Atacama in pursuit of gold, silver, and slaves. The governor and captain general of Chile (after 1589, the viceroy of Perú), García Hurtado de Mendoza (1535–1609), dispatched Juan Ladrillero (1495–1559) southward and extended these routes into Patagonia to the western terminus of the Strait of Magellan. Francisco Vázquez de Coronado's expeditions began a two-year exploration of what would become the western United States in 1540, sighting the Grand Canyon and reaching into western Kansas.[6] The Spanish eventually connected their colonial tributaries to the 1,800-mile North American *Camino real* trail system, which had affixed the Aztec Empire and other great Mesoamerican civilizations to the regional trading center at Casas Grandes in northern Chihuahua.[7] Five successive waves of Spanish colonization, beginning in 1598 eventually extended the Spanish empire's farthest northern reach to its outpost north of Santa Fe (New Mexico).[8] Similarly, extensive ancient pathways across the Atacama contributed to the consolidation of the massive Iberian trail

---

www.dmns.org/press-room/press-releases/modern-science-unravaels-mysteries-in-mummies-new-secrets-from-the-tombs/ (exploring ancient mummification traditions)

3. Francisco Javier Garrido Escobar, "Mining and the Inca Road in the Prehistoric Atacama Desert," Chile 1 (exchange nexus), 27 (prestige goods) (PhD dissertation, Dietrich School of Arts and Sciences, University of Pittsburgh, 2015).

4. Axel E. Nielsen, "Pastoralism and the Non-Pastoral World in the Late Pre-Colombian History of the Southern Andes (1000–1535)," 13 NOMADIC PEOPLES 17, 23 (2009).

5. Francisco Javier Garrido Escobar, "Mining and the Inca Road in the Prehistoric Atacama Desert," Chile 7 (discussing nodal sites), 14 (discussing administrative objectives) (PhD dissertation, Dietrich School of Arts and Sciences, University of Pittsburgh, 2015).

6. *See* DAVID ROBERTS, ESCALANTE'S DREAM: ON THE TRAIL OF THE SPANISH DISCOVERY OF THE SOUTHWEST 7–10 (2019) (discussing Coronado's first European exploration of the American Southwest with an army of 400 men).

7. *See generally* Douglas Preston, *The Granddaddy of the Nation's Trails Began in Mexico* (El Camino Real de Tierra Adentro), 26 SMITHSONIAN 140 (1995) (discussing the so-called Royal Road of the Interior). *See also* DOUGLAS PRESTON & JOSÉ ANTONIO ESQUIBEL, THE ROYAL ROAD: EL CAMINO REAL FROM MEXICO CITY TO SANTA FE 145 (1998).

8. *See* José Antonio Esquibel, *The People of the Camino Real: A Genealogical Appendix, in* PRESTON & ESQUIBEL, *supra* note 7, at 153–54.

system that would solidify imperial rule for 300 years. Shortly after Spain's early-nineteenth-century departure, the Atacama would begin to unveil more of its hidden resources, making it a focal point for major competition and conflict.

Unlike common representations of the Atacama as desolate and empty, the resources of this region attest to its rich, anything-but-barren composition.[9] Atacama metals and minerals have produced a succession of fortunes: first silver and gold to fuel pre-Hispanic and Spanish Empires, then guano, the first worldwide commercial fertilizer, followed by sodium nitrate (saltpeter) extracted from caliche beds to manufacture gunpowder, and after 1867, dynamite.[10] The Atacama contains huge stores of molybdenum, iron, zinc, and the world's largest supply of copper.[11] Most recently, attention has turned to its world-leading cache of lithium.[12] Lithium is a soft, alkali metal with properties diverse enough to treat multiple mental and physical illnesses,[13] and light and strong enough to manufacture aircraft and power the nuclear industry and information age.[14] Lithium is indispensable to the commonplace production of batteries, electric vehicles, cell phones, and laptops, so there is intense demand for its production.[15]

---

9. For more information on the ethnic diversity of the peoples of the Atacama, see generally Héctor Morales M., *Construcción social de la etnicidad: Ego y alter en Atacama*, 46 ESTUDIOS ATACAMEÑOS 145–64 (2013).

10. *See generally* STEPHEN R. BOWN, A MOST DAMNABLE INVENTION: DYNAMITE, NITRATES, AND THE MAKING OF THE MODERN WORLD (2005) (discussing the invention and significance of dynamite).

11. *See Atacama Desert: Where Copper Is King*, COPPER INVESTING NEWS (Aug. 13, 2018), https://investingnews.com/innspired/copper-mining-in-chiles-atacama-desert-where-copper-is-king/ (noting additionally that Chile's Escondida, Collahuasi, and El Tienente mining complexes rank first, second, and sixth in terms of world copper production and that the world's top gold producer is developing the Pascua Lama area of the Atacama between Argentina and Chile, which is projected to produce 850,000 ounces of gold and 35 million ounces of silver in the first five years following completion of construction).

12. *See* Brian W. Jaskula, *Lithium*, U.S. GEOLOGICAL SURVEY, MINERAL COMMODITY SUMMARIES 1, 99 (Jan. 2018), https://mineralsmakelife.org/wp-content/uploads/2018/06/Minerals_Commodities_Summaries_2018.pdf (identifying 47 million tons of lithium resources worldwide, with 9.8 million tons in Argentina, 9 million tons in Bolivia, and 8.4 million tons in Chile).

13. *See* Michael Bauer, *70 Years of Research and 50 Years of Lithium Clinics: From Serendipity to Gold Standard in Mood Disorders*, 51 PHARMACOPSYCHIATRY 165 (2018) (noting lithium's many clinical uses as the "aspirin of psychiatry").

14. *See Lithium*, WORLD NUCLEAR ASSOCIATION (Oct. 2017), https://www.world-nuclear.org/information-library/current-and-future-generation/lithium.aspx (detailing two nuclear-power uses for lithium isotope Li-7); *Lithium Trading*, COMMODITY.COM., https://commodity.com/precious-metals/lithium/ (charting demand for lithium's multiple industrial uses).

15. *See* Dennis Nguyen, *The White Gold Rush: A Battle for Supremacy in the Lithium Tri-*

The Atacama region thus has a surfeit of mineral riches, the control over which has produced phenomenal wealth and two wars. The first war involved Spain's vanquished attempt to claim the guano-rich Chincha Islands off the Atacama coast of Perú (1864–1866). The second war embroiled Bolivia and Perú against Chile in the so-called "nitrate" war—the War of the Pacific (1879–1883)—which resulted in Chile's annexation of a huge portion of the Atacama. The Atacama Desert's forsaken historical status changed during the nineteenth century because its vast mineral resources stimulated territorializing interests and competitions. The region continues to yield tremendous wealth, but it also generates increasing attention due to a problem of scarcity. Although abundant in mineral resources, it remains bereft of water, and water is used intensively by the mining industry and is needed to sustain the Atacama's indigenous populations. Thus, water is a primary economic and a primal human need in the Atacama.

Addressing the problem of access to water reveals the broader and continuing subtext of rivalry in the region. This subtext contrasts the human rights of indigenous populations against the national economic priorities of Chile, Bolivia, and Argentina. It raises long-standing questions about the remediation of colonial injustices caused by former and current systems of land tenure and resource management.[16] It now involves debates about the pushes and pulls of globalization, domestic control over natural resources, and the dispossessive consequences of neoliberalism and corporate transnationalism. Uncovering the semantic incongruity of standard treatments, which historically view the Atacama as a wasteland even though it long has been at the epicenter of territorializing interests, reveals the continuing aftereffects of Spanish dominium in the New World and the rich yet troubled historical contributions of the Americas to the modern understanding of international law.

* * *

Few powers in all of history "so rapidly acquired as much apparently unchartered territory as the Spaniards did in the first half of the sixteenth century."[17] The enormity of their New World holdings—nearly

angle, ECONOMIST, June 15, 2017, https://www.economist.com/the-americas/2017/06/15/a-battle-for-supremacy-in-the-lithium-triangle (noting that demand is expected to triple by 2025).

16. *See, e.g.*, Barbara Göbel, *La minería del litio en la Puna de Atacama: interdependencias transregionales y disputas locales*, 13 IBEROAMERICANA 135 (2013).

17. David Buisseret, *Spanish Colonial Cartography, 1450–1700*, *in* CARTOGRAPHY IN THE EUROPEAN RENAISSANCE 1143 (David Woodward ed., 2007).

eight million square miles[18]—produced unparalleled challenges on how to control, administer, and map this area. Under Charles V (reign, 1516–1558), Spain set out to demarcate the political division of the New World by borrowing from the practices of the Crown of Aragon in its rule over Italy before its union with the Crown of Castile in 1469. There, it had employed viceroys, Spanish-born executive representatives of the king, to build empire. It would recreate that template[19] in the New World in 1535 with the establishment of the viceroyalty of New Spain in Mexico City,[20] which covered all former Aztec territory north of the Isthmus of Darién (Panama). The viceroyalty of Perú followed in 1542, which initially covered all of Spanish South America except for coastal Venezuela and Brazil, which due to the 1494 Treaty of Tordesillas fell into Portugal's domain.[21] The viceroyalties of New Granada and Río de la Plata were cleaved from the viceroyalty of Perú in 1739 and 1776.[22]

Notwithstanding great delays in the communication of news to the metropolitan center, word soon spread of the Americas' substantial populations and mineral and land-rich wealth. With its profusion of gold and silver mines, Perú became Spain's most valued American possession, and indeed, the source of most of the empire's wealth.[23] To capture this wealth, which was far removed from direct imperial oversight, Spain applied a resourceful, proto-corporatist form of divisible sovereignty. The viceroyalties relied on a system of private capital to extract this wealth with land titles purchased by entrusted Spanish noblemen (*encomenderos*).[24] Enslavement practices and decades of abuse

---

18. Estimating Spain's imperial holdings in South America, Central America, and the western coastal territory of California and the Gulf of Mexico to the peninsula of Florida. Spain's technical claim to all of the territory save for Brazil, amounted to more than seventeen million square miles.

19. Many viceroys were European-born Spanish bureaucrats or military officers. They were elevated to the prestigious position for a relatively short tenure of five to eight years. They reported to the Council of the Indies, the colonial administration located in Spain that reported directly to the monarch. For more, see John Laaman, *Viceroyalty System, in* CONFLICT IN THE EARLY AMERICAS: AN ENCYCLOPEDIA OF THE SPANISH EMPIRE'S AZTEC, INCAN, AND MAYAN CONQUESTS 400, 401 (Rebecca M. Seaman, ed., 2013).

20. *See* JOHN EDWIN FAGG, LATIN AMERICA: A GENERAL HISTORY 163 (2d ed. 1969).

21. *See* Mark A. Burkholder, *Bureaucrats, in* CITIES & SOCIETY IN COLONIAL LATIN AMERICA 77, 79 (Louisa Schell Hoberman & Susan Migden Socolow eds., 1986).

22. *Id.* at 79.

23. C. H. HARING, THE SPANISH EMPIRE IN AMERICA 89 (1947). Indeed, several holdings of the Spanish Empire in the New World, Perú and New Spain specifically, would eventually rival Castile in terms of economics and population. *See* CHRISTOPH ROSENMÜLLER, CORRUPTION AND JUSTICE IN COLONIAL MEXICO, 1650–1755, at 43 (2019).

24. *See* Susan E. Ramírez, *Large Landowners, in* CITIES & SOCIETY IN COLONIAL LATIN AMERICA 19, 21 (Louisa Schell Hoberman & Susan Migden Socolow eds., 1986); CHARLES GIBSON, SPAIN IN AMERICA 49–50 (1966).

and infighting by *encomenderos* prompted the Castilian crown to restrict these charters and substitute a system of central royal authority-by-proxy overseen by the Council of the Indies (1524),[25] followed by the *Leyes nuevas* (New laws, 1542), which imperfectly limited the abuse of indigenous peoples.[26] Hemispheric control would thereafter take the form of a series of viceroyal partitions and subdivisions involving captaincies general, presidencies, a system of thirteen judicial and administrative high courts (*audiencias*), and additional subdivisions into rural districts, or *corregimientos, alcaldías mayors* (magistrateships), *gobernaciónes* (governorates), and *subdelegaciones*—all of which reflected imported Iberian hierarchical and socioeconomic arrangements that required classes of compradors, bureaucrats, and *visitadors* to administer.[27] Although cultivating a colonial gentry, Spanish rulers "curtailed the ability of *criollos* to obtain titles of nobility,"[28] an act that attempted to secure fealty to the crown by vesting hemispheric authority in a form of proprietary birthright obtainable only by *peninsulares,* Spanish-born residents of the New World. Although it temporarily succeeded, it fomented sentiments of superintendency while encouraging racial distinctions and divisions within various subaltern populations. Many familiar capital cities throughout the Americas began as *audiencias,*[29] and their stratified class structures contributed to the social unrest, administrative dysfunction, and *caudillo* culture that followed the retreat of the metropolitan pow-

---

25. Mark A. Burkholder, *Colonies and Empire, in* 1 OXFORD COMPANION TO WORLD EXPLORATION, at 165 (David Buisseret ed., 2007); HARING, *supra* note 23, at 25.

26. Despite the interventions of critics of the encomienda system, such as Friar Bartolomé de Las Casas, abusive practices followed the Spanish conquest whether involving the Tainos or Caribs of the West Indies, the Mayas of the Yucatán, the Aztecs of Mexico, or the Incas of Perú. *See* Rebecca M. Seaman, *Leyes Nuevas 1542–1543, in* CONFLICT IN THE EARLY AMERICAS: AN ENCYCLOPEDIA OF THE SPANISH EMPIRE'S AZTEC, INCAN, AND MAYAN CONQUESTS 215 (Rebecca M. Seaman ed., 2013).

27. *See* Burkholder, *supra* note 21, at 79–80. *Visitadors* were inspectors assigned to an *audiencia* to conduct administrative surveys to keep tabs on households and tributary status. *See* Steven A. Wernke & Thomas M. Whitmore, *Agriculture and Inequality in the Colonial Andes: A Simulation of Production and Consumption Using Administrative Documents,* 37 HUM. ECOLOGY 421, 427–28 (2009).

28. Eric R. Wolf & Edward C. Hansen, *Caudillo Politics: A Structural Analysis,* 9 COMP. STUD SOC'Y & HIST. 168, 168 (1967).

29. The first *audiencia* district was established in the viceroyalty of New Spain in Santo Domingo (1511); others included Mexico City (1527), Guatemala (1543), and Guadalajara (1548). Audiencias established in the viceroyalty of Perú included Panama (1538), Lima (1543), Santa Fe de Bogotá (1548), Charcas (Sucre, 1559), Quito (1563), Chile (1563), Buenos Aires (1661), Caracas (1786), and Cuzco (1787). *See* OSCAR CORNBLIT, POWER AND VIOLENCE IN THE COLONIAL CITY: ORURO FROM THE MINING RENAISSANCE TO THE REBELLION OF TUPAC AMARU (1740–1782) 15 (1995).

er.[30] Spatial distance from the metropolitan center and across this empire resulted in widespread miscegenation, producing within a few generations a numerically dominant *mestizo* class.[31] Race and class distinctions endure as considerations in any discussion of the Atacama. Although they were not borne out of Iberian imperial design, administrative structures created to harness this distant territory projected these distinctions across the Americas and embedded them deeply in hemispheric psyche.

The use of detailed maps to apportion and administer empire developed along with the viceroyalties,[32] but Spanish cartography only inexactly framed the Atacama,[33] as it would the Amazon jungle, the Andes Mountains, and numerous other stretches of the New World. Attempts at mapping created cartographic voids, like the Renaissance depictions of unknown peripheries and interiors of the changing sixteenth-century European worldview. Only in the nineteenth century, with the adaptation of a Roman law line-drawing technique of *uti possidetis* (as you possess, so you may possess), did the enormity of the Spanish Empire's border problems become known. The emerging American system required finality, clarity, order, and respect for territorial borders, above all other considerations. *Uti possidetis* became the emerging system's mortar and grout. It allowed the republican state structure to overlay and adhere to the deteriorating bed of the colonial system. It meant sealing the gaps in political tiling that linked the newborn polities of the reconfigured hemispheric order. *Uti possidetis* became the state system's adhesive, and today it remains fundamental to the foundation on which it rests.

Emerging Latin American republics depended on "vague and sometimes conflicting" authority to demarcate borders, "owing to the lack of

---

30. The resultant *caudillaje* political system developed out of the weak colonial planter class of *criollos*, a political alliance with *mestizos*, the emergence of armed patron-client sets, weak institutionalized means for succession to offices, violence as an element of political competition, and failure of political chieftains to consolidate power. *See id.* at 169.

31. Louis C. Faron, *Effects of Conquest on the Araucanian Picunche during the Spanish Colonization of Chile: 1536–1635*, 7 ETHNOHISTORY 239, 240 (1960).

32. *See* RAYMOND LISTER, ANTIQUE MAPS AND THEIR CARTOGRAPHERS 108 (1970).

33. *See* VICTOR PRESCOTT & GILLIAN D. TRIGGS, INTERNATIONAL FRONTIERS AND BOUNDARIES: LAW, POLITICS AND GEOGRAPHY 256–57 (2008) (noting incongruities in maps and landscapes as applied to the Atacama). Miguel Luis Amunátegui noted "*[t]odos los cronistas de América son mui inexactos en materia de designacion de grados jeográficos I en la avaluacion de las distancias, como que solo en el siglo pasado se practicaron trabajos científicos para determiner la posicion de algunos lugares de las provincias españolas en el Nuevo Mundo.*" MIGUEL LUIS AMUNÁTEGUI, LA CUESTIÓN DE LÍMITES ENTRE CHILE Y BOLIVIA 13–14 (1987).

precise geographical knowledge of the regions affected."[34] In an age before the global grid, superimposing sovereignties on top of uncharted mountains, impenetrable jungles, featureless deserts, and expansive plains necessitated great approximation, more than simple Euclidean meridian lines could accomplish. A border logic informed by physical landscape naturally reflected geographically predestined demarcations.[35] Although sufficient for purposes of internal colonial administration, turning these demarcation lines into specific delimitations at the razor's edge of emerging Latin American sovereignties exposed embedded frictions over strategic territory and resources. Even the leading promoter of Pan-Americanism, the Chilean jurist Álejandro Alvarez (1868–1960),[36] concluded that the peculiar geographical situation of Latin American countries made border wars "inevitable." Indeed, "all the states of America have had boundary disputes with all of their neighbors."[37] This problem would play out multiple times in the history of the Atacama Desert.

On the dissolution of the Spanish colonial empire, the four viceroyalties ceded authority to seven newborn republics: Mexico, the Federal Republic of Central America, Colombia, Perú, Chile, Paraguay, and the Provinces of the Río de la Plata. Ecuador and Venezuela would secede from Colombia by 1830, and the Central American Federation would splinter in the early 1840s into five more independent states (Costa Rica, El Salvador, Guatemala, Honduras, and Nicaragua). By that time, the Spanish administrative legacy had begun to harden into authoritarian and racially shaded encodings of *caudilloism* and creole elitism,[38] "nurtured on the complex socio-political, economic, and religious problems that had arisen in dealing with a large Moorish population in Spain."[39] These traditions deeply contested the public's capacity to uphold the political virtues associated with newborn republicanism,[40] and rampant

34. *See* Álejandro Alvarez, *Latin America and International Law*, 3 AM. J. INT'L L. 269, 290 (1909). *See also* DIRDEIRY M. AHMED, BOUNDARIES AND SECESSION IN AFRICA AND INTERNATIONAL LAW: CHALLENGING UTI POSSIDETIS 25 (2015).

35. *See* Norman Hill, CLAIMS TO TERRITORY IN INTERNATIONAL LAW AND RELATIONS 169 (1945).

36. Juan Pablo Scarfi, *In the Name of the Americas: The Pan-American Redefinition of the Monroe Doctrine and the Emerging Language of American International Law in the Western Hemisphere, 1898–1933*, 40 DIPLOMATIC HIST. 189, 208 (2016).

37. Alvarez, *supra* note 34, at 290.

38. *See id.* at 272.

39. Faron, *supra* note 31, at 241.

40. *See* ROBERTO GARGARELLA, THE LEGAL FOUNDATIONS OF INEQUALITY: CONSTITUTIONALISM IN THE AMERICAS, 1776–1860, at 107–10 (2010).

political instability and unrest reinforced this viewpoint in the eyes of the *caudillos*.

Uti possidetis supported administratively convenient and economically efficient border demarcations, but these demarcations paid little attention to human consequences. *Uti possidetis*'s application bisected cultures, languages, religions, kinships, and resources. It drove a sustaining wedge between indigenous communities and the *caudillo* controllers of the postcolonial land tenure system. This divide continues to condition racial relations among countries of the Andean Cone. Human geography never commingled in ways that could accommodate the abstract Euclidean convenience of this line-drawing principle. Moreover, constructing these elements of national identity pushed border questions to their obvious geographic and political place—the periphery. Here, at the periphery, *uti possidetis* would play tricks on its benefactors.

Remnants of this colonial legacy also inform the international politics and legal developments of the region. The nineteenth century incubated British capital infusions in the Atacama, establishing it as an area subject to foreign control.[41] The twentieth century produced a contested atmosphere of liberal economic reforms imported from North America.[42] These policies diffused throughout Latin America and shaped the natural resource policies of the Andean Cone countries, turning the Atacama Desert into a proving ground for neoliberalism, extractivism, and the twenty-first-century pursuit of mineral resources to propel the information age and energy pursuits. Against the backdrop of the Atacama Desert, an intense and vibrant history of excavation arises to shape and explain contemporary issues, making the Atacama Desert a worthy subject of inquiry.

However, desert wanderings require a frame of reference. Any discussion about the Atacama Desert involves the need for a compass. Directional focus orients the referent by illuminating certain pathways while occluding others. Understanding historical developments from the perspective of this overlooked corner of Latin America brings into focus underappreciated factors that inform our understanding of interna-

---

41. *See* Michael Monteón, *The British in the Atacama Desert: The Cultural Bases of Economic Imperialism*, 35 J. ECON HIST. 117–33 (1975).

42. *See* Rolf Lüders, *La Misión Klein-Saks, los Chicago Boys y la Política Económica* (Instituto de Economía, Documento de Trabajo No. 411, 2012), http://economia.uc.cl/docs/dt_411.pdf; Glen Biglaiser, *The Internationalization of Chicago's Economics in Latin America*, 50 ECON. DEV. & CULTURAL CHANGE 269, 275 (2002); JUAN GABRIEL VALDÉS, PINOCHET'S ECONOMISTS: THE CHICAGO SCHOOL IN CHILE 182 (1995).

tional law and international relations. Spatial and geographic frameworks provide a metaphoric compass, and in this inquiry, so too does the idea of remoteness.

Elements of Remoteness

In common law, the relationship between a wrongful act and its harmful result undergirds the law of negligence. Except in rare cases of strict liability, where harm results from keeping wild animals, or engaging in abnormally dangerous activity, or selling certain commercial products, a breach of duty to take care depends on some finding of fault, and fault attaches to only those consequences deemed reasonably foreseeable, or not too remote. Proximity strengthens the connection between cause and effect, or conduct and its offending consequence. Importantly, the harmfulness of the result conditions the wrongfulness of the conduct. There is no such thing as negligence in the air.

The *Wagon Mound (No. 1)* case[43] monumentalized the relationships between fault and harm, cause and effect, and proximity and remoteness. Here, a distant freighter's careless discharge of oil into a bay drifted to the underside of a wooden wharf. Acetylene-torch-bearing welders on the wharf, repairing dry-docked vessels, carelessly dripped molten metal into the bay. The red-hot drippings ignited cotton flotsam under the wharf. The floating pyre then ignited the oily water, which set the wharf ablaze. The unforeseeable remoteness of the chain of events barred recovery for the aggrieved wharf owner in an action against the freighter company. While introducing the foreseeability standard to tort law (thus problematizing the assignment of blame for the cause of the fire), the case held that negligence does not exist at large, or in the abstract. It is a term of relation. And it is an ordered relation. Without a showing of harm, there is no cause of action. No harm, no foul—in that sequence. "Proof of negligence in the air, will not do."[44]

The case suggests that time and space factor into the assignment of responsibility and frame the boundaries of remoteness. Distances

43. Overseas Tankship (UK) Ltd. v. Morts Dock & Eng'g Co., Ltd. [1961] AC 388 (PC) (commonly known as the Wagon Mound [No.1]).

44. The exact Common law phrase is: "Proof of negligence in the air, so to speak, will not do." SIR FREDERICK POLLOCK, THE LAW OF TORTS 455 (11th ed. 1920). The American judge and later Supreme Court justice, Benjamin Cardozo, famously helped to formulate the concept in Martin v. Herzog, 126 N.E. 814, 816 (N.Y. 1920), and Palsgraf v. Long Island R. Co., 162 N.E. 99, 102 (N.Y. 1928).

between time and space, between cause and effect, create attenuations—they muddle foreseeable consequences, cloud proximate causes, and stretch timelines.[45] Remoteness stalks the law of state responsibility, suggesting that cause might originate in an overdetermined number of wrongdoers, thus hampering the credibility and conclusions of judicial authority, which attempt to pinpoint responsibility.[46] However attenuated, one clear Leibnizian proposition rings true. Things are not remote in themselves but only in relation to other things.

* * *

Remoteness problematized the philosophy of the ancient Greeks. The universe presented an atomized *plenum formarum* in which all things big and small were connected by ideas of continuity and gradation, which Arthur O. Lovejoy masterfully explored in his ontological discourse on intellectual history, *The Great Chain of Being* (1936).[47] Atomized views of space informed Lucretius's materialist *De Rerum Natura.*[48] Hesiod's creation story, *Theogony*, mythologized the progression of world order from primeval Chaos to Cosmos. The union of Earth (Gaia) and Sky (Ouranos) produced the Titans who ruled over the corners of the earth, constellations and light, the ether, the moon, mortality, fairness, motherhood, memory, and water. Hesiod provided little commentary about the birth of these Titans, except for the arrival of Time (Kronos). Kronos was the last issue of Earth and Sky, the attenuated tether connecting the Titans and the Cosmos. Hesiod introduced Kronos as "warped" and "wily," and the "[m]ost terrible of sons."[49] Kronos's late arrival disrupted the cosmogony of Hesiod's ancient world. It disturbed his understanding of natural order, which never revealed the "world as a unified whole." At best, Hesiod understood the world as a poetic of "relative order,"[50] with discontinuities, interruptions, and unexplained sudden arrivals to dis-

45. *See generally* Ilias Plakokefalos, *Causation in the Law of State Responsibility and the Problem of Overdetermination: In Search of Clarity*, 26 EUR. J. INT'L L. 471, 478 (2015) (discussing problematic applications of causal usages involving remoteness, foreseeability, or causation in law).

46. *Id.*

47. *See generally* ARTHUR O. LOVEJOY, THE GREAT CHAIN OF BEING: A STUDY OF THE HISTORY OF AN IDEA (1936) (tracing the intellectual development from antiquity to the eighteenth century of the concepts of plenitudinism, continuity, and gradation).

48. *See* LUCRETIUS DE RERUM NATURA 1. 483–550 (William Ellery Leonard trans., 1921) (discussing the character of the atoms).

49. HESIOD, THEOGONY AND WORKS AND DAYS: A NEW BILINGUAL EDITION 17, verse 130 (Kimberly Johnson trans., 2017).

50. DONNA J. PEUQUET, REPRESENTATIONS OF SPACE AND TIME 13 (2002).

rupt the space-time dimension.[51] For Hesiod, remoteness, too, was a relational term.

Remoteness is the unredeemable, often unavoidable element of interaction. It occupies a central place in philosophy, in negligence law, and in historical international relations, although not in the neatly ordered sequence of negligence law. The distance between person and place, or subject and object, affects the image-building process of international relations and the construction of its geography and spatial order.[52] Remoteness casts shadows over problems of historiography, or how scholars contextualize, sequence, and transmit readings of the past. These shadows may lead to the jumbling of past events and contribute to their disordered reshelving. Such out-of-time reorderings result in the baneful charge of anachronism. This charge persistently haunts the study of history. Historians avoid it at all cost. A satirist once wrote, "though God cannot alter the past, historians can."[53] For this reason, anachronism is the ultimate sin that historians can never forgive.

Temporal Remoteness and the Problem of Periodization

Remoteness haunts the temporality of international relations study. Framed in terms of time, remoteness revisits the search for facts and conjures up apparitions, which beggar historians when they improperly contextualize, abridge facts, apply metaphors that do not fit, and disjointedly retell the past. The spirit of remoteness hovers over the implied continuity of traditions. It subverts the invariance or transhistorical significance of meta-theories and sometimes treats them as wishful and triumphal revenants of ideological present-centeredness. Herbert Butterfield labeled this kind of thinking *whiggish*.[54] Dipesh Chakrabarty compared this imaginary to the sin of all sins—*nostalgia*.[55]

Temporal remoteness unveils the plasticity of historical inquiry. This plasticity selectively assimilates preceding events. It underexamines the examiners' biases and diminishes historians' belief that calendrical sepa-

---

51. According to Hesiod, Chaos reigned "in the beginning." Next came Gaia, but with no explanation about whence it came. HESIOD, *supra* note 49, at 15, verse 120.

52. *See* PETER GOULD & RODNEY WHITE, MENTAL MAPS 17 (1974).

53. SAMUEL BUTLER, EREWHON AND EREWHON REVISITED 468 (1933) (adding that "painters can do all that historians can do, with even greater effect"). *Id.* at 469.

54. *See* HERBERT BUTTERFIELD, THE WHIG INTERPRETATION OF HISTORY v (1931) (discussing the whiggish tendency to glorify the present).

55. DIPESH CHAKRABARTY, PROVINCIALIZING EUROPE: POSTCOLONIAL THOUGHT AND HISTORICAL DIFFERENCE 27 (2000).

ration provides the clutter-free environment in which disinterested historical review can take place.[56] It turns history itself into an artifice, like a form of molded art.

Temporal remoteness undermines spatial cognition—our encodings and knowledge about "where we are" when we revisit guideposts of history.[57] It questions the clarity and purpose of grand narrative, convolutes the periodization of history, and complicates the semantic transformations of conceptual history (*Begriffsgeschichte*).[58] It leads to misapplied linguistic usages and vocabularies appropriate perhaps only to another age,[59] and casts doubt on the reliability of sources, both primary and archival.

The specter of remoteness and the plasticity of history frequent the periodization of history, making it an "occupational hazard of the historian"[60] and one of historiography's most "underestimated questions."[61] Even between the closely related studies of international legal history and international relations history, a disciplinary divide widens over debates about what and when to periodize.[62] Jacques Le Goff

---

56. *See* MARK SALBER PHILLIPS, ON HISTORICAL DISTANCE 9 (2013) (discussing plasticity); *see generally* CHRISTOPHER R. ROSSI, SOVEREIGNTY AND TERRITORIAL TEMPTATION: THE GROTIAN TENDENCY ch. 1 (2017) (reviewing problems of historical review).

57. *See generally* ROBERT LLOYD, SPATIAL COGNITION: GEOGRAPHIC ENVIRONMENTS (1997) (explaining the spatial behavior of humans through the acquisition and use of spatial information); THE CONSTRUCTION OF COGNITIVE MAPS (Juval Portugali ed., 1996) (discussing the cognitive processes involved in constructing cognitive maps).

58. *See* D. Timothy Goering, *Concepts, History and the Game of Giving and Asking for Reasons: A Defense of Conceptual History*, 7 J. PHIL HIST. 426, 427 (2013). For a discussion of conceptual history generally, see REINHART KOSSELECK, BEGRIFFSGESCHICHTEN (2006).

59. *See generally* J. G. A. POCOCK, THE MACHIAVELLIAN MOMENT: FLORENTINE POLITICAL THOUGHT AND THE ATLANTIC REPUBLICAN TRADITION (1975) (discussing the situatedness of language and speech acts).

60. Randall Lesaffer, *The End of the Cold War: An Epochal Event in the History of International Law? in* SELECT PROCEEDINGS OF THE EUROPEAN SOC'Y INT'L L., VOLUME 3, at 45 (James Crawford & Sarah Nouwen eds., 2012).

61. Oliver Diggelmann, *The Periodization of the History of International Law, in* THE OXFORD HANDBOOK OF THE HISTORY OF INTERNATIONAL LAW 997 (Bardo Fassbender & Anne Peters eds., 2012). For discussion on problems of periodization, see generally Ignacio de la Rasilla, *The Problem of Periodization in the History of International Law*, 37 LAW & HIST. REV. 275, 277–78 (2019); NICHOLAS GREENWOOD ONUF, THE MIGHTIE FRAME: EPOCHAL CHANGE AND THE MODERN WORLD (2018); William A. Green, *Periodization in European and World History*, 3 J. WORLD HIST. 13 (1992).

62. William Elliott Butler, *Periodization and International Law, in* RESEARCH HANDBOOK ON THE THEORY AND HISTORY OF INTERNATIONAL LAW 379 (Alexander Orakhelashvili ed., 2011). The periodization dispute in the disciplines of international law and international relations forms part of a broader (and not necessary) dispute, which David Bederman likened to "bickering spouses in a paradigmatic dysfunctional family." David J. Bederman, *Constructivism, Positivism, and Empiricism in International Law*, 89 GEO. L. J. 469, 469 (2001).

warned that "there is nothing neutral, or innocent, about cutting time up into smaller parts,"[63] perhaps to suggest that the act of periodizing history also clips or peripheralizes other events of history.[64] Constantine Fasolt noted that the division of time into past and present does not arrive in a convenient package,[65] compounding even the separation of contemporary history from what came before.

A Nearby Example of Problematic Periodization: How Remote Is the Cold War?

International relations specialists periodized the Cold War between 1946 and 1991. Even with the historiographic treatment of this familiar time zone, complications arise. Randall Lesaffer explored the difficulty of packaging the Cold War when assessing whether its end heralded the beginning of a new post–Cold War epoch.[66] Even though Lesaffer recognized that the post–Cold War Age has not yet ended, the bundling of this nearby history can unravel or fray and present for inspection a less than tightly bound parcel. Did the Cold War ever really end?

Consider the possibility of the Cold War's revisitation. For more than one decade, Russia has been militarizing the Arctic. In 2014, Russia took Crimea from Ukraine. Since then it also has fomented rebellion in Ukraine's eastern region of Donbass, including the self-proclaimed Donetsk and Luhansk People's Republics. In 2015, Russia began its successful intervention in the Syrian civil war, which has destabilized the United States's standing in the region. Russia's interference with elections in the United States portends national security problems for all Western democracies. Recently, the Trump administration declared dead the thirty-year-old Intermediate-Range Nuclear Forces Treaty (1987), forecasting the prospect of a new arms race, to join the digital arms race and global cyberwar that are well underway. In 2019, the Trump administration actively encouraged the failed *coup d'état* in Venezuela, with Russia actively providing military assistance to the embattled Maduro regime. This encounter suggests a reheating of superpower

---

63. JACQUES LE GOFF, MUST WE DIVIDE HISTORY INTO PERIODS? 2 (M. B. DeBevoise trans., 2015).

64. Even though periodized as the Middle Ages, Le Goff complained that of its peripheralization and contemptuous treatment as the Dark Ages by the cultural elites of the Renaissance. *See id.* at 59, ch. 6 (discussing the issue under the title "The Middle Ages Becomes the Dark Ages").

65. *See* CONSTANTINE FASOLT, THE LIMITS OF HISTORY 6 (2004).

66. Lesaffer, *supra* note 60, at 4.

proxy confrontation in Latin America, which hemispherically defined the Cold War in the 1980s.

Perhaps the periodization of the post–Cold War era should reconsider Francis Fukuyama's encomium to the *End of History* (1992),[67] or Samuel Huntington's projection articulated in his *Clash of Civilizations* (1993).[68] Both presentations foresaw new but different kinds of world order emerging from the detritus of the Cold War. Are these assessments now passé? Were they ever empirically supportable?[69] Perhaps they were premature, faddish extensions of President George Bush's 1991 articulation of "a unique and extraordinary moment" foretelling "a New World Order."[70] The window of transformational opportunity may have closed too quickly, with the unanticipated consequences to NATO's 1999 bombing of Serbia, the West's recognition of Kosovo's unilateral declaration of independence in 2008, and NATO's empty pieties associated with intensive engagement and eastern expansion rhetoric directed at fledgling eastern European democracies. This rhetoric promised NATO membership for Georgia and Ukraine—four months before Russia launched its 2008 military campaign against Georgia's breakaway territories of Abkhazia and South Ossetia. Mere days after the 2014 pro-West Ukraine Euromaidan Movement ousted the Russian-client government of Viktor Yanukovych, Russia annexed then absorbed Crimea as a Russian federal district.[71] When did the Cold War end? Did it begin anew? Where and when should such lines be drawn? The packaging of history embeds the

---

67. *See generally* FRANCIS FUKUYAMA, THE END OF HISTORY AND THE LAST MAN (1992) (asserting a Hegelian triumph of liberal democracy over authoritarian counterparts following the collapse of the Soviet Union).

68. *See generally* Samuel P. Huntington, *The Clash of Civilizations?* 72 FOREIGN AFF., Summer 1993, at 22 (introducing the thesis that the post–Cold War era would produce civilizational conflict).

69. *See generally* JACQUES DERRIDA, SPECTERS OF MARX: THE STATE OF THE DEBT, THE WORK OF MOURNING, AND THE NEW INTERNATIONAL (1994) (attacking Fukuyama's attempted conjuring away of the ghosts that haunt liberalism, pondering as well, "How can one be late to the end of history?"). *Id.* at 39; CIVILIZATIONS IN WORLD POLITICS: PLURAL AND PLURALIST PERSPECTIVES (Peter J. Katzenstein ed., 2009) (discussing the issue specifically in relation to Huntington's thesis).

70. Videotape: George H. W. Bush, "Address before a Joint Session of Congress" (Sept. 11, 1990) (on file with UVA Miller Center), https://millercenter.org/the-presidency/presidential-speeches/september-11-1990-address-joint-session-congress

71. NATO heads of state agreed at its Bucharest Summit in 2008 to "welcome[] Ukraine's and Georgia's Euro-Atlantic aspirations for membership in NATO. We agree today that these countries will become members of NATO." "Bucharest Summit Declaration Issued by the Heads of State and Government Participating in the Meeting of the North Atlantic Council in Bucharest," NATO (May 8, 2014, 11:10 AM), http://www.nato.int/cps/en/natolive/official_texts_8443.htm

problem of periodization, forever coloring assessments of remoteness even with regard to nearby history.

Much of the history of the Atacama attaches to standard treatment of the War of the Pacific. Its nearby history seems subsumed by grander discourses of neoliberalism or problems of hemispheric democratization, and not by actually focusing in on the geospacer itself. Historians worry about time-slicing when they contemplate problems of periodization. This worriment may presuppose a structural unity to historicism, which has led some theorists to caution that "talk about ages, stages, periods or epochs" need not actually imply that history "is going anywhere in particular."[72] Debating history's directional course dissimulates problems associated with the framing of history. Periodization provides the necessary "skeletal system for historical studies," but it can lead to epochal divisions "too important to be accepted unthinkingly as an intellectual inheritance."[73] Periodization tempts historians to use rigid or reductive classifications, for instance the division of history into ancient/medieval/modern/postmodern times, or the reflexive segmentation of the Atacama into a time frame molded by Perú and Bolivia's war against Chile. These classifications can interrupt continuity, arbitrarily frame relationships, and condition discursive treatments of subjects or regions as central or peripheral, not simply as nearby or remote. Periodization may subtly shade history, cloaking regions such as the Atacama with subsumed status in comparison with such towering themes as the Age of Discovery, Liberalism, Republicanism, Latin Americanism, or Imperialism.

The arbitrariness of frameworks contributes to the derivative status of the Atacama. It is the object of historical activity framed from afar, not a subject of study in itself. These frameworks result from dominant constructions of New World narratives that project standard historiographies and periodizations of metropolitan rulership. Reframing the Atacama Desert as a centerpiece of New World history sheds light and perspective on continuing problems of hemispheric international relations.

International Law's Struggle with Remoteness and Periodization

Periodization in international law provides another good example of the arbitrariness and occluding significance of frameworks. Wilhelm Grewe

72. *See* ONUF, *supra* note 61, at 7 (referencing Foucault as well).
73. Green, *supra* note 61, at 53.

elevated the importance of periodization to the title of his masterwork on sequentialism and the history of international law, *Epochen der Völkerrechtsgeschichte* (1984).[74] In this work, international law's history is portrayed as a succession of great imperial epochs.[75] According to international legal historian Randall Lesaffer, the "most foundational" periodization of international law is the emergence of sovereignty and the state-centric system in Europe.[76] When do international legal scholars think it emerged?

Grewe called its epochal arrival the French Age, which framed Europe as the center of gravity between 1648 and 1815.[77] During this period, the newly discovered continents were only an object of European politics, lacking their own force field and gravitational center.[78] The rise of the United States with its Declaration of Independence in 1776 did not alter the gravitational pull or linguistic usage of the *droit public de l'Europe* because the United States was swiftly and without difficulty integrated into the international legal community as an "offshoot of the Christian-European family of nations."[79] According to Grewe, only after publication of Jeremy Bentham's *Introduction to the Principles of Morals and Legislation* (1789), where Bentham first used the term "civilization" in the context of international law,[80] did a new orbital epoch widen to incorporate a more cosmopolitan group of non-Christian nations.[81] This epoch

---

74. WILHELM G. GREWE, EPOCHEN DER VÖLKERRECHTSGESCHICHTE [THE EPOCHS OF INTERNATIONAL LAW] (1984).

75. Martti Koskenniemi, *Carl Schmitt and International Law*, *in* THE OXFORD HANDBOOK OF CARL SCHMITT 592 (Jens Meierhenrich & Oliver Simons eds., 2017).

76. Lesaffer, *supra* note 60, at 47.

77. On *Das französische Zeitalter*, see GREWE, *supra* note 74, 325ff. Grewe separated the French Age from the preceding Spanish Age, which he periodized between 1494 and 1648. *See id.* 163ff. Central to his portrayal of a "new constellation" was the Peace of Westphalia and the role of France ("*Die Rolle, die Frankreich in Münster und Osnabrück (1648) [Wesphalia] spielt, läßt die neue Konstellation deutlich erkennen*"). *Id.* at 167. "*Spanien rückt aus dem Mittelpunkt des Staatensystems heraus. Eine neue Epoche hebt an, eine Epoche, in der die politische Führung Frankreich zufällt. . . .*" *Id.*).

78. *Id.* at 342 ("*Die neunen Kontinente sind in diesem Zeitabschnitt nur Objekt der eruopäischen Politik. Sie bilden kein eigenes Kraftfeld mit eigenen Gravitationszentren.*").

79. *Id.* at 342–43 ("*. . . denn daß die Aufnahme der Vereinigten Staaten in die Völkerrechtsgemeinschaft so rasch und ohne wesentliche Schwierigkeiten vor sich ging, was doch nur deswegen möglich, weil es sich hier um einen Sproß der christlich-europäischen Völkerfamilie handelte.*") (footnote omitted).

80. *Id.* at 526 ("*In einem völkerrechtlichen Zusammenhang ist der Begriff der Zivilisation zum ersten Male in dem von Bentham in den Jahren 1786–89 verfaßten.*").

81. According to Grewe, no state doubted the legal identities of the widening community states. Although foreign to Europe, Grewe noted that they were rooted in the Christian-European cultural heritage. *Id.* at 541 ("*Niemand mochte die Völkerrechtsfähigkeit*

created the worldwide state system grounded on a scheme of balance of power.[82]

Much of modern international legal theory has construed Westphalia as the dominant period. Postmodern and historiographic scholarship increasingly criticize this conclusion for its eclipsing and misplaced emphasis. It certainly displaces almost 130 years of international legal development in the Americas, which traces its informal birth to the Spanish conquest of the Aztec Empire beginning in 1519. Leo Gross viewed the epochal 1648 Westphalia peace treaties as the "majestic portal" leading from "the old into the new world."[83] Charles Fenwick claimed the treaties introduced coequality and independence as keystones of the international community.[84] Hans Morgenthau asserted that they "made the territorial state the cornerstone of the modern state system."[85] Richard Falk imparted epiphenomenal significance to the Westphalia peace treaties, influentially labeling the sudden appearance of the state system a Grotian Moment.[86] Perhaps Hugo Grotius's (1583–1645) arrival on the scene was the epochal event. His putative title as the father of *modern* international law sparked an intense originary debate in the early twentieth century. Others have depersonalized the debate and have viewed the ontogeny of the state system in pre- and postevolutionary terms, ascribing to Westphalia a diachronic significance connecting to the *cuius regio*

---

dieser neuen, zwar außereuropäischen, aber im christlich-europäischenKulturerbe verwurzelten Staatswesen bezweifeln.").

82. See *id.* at 541. ("*Eine uber den europaischen Kontinent immer mehr hinauswachsende, sich vor allem durch das Band einer gemeinsamen Zivilisation verbunden fuhlende staatengemeinschaft, deren politische Beziehungen durch ein weltweites Gleichgewicht der Macht unter der Vorherrschaft einer maritime-kolonialen Weltmacht. . . .*"). Grewe credited the American Henry Wheaton and publication of his treatise, ELEMENTS OF INTERNATIONAL LAW: WITH A SKETCH OF THE HISTORY OF THE SCIENCE (1836), with influencing Anglo-American adoption of this modern notion of international law as a replacement for the term "*Europäisches Völkerrecht.*" *Id.* at 542.

83. Leo Gross, *The Peace of Westphalia 1648–1948*, 42 AM. J. INT'L L. 20, 28–29 (1948).

84. CHARLES FENWICK, INTERNATIONAL LAW 14 (4th ed. 1965).

85. HANS J. MORGENTHAU & KENNETH W. THOMPSON, POLITICS AMONG NATIONS: THE STRUGGLE FOR POWER AND PEACE 294 (6th ed. rev., 1985).

86. Richard Falk coined the term "Grotian Moment" in 1980. *See* Richard Falk, *Some Thoughts on the Decline of International Law and Future Prospects*, 9 HOFSTRA L. REV. 399 (1980). For influential adaptations of the terms, see Milena Sterio, *A Grotian Moment: Changes in the Legal Theory of Statehood*, 39 DEV. J. INT'L L. & POL'Y 209 (2011); Michael P. Scharf, *Seizing the "Grotian Moment": Accelerated Formation of Customary International Law in Times of Fundamental Change*, 43 CORNELL INT'L L. J. 439 (2010); Boutrous Boutrous-Ghali, *A Grotian Moment: The Role of International Law in the Twenty-First Century*, 18 FORDHAM INT'L L. J. 1609 (1995).

agreement established by the Peace of Augsburg (1555)[87] or tracing "back way beyond the Ages to classical and even pre-classical Antiquity."[88]

International lawyers have long emphasized the importance of Westphalia and 1648. However, this periodization has been problematized by other international relations specialists, some legal scholars included. Benno Teschke rejected the paradigmatic significance of 1648, calling it a "myth" of premodernity and an archaic expression of absolutism.[89] Stuart Elden recognized the arbitrariness of the Westphalian marker, which came about following the conclusion of the Thirty Years' War (1618–1648).[90] He agreed that Westphalia "was not nearly as central as the traditional account suggests," but "not as unimportant as the revisionists would have us believe."[91] Stéphane Beaulac argued in favor of the unmaking of the myth of Westphalia, "in order to show that the mythical reality for which it has long stood is substantially remote from the initial material reality."[92] Andreas Osiander noted that the terms of the treaties contained "little that was serviceable" for the fictional account that they used to reorder the European system with the new rule of sovereignty.[93] The treaties almost exclusively concerned the Holy Roman Empire, making Westphalia's shorthand seventeenth-century identification with sovereignty "really a product of the nineteenth and twentieth century fixation on the concept of sovereignty."[94] If Westphalia

---

87. *Cuius region, eius religio* ("whose realm, his religion") was the principle concluded by the 1555 Peace of Augsburg. It granted princes and free cities of the Holy Roman Empire the power to determine whether their respective lands and inhabitants should be Catholic or Protestant, excluding ecclesiastical territories (the *reservatum ecclesiasticum*). The Peace of Westphalia broadened this unworkable division by also recognizing rights of Anabaptists and Calvinists.

88. Lesaffer, *supra* note 60, at 48 (referencing works by Preiser and Zieger). *See generally* BENNO TESCHKE, THE MYTH OF 1648: CLASS, GEOPOLITICS AND THE MAKING OF MODERN INTERNATIONAL RELATIONS (2003) (contesting the claim that the Treaty of Westphalia, which marked the end of the Thirty Years' War, was an epochal event); STATE SOVEREIGNTY AS SOCIAL CONSTRUCT (Thomas J. Biersteker & Cynthia Weber eds., 1996) (applying constructivist themes to understanding the evolution of state sovereignty); JENS BARTELSON, A GENEALOGY OF SOVEREIGNTY (1995) (addressing sovereignty as a contingent, elusive parergon).

89. TESCHKE, *supra* note 88. *See also* Andreas Osiander, *Sovereignty, International Relations, and the Westphalian Myth*, 55 INT'L ORG. 251 (2001).

90. STUART ELDEN, THE BIRTH OF TERRITORY 309 (2013).

91. *Id.* at 310.

92. STÉPHANE BEAULAC, THE POWER OF LANGUAGE IN THE MAKING OF INTERNATIONAL LAW: THE WORD *SOVEREIGNTY* IN BODIN AND VATTEL AND THE MYTH OF WESTPHALIA 64 (2004).

93. Osiander, *supra* note 89, at 264.

94. *Id.* at 251.

did indeed usher in the new epoch of the state system, it is worth remembering that the preceding political order of the Holy Roman Empire managed to maintain its identity for another 158 years.[95]

David Kennedy argued that the consolidation of sovereignty and the state during the nineteenth century had been usurped by early-twentieth-century turmoil and the false hopes of the League of Nations. He inverted the idea of remoteness, upsetting the semblance of a sequential order by making the nineteenth century seem more distant than the formative problems of statehood confronting the great publicists of the seventeenth and eighteenth centuries.[96] "It would be easy to study international law today and learn next to nothing about the nineteenth century,"[97] he argued. This point certainly helps to explain the general abridgment of international law's history in the Americas, which underwent its nineteenth-century state-building project in a manner presumed to follow the channel established by Europeans' misleading Westphalian portal.

Kennedy postdated the crystallization of the classical state-centric system to the 1920s, in line with its modernist replacement of formalist doctrine with functional, practical arrangements.[98] Regarding international law's nineteenth-century memory lapse, Kennedy noted today's international law "is largely a twentieth century tale, rooted in great principles from the mid-seventeenth century break to a state system in Europe."[99] He felt that the traditional narrative of international law "has always had a problem with dates."[100]

Martti Koskenniemi thought the nineteenth and twentieth centuries ought to be read together as one epoch of international legal thought.[101] Disputes over the causal sequencing of periodic markers led Jean d'Aspremont to observe that the pedigree of contemporary international legal thought traced to "a past more immediate than the remote humanist past to which interwar international lawyers, in particular, had traced their roots."[102]

---

95. The Holy Roman Empire ceased to exist following Napoleon's crushing victory at the Battle of Austerlitz in 1805. *See generally* THE HOLY ROMAN EMPIRE, 1495–1806: A EUROPEAN PERSPECTIVE (R. J. W. Evans & Peter H. Wilson eds., 2012) (reworking histories of the empire).

96. See David Kennedy, *International Law and the Nineteenth Century: History of an Illusion*, 17 QUINNIPIAC L. REV. 99, 100 (1997).

97. *Id.* at 105.

98. *Id.* at 108, 109–10.

99. *Id.* at 105.

100. *Id.* at 103.

101. Jean d'Aspremont, *Critical Histories of International Law and the Repression of Disciplinary Imagination*, 7 LONDON REV. INT'L L. 89, 102 (2019) (citing Koskenniemi).

102. *Id.* at 102–3.

The point here is not to identify the genealogy of the state system as ancient or modern, as a crystallized creation of 1648, as an epiphenomenal Grotian Moment, as an ontological expression of diachronicity, or as an emblem of historical amnesia about the Thirty Years' War. It is to heighten awareness about the challenges associated with problems of remoteness and its connection to periodization. And yet, remoteness acts as a residual negative principle for problems of periodization. It is a metaphoric default receptacle into which much Latin American history has been placed, certainly with regard to Andean countries. In the abstract, periodization is a memory construct utilized to support or disrupt linear succession. It deals with the act of returning to a *frequented* signpost to begin a new chapter. As Jacques Derrida would have it, periodization is like a specter, it "begins by coming back."[103]

Two Current Problems of Remoteness: Globalization and the Anthropocene

Globalization brings us back to the problem of remoteness and periodization. It generates problems about communication and absorption;[104] it de-centers geographical models of core and periphery, or First, Second, and Third World;[105] it highlights disputes about the destabilization of the sovereign era in view of new technologies, mass migration, climate change, sinking island states, coastal inundations, food (in)security, the fragilities of the global economic system, and cross-border threats of nonstate actors.[106] Some of these issues of the globalized world have only recently emerged on the horizon of international relations, and they relate to the problem of the Anthropocene, a term only coined in 2000 by an atmospheric scientist to introduce the geological epoch.[107] The Anthropocene, too, presents a problem of periodization.

These new issues challenge the constructs and vocabularies of remoteness in international relations and international law. For example, time-

---

103. Derrida, *supra* note 69, at 37.

104. LE GOFF, *supra* note 63, at 116.

105. *See* DENIS COSGROVE, APOLLO'S EYE: A CARTOGRAPHIC GENEALOGY OF THE EARTH IN THE WESTERN IMAGINATION ix–x (2001).

106. *See* Daniel Bethlehem, *The End of Geography: The Changing Nature of the International System and the Challenge to International Law* 25 EUR. J. INT'L L. 9, 18 (2014). *See also* Catherine Dauvergne, MAKING PEOPLE ILLEGAL: WHAT GLOBALIZATION MEANS FOR MIGRATION AND LAW (2008); SASKIA SASSEN, LOSING CONTROL? SOVEREIGNTY IN THE AGE OF GLOBALIZATION (1996).

107. Paul J. Crutzen, *The "Anthropocene," in* EARTH SYSTEM SCIENCE IN THE ANTHROPOCENE: EMERGING ISSUES AND PROBLEMS 13 (Eckart Ehlers & Thomas Krafft eds., 2000).

series aerial and satellite imagery captured for the first time in 2016 the disappearance of vegetated reef islands belonging to the Solomon Islands. The disappearance may have resulted from rising sea levels due to human-induced climate change. Together with episodes of severe drought, storm surges, tidal forcings, and topographic and groundwater contamination by seawater, the question now arises of whether we are entering the age of climate refugees and the disappearing state.

To Plato (c. 428–348 BCE), the lost city of Atlantis was the subject of allegory.[108] Today we begin to periodize it as reality. However, the concept of statehood does not accommodate Atlantis-like deterritorializations, and the structure of international refugee law does not legally recognize mass migratory border crossings caused by natural disasters.[109] These scenarios have been too remote to contemplate. The Atlantis scenario conceptually challenges the closed circuit of rootedness that forms the telluric underpinning of statehood. This circuit construes statelessness as a condition resulting from discrimination and gaps in nationality laws, the emergence of new states, or changes in borders between existing states. The primordial logic of statehood never contemplated the submergence of extant states, or even the remote idea of statehood *sans* territory.[110] Pressures of the globalized world and the Anthropocene now give rise to remote possibilities that suddenly outpace the legal and political means of regulating their arrival. It produces new idioms such as the climate refugee, which stretches the vocabulary of international law to cover objects and purposes of unintended nearby conventional law. It creates gaps and uncertainties in the application of law, which either weakens international law's credibility or forces its recognition of the Wittgenstein-like *non liquet* proposition that "Whereof one cannot speak, thereof one must be silent."[111]

The physically disappearing state—or other weather-related displacements associated with submerging deltas, desertification, and thawing permafrost—also presents contextual challenges to the border logic of international law. At most, the onset of migratory disruptions, presumably created by sudden circumstances, threatened the understood spa-

108. *See* PLATO, TIMAEUS, *in* PLATO: TIMAEUS AND CRITIAS 13 (Robin Waterfield trans., 2008).

109. See Christopher R. Rossi, *The Nomos of Climate Change and the Sociological Refugee in a Sinking Century*, 50 GEO. WASH. INT'L L. REV. 613, 615–17 (2018).

110. Abhimanyu George Jain, *The 21st-Century Atlantis: The International Law of Statehood and Climate Change–Induced Loss of Territory*, 50 STAN. J. INT'L L. 1, 3, 49 (2014).

111. I refer to LUDWIG WITTGENSTEIN, TRACTATUS LOGICO-PHILOSOPHICUS 90 (Bertrand Russell intro., 1922) ("*Wovon man nicht sprechen kann, darüber muß man schweigen.*").

tial peripheries of the state. However, projected climate-induced human displacements do little to stimulate the crisis sensitivity of the bracketed international legal mindset, which has been built on the geographically centered landscape of interwar Europe, not on perturbations to the system arising from the non-European periphery.

The institutional societal response to forced cross-border movement began after World War I, with the birth of the High Commission for Refugees under the direction of Fridtjof Nansen and within the legal framework of the League of Nations and the International Labor Organization.[112] In addition to the 1954 and 1961 statelessness conventions, the Refugee Convention (1951) created a new *dispositif*—a watchful European panopticon to contain the acute spread of migratory unease and spatial disorder through the creation of an exceptional classification of the modern refugee.[113] This panopticon restricted protections to those bracketed persons fleeing persecution mostly from within a European line of amity. It extended protections to persons able to show a well-founded fear of persecution owing to affiliation with a race, religion, nationality, or membership of a particular social group or political opinion.[114] It assumed a sequential harm caused by some state or person—an agent—not a diffuse or indiscriminate environmental condition. Importantly, it temporalized the objective fear of persecution, situating the threat in the present passive tense to thwart stale, remote, or inchoate claims. Historical treatment or future concerns do not activate the designation of refugee status, nor does a person's subjective state of mind. It is individualized and arises from the condition of *being persecuted*.

However, more than one million migrants and refugees from mostly Muslim-majority countries beyond the line of European amity suddenly entered Europe through Balkan corridors or Mediterranean Sea crossings between 2015 and 2016. This influx created massive problems and divisions within the European Union. A collapsing refugee legal structure, beholden to the vocabulary of a bounded spatial design predicated on European interwar thinking, transposed into a reordered peripheral space that fortified borders, non-entrée procedures, interception and interdiction techniques, and offshore processing centers. Elsewhere, as

---

112. *See* Rossi, *supra* note 109, at 626.

113. *See* Didier Bigo, *Globalized (in)Security: The Field and the Ban-Opticon*, *in* TERROR, INSECURITY AND LIBERTY: ILLIBERAL PRACTICES OF LIBERAL REGIMES AFTER 9/11, at 10 (Didier Bigo & Anastassia Tsoukala eds., 2008).

114. Convention Relating to the Status of Refugees, art. 1(A)(2), July 28, 1951, 19 U.S.T. 6259, 189 U.N.T.S. 150.

in the United States, it transmuted into a "build-a-wall" political platform.[115] These responses intend to establish an extraterritorial trip wire to thwart application of *non-refoulement,* the established international legal proscription against forcing refugees to return to frontiers where they will face threats to life or freedom.

This security network preserved the spatial grip of statehood that could not otherwise withstand the nihilistic consequences of normalizing multitudes of people outside the full scope of statehood's protective shell. The restrictive measures implemented by receiving states, together with innate definitional ambiguities and ambivalence toward the refugee, call into question whether the Refugee Convention is still fit for its purpose.[116] Is the international legal *dispositif* now defined more by the disintegrating order it seeks to uphold, or by the gaps it cannot address or even foresee? Problems of globalization and the Anthropocene will produce future debates on periodization and rearrange *rooted* conceptions of space that implicitly define remoteness as the study of international relations broadens beyond the building block of the state.

Geographic Remoteness

As already suggested by problems of globalization and the Anthropocene, historiographic problems of temporality have a companion. The revenant of remoteness intrudes on the study of international relations in the form of geographic spatiality. Globalization literature asserts that the hypermobility of capital, labor, technology, and information has compressed time and space, eclipsing old industrial cores with new centers of production—while creating new peripheries.[117] The unsecured political geographies of the world (and beyond), for instance the deep seabed, outer space, Antarctica, and ice-encrusted transpolar sea-lanes, are becoming less remote.

Jurisdictional claims over areas once considered beyond the limits of national jurisdiction have been expanding for almost one century. This encroachment has been particularly robust in the law of the sea, with the

---

115. COMMITTEE ON ARRANGEMENTS FOR THE 2016 REPUBLICAN NATIONAL CONVENTION, REPUBLICAN PLATFORM 2016, at 26 (2016) ("[W]e support building a wall along our southern border and protecting all ports of entry.").

116. Rossi, *supra* note 109, at 635.

117. *See, e.g.,* KEVIN R. COX, *Introduction: Globalization and Its Politics in Question, in* SPACES OF GLOBALIZATION: REASSERTING THE POWER OF THE LOCAL 1 (Kevin R. Cox ed., 1997).

twentieth-century extension of the territorial sea, the development of the contiguous zone, the continental-shelf doctrine, archipelagic waters, exclusive fishing zone claims, the exclusive economic zone, and now twenty-first-century extended continental-shelf submissions. They find increasingly contested expression in sovereign claims over the Northeast Passage across Eurasia, its lesser-included stretch called the Northern Sea Route, the Northwest Passage atop North America, the waters and continental shelf adjacent to Svalbard, and the South China Sea, the fifth-largest body of water in the world. In the seventeenth century, Hugo Grotius overlooked the North Sea and considered the waters too vast to be possessed.[118] Today, 36 percent of the area of the world's oceans (containing 90 percent of fish stocks and 87 percent of the world's oil and gas deposits) fall under some form of coastal state authority.[119]

These sovereign-like claims and creeping enclosures invite an array of reterritorialization schemes, by states, transnational corporations, and even business elites. The ledger technology of bitcoin and cryptocurrencies reveals a new power that is shaking staid financial institutions and central banking systems, leading them into crypto experimentation.[120] The next great space race may be between the United States and China.[121] Could it already be taking place among billionaires Elon Musk, Jeff Bezos, and Richard Branson?[122] Metadata surveillance schemes and signals intelligence activities pose distant national security, foreign policy, and privacy concerns affecting information and communications technologies.[123] Pressures to reconfigure and territorialize the shrinking

118. HUGO GROTIUS, MARE LIBERUM 1609–2009, at 81 (Robert Feenstra ed., with a general introduction by Jeroen Vervliet, 2009) (1609).

119. Garry Taylor, *The Law of the Sea and "Creeping Jurisdiction of Coastal States,"* LINKEDIN, https://www.linkedin.com/pulse/law-sea-creeping-jurisdiction-coastal-states-garry-taylor

120. For instance, US banking conglomerate J. P. Morgan Chase & Company's digital asset stablecoin (JPM Coin) and its competitor, Ripple's XRP.

121. *See generally* David A. Koplow, *The Fault Is Not in Our Stars: Avoiding an Arms Race in Outer Space*, 59 HARV. INT'L L. J. 331 (2018) (focusing on the coming competitions to control outer space); Matthew Burris, *Astroimpolitic: Organizing Outer Space by the Sword*, 7 STRAT. STUD. Q. 108 (2013) (noting that intense competition (with China) for control of outer space need not result in conflict).

122. *See* Peter H. Diamandis, *The Next Space Race: Bezos vs. Musk*, SINGULARITYHUB (May 24, 2019), https://singularityhub.com/2019/05/24/the-next-space-race-bezos-vs-musk/; Jackie Wattles, *Richard Branson's Virgin Galactic Is Finally Moving to Its Space Tourism Headquarters*, CNNBUSINESS (May 10, 2019), https://www.cnn.com/2019/05/10/tech/richard-branson-virgin-galactic-space-tourism-spaceport-america/index.html

123. Exec. Office of the President, Presidential Policy Directive 28: Signals Intelligence Activities (2014); Privacy and Civil Liberties Oversight Bd., Exec. Office of the Presi-

global commons suggest coming conflicts between newly reshaped cores and peripheries, among forces of globalization, governance, and transnational capital writ large. In a world of scarcity, these reconfigurations of geographic spatiality will play out against the ever-evolving backdrop of coercive violence and socialized forms of political control.[124]

Territorializing Remoteness

Reterritorializing the increasingly less remote global commons presupposes an idea of territory itself, and the prime position it occupies in international relations discourse and state formation.[125] The rise of transnational, supranational, substate, and nonstate actors adds multilayered edges to the traditional political imagination of bounded territorial space.[126] According to Nikolas Rajkovic, this traditional and notional idea of territory has labored since roughly the sixteenth century under the "brute and geological" majesty of international law's limited spatial geo-epistemology.[127] He argued that the "inescapable decay" of cartographic representations required consideration of "non-territorialized configurations" involving "material and social practices" in understanding the territorial matrix.[128]

In *The Birth of Territory* (2013), Stuart Elden excavated the genealogy of the political-territorial order, locating its constant evolution across time, and its significance as a tool of historical agrimensors. Through his critical examination of historical texts dating to Greco-Roman traditions (*khôra*/χώρα, *polis*, *terra*), he emphasized its association with the majesty of the king in early modern Europe, where fealty was established in relation to the person of the king more than the surrounding realm. "[T]he emergence of territory at Westphalia was not tied to some absolute

dent, Report on the Surveillance Program Operated Pursuant to Section 702 of the Foreign Intelligence Surveillance Act (2014).

124. *See* Matthew Sparke, *Political Geography: Political Geographies of Globalization (2)—Governance*, 30 PROGRESS IN HUM. GEOGRAPHY 357 (2006).

125. *See, e.g.*, ROY E. H. MELLOR, NATION, STATE, AND TERRITORY 53 (1989) ("Human societies have a strong attachment to territory, seeking to exercise absolute control over tracts of country regarded as vital living space.").

126. Anssi Paasi, *Reading Stuart Elden's The Birth of Territory*, 46 POL. GEO. 93, 97 (2015).

127. Nikolas M. Rajkovic, *The Visual Conquest of International Law: Brute Boundaries, the Map, and the Legacy of Cartogenesis*, 31 LEIDEN J. INT'L L. 267, 271 (2018).

128. *Id.* at 268.

notion of sovereignty, as is often supposed," wrote Elden.[129] State formation developed as a sociological project that transformed the uncentered, un-unified peripatetic wanderings of the king and his cortège ultimately into a dimension of fixity and internal rulership.[130] However, the concept of territory had to develop into the idea of bounded space, and this development had to first dissolve or depersonalize the status tidings accorded to the personage of the *seignor.* Only after Westphalia did the depersonalized concept of territory begin to coalesce. It first had to form a spatial framework for the European exportation of a new political technology of land division that relied on calculative measurements extending to the territorial periphery. In his historical review of the idea of territorial space, Elden concluded that "[t]erritory can be understood as the political counterpart to this notion of calculating space."[131] Territorial space is something more than bounded space.

Lines and Maps

An inexact foretelling of this politicized method of calculating space found expression with the cartographic division of the world into Portuguese and Spanish halves with the Treaty of Tordesillas (1494).[132] The crudity of this late medieval depiction of *nomos,* more telling perhaps as "cultural text"[133] within the fraying ranks of Christendom,[134] suggested the beginnings of an understanding in Europe of the internal homogeneities of space crafted from linear, calculated, division.[135] It mattered

---

129. ELDEN, *supra* note 90, at 313.

130. Michael Biggs, *Putting the State on the Map: Cartography, Territory, and European Sate Formation,* 41 COMP. STUD. SOC'Y & HIST. 374, 375 (1999).

131. ELDEN, *supra* note 90, at 322.

132. *See* J. B. Harley, *Deconstructing the Map, in* 26 CARTOGRAPHICA 1, 12 (1989) (noting that centers of political power always have exerted political influence on cartography: "Monarchs, ministers, state institutions, the Church, have all initiated programs of mapping for their own ends."). The treaty divided newly discovered land as between Portugal and the Crown of Castile. Land east of the demarcation would belong to Portugal; land west of the demarcation would belong to Spain.

133. "Maps are a cultural text." *Id.* at 7.

134. *See* J. Leitch Wright, Jr., *Sixteenth Century English-Spanish Rivalry in La Florida,* 38 FL. HIST. Q. 265, 265 (1960) (noting Spain's protest of John Cabot's 1498 coastal exploration of North America, commissioned by Henry VII of England). *See generally* JESÚS VARELA MARCOS, EL TRATADO DE TORDESILLAS EN LA POLÍTICA ATLÁNTICA CASTELLANA (1997) (discussing the struggles for the succession to the Crown of Castile and the disputes with Portugal).

135. J. B. Harley encouraged an epistemological shift in interpreting cartography.

little that the measurement of longitude at sea remained elusive at this time.[136] It would matter only later that neither country knew where the line fell in the east—the dark side of the earth—as the division intended to run north-south fully around the globe.[137] Alexander VI's 1493 *Inter caetera* papal bull establishing the north-south demarcation line 100 leagues west of the Cape Verde Islands,[138] adjusted by the treaty to accommodate Portugal's protest and settling on a mutually agreed-on demarcation line 370 leagues west of the Cape Verde Islands,[139] displayed embryonic regard for the technical processes that would extend cartography as a mathematical expression of control.[140] By claiming the Atlantic Ocean

---

Mappers have always engaged in the unquestioned form of knowledge creation, however "cartography is seldom what cartographers say it is." Harley, *supra* note 132, at 1. On the central role of linearity in the disciplinary paradigm of international law, see Zain Sardar, "The Horizon of International Law: Earth-Thinking, Ordering and Disciplinary International Law in the Colonial/Modern World-System" 15 (PhD dissertation, University of London [Birkbeck], 2018).

136. *See generally* W. G. L. Randles, *Portuguese and Spanish Attempts to Measure Longitude in the 16th Century*, 28 VISTAS IN ASTRONOMY 235–241 (1985) (tracing the befuddling astronomical and mathematical problems of longitude measurement for purposes of navigation and cartography). Longitude would remain elusive for centuries, and not well understood even after the eighteenth-century clockmaker John Harrison invented the first accurate marine chronometer. *See generally* DAVA SOBEL, LONGITUDE: THE TRUE STORY OF A LONE GENIUS WHO SOLVED THE GREATEST SCIENTIFIC PROBLEM OF HIS TIME (1995) (discussing Harrison's forty-year quest to invent a chronometer to keep accurate time for navigation purposes); Henry Jones, *Lines in the Ocean: Thinking with the Sea about Territory and International Law*, 4 LONDON REV. INT'L L. 307–43 (2016) (discussing problems relating to constructing space at sea).

137. DAVID BUISSERET, THE MAPMAKERS' QUEST: DEPICTING NEW WORLDS IN RENAISSANCE EUROPE 77 (2003). Disputes erupted between Spain and Portugal in the 1520s over where the Treaty of Tordesillas's eastern line fell due to problems relating to the calculation of longitude. These problems would persist into the eighteenth century's introduction of a reliable maritime chronometer. *Id. See also* STEPHEN R. BOWN, 1494: HOW A FAMILY FEUD IN MEDIEVAL SPAIN DIVIDED THE WORLD IN HALF 157 (2012) ("no one had any real idea of what was being divided").

138. For an English translations, see *The Doctrine of Discover, 1493: A Spotlight on a Primary Source by Pope Alexander VI*, HISTORY NOW (Gilder Lehrman Institute of American History, https://www.gilderlehrman.org/content/doctrine-discovery-1493 (last visited Aug. 21, 2019).

139. The treaty granted title to Portugal of all new land north and east of the line; Spain assumed possession of all new territories south and west of the line. The division essentially secured the North African coast east of Morocco for Spain while allowing Portugal to retain interests in West Africa. *See* JOHN EDWARDS, THE SPAIN OF THE CATHOLIC MONARCHS 1474–1520, 246 (2000).

140. The treaty did recognize the mathematical application of longitude as the division line running west of the Azores and Cape Verde, but was completely silent as to the assignment of space pertaining to the sea zones. *See* ARTHUR JAY KLINGHOFFER, THE POWER OF PROJECTIONS: HOW MAPS REFLECT GLOBAL POLITICS AND HISTORY 61 (2006). Assertions of *dominium* over sea space would not crystallize until Cornelius van Bynkershoek's doctrinal expression of the territorial sea in the early eighteenth century.

as a European geopolitical space,[141] the Treaty of Tordesillas began to foreshadow the developing "jigsaw of territorial states" that created a depiction unknown to medieval Christendom, where maps were rarely used to represent geographical information.[142] Jerry Brotton noted that "[l]ate fifteenth- and sixteenth-century geography had only ever really been based on the ability to speculate and conjecture on the imaginative possession of distant territories." In terms of the Treaty of Tordesillas, that speculation covered half of the world. However, this difficulty in picturing remoteness did not make the depictions "any less effective and valuable in the eyes" of those who used them.[143]

The Contarini-Rosselli 1506 world map,[144] the first printed map of the New World,[145] connected the coast of America to the Asian mainland,[146] erroneously supporting Columbus's conclusion that he had discovered a new pathway to Asia. Martin Waldseemüller's (1470–1520) 1507 twelve-block woodcuts,[147] forming the oldest known printed map to use the toponym "America,'"[148] separated the New World from Asia and depicted a map of 360 degrees of world circumference, suggesting the Pacific Ocean (*Mar del Sur*) as a separate body of water before the overland

---

141. COSGROVE, *supra* note 105, at 84.

142. Biggs, *supra* note 130, at 374. Referencing Harvey, Biggs noted that "[m]edieval Christendom was essentially a mapless world, with no conception of states, scale, or "any kind of graphical depiction of the earth's surface." *Id.* at 376–77. Most familiar to rulers would have been the *mappaemundi*, a sacred depiction of cosmological space orienting Earth to Heaven." *Id.* at 374–75.

143. JERRY BROTTON, TRADING TERRITORIES: MAPPING THE EARLY MODERN WORLD 186 (1998).

144. Giovanni Matteo Contarini & Francesco Rosselli (engraver), *Mundu* [sic] *spericum . . . cognosces diligentia joani mathei Contareni, arte et ingenio francisci Roselli florentini 1506 notũ* (1506), *available at* Brit. Lib., https://www.bl.uk/collection-items/first-known-printed-world-map-showing-america

145. *Mundu* [sic] *spericum . . . cognosces diligentia joani mathei Contareni, arte et ingenio francisci Roselli florentini 1506* notũ. Brit. Lib. [catalogue detail], Brit. Libr., http://explore.bl.uk/primo_library/libweb/action/dlDisplay.do?vid=BLVU1&search_scope=LSCOP-ALL&docId=BLL01004961342&fn=permalink. ("This is believed to be the first printed map of the world showing any part of America.")

146. LISTER, *supra* note 32, at 110.

147. Martin Waldseemüller, *Universalis cosmographia secundum Ptholomaei traditionem et Americi Vespucii alioru[m]que lustrationes* (1507). The only extant version of this map is housed at the Library of Congress in Washington, DC, and is available for digital viewing at https://www.loc.gov/item/2003626426/

148. Giovanni Matteo Contarini & Francesco Roselli (engraver), *Mundu* [sic] *spericum . . . cognosces diligentia joani mathei Contareni, arte et ingenio francisci Roselli florentini 1506 notũ* (1506); Lister, *supra* note 32, at 110. It has been referred to as the baptismal certificate of the New World. Hans Wolff, *Martin Waldseemüller: The Most Important Cosmographer in a Period of Dramatic Scientific Change, in* America: Early Maps of the New World 111, 112 (Hans Wolff ed., 1992).

sighting of Balboa in 1513 and Magellan's arrival from the South Atlantic in 1520. This depiction radically altered the classical world of Ptolemaic geography, which portrayed only the continents of Europe, Africa, and Asia.[149] Curiously, a subsidiary map on Waldseemüller's same sheet contains a planisphere of the Western Hemisphere that omits the strait across the Central American isthmus, suggesting "how speculative and tentative geographical knowledge was at the time, especially with regard to the most important questions about the structure of the New World and the sea route to the 'Indies.'"[150]

Florentine cosmographer Amerigo Vespucci (1454–1512) deeply influenced Waldseemüller.[151] Sailing under Portuguese authority, Vespucci provided a travel account of his 1501–1502 New World voyage in a letter to Lorenzo Pietro di Medici; when reworked, it then circulated in Paris as the famous 1503 *Mundus Novus* letter ("And these [new regions] we may rightly call a new world").[152] Based on Vespucci's account, Wald-

---

149. Ancient geography and astronomical science depended heavily on Claudius Ptolemy (c. 100) and his famous work, GEOGRAPHIA, also known as COSMOGRAPHIA. Ptolemy conceived of the Earth as a mathematically measurable. His views dominated Western science for fourteen centuries, although he underestimated the Earth's circumference by 18,000 miles. *See* Hans Wolff, *The Conception of the World on the Eve of the Discovery of America—Introduction, in* AMERICA: EARLY MAPS OF THE NEW WORLD 10 (Hans Wolff ed., 1992).

150. *Id.* at 114. *See also* EVIATAR ZERUBAVEL, TERRA COGNITA: THE MENTAL DISCOVERY OF AMERICA 40–41 (1992) (noting the difficulties encountered by sixteenth-century European cosmographers on settling on the proposition that the New World presented a single landmass).

151. Vespucci and Ptolemy are the two principal influencers of Waldseemüller's 1507 map. Their images adorn the top of the map. *See* plate 3, *Universalis cosmographia,* LIBR. CONG., https://www.loc.gov/resource/g3200.ct000725C/?r=0.215,-0.004,0.748,0.371,0

152. *Et inuenimus quales nouū mūdu appellare licet. . . . Sed hanc eorum opinionem esse falsam et veritati omnino contrariam hec mea ultima navigatio declaravit, cum in partibus illis meridianis continentem invenerim frequentioribus populis et animalibus habitatam quam nostrum Europam seu Asiam vel Africam. . . . Ibi eam terram cognovimus non insulam, sed continentem esse, quia et longissimis producitur litoribus non ambientibus eam et infinitis habitatoribus replete est. . . .* [And these (new regions) we may rightly call a new world. . . . But that this their opinion is false and utterly opposed to the truth, this my last voyage has made manifest; for in those southern parts I have found a continent more densely peopled and abounding in animals than our Europe or Asia or Africa. . . . We knew that land to be a continent and not an island both because it stretches forth in the form of a very long and unbending coast, and because it is replete with infinite inhabitants]. MUNDUS NOVUS: LETTER TO LORENZO PIETRO DI MEDICI 1 (George Tyler Northrup trans., 1916); MUNDUS NOVUS: EIN BERICHT AMERIGO VESPUCCI'S AN LORENZO DE MEDICI ÜBER SEINE REISE NACH BRASILIEN IN DEN JAHREN 1501/1502, at 29 (in Faksimile und mit einleitungen herausgegeben von Emil Sarnow & Kurt Trübenbach, Strassburg im Elsass, 1903) [Latin text]. Waldseemüller was part of a group of humanist clerics who formed an intellectual circle at the Gymnasium Vosagense in Saint-Dié,

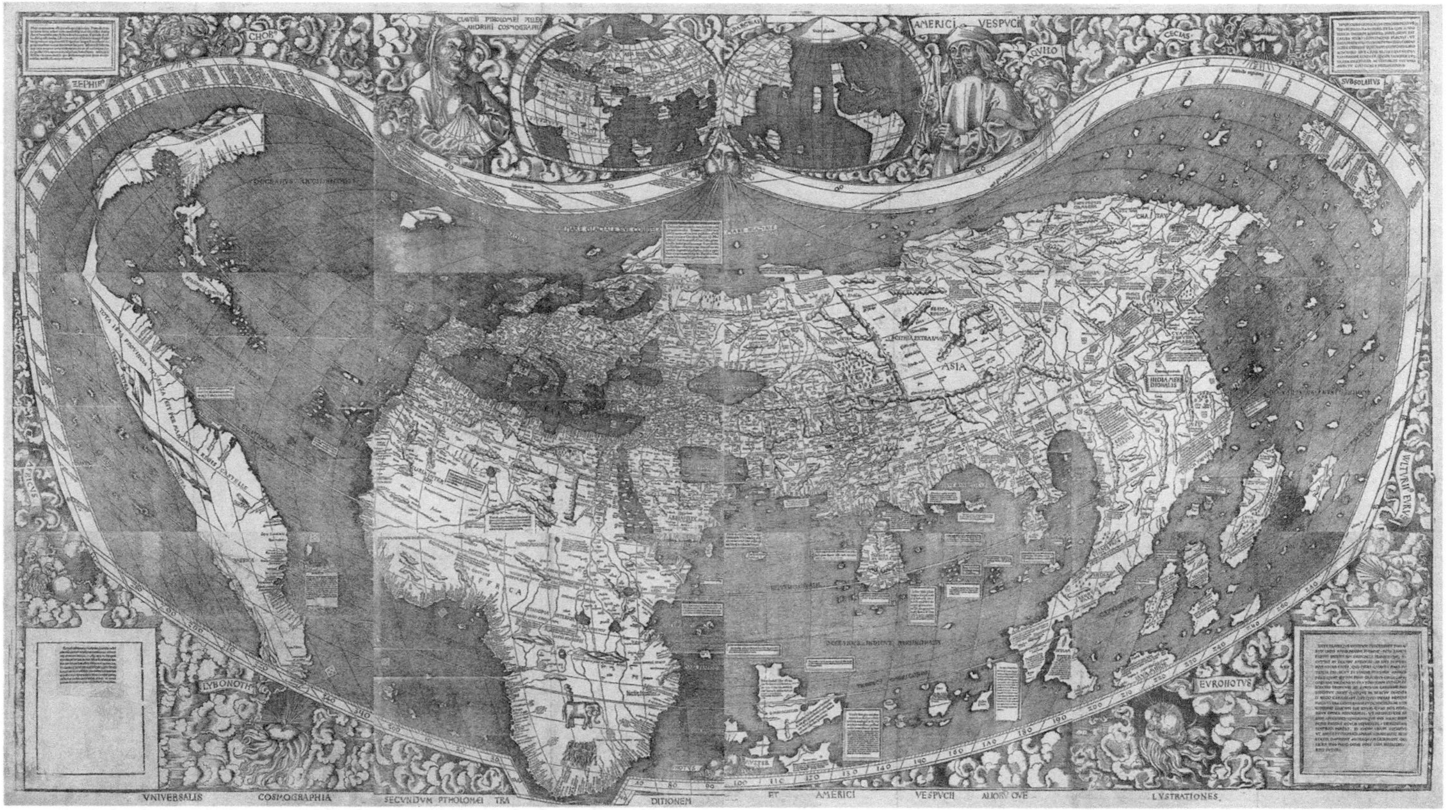

Fig. 1: *Universalis cosmographia,* Martin Waldseemüller, cartographer, 1507. Image courtesy of Geography and Map Division, Library of Congress.

seemüller's 1507 map depicted open water separating the southern continent from the northern landmass, or "the continents of North and South America as we recognize them today."[153] The map also suggested a possible northern route to Asia atop the North American continent.[154] He created woodcut gores for a three-inch-diameter terrestrial globe intended as an ensemble package of his *Cosmographiae introductio.*[155] Two of these 1507 globe gores survive,[156] and, unlike his map, they also suggest a southern and westward passageway to Asia around the headland of what would become the Cape of Good Hope.[157] However, these aspects

---

France. The group acquired a French translation of the *Mundus Novus*, leading Waldseemüller to believe Vespucci's voyages were principally responsible for the discovery of the New World. *See* John R. Hébert, *The Map that Named America*, LIBR. CONG (Sept. 2003), https://www.loc.gov/loc/lcib/0309/maps.html

153. John W. Hessler, *"An Island . . . Surrounded on All Sides by Sea": The World Map 1507*, *in* JOHN W. HESSLER & CHET VAN DUZER, SEEING THE WORLD ANEW: THE RADICAL VISION OF MARTIN WALDSEEMÜLLER'S 1507 & 1516 WORLD MAPS 13 (2012). Waldseemüller wrote, "The earth is now known to be divided into four parts, the first three are continents, but the fourth part is an island, because it has been found to be surrounded on all sides by sea." *Id.* at 16 (quoting Waldseemüller's *Cosmographiae introductio*).

154. Cartographers debate the significance of the northern landmass as a depiction of North America. Columbus's fourth and last voyage to the New World in 1502 patrolled the coasts of present-day Nicaragua, Costa Rica, and Panama for the western passage to the Pacific Ocean and proved that a strait did not exist between North and South America. A navigable northern route across North America would have been a matter of pure conjecture. Neither of these routes would be known to exist for another 400 years. Cartographers debate the significance of the northwest landmass and differences between Waldseemüller's 1507 and 1516 maps owing to the theory that Waldseemüller may have come around to the erroneous idea that the northwest landmass was actually Cuba (Columbus's Asia). *See* Video, *The Carta Marina at 500*, LIBR. CONG. (Oct. 6, 2016), https://www.loc.gov/item/webcast-7672 (time mark 31:16), Donald McGuirk, *How the Waldseemüller Carta Marina Answers "Perhaps the Greatest Unsolved Cartographic Puzzle of the Period."* Interestingly, Waldseemüller's 1507 map also depicts the Rocky Mountains and the Andes extending down the western side of both continents. "It is not clear whether his accuracy was due to lost or secret information or was in fact coincidence or intuition." Wolff, *supra* note 148, at 114. The Panama Canal forged the fabled waterway between the oceans in August 1914, following the initiation of the project by the French in the 1880s. The Norwegian discoverer Roald Amundsen and his *Gjøa* expedition (1906) confirmed as correct Waldseemüller's depiction of an open-water passageway across the North American landmass, however it took Amundsen three years of often ice-bound exploration to find the route.

155. Ute Obhof, *The Terrestrial Globe that Named America: On Historical Preservation of Martin Waldseemüller's Gores*, 55/56 GLOBE STUD. 13, 13 (2009).

156. No assembled Waldseemüller globe gores survive, however the two paper globe gores are housed in the Bavarian State Library in Münich and the James Ford Bell Library at the University of Minnesota. For a detailed image, see EDWARD H. DAHL & JEAN-FRANÇOIS GAUVIN, SPHÆRÆ MUNDI: EARLY GLOBES AT THE STEWART MUSEUM 22–23 (2000). The globes are the first printed globes in history. *See* Wolff, *supra* note 148, at 116.

157. I thank Chet Van Duzer for bringing this point to my attention. Waldseemüller's 1507 map depicts the southern continent as extending to the edge of the map, thus block-

of his cartographic portrayal, although prescient, were purely speculative when they were not otherwise simply false (as with Waldseemüller's depiction that the New World contained separate land masses[158]). Perhaps they were based on unrevealed information or voyages unrecorded, although there is no evidence, only extreme historical controversy about the riddles presented by some of Waldseemüller's cartographic depictions and conclusions.[159] Waldseemüller did classify the territory, and by implication what lay beyond, as *terra ultra incognita* or *terra ulteri incognita,* nevertheless recognizing it as belonging to the Crown of Castile (*Tota ista provincia inventa est per mandatum regis castelle*).

As is the case with all maps, Waldseemüller's depictions embedded a history he helped to construct.[160] These depictions embedded political motivations even with their depictions of remoteness. Around 1500, the Portuguese set up a charting center (the *Armazém da Guiné*) to facilitate their growing seaborne political and commercial interests. Several nautical charts, most famously the Cantino map (1502), propelled Portuguese trade to Brazil and the Spice Islands. The Cantino map was a probable product of this navigation center, and its maps were guarded with care and demanded back on return because of their great political value.[161]

---

ing any western sea route to Asia around South America. Waldseemüller's depiction of the southern tip of Africa, however, bends the map border to make additional room for an eastern route around Africa to India to accommodate what was known about Vasco da Gama's discovery of this route from his 1497 voyage. The negative implication here is that Waldseemüller could have used the same technique to craft a route around South America. He did so, not with his map, but with his globe gores; he did do so with his globe gores. Van Duzer points out that in many cases it is difficult if not impossible to know what Waldseemüller was thinking.

158. Columbus's fourth and last voyage to the New World in 1502 patrolled the coasts of present-day Nicaragua, Costa Rica, and Panama for the western passage to the Pacific Ocean and proved that a strait did not exist between North and South America. Waldseemüller thought in 1507 that Amerigo Vespucci was much more important than Columbus in the European discovery of the New World. He may have been relying on Vespucci's view that the New World formed an island. He would change his opinion about Vespucci nine years later with the publication of the 1516 *Carta marina,* which promoted Columbus's views. *See* Chet Van Duzer, correspondence, on file with the author.

159. *See* Hessler, *supra* note 153, at 16.

160. *See* DENIS WOOD (WITH JOHN FELS), THE POWER OF MAPS 28 (1992) ("Maps are embedded in a history they help to construct.").

161. BUISSERET, *supra* note 137, at 77 (THE MAPMAKERS' QUEST). Maritime knowledge about pathways to Asia and the New World would remain highly valued for more than one century. As an example, shortly after a Dutch East India Company vessel captured a Portuguese carrack harbored at the Johor River in Malaysia (the *Santa Catarina* incident, 1603), offended Frisian and Mennonite shareholders, who viewed the taking as an act of piracy, approached Henry IV, king of France, with a proposal to create a Franco-Dutch East India Company. France had no entry into eastern waters because it lacked the maritime compe-

Martin Lehmann argued that Waldseemüller's 1507 map forwarded the political and economic interests of the Portuguese Crown and its German financiers. He claimed the Spanish Crown must have viewed it as a setback in its search for a westward route to Asia. Waldseemüller's map depicted the southern hemispheric landmass as functionally blocking a western backdoor route to Asian emporia.[162] The discovery of such an opening also would have deeply upset Portuguese interests and the southern German merchant families financially connected to the Portuguese royal house, given its eastern-route monopoly over the spice trade.[163] Deciphering Waldseemüller's early-sixteenth-century mindset presents problems, however it is known that his later visually detailed, annotated, and exoticized map, the *Carta marina* (1516),[164] retracted 128 degrees of spatial projection by deleting the Pacific Ocean, the west coast of the New World, much of South America, and even the toponym that provided the Western Hemisphere's birth certificate.[165] He renamed the

---

tency to navigate such a course. The prospect of gaining access to the shareholders' seasoned captains created a huge problem for the United Provinces and required the expenditure of a great deal of diplomatic capital to thwart. *See* ROSSI, *supra* note 56, at 62–63. Similarly, Sir Francis Drake, the English sea captain, gentleman, and plunderer, obtained sea charts of inestimable value in 1579 raids off the Pacific coast of Central America, "opening up the coasts of Mexico and California and showing a route to him of the Indies to the Cape of Good Hope." George Davidson, *Francis Drake on the Northwest Coast of America in the Year 1579*, 5 TRANSACTIONS & PROC. GEOGRAPHICAL SOC'Y PAC. 1, 35 (1908).

162. Martin Lehmann, *The Depiction of America on Martin Waldseemüller's World Map from 1507—Humanistic Geography in the Service of Political Propaganda*, 3 COGENT ARTS & HUMAN. 10 (2016).

163. *See id.* at 11 (noting the importance of the Welser, Hirschvogel, and Imhoff merchant families of Nuremberg and the Fugger trading house of Augsburg).

164. Martin Waldseemüller, *Carta marina navigatoria portugallen navigationes, atque tocius cogniti orbis terre marisque formam naturam situs et terminos nostris temporibus recognitos et ab antiquorum traditione differentes, eciam quor vetusti non meminerunt autores, hec generaliter indicat* (1516) [A nautical chart that comprehensively shows the Portuguese voyages and the shape of the whole known world, both land and sea, and its nature, its regions, and its limits as they have been determined in our times, and how they differ from the traditions of the ancients, and also areas not mentioned by the ancients], *available at* https://www.loc.gov/resource/g3200m.gct00046/?st=gallery [hereinafter *Carta marina*]. The full name appears across the tops of plates 1, 2, 3, and 4. I thank Ryan Moore, cartographic specialist, Geography and Map Division, Library of Congress, for assistance in securing enhanced images of the *Carta marina*. *See also* Chet Van Duzer, *"Land of Cuba, Part of Asia: The Carta Marina 1516," in* JOHN W. HESSLER & CHET VAN DUZER, SEEING THE WORLD ANEW: THE RADICAL VISION OF MARTIN WALDSEEMÜLLER'S 1507 & 1516 WORLD MAPS 49 (2012) [hereinafter *"Land of Cuba, Part of Asia"*].

165. Chet Van Duzer, *Portraying the World Anew: Martin Waldseemüller's Carta Marina (1516)*, JOHN CARTER BROWN LIBR. (June 11, 2014), https://www.brown.edu/academics/libraries/john-carter-brown/media/martin-waldseem%C3%BCllers-carta-marina-1516 (time mark 16:52, Waldseemüller's 1516 *Carta marina* renamed (South) America *Terra Nova*).

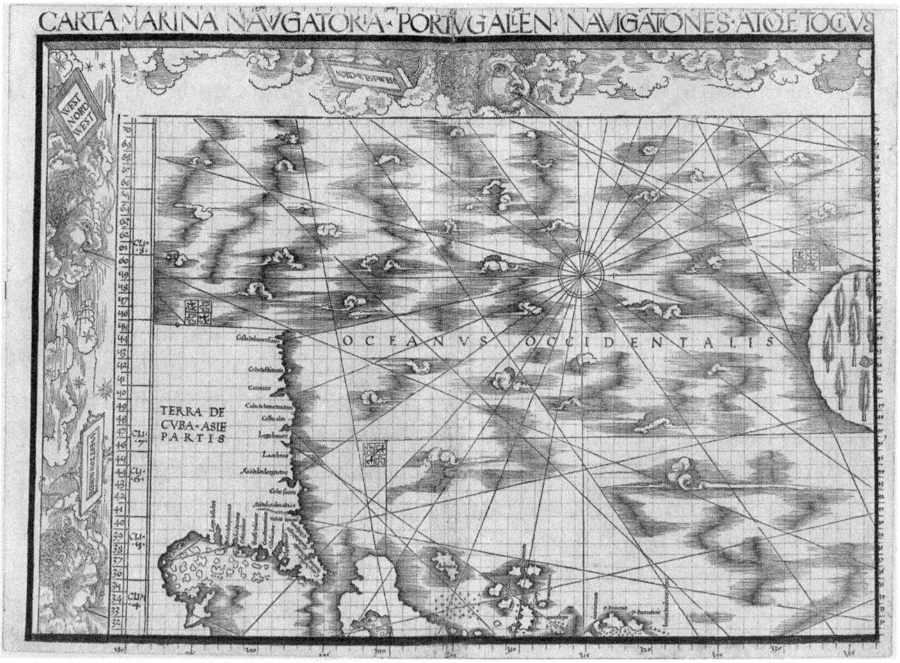

Fig. 2: *Carta marina* (detail), Martin Waldseemüller, cartographer, 1516. Image courtesy of Geography and Map Division, Library of Congress.

landmass that suggested a North American continent *Terre De Cuba Asie Partis* (Land of Cuba, Part of Asia).[166]

Rather than construe this rescission as an aberration of Renaissance thinking, geographers pay increasing attention to Waldseemüller's 1516 masterpiece in view of its more famous 1507 philological counterpart. In the space of nine years, he radically transformed the cartographic conversation he revolutionized in 1507. His turn to Asia not only abandoned the idea of depicting the whole circumference of the world, he deviated from his principal source of cartographic inspiration, Nicolay de Caverio's map of the world (c. 1503), by diminishing Caverio's depictions of the northeast corner of continental Asia, which included China and Japan.[167] Waldseemüller's *Carta marina* projected the functional utility of cartography as a "zoomed-in"[168] political medium. Using portolan tech-

---

166. WALDSEEMÜLLER, *Carta marina*, LIBR. CONG., https://www.loc.gov/resource/g3200m.gct00046/?sp=1 (Plate 1).

167. Van Duzer, *"Land of Cuba, Part of Asia," supra* note 164, at 50 (Caverio's map as principal source of the *Carta marina*), 53 (diminishment of northeast corner of Asia).

168. *Id.* at 53.

niques, he charted the pathway to Asia of interest to the Portuguese *Fidalgos* (noblemen) and the *Estado da Índia* by emphasizing "only the parts of the world where Europeans traveled, and where trade was known to occur."[169] Moreover, with its focus on coastlines, Caverio's map depicted little interior information, except for conventional markings such as the Nile River and the Mountains of the Moon.[170] Waldseemüller's *Carta marina* exploded with interior decoration and detail, including depictions of rivers, mountains, cities, sovereigns, peoples, and detailed text blocks listing sources and the latest information available to him.[171] It represented a tremendous compendium of information assimilated in only nine years by his learned group of humanist associates at the Gymnasium Vosagense in Saint-Dié, France, where he worked. Cartographic historian Chet Van Duzer described it as a "complete, radical updating of his image of Asia" centuries removed from the chief sources of information on his 1507 map culled from Ptolemy and Marco Polo.[172]

In the interceding nine years, Waldseemüller's *Carta marina* demonstrated that the political orientation of the Western world had decidedly turned toward a practical focus on the sea-lanes leading to Asia trade. This map expressly emphasized Portuguese seaborne advances in its fuller title—*A Nautical Chart that Comprehensively Shows the Portuguese Voyages.*[173] Led by King Manuel of Portugal, who was portrayed on the map as having tamed the seas (by harnessing a sea monster while rounding the southern tip of Africa),[174] Waldseemüller produced the first printed nautical map,[175] radically altering ancient principles of Ptolemaic cartography.[176]

169. *Id.*

170. See W. G. L. Handles, *South-East Africa as Shown on Selected Printed Maps of the Sixteenth Century*, 13 IMAGO MUNDI 69, 70 (1956).

171. WALDSEEMÜLLER, *Carta marina*, LIBR. CONG., https://www.loc.gov/resource/g3200m.gct00046/?sp=9&r=-0.01,0.129,1.633,0.811,0 (plate 9). *See* Van Duzer, *"Land of Cuba, Part of Asia," supra* note 164, at 55 (noting Waldseemüller's inclusion of de Varthema and his travelogue as a source, detailing Varthema's journey to the East in 1502–1508).

172. Van Duzer, *supra* note 165 (time mark 21:03).

173. *See* WALDSEEMÜLLER, CARTA MARINA, *supra* note 164.

174. WALDSEEMÜLLER, *Carta marina*, LIBR. CONG., https://www.loc.gov/resource/g3200m.gct00046/?sp=11&r=-0.287,-0.024,1.642,0.815,0 (plate 11). For more on this symbolic political imagery, see CHET VAN DUZER, SEA MONSTERS ON MEDIEVAL AND RENAISSANCE MAPS 76 (2013).

175. *Exploring the Early Americas, Waldseemüller Maps*, LIBR. CONG., https://www.loc.gov/exhibits/exploring-the-early-americas/interactives/waldseemuller-maps/cartamarina1516/index.html

176. On comparisons between Ptolemaic and nautical cartographic systems, see video, *The Carta Marina at 500*, LIBR. CONG. (Oct. 6, 2016), https://www.loc.gov/item/web-

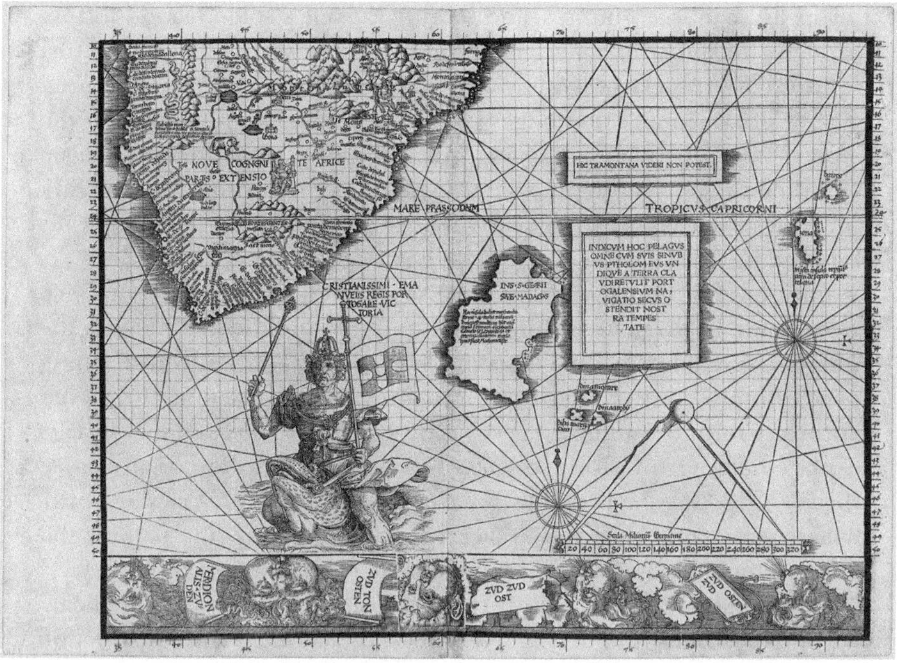

Fig. 3: *Carta marina* (detail), Martin Waldseemüller, cartographer, 1516. Image courtesy of Geography and Map Division, Library of Congress.

The *Carta marina* included a detailed descriptive cartouche of spices and prices, woods, and precious stones from the Calicut trade,[177] which reflected the increasing Western orientation toward commerce and the spice trade.[178] This orientation would indeed help periodize successive

cast-7672 (Joaquim Gaspar, *Maps and Nautical Charts in the Medieval and Early Modern Ages: Two of a Kind or Different Cartographic Paradigms? Facts or Fictions: Debating the Mysteries of Early Modern Science and Cartography*, time mark 2:26). On Waldseemüller's intentional setting aside of Ptolemy and employment of the entirely different nautical cartographic system, see LIBR. CONG., *The Carta Marina at 500*, YOUTUBE (Oct. 6, 2016), https://www.youtube.com/watch?v=PmCwJN6ea5A&feature=youtu.be (*Chet Van Duzer on Martin Waldseemüller's Carta Marina: Its Originality and Diffusion, Facts or Fictions: Debating the Mysteries of Early Modern Science and Cartography*, time mark 1:04:09) [hereinafter *Facts or Fictions*].

177. WALDSEEMÜLLER, *Carta marina*, LIBR. CONG., https://www.loc.gov/resource/g3200m.gct00046/?sp=12&r=0.039,0.071,0.944,0.469,0 (plate 12). Included in his list of spices were nutmeg, cinnamon, ginger, pepper, cloves, spikenard, sandalwood, amber, white coral, and reed coral.

178. Chet Van Duzer, *A Northern Refuge of the Monstrous Races: Asia on Waldseemüller's 1516 "Carta Marina,"* 62 IMAGO MUNDI 221, 226–27 (2010); Chet Van Duzer, *Facts or Fictions*, *supra* note 176 (time mark 1:26:33).

European seaborne empires, and solidify Europe's role in world history through the spread of biota, culture,[179] and the world's forgotten first world war.[180] In acknowledging Foucault's revelation of the omnipresence of power in all knowledge, J. B. Harley attacked not so much the imprecision of early mappings, but the dismissive scientific chauvinism regarding the now more precise "true map," behind which may still lurk "an army of inaccurate, heretical, subjective, valuative, and ideologically distorted images."[181]

Cartographic confusion about the New World, particularly its western coast, would begin to lift within a generation,[182] and the scramble for the Americas would begin.[183] This scramble would first start by transforming space into place with the European toponymic construction of the New World as a form of languified geography. Paul Carter argued that this act of place-naming transformed space symbolically into imperial history, whereby the "namer inscribes his passage permanently on the world, making a metaphorical word-place which others may one day inhabit and by which, in the meantime, he asserts his own place in history."[184] This imperial treatment of the New World did not simply convert meaningless landscapes into descriptive places, it facilitated the construction of historical landscapes, preferencing received European notions of what the New World should become or reflect, as opposed to the characterizations indigenously formed. David J. Robinson noted that this European project of place-naming revealed much about "the context of [the] historic enterprise." It is no wonder that Columbus rank-ordered the first newly discovered landings the Savior (San Salvador), the Virgin

---

179. Felipe Fernández-Armesto, *Maritime History and World History*, *in* MARITIME HISTORY AS WORLD HISTORY 7, 30 (Daniel Finamore ed., 2004).

180. C. R. BOXER, THE PORTUGUESE SEABORNE EMPIRE: 1415–1825, at 2 (1969) (discussing the Dutch-Iberian battles of the seventeenth century, "fought over four continents and on seven seas").

181. *See* Harley, *supra* note 132, at 3, 4–5.

182. For instance, the oval world maps of Sebastian Münster (c. 1540) and Sebastian Cabot (1544), inaccuracies aside, provided examples of increasing articulation of the western coast of the Americas, to the Baja and beyond. *See* Hans Wolff, *Sixteenth-Century Printed Maps of the World*, *in* AMERICA: EARLY MAPS OF THE NEW WORLD 72–75 (Hans Wolff ed., 1992). Waldseemüller had produced in 1513 the *Tabula Terre Nove*, the first printed map to focus on the New World (the Admiral's Map), however it focused on a continuous portion of the eastern coastline of North and South America.

183. *See* LYLE N. MCALISTER, SPAIN AND PORTUGAL IN THE NEW WORLD: 1492–1700, at 93 (1984) (discussing the collapse of Columbian cosmography and the advances of sixteenth-century Spanish, Portuguese, English, and French coastal expeditions).

184. PAUL CARTER, THE ROAD TO BOTANY BAY: AN EXPLORATION OF LANDSCAPE AND HISTORY xxiv (1987).

Mary (Santa María de la Concepción), the king (Fernandina), the queen (Isabela), and finally, the royal prince (Juana).[185]

Cartography would simultaneously undergo an internal zooming-in process that would influence the development of the state, its emerging periphery, and the idea of remoteness. James Scott noted that "[t]he premodern state was, in many crucial respects, partially blind." Not only did it know little if anything about continental *terra ultra incognita*, "it knew precious little about its subjects, their wealth, their landholdings and yields, their location, their very identity. It lacked anything like a detailed 'map' of its terrain and its people."[186] The early modern state had to standardize if not decipher the hieroglyphics of measurement, to achieve food and state security, to collect taxes, to end tax evasion, and to monitor and control public plans.[187] Much of this ignorance facing the premodern state would begin to change in the fifteenth century, through the synoptic power of geographic communication. The intellectual impact of Gutenberg's printing press (1450) operationalized the industrial production of paper, which had started before Gutenberg.[188] The experimental use of woodcut blocks, and then the development in the second third of the fifteenth century of fine-line copperplate engraving,[189] "[p]layed a central role" in sixteenth- and seventeenth-century scientific renewal.[190] Feudal and local maps gave way to larger regional and national representations throughout sixteenth-century Europe.[191] Olaus Magnus produced the first large-scale regional map of Europe (Scandinavia) in 1539, "one of the first maps to show whole" nationalistic units.[192] Maurice Bouguereau published *Le Théâtre Français* in 1594—a compendium of forty-eight town plans "for the pleasure of learned men, for the use of martial men and of the king's tax gatherers

185. David J. Robinson, *The Language and Significance of Place in Latin America*, *in* THE POWER OF PLACE: BRINGING TOGETHER GEOGRAPHICAL AND SOCIOLOGICAL IMAGINATIONS 157, 160 (John A. Agnew & James S. Duncan eds., 1989).The practice at that time was to feminize toponyms attaching to new territory (hence Fernandina for Fernando, Jaua for Juan, and of course, America for Americo Vespucci).

186. JAMES SCOTT, SEEING LIKE A STATE: HOW CERTAIN SCHEMES TO IMPROVE THE HUMAN CONDITION HAVE FAILED 2 (1998).

187. *See id.* at 27–30.

188. CHRISTIAN JACOB, THE SOVEREIGN MAP: THEORETICAL APPROACHES IN CARTOGRAPHY THROUGHOUT HISTORY 54 (2006).

189. *Id.*

190. *Id.* at 55.

191. JOHN RENNIE SHORT, THE WORLD THROUGH MAPS: A HISTORY OF CARTOGRAPHY 112 (2003).

192. *Id.*

and treasurers."[193] Christopher Saxton published *An Atlas of England and Wales* (1579), and shortly after Timothy Pont produced seventy-seven maps of Scotland (1583–1596).[194] Remoteness in the late medieval period meant clarifying the nearby environment as much as filling the interior continental voids with geographic information, not simply decorative art and allegory.

Scott assigned much significance to the development of the cadastral map, which bounded land ownership in the form of a registry, which rationalized "the fiscal take of the state" by eliminating illegible forms of "fiscal feudalism."[195] This map inverted the peripheries of statehood, defining as most important the land tenure demarcations among internal inhabitants. This inversion facilitated accounting, internal control, valuation, and revenue accumulation—elements supervening authority needed in order to grow into the state. *The Sovereign Map,* to borrow from the title of Christian Jacob's exploration of the history of cartography, became a "tool for power"[196]—a "formal mechanism of enunciation"[197]—that imposed on "a province, a nation, a kingdom, an empire, protecting or conquering a territory . . . the rationality of an administrative grid."[198] Elden argued that the development of mathematical means of rationalizing the grid created a powerful tool that the state system could use as an intellectual weapon.[199] Jacob noted that cartography transformed "the indistinct, indeterminate, and formless" into a materialized metonymy of power; it provided "the objectification of a reality that becomes identical for everyone . . . [a] geographical discourse with a referent,"[200] with obvious refinements to the idea of remoteness and its implications for the historical study of international relations.[201] These works contributed to the contemporary understanding of the historiography of the state through their emphases on the determinants of geography, measurement, and land tenure that contributed to the development of the state's spatial capacity and the need to define its core assets along with its tendrils radiating to the periphery.

---

193. *Id.*

194. *Id.*

195. SCOTT, *supra* note 186, at 38.

196. JACOB, *supra* note 188, at 30.

197. *Id.* at 30.

198. *Id.* at xviii.

199. ELDEN, *supra* note 90, at 325 (quoting Harley on maps "being appropriated as an intellectual weapon of the state system").

200. JACOB, *supra* note 188, at 30.

201. *See id.* at xvii–xviii.

This calculative and rational method would extend over the eighteenth century with the development of large estate maps as means of organizing and "seeing" land use.[202] State formation encountered a twofold process of discovery, including an accounting of resources proximate to its core that would contribute to internal management and a more refined articulation of the bounded space that would emerge at the periphery.

Doctrinal Remoteness

This geographic framing brings to light doctrinal criticisms of the study of international relations and its disproportionate emphasis on core subject and geographic areas. This skewing forms a basis of complaint from postcolonial perspectives, where the disciplinary cartography "constructs borders around the spaces recognized as law, privileging particular spaces and excluding, or rendering invisible, other spaces and the interactions within these spaces from the ambit of 'international law.'"[203] The peripheralization of international relations subscribes to a semiotic form of coloniality, which projects the cosmology of its Western Enlightenment–based orientation. Chakrabarty argued that although the project of subaltern studies is to reapportion the narrative and to generate the capacity for muffled voices to represent themselves, Europe "remains the sovereign, theoretical subject of all histories, including the ones we call 'Indian,' 'Chinese,' 'Kenyan,' and so on,"[204] including, presumably "Andean." Here, geographic spatiality preferences narratives and norms nearer to the physical and ideological centers of dominant discourse and information production, nearer to core power structures and regions, nearer to the discursive *lingua franca* of international relations, and nearer to the light-limiting architecture of its established, monetized, and gendered education hubs, department faculties, and professional societies.

One subdivision of international-relations study involves international law, which has a long, established, and increasingly dissected association with the light-limiting strictures of international relations' geographic orientation. The geospatial anatomy of international law's Enlightenment project pinpoints a dominant Western epicenter. This epicenter invites criticisms about its Eurocentric story and its implied

202. Henry Jones, *Property, Territory, and Colonialism: An International Legal History of Enclosure*, 39 LEGAL STUD. 187, 190 (2019).

203. Pearson, *supra* note 1, at 490.

204. DIPESH CHAKRABARTY, PROVINCIALIZING EUROPE: POSTCOLONIAL THOUGHT AND HISTORICAL DIFFERENCE 27 (2000).

crowding out or peripheralization of trans-civilizational contributions, and the subordination of these encounters to presumptions of Europe's grander civilizing mission.[205] Critical scholars, in their turn to history, attempt to relocate international law's historical center, or expand its *locus*, to include attenuated, subaltern voices. These voices may reveal myths about international law's cosmopolitan and universal appeal. They may add coloration and complexity to received historical narratives as they seek to address historical incongruities projected by the dominant Western partial-retellings of history's complex, multitextured story. Evidence of this growing literature extends beyond critical approaches and embraces pluralistic views that also attempt to reconceptualize normative frameworks of international law.[206]

Ideological, physical, and geographic patterns of dominance and proximity now stimulate questions about the *collegium* of international relations specialists and their intimate self-referential vocabulary, groupings, and subdivisions. This intimacy leads to charges that the study of the international is less international than it purports to be,[207] more value-oriented than its structures, organizational forms, and system suggest,[208] and unduly constricted in terms of the normative viewpoints that characterize the field.

Already a process of historiographic self-examination is underway in postcolonial circles. The theoretical unfolding in decolonial thinking has noted the unwitting attention to subaltern critiques expressed in English and housed in elite, Western academic citadels.[209] In his specific

---

205. *See generally* MARTTI KOSKENNIEMI, THE GENTLE CIVILIZER OF NATIONS: THE RISE AND FALL OF INTERNATIONAL LAW 1870–1960 (2002); Kinji Akashi, *(Re-)Examination of "the Eurocentric Story of International Law" through the Japanese Experience*, 107 PROC. AM. INT'L L. 379 (2013).

206. Important reconceptualizations from Latin American perspectives include JUAN PABLO SCARFI, THE HIDDEN HISTORY OF INTERNATIONAL LAW IN THE AMERICAS: EMPIRE AND LEGAL NETWORKS (2017); ARNULF BECKER LORCA, MESTIZO INTERNATIONAL LAW: A GLOBAL INTELLECTUAL HISTORY 1842–1933 (2015); Liliana Obregón, *Between Civilisation and Barbarism: Creole Interventions in International Law*, 27 THIRD WORLD Q. 815 (2006).

207. *See generally* ANTHEA ROBERTS, IS INTERNATIONAL LAW INTERNATIONAL? (2017) (identifying distinct scholarly silos of dominance among the purportedly universalist community of international lawyers).

208. *See generally* BENJAMIN ALLEN COATES, LEGALIST EMPIRE: INTERNATIONAL LAW AND AMERICAN FOREIGN RELATIONS IN THE EARLY TWENTIETH CENTURY (2016) (emphasizing the ideological motivations of practitioners of international law). Dike is the blindfolded figurine of Greek mythology, ancient Greece's goddess of justice.

209. Iver Neumann elevated this problem to the ranks of all present-day academics (not simply expositors of postcolonial viewpoints), who are for the most part products of Western education and in this sense more or less Eurocentric. IVER B. NEUMANN, CON-

examination of subalternity in Latin America, John Beverley pointed out that the subaltern perspective is itself implicated in the Western academic practices that have constructed the subaltern.[210] Walter Mignolo applauded the attention that decolonial scholarship in the Americas pays to Spanish or Latin American authors writing in English, but lamented the absence of attention paid to the viewpoints of Aymaras, Quechuas, and Quichuas, even when they are expressed in English.[211] Finding the missing parts to the postcolonial story may require an excavation of ethnocentric predispositions within the Eurocentric geography of decolonial scholarship. This irony already has been self-consciously suggested by Gayatri Chakravorty Spivak in view of her exalted academic career in the West:[212] "With what voice-consciousness can the subaltern speak?"[213] The fact that she is heard implicates the conclusion that they cannot speak.[214] The ironic implications within intramural circles of postcoloniality should not mask the sustaining observation that self-awareness of history's incongruities and discontinuities is key to minimizing the inherent pitfalls of historiography.

Independent of this introspective debate, subaltern perspectives maintain that their discourses are actually central to the understanding of the discipline. As with negligence and remoteness, their understanding of the periphery is also relational. Postcolonialists see no such thing as "periphery in the air." Subaltern voices have been rendered peripheral only in relation to the dominant Eurocentric viewpoint, and to international law's heteronormative hierarchy and teaching.[215] Indeed,

---

CEPTS OF INTERNATIONAL RELATIONS, FOR STUDENTS AND OTHER SMARTIES 73 (2019) (noting that postcolonialists such as Edward Said, Homi Bhabha, Gayatri Chakravorty Spivak, Achille Mbembe, and Mahmood Mamdani are all products of Western universities).

210. *See generally* JOHN BEVERLEY, SUBALTERNITY AND REPRESENTATION: ARGUMENTS IN CULTURAL THEORY (1999) (presenting considerations on subordination brought about by colonization and access to representation).

211. *See* Walter Mignolo, *Dispatches from Hong Kong 5: Doubtful Postcolonial/Decolonial Scholarship* (June 23, 2012) http://waltermignolo.com/dispatches-from-hong-kong-5-doubtful-postcolonialdecolonial-scholarship/ (noting that decolonial scholarship in the Americas pays attention, for instance, to Spanish or Latin American authors writing in English but misses viewpoints of the Aymaras, Quechuas, and Quichuas).

212. For more on this irony, see Ambesange Praveen V., *Postcolonialism: Edward Said & Gayatri Spivak*, 5 RES. J. RECENT SCI. 47, 48–49 (2016).

213. Gayatri Chakravorty Spivak, *Can the Subaltern Speak?*, *in* MARXISM AND THE INTERPRETATION OF CULTURE 271, 285 (Cary Nelson & Lawrence Grossberg eds., 1988).

214. *See id.* at 308 ("The subaltern cannot speak.").

215. *See generally* Dianne Otto, *Handmaidens, Hierarchies, and Crossing the Public-Private Divide in the Teaching of International Law*, 1 MELBOURNE J. INT'L L. 35–69 (2000) (discuss-

if subaltern voices could actually speak in a way that really *mattered*, they would not be subaltern.[216] The subaltern project seeks to resituate ideological discourse, reform dominantly constructed norms of international law,[217] and counter its own marginalization due to international law's disproportionate Western influences and dominant Euro-geographic physicality.

Voices populating and interrogating international law's periphery include Third World approaches to international law (TWAIL),[218] feminist approaches to international law (FAIL),[219] postcolonial[220] and regional perspectives,[221] the *dependencia* school,[222] world systems

ing hierarchy in the teaching and learning of international law and its effects on the practice of international law).

216. BEVERLEY, *supra* note 210, at 1. *See also* Dianne Otto, *Subalternity and International Law: The Problem of Global Community and the Incommensurability of Difference*, 5 SOC. & LEG. STUD. 337, 359 (1996) (noting that law has the constitutive power to disqualify certain forms of speech).

217. *See, e.g.*, Antony Anghie, *The Evolution of International Law: Colonial and Postcolonial Realities*, 27 THIRD WORLD Q. 739, 739 (2006) (referencing specifically the Eurocentric (traditional) understanding of international law regarding colonialism).

218. *See, e.g.*, B. S. Chimni, *Third World Approaches to International Law: Manifesto*, 8 INT'L COMM. REV. 3 (2006); M. Matua & Anthony Anghie, *"What Is TWAIL?,"* 94 AM. SOC. INT'L. PROC. 31 (2000).

219. *See, e.g.*, Kiran Grewal, *Can the Subaltern Speak within International Law? Women's Right Activism, International Legal Institutions and the Power of "Strategic Misunderstanding," in* NEGOTIATING NORMATIVITY 27 (N. Dhawan et al. eds., 2016).

220. *See, e.g.*, PRABHAKAR SINGH AND BENOÎT MAYER, CRITICAL INTERNATIONAL LAW: POSTREALISM, POSTCOLONIALISM, AND TRANSNATIONALISM (2014); SUNDHYA PAHUJA, DECOLONISING INTERNATIONAL LAW: DEVELOPMENT, ECONOMIC GROWTH AND THE POLITICS OF UNIVERSALITY (2011); ACHILLE MBEMBE, ON THE POSTCOLONY (2001).

221. *See, e.g.*, JUAN PABLO SCARFI, THE HIDDEN HISTORY OF INTERNATIONAL LAW IN THE AMERICAS: EMPIRE AND LEGAL NETWORKS (2017); ARNULF BECKER LORCA, MESTIZO INTERNATIONAL LAW: A GLOBAL INTELLECTUAL HISTORY 1842–1933 (2014); Liliana Obregón, *Completing Civilization: Creole Consciousness and International Law in Nineteenth-Century Latin America, in* INTERNATIONAL LAW AND ITS OTHERS 247 (Anne Orford ed., 2006); Lauri Mälksoo, *The History of International Legal Theory in Russia: A Civilizational Dialogue with Europe*, 19 EUR. J. INT'L L. 211 (2008); RAM PRAKASH ANAND, STUDIES IN INTERNATIONAL LAW AND HISTORY: AN ASIAN PERSPECTIVE (2004); Alfred M. Boll, *The Asian Values Debate and Its Relevance to International Humanitarian Law* 841 INT'L REV. RED CROSS 45 (2001); James Thuo Gathii, *Africa and the History of International Law, in* OXFORD HANDBOOK OF THE HISTORY OF INTERNATIONAL LAW 407 (Bardo Fassbender & Anne Peters eds., 2012); A. Peter Mutharika, *The Role of International Law in the Twenty-First Century: An African Perspective*, 18 FORDHAM INT'L L. J. 1706 (1994); T. O. ELIAS, AFRICA AND THE DEVELOPMENT OF INTERNATIONAL LAW (1988).

222. *See, e.g.*, Theotonio Dos Santos, *The Structure of Dependence*, 60 AM. ECON REV. 231 (1970); Osvaldo Sunkel, *National Development Policy and External Dependence in Latin America*, 6 J. DEV. STUD. 23 (1969); Andre Gunder Frank, *The Development of Underdevelopment*, 18 MONTHLY REV. 17 (1966);

theorists,[223] a litany of radical theories of imperialism,[224] and emerging viewpoints rooted in the gender expressions and experiences of nonheterosexual sexualities.[225] Added to these views is the field of cultural memory studies. Although undernourished in international relations studies, this field draws into question the shadings of historical recall that imperfectly distinguish the temporalities of past, present, and future.[226] Cultural memory is socially constructed. It aggregates distributed, fragmented, yet dynamic societal "beliefs, feelings, moral judgments, and knowledge about the past."[227] This knowledge is not known singly; it is known in comparison to individuals "situated in conflicting groups."[228] Cultural memory is also relational, and it profoundly influences the study of international relations in the Americas,[229] most particularly in the Atacama.[230]

---

223. *See, e.g.*, Immanuel Wallerstein, *Semi Peripheral Countries and the Contemporary World Crisis*, 3 THEORY & SOC'Y 461 (1976); IMMANUEL WALLERSTEIN, THE MODERN WORLD-SYSTEM, VOLUME 1 (1974).

224. *See, e.g.*, JOHN A. HOBSON, THE EVOLUTION OF MODERN CAPITALISM: A STUDY OF MACHINE PRODUCTION (1894); V. I. LENIN, IMPERIALISM, THE HIGHEST STAGE OF CAPITALISM: A POPULAR OUTLINE (1939).

225. *See, e.g.*, Dianne Otto ed., QUEERING INTERNATIONAL LAW: POSSIBILITIES, ALLIANCES, COMPLICITIES, RISKS (2017); CYNTHIA WEBER, QUEER INTERNATIONAL RELATIONS: SOVEREIGNTY, SEXUALITY, AND THE WILL TO KNOWLEDGE (2016); Dianne Otto, *"Taking a Break" from "Normal": Thinking Queer in the Context of International Law*, 101 PROC. AM SOC'Y INT'L L. 119 (2007).

226. BERBER BEVERNAGE & CHRIS LORENZ, EDS., BREAKING UP TIME: NEGOTIATING THE BORDERS BETWEEN PRESENT, PAST AND FUTURE (Berber Bevernage & Chris Lorenz eds., 2013); Benita Parry, *Aspects of Peripheral Modernisms*, 40 ARIEL 27 (2009); DIPESH CHAKRABARTY, PROVINCIALIZING EUROPE: POSTCOLONIAL THOUGHT AND HISTORICAL DIFFERENCE (2000); JOHANNES FABIAN, TIME AND THE OTHER. HOW ANTHROPOLOGY MAKES ITS OBJECT (2002) [1983]. The false dichotomy between diachronic continuity and rupture has been accentuated by the work of Reinhart Koselleck. For more, see Javiér Fernández Sebastián & Juan Francisco Fuentes, *Conceptual History, Memory, and Identity, An Interview with Reinhart Koselleck* 2 CONTRIBUTIONS TO HIST. CONCEPTS 99 (2006).

227. Barry Schwartz, *Collective Memory*, *in* ENCYCLOPEDIA OF SOCIOLOGY 588 (2007).

228. *Id.*

229. *See, e.g.*, Fernando García Argañarás, *Memory, History and Identity in Bolivia's Foreign Policy toward Chile Under Morales*, *in* CONFLICT, MEMORY, AND RECONCILIATION: BRIDGING PAST, PRESENT, AND FUTURE, KIGALI, RWANDA, 2012); Franck Gaudichaud & Mariana Ortega Breña, *Popular Power, Oral History, and Collective Memory in Contemporary Chile*, 36 L. AM. PERSP. 58 (2009); JEANETTE RODRÍGUEZ & TED FORTIER, CULTURAL MEMORY: RESISTANCE, FAITH, AND IDENTITY (2007); RITA ARDITTI, SEARCHING FOR LIFE: THE GRANDMOTHERS OF THE PLAZA DE MAYO AND THE DISAPPEARED CHILDREN OF ARGENTINA (1999); GUILLERMO BONFIL BATALLA, MÉXICO PROFUNDO: RECLAIMING A CIVILIZATION (1987).

230. *See, e.g.*, Paulo Drinot, *Website of Memory: The War of the Pacific (1879–84) in the Global Age of YouTube*, 4 MEMORY STUD. 370 (2011).

Demarginalizing the Desert

Discussion of the Atacama Desert and its importance to the study of international relations covers a wide expanse, and no part of it is more debilitating than the imagery associated with deserts. Isaiah Bowman listed deserts among the main fields of historical exploration, along with polar regions, mountains, tropical forests, islands, and rivers.[231] Borderlands evoke areas defined by administrative and political delimitations of territory, frontiers represent open spaces populated by creative ingenuity, marginal areas "may be out of the way but not necessarily poorly connected," and wilderness implies nature management and the absence of people.[232] And the term *desert* conjures up spatial usages of exoticized marginality, a place for soul-searchers, wanderers, biblical devotionalists,[233] and personal encounters with evil and temptation.[234] These depictions are not those of geographers, anthropologists, zoologists, climatologists, or indigenous inhabitants, but they exist deep in the Western mindset. A vertebrate biologist faintly captured the exoticized significance of the desert in popular culture. He asked, "Why are so many Westerns set in the deserts?"[235]

The answer, in part, traces back to the latter period of the fifteenth century and the first dozen years of the sixteenth century,[236] to a rising European fascination in the landscapes of the Holy Land and their topography as "being distant from Europe."[237] During this period, European narratives of the pilgrimage to the Holy Sepulcher began to circulate in the form of a burgeoning literary genre, the travelogue.[238] An industry of packaged tours, inspired by the publication of *Mandeville's Travels* (1357),[239] grew into annual pilgrim fleets sailing from Venice to

231. Isaiah Bowman, Desert Trails of Atacama 3 (1924).

232. SHAFQAT HUSSAIN, REMOTENESS AND MODERNITY: TRANSFORMATION AND CONTINUITY IN NORTHERN PAKISTAN 4 (discussing marginality), 5 (discussing other remote spatial concepts) (2015).

233. *See, e.g.*, Exodus 2:11–15, Leviticus; Book of Numbers; Deuteronomy 1:1; Acts 7:30.

234. *See, e.g.*, LUKE 4:1–13; MATTHEW 4:1–11; MARK 1:13

235. ENCYCLOPEDIA OF DESERTS xi (Michael A. Mares ed., 1999),

236. H. F. M. PRESCOTT, ONCE TO SINAI: THE FURTHER PILGRIMAGE OF FRIAR FELIX FABRI 18 (1957).

237. RICHARD V. FRANCAVIGLIA, IMAGINING THE ATACAMA DESERT: A FIVE-HUNDRED-YEAR JOURNEY OF DISCOVERY 56 (2018).

238. For a detailed discussion of the geographical material provided by European religious pilgrims, see LLOYD A. BROWN, THE STORY OF MAPS ch. 4 (1949).

239. MANDEVILLE'S TRAVELS was an early secular medieval account of the East, with large portions devoted to descriptions of the Holy Land. It overshadowed the popularity of Marco Polo's *Divisament dou Monde* notwithstanding numerous inaccuracies, enough to

the Holy Land. Four fleets sailed in 1479 and five in 1483.[240] While most pilgrimages involved the journey to Jerusalem, a few wealthy merchants, soldiers, and priests added to their journey a visit to St. Catherine's Monastery at the base of Mount Sinai (Gebel Musa). Employing Saracen guides,[241] they requisitioned the necessary provisions to supply the thirty days passage from Jerusalem to the locus of the Abrahamic religions. This caravan took them deep into the Arabian Peninsula, first across the dune sheet and massifs leading to the Tîh Plateau—the biblical Desert of the Exodus[242]—and then across the escarpments to the Mount, thereafter across more desert to the Red Sea, then to Cairo, and finally Alexandria, where Venetian spice traders would portage them homeward.[243]

Several of the most famous accounts took place during the eventful pilgrimage sailings between 1479 and 1483, including those of the Swiss Franciscan friar Paul Walther of Guglingen's *Itinerarium* (c. 1484)[244] and the German cleric Bernhard von Breydenbach's *Peregrinatio in Terram Sanctam* (1486).[245] Joos van Ghistele, a contemporary Flemish nobleman, also contributed a popular account of the Levant, however his posthumous work, *Tvoyage van Mher Joos van Ghistele*, was reworked by Ambrosius Zeebout and did not appear until published in Ghent in 1557.[246]

"make it extremely improbable that its author ever left his native Europe." MANDEVILLE'S TRAVELS xiv (Michael Seymour ed., 1967). The book has been called perhaps the most popular book in Europe in its own day, see TAMARAH KOHANSKI, THE BOOK OF JOHN MANDEVILLE vii (Tamarah Kohanski & C. David Benson eds., 2001), and "an international blockbuster that combined romance, fiction and travel stories in the form of a traditional pilgrimage narrative." *Id.*; KATHRYNE BEEBE, PILGRIM AND PREACHER: THE AUDIENCES AND OBSERVANT SPIRITUALITY OF FRIAR FELIX FABRI (1437/8–1502), at 39–40 (2014).

240. JONATHAN SUMPTION, THE AGE OF PILGRIMAGE: THE MEDIEVAL JOURNEY TO GOD 373–74 (2003).

241. *See* PRESCOTT, *supra* note 236, at 21.

242. NED H. GREENWOOD, THE SINAI: A PHYSICAL GEOGRAPHY 31 (1997).

243. For pilgrims' articulation of the deserts of the Holy Land, see FRANCAVIGLIA, *supra* note 237, at 56.

244. FRATRIS PAULI WALTHERI VON GUGLINGEN, GUGLINGENSIS ITINERARIUM IN TERRAM SANCTAM ET AD SANCTAM CATHARINAM (Herausgegeben und mit erläuterungen versehen von Matthias Sollweck, 1892). The travelogue is kept at the Staatlichen Bibliothek in Neuburg and der Donau. Its provenance is not known prior to its discovery by Sollweck, however it was probably written after Guglingen's return home in 1484. He died in 1496. Lost versions of his manuscript were known to circulate. *See* Marianne P. Ritsema Van Eck, *Encounters with the Levant: The Late Medieval Illustrated Jerusalem Travelogue by Paul Walter von Gugligen*, 32 MED. HIST. REV. 153, 155 (2017).

245. BERNHARD VON BREYDENBACH, PEREGRINATIO IN TERRAM SANCTAM, EINE PILGERREISE INS HEILIGE LAND, FRÜHNEUHOCHDEUTSCHER TEXT UND ÜBERSETZUNG (Herausgegeben von Isolde Mozer, 2010).

246. AMBROSIUS ZEEBOUT, TVOYAGE VAN MHER JOOS VAN GHISTELE (R. J. G. A. A. Gaspar ed., 1998) (1557). Book 4 details van Ghistele's trip through Arabia to the Monastery of St.

Together, these accounts illuminated nonreligious facets of the late medieval pilgrimage experience, intermixing descriptive commentary and visual art,[247] and they appear as a bridge from cartography's complex transitional period of the early modern age.[248] They helped to establish a travelogue genre that interspersed illustrations of flora and fauna with recordings of cities and Islamic spaces as well as reverential Christian sanctuaries.[249] When they did not prejudice its construction, they helped to demystify the periphery. Pilgrimage literature of the Holy Land "has long been seen as the initial step toward the Renaissance literature of discovery" with its specific attachments to individual identity,[250] and to the development of the novel.[251] Pilgrims' logs, itineraries, diaries, and guidebooks grew into luxurious narratives of self-realization. They also must be viewed as a late-medieval template for the sixteenth- and early seventeenth-century Western interest in exploration of the New World, where the principal interests of explorers as route finders intermixed with "scientific, prospecting, evangelizing, military, surveying, legal, and political motives."[252] Chroniclers of sixteenth- and seventeenth-century exploration provided the "telescope in which to view a gone world," a world as remote as outer space.[253]

Catherine at the foot of Mt. Sinai. Zeebout did not accompany Ghistele on his pilgrimage, which included the Holy Land, Egypt, the Sinai, some Aegean islands, Sicily, Tunis, Carthage, Aden, and Tabriz, but became Ghistele's confessor and was commissioned to write the report. It was not an eyewitness account and "formed part of the nobelman's official self-presentation"). *See also* Stefan Schröder, *The Encounter with Islam between Doctrinal Image and Life Writing: Ambrosius Zeebout's Report of Joos van Ghistele's Travels to the East 1481–1485*, *in* FEAR AND LOATHING IN THE NORTH: JEWS AND MUSLIMS IN MEDIEVAL SCANDINAVIA AND THE BALTIC REGION 83, 86—87, 88 (Cordelia Heß & Jonathan Adams eds., 2016).

247. *See* Robert Bork & Andrea Kann, *The Art, Science, and Technology of Medieval Travel*, *in* THE ART, SCIENCE AND TECHNOLOGY OF MEDIEVAL TRAVEL 1, 6–7 (Robert Bork & Andrea Kann eds., 2008).

248. *See* Pauline Moffitt Watts, *The European Religious Worldview and Its Influence on Mapping*, *in* HISTORY OF CARTOGRAPHY, VOLUME 3 (PART 1), CARTOGRAPHY IN THE EUROPEAN RENAISSANCE 382, 382 (David Woodward ed., 2007) (locating this transitional period from 1400 to 1460).

249. Van Eck, *supra* note 244, at 153–54. Van Eck notes other important but less noted illustrated accounts of pilgrims, including Arnold von Harff, Konrad Grünemberg, and Niccolò da Poggibonsi. *See id.* at 153.

250. Beebe, *supra* note 239, at 3.

251. *See generally* PERCY G. ADAMS, TRAVEL LITERATURE AND THE EVOLUTION OF THE NOVEL (1983) (analyzing the connection between prose and fiction and the influences of travel literature on society in general).

252. Felipe Fernández-Armesto, *Maps and Exploration in Sixteenth and Early Seventeenth Centuries*, *in* 3 THE HISTORY OF CARTOGRAPHY, CARTOGRAPHY IN THE EUROPEAN RENAISSANCE 738 (David Woodward ed., 2007).

253. DONALD R. HOWARD, WRITERS AND PILGRIMS: MEDIEVAL PILGRIMAGE NARRATIVES AND THEIR POSTERITY 2 (1980).

Famous compilers of these New World exploits included the vehemently anti-Spanish Richard Hakluyt (1552–1616), who enthusiastically promoted the English voyages of John Hawkins, Francis Drake, Thomas Cavendish, and Walter Raleigh;[254] Antonio de Herrera (1549–1625), named by Philip II in 1596 the Coronista mayor de las Indias, y Coronista de Castilla (national historian of the Americas and of Castille),[255] who compiled in eight volumes detailed data about the first six decades of the Spanish conquest of the Americas (from 1492–1554),[256] and published the second atlas of the Americas;[257] the French hydrographer Amédée François Frézier (1682–1773), who the king of Spain commissioned to reconnoiter Pacific-coast Spanish fortifications around Chile, Perú, and involving the Atacama;[258] the English buccaneer William Dampier (c. 1650–1715), who produced a three-volume account of *A New Voyage round the World* (1692);[259] and Samuel Purchas (1577–1626), who adapted the medieval pilgrimage idea into the title of his four-volume work, *Purchas His Pilgrims* (1625),[260] the largest book ever published in England up to that time.[261] Drake's passage into the South Sea on the *Golden Hind* net-

254. *See* RAYMOND JOHN HOWGEGO, ENCYCLOPEDIA OF EXPLORATION TO 1800, at 474 (2003) (noting Hakluyt hated the Spanish). Hakluyt's greatest works include DIVERS VOYAGES TOUCHING THE DISCOVERY OF AMERICA AND THE ILANDS ADIACENT UNTO THE SAME, MADE FIRST OF ALL BY OUR ENGLISHMEN AND AFTERWARDS BY THE FRENCHMAN AND BRITONS (1582); and THE PRINCIPALL NAVIGATIONS, VOIAGES AND DISCOVERIES OF THE ENGLISH NATION, MADE BY SEA OR OVER LAND, TO THE MOST REMOTE AND FARTHEST DISTANT QUARTERS OF THE EARTH AT ANY TIME WITHIN THE COMPASS OF THESE 1500 YEARES (1589). Hakluyt's having impressed men of letters, mostly from the Royal Geographical Society, led to the creation in 1846 of the Hakluyt Society, which grew far beyond its original devotion to the writings of "medieval travelers, cosmographers, . . . [and] narratives of the age of the great discoveries." ALAN EDWIN DAY, DISCOVERY AND EXPLORATION: A REFERENCE HANDBOOK, THE OLD WORLD 92–93 (1980).

255. *See* María de Carmen Martínez Martínez, *Pro defensione veritatis: Antonio de Herrera, Cronista Mayor de Indias*, E-SPANIA (Juin 18, 2014), https://journals.openedition.org/e-spania/23687

256. ANTONIO DE HERRERA, HISTORIA GENERAL DE LOS HECHOS DE LOS CASTELLANOS EN LAS ISLAS Y TIERRA FIRME DE MAR OCEANO (1601).

257. ANTONIO DE HERRERA, DESCRIPCION DE LAS ISLAS, Y TIERRA FIRME DEL MAR OCEANO, QUE LLAMAN INDIAS OCIDENTALES. For the first atlas of the Americas, see CORNELIUS WYTFLIET, PTOLEMAICAE AUGMENTUM (1597).

258. AMÉDÉE FRANÇOIS FRÉZIER, A VOYAGE TO THE SOUTH-SEA AND ALONG THE COASTS OF CHILI AND PERU IN THE YEARS 1712, 1713, AND 1714, PARTICULARLY DESCRIBING THE GENIUS AND CONSTITUTION OF THE INHABITANTS, AS WELL . . . (1717).

259. CAPTAIN WILLIAM DAMPIER, A NEW VOYAGE ROUND THE WORLD . . . (1717) (1692).

260. SAMUEL PURCHAS, HAKLUYTUS POSTHUMUS, OR PURCHAS HIS PILGRIMES, CONTAYNING A HISTORY OF THE WORLD, IN SEA VOYAGES & LANDE TRAVELS, BY ENGLISHMEN AND OTHERS (1625).

261. Anthony Payne, *Samuel Purchas*, *in* 2 THE OXFORD COMPANION TO WORLD EXPLORATION 180 (David Buisseret ed., 2007).

ted him 90,000 pounds of treasure, having plundered Tarapacá, Arica, Callao, Lima, and other Spanish possessions to 150 leagues south of Panama.[262] The French Huguenot pirate-historian-surgeon Alexander Esquemelin (1645–1707) would publish his masterpiece *Bucaniers of America* (1678),[263] which is of immense historical value serving also as "the prime, and indeed almost the only comprehensive source of information for pirate activities" in the entire seventeenth century.[264]

Seventeenth-century intrusions into the Spanish South Sea (Pacific Ocean) by Dutch sea dogs, English buccaneers, and French corsairs sparked an interest in Atacama coastal ports as waystations for freshwater replenishment and springboards for plunder against the Spanish fleet.[265] Agents of the formidable Dutch East India Company rounded South America in 1614 and plied waters from Chile to Mexico, searching to abduct the viceroy of Perú.[266] Spain undertook costly expenditures to garrison key South Sea ports. By 1712, Spain specifically commissioned Frézier to study the coastal defenses of Chile and Perú against the enemies of the Bourbon monarchy.[267] He found that the Spaniards "indiscreetly neglect[ed] the Defences" even against the rebellion of the Indians, "who only want an Opportunity to destroy them, whatever Appearance of Peace there be among them."[268] The Atacama port city of Arica, close to a fresh water source, repeatedly came under attack in 1681 by the romanticized swashbucklers Bartholomew Sharp, Basil Ringrose, and John Watling.[269] Dampier also attacked the town as part of 1680 seaborne raids stretching from the Ilo River in Perú to Coquimbo and the

---

262. ROBERT GRANT WATSON, 1 SPANISH AND PORTUGUESE SOUTH AMERICA DURING THE COLONIAL PERIOD, 294–95 (1884).

263. JOHN EXQUEMELIN, THE BUCANIERS OF AMERICA: OR, A TRUE ACCOUNT OF THE MOST REMARKABLE ASSAULTS COMMITTED OF LATE YEARS UPON THE COASTS OF THE WEST-INDIES, BY THE BUCANIERS OF JAMAICA AND TORTUGA, BOTH ENGLISH AND FRENCH (1684).

264. HOWGEGO, *supra* note 254, at 357.

265. *See* FRANCAVIGLIA, *supra* note 237, at 106 (noting Atacama coastal ports developed where meagre small streams managed to reach the coast); FRÉZIER, *supra* note 258, at 148–51 (describing the strategic value of Arica).

266. ROSSI, *supra* note 56, at 206.

267. FRÉZIER, *supra* note 258, at 150–51 (on, for example, Arica); HOWGEGO, *supra* note 254, at 399 (on Frézier's commission).

268. FRÉZIER, *id.* at 55.

269. *See* EXQUEMELIN, *supra* note 263. A separate work, conceived of as a second volume but sometimes appended to Esquemeling's work, is 2 BASIL RINGROSE, BUCANIERS OF AMERICA. THE SECOND VOLUME. CONTAINING THE DANGEROUS VOYAGE AND BOLD ATTEMPTS OF CAPTAIN BARTHOLOMEW SHARP, AND OTHERS; PERFORMED UPON THE COASTS OF THE SOUTH SEA, FOR THE SPACE OF TWO YEARS, . . . (William Crooke, at the Sign of the Green Dragon without Temple-bar, 1685).

Juan Fernandez archipelago in Chile.[270] Geographer Richard Francaviglia credited Dampier with providing through his narrative an early cartographic description of the region, which not only sparked a revolution in map-making ("and careers such as that of map-maker Herman Moll"), but contributed scientific observations about wind and ocean currents, atmospheric phenomena, hydrology, and cultural ecology.[271] Famous seafarers James Cook, Richard Howe, and Horatio Nelson relied on his 1699 discourse on winds, storms, seasons, and tides, and it "continued to be used in the compilation of *Admiralty Sailing Directions* well into the twentieth century."[272] "Alexander von Humboldt [1769–1859] and Charles Darwin [1809–1882] acknowledged their admiration for Dampier's volume."[273] Dampier's account of his "roving way of life," which loosely described his twelve-year freebooting campaign against Spanish shipping and settlements in the Caribbean and South Sea (and later in Southeast Asia), went through three editions in its first year of publication and helped to make British travel writing in the eighteenth century second only to theology in terms of public popularity.[274] And yet his Baconian attraction to empirical detail and pre-Linnacan classificatory regard for observation has been credited for inaugurating a tradition of scientific travelogue literature.[275]

More formally trained European cartographers began charting the Atacama landscape in 1703.[276] Darwin explored the terrain in May and June 1835, during his famous *HMS Beagle* expedition. He described it as "a barrier far worse than the most turbulent ocean."[277] Darwin deeply admired the Prussian naturalist and polymath Alexander von Humboldt,

---

270. 1 DAMPIER, *supra* note 259, at iv (discussing the raids).

271. FRANCAVIGLIA, *supra* note 237, 108 (discussing Moll), 108–09 (discussing Dampier's scientific observations). *See also* HERMAN MOLL, A SYSTEM OF GEOGRAPHY: OR, A NEW ACCURATE DESCRIPTION OF THE EARTH IN ALL ITS EMPIRES, KINGDOMS AND STATES (1701).

272. James Kelly, *William Dampier, in* OXFORD COMPANION TO WORLD EXPLORATION 222, 225 (David Buisseret ed., 2007).

273. *Id.*

274. Carl Thompson, *William Dampier (1651–1715): English Buccaneer, Explorer, and Travel Writer,* in LITERATURE OF TRAVEL AND EXPLORATION: AN ENCYCLOPEDIA. VOLUME ONE: A TO F 312 (Jennifer Speake, ed., 2003). It went through two further editions by 1705.

275. *See id.*

276. *See* Richard Francaviglia, *Demystifying Desolation: A Cartographic History of the Atacama Desert, 1700–1900,* SOC'Y FOR THE HISTORY OF DISCOVERIES, https://www.sochistdisc.org/annual_meeting_2018_abstracts.htm (last visited Jan. 3, 2019) (noting Guillaume Delisle's map published in Paris in 1703/1708–1718, and Juan Cruz de la Cano's 1775 América Meridional map).

277. Charles Darwin, *The Voyage of the Beagle* 351–52 (ann. & with an introduction by Leonard Engle, 1962) (1839).

particularly Humboldt's multivolume account of the Southern Hemisphere.[278] Darwin took Humboldt's book with him on his *Beagle* voyage.[279] "If you really want to have a notion of tropical countries," wrote Darwin, "*study* Humboldt. Skip the scientific parts."[280]

Humboldt was the premier scientist of his day, "the greatest scientific traveler who ever lived," according to Darwin.[281] With travel documents provided by Spain's monarchy, he and French physician/botanist Aimé Bonpland (1773–1858) gained unimpeded access to South America's interior. Over the course of five years, they charted the physical, organic, and human landscapes of Venezuela, Colombia, Ecuador, Perú, Mexico, and Cuba.[282] Humboldt namesakes appear throughout South America, attaching for instance to the cold, low-salinity ocean current off the coast of the Atacama, a species of penguin populating this water (the Humboldt Current/Humboldt Penguin), Venezuela's second-highest mountain and its rapidly receding glacier (Pico Humboldt/Humboldt Glacier), tree species (the Andean oak (*Quercus humboldtii*), a South American willow (*Salix humboldtiana*)), and more.[283]

---

278. ALEXANDER VON HUMBOLDT & AIMÉ BONPLAND, PERSONAL NARRATIVE OF TRAVELS TO THE EQUINOCTIAL REGIONS OF THE NEW CONTINENT, DURING THE YEARS 1799–1804 (1819–1829, 7 vols). The study appeared originally in "thirty lavish folio editions and numerous smaller and abridged editions" between 1805 and 1838. Vera M. Kutzinski & Ottmar Ette, *The Art of Science: Alexander von Humboldt's Views of the Cultures of the World*, *in* ALEXANDER VON HUMBOLDT: VIEWS OF THE CORDILLERAS AND MONUMENTS OF THE INDIGENOUS PEOPLES OF THE AMERICAS: A CRITICAL EDITION xiv (Vera M. Kutzinski & Ottmar Ette eds., J. Ryan Poynter trans., 2012).

279. *See* Christian Helmreich, *Geschichte der Natur bei Alexander von Humboldt*, 10 INTERNATIONALE ZEITSCHRIFT FÜR HUMBOLDT STUDIEN 54 (2009): 54 (noting Darwin's copy of Humboldt's work, "*die Darwin mit auf die Reise genommen hatte*").

280. Charles Darwin, *The Voyage of the Beagle* (Nora Barlow ed., London: Pilot Press Ltd., 1945), 56.

281. [Letter from] *C. Darwin to J. D. Hooker, August 6, 1881*, *in* 3 LIFE AND LETTERS OF CHARLES DARWIN, INCLUDING AN AUTOBIOGRAPHICAL CHAPTER 247 (Francis Darwin ed., 1887) (agreeing with J. D. Hooker's assessment).

282. *See generally* HUMBOLDT & BONPLAND, *supra* note 278. *See also* Anna Maria Gillis, *Humboldt in the New World*, 33 *Humanities* (Nov./Dec., 2012), https://www.neh.gov/humanities/2012/novemberdecember/feature/humboldt-in-the-new-world. Beginning in 1799, Humboldt spent three years and two months exploring Venezuela, Colombia, Ecuador, and Perú, one year in Mexico, four months in Cuba, and four months sailing from one Spanish American port to another; and Arthur P. Whitaker, *Alexander von Humboldt and Spanish America*, 104 PROC. AM. PHIL. SOC'Y 320 (June 1960).

283. Note national forests and parks in Perú and Cuba (Bosque Nacional Alexander von Humboldt en Irazola/Parque Nacional Alejandro de Humboldt), the Amazon river dolphin (*Inia geoffrensis humboldtiana*), Venezuela's enormous sinkhole (Sima Humboldt), and numerous other botanical, biological, communal, institutional, terrestrial, aqueous, lunar, orbital, and space namesakes.

Humboldt notably "cast a net across the cultures of the world." However, his filtration of firsthand experiences "still originated in a very specific cultural perspective," decidedly within the bounded traditions of Western civilization.[284] Accordingly, he contributed to "cognitive dichotomies" that contrasted Spanish America as a land of darkness with enlightened Europe while also exposing the tensions between popular travel literature and earnest scientific engagement.[285]

Humboldt stimulated imagination beyond the realm of science, artfully presenting his narrative as a popular, if neglected, literary form.[286] Although acclaimed as the scientific discoverer of America, Humboldt's writings profoundly influenced writers, artists, and the public at large.[287] He was the archetypical figure among a new order of heroic scientist-adventurers who brought a cultural dimension of "local color" and wonder-seeking dignity to the New World.[288]

Along with his near contemporaries, Johann Baptist von Spix (1781–1826) and Carl Friedrich Philipp von Martius (1794–1868), who explored the Brazilian Amazon in 1814,[289] and later, Johann Jakob von Tschudi (1818–1889), who dubiously asserted the discovery of three pre-Incaic races based on a review of ancient cranial evidence and parietal protuberances,[290] a popularized early-nineteenth-century travel literature arose. Much of this literature aestheticized the descriptive format and exoticized the Latin American landscape while subjecting it to European Enlightenment values and examination. This travel literature

---

284. Kutzinski & Ette, *supra* note 278, at xviii.

285. Ricardo D. Salvatore, *Re-discovering Spanish America: Uses of Travel Literature about South America in Britain*, 8 J. LAT. AM. CUL. STUD. 200 (1999).

286. *See generally* Hajo Greif, *The Darwinian Tension: Romantic Science and the Causal Laws of Nature*, 53 STUD. HIST. & PHIL. BIO. & BIOMED. SCI. 53–61 (2015) (contrasting early Victorian natural science and its descendants, including Herschel, Lyell, and Malthus, and the German romantic approach to science embraced by Humboldt and Goethe); ALFRED I. TAUBER, ED., THE ELUSIVE SYNTHESIS: AESTHETICS AND SCIENCE (1996).

287. Sandra Nichols, *Why Was Humboldt Forgotten in the United States?* 96 GEO. REV. 399–401 (July 2006) (listing Humboldt's influences on Ralph Waldo Emerson, Henry David Thoreau, Edgar Allan Poe, Washington Irving, Walt Whitman, Julia Ward Howe, Oliver Wendell Holmes, and William Prescott; on the Hudson River School of landscape painters; on education, academic geography, and zoology; and American political leaders, especially Jefferson and Madison. It frames Humboldt's significance in the popular imagination).

288. Ronald Hilton, *The Significance of Travel Literature, with Special Reference to the Spanish- and Portuguese-Speaking World*, 49 HISPANIA 839 (Dec. 1966).

289. Kutzinski & Ette, *supra* note 278, at xviii.

290. *See* MARIANO EDWARD RIVERO & JOHN JAMES VON TSCHUDI, PERUVIAN ANTIQUITIES 26 (Francis L. Hawks trans., 1853); JOHANN JAKOB VON TSCHUDI, TRAVELS IN PERU, DURING THE YEARS 1838–1842, ON THE COAST, IN THE SIERRA, ACROSS THE CORDILLERAS AND THE ANDES, INTO THE PRIMEVAL FORESTS (1847).

implicitly fortified the bounded geographic line of amity separating refined Europe and the untamed New World.

Hiram Bingham (1875–1956), the Yale University adventurer and serious, self-trained anthropologist, portaged this tradition into the twentieth century. He helped to introduce European and North American readers to the Atacama landscape in the early twentieth century. Bingham retraced the trodden pre-Incan and Spanish route connecting Buenos Aires to Lima via Potosí, and subsequently conducted extensive research as part of Yale University's Peruvian Expedition of 1911–1915.[291] He reminded his audience that the riches portaged over the route—"[t]wo billion ounces of silver is the record of its output and the tale is not yet told"—surpassed tales of the Arabian Nights and the dream of Midas.[292] In 1911, he "discovered" the long-rumored royal Incan ruins of Machu Picchu, which the press touted as the "Lost City in the Clouds."[293] It was never lost to the Quechua-speaking boy who, on instruction from a local muleteer, showed him where it was.[294]

Slightly more than one century before Bingham's ascent to Machu Picchu, Humboldt, as part of his five-year sojourn in the Americas, descended from the Peruvian highlands to the Atacama coast, where he encountered heavy Pacific Ocean barge traffic laden with guano mined from the Chincha Islands. Frézier had observed the same industry as early as 1717, noting that mule trains then portaged the guano to "the Vines and plow'd Lands of Tarapacá, Pica, and other Neighbouring Places."[295] Frézier did not understand guano's significance: "some believe, that it is a peculiar Sort of Earth: For my part, I am not of that Opinion."[296] However, Humboldt suspected differently. Others had begun to take note of the substance "Out of the Islands in the South-Sea,

---

291. *See generally* Ricardo D. Salvatore, *Local Versus Imperial Knowledge: Reflections on Hiram Bingham and the Yale Peruvian Expedition*, 4 NEPLANTLA: VIEWS FROM SOUTH 67–79 (2003) (discussing the scientific expedition launched from Yale University).

292. HIRAM BINGHAM, ACROSS SOUTH AMERICA; AN ACCOUNT OF A JOURNEY FROM BUENOS AIRES TO LIMA BY WAY OF POTOSÍ, WITH NOTES ON BRAZIL, ARGENTINA, BOLIVIA, CHILE, AND PERU 115 (1911).

293. CHRISTOPHER HEANEY, CRADLE OF GOLD: THE STORY OF HIRAM BINGHAM, A REAL-LIFE INDIANA JONES, AND THE SEARCH FOR MACHU PICCHU 166 (2010).

294. *See* HIRAM BINGHAM, LOST CITY OF THE INCAS: THE STORY OF MACHU PICCHU AND ITS BUILDERS 159–67 (1948).

295. FRÉZIER, *supra* note 258, at 147 ("The Island of Iquique is also inhabited by Indians and Blacks, who are there employ'd to gather Guana, being a yellowish Earth thought to be the Dung of Birds . . . for during the Space of a hundred Years past, they have laden ten or twelve Ships every Year with it, to manure the Land").

296. *Id.*

not far from the City of Arica" where "they fetch [a white] Earth . . . called *Guano* . . . because of it's admirable Virtue in making ploughed Ground fertile."[297] Humboldt's guano samples, taken back to Europe in 1803, were found to contain high concentrations of uric acid, and the world quickly learned of the soluble, nitrogen-rich powers of this fertilizer. By the 1850s, demand for Peruvian guano intensified internationally,[298] providing Perú with almost all of its hard currency[299] and a monopoly over an export resource in tremendous demand from the dominant agriculturally based economies of the world. Humboldt credited Perú's indigenous peoples with the discovery of guano's importance.[300] However, the publication of guano's application as fertilizer would eventually serve as a pretext for war.

The unveiling of knowledge in these tales would establish geography as "overwhelmingly a European discipline."[301] It would expand in the eighteenth and nineteenth centuries due largely to the formalizing influences of Immanuel Kant's *Physische Geographie* (1803),[302] Humboldt and Bonpland's five-year exploration of the Americas,[303] and Darwin's *Beagle* expedition.[304]

Much of this literature aestheticized the descriptive format and exoticized the Latin American landscape while subjecting it to Euro-

297. For other accounts of the guano trade off the western coast of South America, along with emerging scientific descriptions of its powers as a fertilizer, see ALVARO ALONSO BARBA, A COLLECTION OF SCARCE AND VALUABLE TREATISES UPON METALS, MINES, AND MINERALS. CONTAINING, I. CURIOUS OBSERVATIONS ON MINES AND THE SEVERAL . . . 13 (2d ed. 1740); MAJOR-GENERAL ALEXANDER BEATSON, TRACTS RELATIVE TO THE ISLAND OF ST. HELENA; WRITTEN DURING A RESIDENCE OF FIVE YEARS 21 (1816).

298. *See* Brett Clark & John Bellamy Foster, *Ecological Imperialism and Global Metabolic Rift: Unequal Exchange and the Guano/Nitrates Trade*, 50 INT'L J. COMP. SOC. 318 (2009).

299. *See* WILLIAM COLUMBUS DAVIS, THE LAST CONQUISTADORES: THE SPANISH INTERVENTION IN PERU AND CHILE, 1863–1866, at 52 (1950).

300. *See* GREGORY T. CUSHMAN, GUANO AND THE OPENING OF THE PACIFIC WORLD: A GLOBAL ECOLOGICAL HISTORY 25–26 (2013).

301. D. R. STODDART, ON GEOGRAPHY AND ITS HISTORY 39 (1986).

302. Michael Church, *Immanuel Kant and the Emergence of Modern Geography*, *in* READING KANT'S GEOGRAPHY 22 (Stuart Elden & Eduardo Mendieta eds., 2011) (noting the structure of Kant's "organized compendium" compiled from travelogues, navigators' maps and empirically grounded sources). In 1755, Kant qualified as *Magister* at the university of Köningsberg and, as *Privatdozent*, delivered his lectures on geography forty-six times over the next forty years, "more frequently than any course except logic and metaphysics." *Id.* at 20. Humboldt "carried forward the tradition of intellectual geography in the immediately post-Kantian period." *Id.* at 27.

303. *See* HUMBOLDT & BONPLAND, *supra* note 278. The study appeared originally in "thirty lavish folio editions and numerous smaller and abridged editions" between 1805 and 1838. *See* Kutzinski & Ette, *supra* note 278, at xvi.

304. Darwin, *supra* note 277.

pean Enlightenment values and examination. This travel literature implicitly fortified the bounded geographic line of amity separating refined Europe and the untamed New World. While it contributed to the Enlightenment project of expanding consciousness and identity through discovery and examination, this geographic division, and geography itself, remained a "vanguard colonial discipline" that would closely associate geographers with imperialism.[305] It contributed to international law's co-opting of the idea of civilization and its missionary exportation of a European standard of civilization. While international lawyers of the nineteenth century deployed to justify the exportation of a European standard of civilization, they followed the rationalized and romanticized path charted by conqueror-discoverers, buccaneer-cartographer-geographers, and scientists doubling as travelogue expositors. An immense, indirect body of knowledge associated with geography contributed to the law of nations' late scholastic and early modern development. This knowledge was often packaged in the descriptions of travelogue literature and the recordings of gentlemen freebooters.

The visual and descriptive narratives of travel literature—part of the rise of graphicacy in the early Middle Ages[306]—contrasted with the allegorical nature of medieval cartographic prototypes, as influentially represented by Pierre Eskrich's *Mappe-monde nouvelle papistique* (1566), which surrounded the walled papal kingdom and the city of Rome with the "hideously disarticulated jaws of the devil fame" and the primeval chaos beyond the border of sanctuary.[307] Herodotus, Pliny the Elder, and numerous other Greco-Roman narrators populated the edges of the Western world with monstrous creatures, animalistic forms, and exotica.[308] Waldseemüller's *Carta marina* portrays a cynocephalus (dog-headed) creature patrolling the conjoined mountains, forests, and

305. Tayyab Mahmud, *Geography and International Law: Towards a Postcolonial Mapping*, 5 SANTA CLARA J. INT'L L.531 (2007).

306. W. G. V. Balchin and Alice M. Coleman coined the term "graphicacy" in the mid-1960s to define a specific mode of visual communication by means of nonverbal or numerical formats, such as diagrams, maps, sketches, graphs, and drawings. Graphicacy is central to the study of geography and cartography and is analogous to the study of literacy, numeracy, and articulacy. *See* W. G. V. Balchin & Alice M. Coleman, *Graphicacy Should Be the Fourth "Ace" in the Pack*, TIMES EDUCATIONAL SUPPLEMENT 23, Nov. 5, 1965. On its historical appearance and significance to the late Roman and post-Roman worlds, see Ildar Garipzanov, *The Rise of Graphicacy in Late Antiquity and the Early Middle Ages*, 46 VIATOR 1 (2015).

307. Moffitt Watts, *supra* note 248, at 390.

308. *See* Van Duzer, *supra* note 178, at 221.

"*Desertum*" of Asia,[309] while an entire subgenre of cartography and *mappaemundi* projected the theme of Apocalypticism.[310]

Breydenbach's account revolutionized and "reconceptualized the form and making of a book."[311] He took with him on his pilgrimage in 1483–1484 the skillful Dutch woodcutter and printer Erhard Reuwich, who created an impressively detailed woodcut of Venice and the earliest published panoramic of Jerusalem, along with woodcuts of other city ports ("composed with rare topographical accuracy"), images of peoples of the Levant, animals, and holy sites.[312] The book "self-consciously constructed eyewitness views" using "the visual rhetoric of perspective" as a model of knowledge dissemination. And it was an instant success, appearing in Latin, German, and Dutch by 1488, French, Spanish, and Czech before 1500, and thirteen editions in total before 1522.[313] It contributed to Breydenbach's reputation as having created the first illustrated travel book.[314]

Guglingen's travelogue is also important for its inclusion of maps and illustrations, descriptions of crocodiles, a sea monster (possibly a sea cow), and exotic trees, all of which evidence a rising "empirical curiosity" in the natural, cultural, and secular world.[315] He made no attempt to Christianize his personal encounters with Islamic spaces, making his travelogue "truly exceptional."[316] He, too, described his encounter with the desert, however his contemplative account did not make this a focal point of his travel diary.[317] These accounts would contribute to stylized

309. WALDSEEMÜLLER, *Carta marina*, LIBR. CONG., https://www.loc.gov/resource/g3200m.gct00046/?sp=3&r=-0.151,-0.213,1.138,0.565,0 (plate 3). Barking cynocephali represented gibberish speakers, a term which derived from the ancient Greek *barbarous* [barbarian]. *See* Dana Rehn, *Going to the Dogs: The Foreign and Religious Other in German Renaissance Prints*, 5 OTHERNESS: ESSAYS & STUD. 111, 113 (2016).

310. *See generally* CHET VAN DUZER & ILYA DINES, APOCALYPTIC CARTOGRAPHY: THEMATIC MAPS AND THE END OF THE WORLD IN A FIFTEENTH-CENTURY MANUSCRIPT (2016) (presenting depictions of religious history and events of the last days from an unstudied manuscript in the Huntington Library).

311. ELIZABETH ROSS, PICTURING EXPERIENCE IN THE EARLY PRINTED BOOK: BREYDENBACH'S PEREGRINATIO FROM VENICE TO JERUSALEM 1 (2014).

312. *Id.* at 2.

313. *Id.* at 3. Additionally, Reuwich's original woodcuts circulated and were copied in Mainz, Lyons, Speyer, and Zaragoza. *Id.*

314. *Id.* at 1.

315. Van Eck, *supra* note 244, at 156. *See also id.* at 159 (crocodile), 160 (sea monster), 161–62 (exotic trees), 154 (maps and illustrations).

316. *Id.* at 176.

317. *See also* PRESCOTT, *supra* note 236, at 17–18 ("[h]is inward-turning eye found little to interest it in the desert, and even looked with indifference upon the crowding experiences of Egypt").

and descriptive treatments of the New World by a succeeding generation of explorers and plunderers—proto international lawyers—who would encounter the deserted west coast topography of the Atacama in the sixteenth century.

However, the depictions of the desert that perhaps had the most impact on the European mindset came from the Swiss Dominican friar, Felix Fabri (c. 1441–1502). Fabri paid attention to the quotidian particulars of his journey and did so with levity and with a mind toward dissemination among multiple audiences. He was "the Proust of the genre"[318] and made two trips to the Holy Land, in 1480 and 1483–1484. He noted to his readers that he had also visited all three parts of the then known world, implying that he was an almost unparalleled expert on the peripheries of the world.

He also wrote for different audiences,[319] adding a multiplier effect to his historical significance. For his Dominican brethren, he spent ten years compiling the *Evagatorium in Terrae Sanctae, Arabiae et Egypti peregrinationem.*[320] For his secular patrons, he wrote about his first pilgrimage in rhyme and in Swabian-German (*Gereimtes Pilgerbüchlein*). For his noble patrons, he produced the vernacular *Pilgerbuch* about "[h]is second, longer journey."[321] And for the Observant Sisters of the Cloisters of Medingen and Medlingen, he produced in 1491 *Die Sionpilger,* a spiritual guide so that "despite their enclosure, they too might make a journey to the Holy Land."[322]

Fabri provided detailed accounts of the wilderness from the Holy Land to Arabia and the Sinai. His paths crossed with Breydenbach and Guglingen, but he described the nature of the desert in much more detail than any other travelogue diarist, imparting to Western audiences an onslaught of first depictions—all of them bleak. He described the Sinai as "an unfruitful and exceeding bad land . . . a land deserted by God . . . deserted by mankind . . . a lonesome place . . . unfrequented by men . . . wherein neither men, beasts, nor birds can live." He related that

318. HOWARD, *supra* note 253, at 38. "Brother Felix's book covers everything and covers it in more detail than anyone else had. Coming at the end of a tradition of writing, he produces its ultimate exemplar by sheer inclusiveness." *Id.* at 45.

319. *See generally* BEEBE, *supra* note 239, at ch. 4, 93ff.

320. Kathryn Beebe, *Reading Mental Pilgrimage in Context: The Imaginary Pilgrims and Real Travels of Felix Fabri's "Die Sionpilger,"* 25 ESSAYS IN MEDIEVAL STUDIES 39, 39 (2008).

321. *Id.* at 39.

322. *Id. See also* Ora Limor, *Placing an Idea: The Valley of Jehoshaphat in Religious Imagination, in* BETWEEN JERUSALEM AND EUROPE: ESSAYS IN HONOUR OF BIANCA KÜHNEL 280, 294 (Renana Bartal & Hanna Vorholt eds., 2015).

"no such wilderness is to be found in Germany, France, or Italy," and confirmed numerous passages in the Hebrew Bible describing it as a wasteland "of exceeding great width and length . . . so great, so long, and so wide, that it cannot be crossed, and no man can be found/who has reached its boundaries . . . there is no water . . . [it is the] . . . the image of death . . . barren . . . pathless."[323]

The association of deserts with parched and barren landscapes carried with it subtle shadings of Western geographic marginality. Francaviglia credited Fabri with fashioning a depiction of the desert as a place that God created through subtraction, redistributing the bounty of the world elsewhere.[324] The forsaken quality of the desert landscape has remained at the forefront of Western imagery, notwithstanding complaints about such depictions. Earlier it was noted that topophilia grows in gardens, not deserts. In humanistic terms, it grows wherever human emotions intermix with landscape. Bowman's seminal 1924 geographic study of the Atacama began with the observation that "every desert has a great many people in it," noting that the Sahara alone supported two million people within its borders at that time.[325] Francaviglia observed that Aboriginal Australians "do not consider themselves to be living in a desert, but rather a complex land that offers resources in abundance." The Shoshone of North America have long resented the external assignment of their *nomos* to Death Valley.[326] One should not expect indigenous populations of the Atacama to think differently about external characterizations of their environment.

Conclusion

The remoteness of the Atacama Desert reveals temporal, geographic, cartographic, and doctrinal depictions of marginalization. These treatments have been reinforced by historical depictions of deserts within the European mindset and by historiographic problems of periodization, which present the genealogy of international law in terms of bracketed parameters informed by debates on the birth and meaning of sovereignty and the Westphalian state system. A telluric attachment to a European *nomos* eventually zoomed inward to account for cadastral and

---

323. 2 FELIX FABRI, EVAGATORIUM, OR WANDERINGS OF FELIX FABRI, 460–73 (X Palestine Pilgrims' Text Society, 1897).

324. FRANCAVIGLIA, *supra* note 237, at 57.

325. BOWMAN, *supra* note 231, at 5.

326. *Id.* at 55.

managerial valuations that closed administrative gaps of accountancy and fiscal valuation. This shift toward the core attributes of statehood later radiated outward to hone, imperfectly, the razor's edge of bounded peripheries that make up the state-centric jigsaw puzzle. Although partially blind to the forces informing their own process of state formation, metropolitan powers nevertheless exported unwitting notions of geospace to the New World, in the process capturing unfathomable swaths of territory under a rubric guided by proximity and aggrandizement. Left for future development were the legal tools and techniques of territorial division, followed by the telluric considerations of land appropriation and human geography that have hampered the application of these legal tools and techniques, which has contributed to much turmoil in the Americas ever since. Reorienting the discussion of the international relations history of the Americas by zooming in on the remote status of the Atacama Desert helps to examine the enduring problems of American hemispheric relations and their turbulent encounter with international law. The remoteness of the Atacama Desert contributes to a better understanding of the globalized and racialized pressures of Southern Cone relations. The Atacama is at the intersection of international law and geography. In important ways, it is the *locus classicus* of the hemispheric outpost, where "'peripheral,' resource-rich countries" are drawn to a type of extractivism that harbors "negative socio-environmental implications as well as relations of unequal exchange at the global scale."[327]

Remoteness needs to be dissected. It needs to be separated from the geospatial anatomy of the Western encounter with the Americas. Such a separation helps one view more clearly the structural difficulties presented by international law's hemispheric encounter. This separation elevates the importance of the Atacama from the shadows of peripheralization and European periodization. It allows for the exploration of historical incongruities projected onto the topography of the Americas. It begins to address the skewing of perspective clearly acknowledged by any cartographic framework but sublimated by Western thought production, the European concept of civilization, and semiotic expressions of doctrinal coloniality.

Overlooked by grander themes of historiographic emphasis and periodization, the Atacama Desert nevertheless contains, aside from its min-

327. Diego Andreucci & Isabella M. Radhuber, *Limits to "Counter-Neoliberal" Reform: Mining Expansion and the Marginalisation of Post-Extractivist Forces in Evo Morales's Bolivia*, 84 GEOFORUM 280 (2017).

eral wealth, underexplored narratives. These narratives teach of territorialization, neoliberalism, transnational corporatism, human rights, condominium, and indigenous rights. Perhaps the Atacama provides a template for harmonizing these competitive themes. If so, we would first need to better deal with the eclipsing insignificance of its remote status through a reexamination of the idea of remoteness in international law.

THREE

Nomos

Glacial geologists searching for traces of the radioactive isotope beryllium-10 declared the Dry Valleys west of McMurdo Sound in Antarctica the driest place on earth. The valleys have received little or no precipitation for millions of years.[1] The Atacama Desert, narrowly situated between the Pacific Ocean and the Andes Mountains, rivals that harsh environment as the driest nonpolar desert on earth. The prevailing moisture-bearing winds blow from the Atlantic Ocean, placing the Atacama in the rain shadow of the Andes, in essence on the leeward side of the range. Off its Pacific coast, a subtropical high-pressure center meets the cold, northward-flowing Humboldt Current to create a constant temperature inversion that is penned in by offshore winds (the Pacific anticyclone flow), the Andean rain shadows from east of the Cordillera, and the Chilean Coast Range, the western coastal mountain range that intercepts Pacific Ocean weather systems.[2] Mountains, winds, ocean currents, atmospheric pressure, and temperature combine to deprive the Atacama of rain, making its forbidding beauty comparable to that of desolate Antarctica.[3]

1. *See* L. R. McHargue & P. E. Damon, *The Global Beryllium 10 Cycle*, 29 REVIEWS OF GEOPHYSICS 141, 141–158 (1991); Becky Oskin, *Antarctic Hills Haven't Seen Water in 14 Million Years*, LIVESCIENCE (Nov. 1, 2013), https://www.livescience.com/40890-antarctic-dry-valleys-no-water.html. Beryllium-10 serves as a proxy indicator of precipitation. A higher reading in soil samples indicates more rain.

2. *See* Alan T. Bull et al., *The Atacama Desert: Technical Resources and the Growing Importance of Novel Microbial Diversity*, 70 ANNU. REV. MICROBIOL., 215, 215 (2016).

3. *See, e.g.*, Christopher P. McKay et al., *High-Frequency Rock Temperature Data from Hyper-Arid Desert Environments in the Atacama and the Antarctic Dry Valleys and Implications for Rock Weathering*, 110 GEOMORPHOLOGY 182 (2009). Geologists recounting the 1958 Cambridge University Atacama Desert Expedition noted that their other option for field work was to join the Antarctic exploration of James Wordie and Vivian Fuchs, other Cambridge associ-

Defined broadly, the Atacama Desert spreads across Perú's coastal desert (the southern *Chala*), the *precordillera* and high mountain plateaus of Bolivia (the *Altiplano*) and Argentina (*Puna de Atacama*), and the region north of Santiago, Chile (*Norte Chico*).[4] It forms part of a 3,700 km stretch of desert coastland that begins in southern Ecuador near Perú's northern coastal town of Chiclayo and extends southward through Perú's Sechura Desert to the Santiago area of central Chile.[5] Its driest area stretches nearly 1,000 km along the western coast from the Chilean-Peruvian border around Tacna and Arica to Copiapó at 27 degrees south latitude. Dry basins (*salars*), alluvial fans, and extensive salt beds form this topography, with three tropical oases at Arica, Calama, and Atacama (Cobija) situated along the only watercourses that reach the Pacific. The driest portions of the Atacama receive on average less than one millimeter of annual precipitation.[6] Southward from Copiapó to Illape (31.5 degrees south latitude, a distance of about 650 km) some rain may occasionally fall.[7]

Although popularly depicted as open and flat, much of the Atacama is hilly to mountainous.[8] Isaiah Bowman framed its entire geographical picture by extending its perimeter to the high ranges and plateaus of the central Andes bounded by the Puna de Atacama on the south to the Chaco or grasslands of northeastern Argentina and adjacent Bolivia. He did so "because the currents of business flow naturally from these border settlements across the Atacama country and deeply affect its life."[9] This adjacent *Altiplano* area rises to an elevation higher than 3,500 meters and "supports vegetation that includes *bofedales*, unique peatlands," geyser fields, high plateaus, and cave systems.[10]

---

ates and fabled explorers. See JOHN AARONS & CLAUDIO VITA-FINZI, THE USELESS LAND: A WINTER IN THE ATACAMA DESERT 9 (1960).

4. The classical account of the geography of the Atacama remains ISAIAH BOWMAN'S DESERT TRAILS OF ATACAMA (1924). *See also* geographer Richard V. Francaviglia's account, IMAGINING THE ATACAMA DESERT: A FIVE-HUNDRED-YEAR JOURNEY OF DISCOVERY 37 (2018) (describing and noting the Atacama's borders, which, like all deserts, defy precise cartographic depiction).

5. JULIE LAITY, DESERTS AND DESERT ENVIRONMENTS 35 (2008).

6. *Id.* at 33.

7. *See* Michael A. Mares ed., ENCYCLOPEDIA OF DESERTS 54 (1999).

8. FRANCAVIGLIA, *supra* note 4, at 13.

9. BOWMAN, *supra* note 4, at v. Bowman described the Puna de Atacama as "the collective name given to the basins, valleys, salt-covered basin floors, mountain knots, chains, and alluvial piedmont deposits that are the chief topographic and drainage features of a belt of exceedingly high and cold country that lies between the main chain of the Andes . . . and the eastern mountain wall." *Id.* at 257.

10. Bull et al., *supra* note 2, at 217.

Like the difficult-to-define American Middle West,[11] experts dispute what the Atacama region signifies, leading one of its leading geographers to conclude that "there is no right and wrong way to determine where this desert lies, just an array of perceptions that have varied through time."[12] Historians understand regional identity in terms of geographic coherence, intersecting historical issues, and common cultural touchstones.[13] Social anthropologists look to personality features acquired in childhood derived from selfsameness as interpreted in relation to others.[14] Sociologists link territorial identity to local community,[15] a spatial context better marked by fluidity rather than fixity.[16] Followers of John Locke (1632–1704) associated *dominium*, or the power to possess, with the ability to make productive only that territory that came under actual possession subject to human improvement.[17] International lawyers rely on principles of sovereignty, boundaries, and self-rule, enshrined in the 1933 Montevideo Convention: in legal terms, a state must possess a permanent population, a defined territory, a government, and the capacity to enter into relations with other states.[18] These features reflect telluric underpinnings that have galvanized the attention of theorists when reduced to one problematic word: *nomos*.

Carl Schmitt and Nomos

With use of metaphor, analogy, history, and "an abundance of physical inscriptions,"[19] perhaps no modern theorist of international relations

---

11. *See generally* ANDREW R. L. CAYTON & PETER S. ONUF, THE MIDWEST AND THE NATION: RETHINKING THE HISTORY OF AN AMERICAN REGION (1990) (presenting the state of scholarship on the idea of the Midwest to mark the bicentennial of the Northwest Ordinance).

12. FRANCAVIGLIA, *supra* note 4, at 19–20.

13. *See* THE AMERICAN MIDWEST: ESSAYS ON REGIONAL HISTORY 1 (Andrew R. L. Cayton & Susan E. Gray eds., 2001).

14. Martin Sökefeld, *Debating Self, Identity, and Culture in Anthropology*, 40 CURRENT ANTHROPOLOGY 417 (1999).

15. *See, e.g.*, Manuel Castells, *The Power of Identity: The Information Age-Economy*, SOC'Y & CULTURE 63 (2d ed. 2010).

16. Cristian Olmos Herrera, *Territory's Fragmentation: The Territory of Aboriginal Communities in the Process of Mining Expansion: The Case of the Atacama Desert, Chile*, https://www.researchgate.net/publication/280038214_TERRITORY'S_FRAGMENTATION_The_territory_of_aboriginal_communities_in_the_process_of_mining_expansion_The_case_of_the_Atacama_Desert_Chile

17. *See* John Locke, *The Second Treatise of Government* (1689), *in* JOHN LOCKE, POLITICAL WRITINGS ch. 5 (David Wootton ed., 1993) ("Of Property").

18. Convention on the Rights and Duties of States Adopted by the Seventh International Conference of American States art. 1, Dec. 26, 1933, 49 Stat. 3097, 165 L.N.T.S. 19 [hereinafter Montevideo Convention].

19. François Debrix, *The Virtual Nomos?*, *in* SPATIALITY, SOVEREIGNTY AND CARL SCHMITT: GEOGRAPHIES OF THE NOMOS 220 (Stephen Legg ed., 2011).

invigorated a closer connection of international law to the earth than did Carl Schmitt (1888–1985). He employed the term *nomos* to represent "true law," which developed in an enclosed location bound to the soil (*Boden*).[20] Law creation was a process involving land appropriation, whereby "soil that is cleared and worked by human hands manifests firm lines, whereby definite divisions become apparent. Through the demarcation of fields, pastures, and forests, these lines are engraved and embedded. . . . In these lines, the standards and rules of cultivation of the earth become discernable."[21] *Nomos* was "the immediate form in which the political and social order of a people becomes spatially visible;" he regarded *nomos* as "the *measure* by which the land in a particular order is divided and situated."[22]

To Schmitt, *nomos* represented the spatial consciousness that produced "a spatially concrete" orientation, which stood behind the creation of legal order.[23] If separated from its concrete, telluric base, *nomos* lost its "orientation," and resulted in "nihilism."[24] Nihilism expressed a form of legal normativity that separated *is* and *ought* and relied on abstractions that disregarded the spatial structure of a concrete order.[25] Mark Antaki noted that "[n]orms without a *nomos* do not constitute law proper. Laws cannot be understood as mere oughts detached from time and place."[26] Mika Ojakangas summarized that law could never be universal to Schmitt as it "exists only in a particular place and consists of what is within its own boundaries."[27] "True and authentic fundamental order [*nomos*] is based, at its essential core, on certain spatial limits and delimitations, on certain measures and a certain partitioning up of the earth."[28]

Schmitt's spatial and political writings have generated keen interest among critical scholars,[29] particularly critics of liberalism's value-ori-

20. Mika Ojakangas, *Carl Schmitt and the Sacred Origins of Law*, 147 TELOS 34, 35 (2009).

21. CARL SCHMITT, NOMOS OF THE EARTH AND THE INTERNATIONAL LAW OF THE JUS PUBLICUM EUROPAEUM 42 (2006) [hereinafter Schmitt, Nomos].

22. *Id.* at 70.

23. *Id.* at 78.

24. *Id.* at 66.

25. *See id.* at 69.

26. Mark Antaki, *Carl Schmitt's Nomos of the Earth*, 42 OSGOODE HALL L. J. 317, 322 (2004).

27. Ojakangas, *supra* note 20, at 37.

28. *Id.* at 37 (quoting Schmitt's LAND AND SEA, translation modified).

29. *See* Claudio Minca & Rory Rowan, *The Question of Space in Carl Schmitt*, 39 PROGRESS HUM. GEOGRAPHY 268, 269 (2014) (noting the reapportionment of Schmitt's spatial concepts by the Left and his critique of neoliberal ideology). *But see* Mark Neocleous, *Friend or Enemy? Reading Schmitt Politically*, 79 RADICAL PHIL. 13, 21 (1996) (chastising socialist theorists for utilizing Schmitt's antiliberalism teachings and turning him into a debating adversary).

ented premise, which professes Enlightenment principles of universal citizenship but expresses instead contradictions that promote its own kind of imperialism.[30] This critique of liberalism would grow to hold sway in Latin America.

German social and political philosopher Jürgen Habermas noted that Schmitt's persona "represents a division in the intellectual world."[31] Writing in 1989, Habermas did not think Schmitt's writings would have "a similar power of contagion in the Anglo-Saxon world" as they generated in continental discussions.[32] Two decades later, however, Benno Teschke labeled that prediction "naïve."[33] By 2000, Raphael Gross claimed that bibliographic material on Schmitt would "require a book of its own."[34] Habermas's lengthy intellectual engagement with Schmitt "would ultimately recognize as meritorious his diagnosis of the interaction of international law and international politics."[35] Teschke called Schmitt's principal text on international law, *Nomos of the Earth in the International Law of Jus Publicum Europaeum* (1950), a "modern classic on the executive state," as well as a screed against Kantian liberal universalism.[36] In its final section, it charted the development of a post-European international legal epoch—in Schmittian terms, a new version of the

30. *See, e.g.*, Seyla Benhabib, *Carl Schmitt's Critique of Kant: Sovereignty and International Law*, 40 POL. THEORY 688–713 (2012); WILLIAM HOOKER, CARL SCHMITT'S INTERNATIONAL THOUGH: ORDER AND ORIENTATION (2009); Roland Axtmann, *Humanity or Enmity? Carl Schmitt on International Politics*, 44 INT'L POL. 531, 531–51 (2007); Martti Koskenniemi, *International Law as Political Theology: How to Read* Nomos der Erde?, 11 CONSTELLATIONS 492–511 (2004).

31. Jürgen Habermas, *The Horrors of Autonomy: Carl Schmitt in English*, *in* THE NEW CONSERVATISM: CULTURAL CRITICISM AND THE HISTORIANS' DEBATE 128 (Shierry Weber Nicholsen ed. & trans., 1989).

32. *Id.* at 135.

33. Benno Teschke, *Decisions and Indecisions: Political and Intellectual Receptions of Carl Schmitt*, 67 NEW LEFT REV. 61, 61 (2011).

34. RAPHAEL GROSS, CARL SCHMITT AND THE JEWS: THE "JEWISH QUESTION," THE HOLOCAUST, AND GERMAN LEGAL THEORY 3 (Joel Golb trans., 2007).

35. Roberto Orsi, "Rethinking the Concept of Order in International Politics: Carl Schmitt and Jürgen Habermas," at 220 (Oct. 2012) (unpublished PhD dissertation, London School of Economics and Political Science), *available at* http://etheses.lse.ac.uk/750/1/Orsi_rethinking_concept_order.pdf

36. Teschke, *supra* note 33, at 62.

katechon,[37] or restrainer[38]—which would take the form of neoliberalism's insidious and domineering land appropriation.[39]

Elements of Schmitt's constitutional theory (*Verfassungslehre*) caught the attention of Ernst-Wolfgang Böckenförde, the distinguished constitutional scholar and former judge of Germany's Federal Constitutional Court (*Bundesverfassungsgericht*).[40] Schmitt's work also has informed Reinhart Koselleck's approach to conceptual history (*Begriffsgeschichte*)[41] and Giorgio Agamben's political thought.[42] Schmitt's multifaceted political and spatial theories, apart from his abhorrent personal beliefs and Axis-power association, resonate across a wide spectrum.[43]

---

37. The *katechon* appears in Paul's *Second Letter to the Thessalonians* (2:2), introducing the *katechon* as the restraining force that delays the advent of the Antichrist (lawless one). Numerous political theorists have contemplated the emergence of a radically different world politics as a form of messianism, where the restraining influences of the *katechon* are converted into violence and nihilism. *See generally* Sergei Prozorov, *The Katechon in the Age of Biopolitical Nihilism*, 45 CONTINENTAL PHIL. REV. 483 (2012); Nicholas Guilhot, *American Katechon: When Political Theology Became International Relations Theory*, 17 CONSTELLATIONS 224 (2010) (addressing the messianic turn in continental philosophy).

38. SCHMITT, NOMOS, *supra* note 21, at 59. Described as Schmitt's most enigmatic concept, the *katechon* represented Schmitt's attempt at imperial ruin-gazing, his retheorization of the trope of imperial decline in terms of Europe's post-(Roman) empires, which are "haunted by the knowledge that all empires end in ruins." Julia Hell, *Katechon: Carl Schmitt's Imperial Theology and the Ruins of the Future*, 84 GERMANIC REV.: LITERATURE, CULTURE, THEORY 283, 283–84 (2010).

39. *See* Carl Raschke, *What Is the New "Nomos of the Earth"? Reflections on the Later Schmitt*, POL. THEOLOGY (Sept. 3, 2016), https://politicaltheology.com/what-is-the-new-nomos-of-the-earth-reflections-on-the-later-schmitt-carl-raschke/

40. *See* ERNST-WOLFGANG BÖCKENFÖRDE, STATE, SOCIETY AND LIBERTY: STUDIES IN POLITICAL THEORY AND CONSTITUTIONAL LAW 89 (J. A. Underwood trans., 1991) (outlining Schmitt's constitutional theory separating constitutional and parliamentary monarchy).

41. *See, e.g.*, Niklas Olsen, *Carl Schmitt, Reinhart Koselleck and the Foundations of History and Politics*, 37 HIST. EUR. IDEAS 197, 197 (2011).

42. *See generally* GIORGIO AGAMBEN, HOMO SACER: SOVEREIGN POWER AND BARE LIFE (Daniel Heller-Roazen trans., 1995) (investigating the relationship between human life and state power).

43. *See* Matilda Arvidsson, Leila Brännström, & Panu Minkkinen, *Editors' Introduction*, *in* THE CONTEMPORARY RELEVANCE OF CARL SCHMITT: LAW, POLITICS, THEOLOGY 1, 5 (Matilda Arvidsson et al. eds., 2016) (reviewing Schmitt's widely divergent academic appeal); Christian J. Emden, *The Brilliant Fascist? Carl Schmitt and the Limits of Liberalism*, H-NET REVIEWS 1 (2005), https://www.h-net.org/reviews/showpdf.php?id=10599 (reviewing scholarship on Schmitt and noting serious questions posed by Schmitt "for any discussion of liberalism and parliamentary democracy" in view of the historical and political distance separating his repulsive personal views); PAUL EDWARD GOTTFRIED, CARL SCHMITT: POLITICS AND THEORY 2 (1990) (referencing "cross-political support" for Schmitt's schol-

Neoconservatives read him for his embrace of executive authority beyond the bounds of the constitutional order during times of emergency ("Sovereign is he who decides on the [state of exception]").[44] Realists read him for his concept of the political, which polemicizes against liberalism's treatment of concrete threats as competitions or debating adversaries,[45] as well as for his concrete depiction of the friend/enemy distinction, which rationalizes the public enemy as *hostis* (who must be dealt with as an equal adversary) as distinct from the private "adversary whom one hates" (*inimicus*).[46] Ethicists and Christian theologians focus on his depoliticized construct of global civil society, technocratic capitalism's abnegation of personhood, and the "anomic borderlessness" caused by humanity's displacement from nature.[47] International relations scholars read him for his reconstruction of grand history.[48] Postcolonialists pick up on his theme that Europe "had bought peace within the continent by externalizing warfare into the colonies" in accordance with the principle "no peace beyond the line."[49] This thesis consolidated the postcolonial view of Europe's exportation of a spatial order of "global overlordship."[50] Critical theorists read him for his critique of liberalism as a shibboleth for pan-interventionism,[51] which transmutes into an international economic policy consensus serving hegemonic

---

arship in Spanish and German journals such as *Razón Españolo* and *Criticon,* his "mark on the political Left as well as on the political Right" in Italy and France, and his impress on influential political theorists such as Norberto Bobbio, Carlo Galli, and Frankfurt-style Marxists, including the editors of *Telos,* who began circulating his views of the "decrepitude of bourgeois society" in the late 1980s).

44. CARL SCHMITT, POLITICAL THEOLOGY: FOUR CHAPTERS ON THE CONCEPT OF SOVEREIGNTY 5 (George Schwab trans., 1985). This famous expression forms the core of Schmitt's theory of decisionism, the belief that political action forms a value in itself and that exigent situations create their own legality by obviating normative law. *See* JEFFREY HERF, REACTIONARY MODERNISM: TECHNOLOGY, CULTURE, AND POLITICS IN WEIMAR AND THE THIRD REICH 44 (1984).

45. *See* CARL SCHMITT, THE CONCEPT OF THE POLITICAL 28 (2007), at 28.

46. *Id.*

47. *See, e.g.,* MICHAEL S. NORTHCOTT, A POLITICAL THEOLOGY OF CLIMATE CHANGE 304–05 (2013); *see also* BRUNO LATOUR, FACING GAIA: EIGHT LECTURES ON THE NEW CLIMATIC REGIME 228 (Catherine Porter trans., 2017) (especially the seventh lecture section "On the proper dosage of Carl Schmitt").

48. *See, e.g.,* Benno Gerhard Teschke, *Fatal Attraction: A Critique of Carl Schmitt's International Political and Legal Theory* 3 INT'L THEORY 179–227 (2011).

49. Martti Koskenniemi, *Carl Schmitt and International Law, in* THE OXFORD HANDBOOK OF CARL SCHMITT 594 (Jens Meierhenrich & Oliver Simons eds., 2017).

50. *Id.*

51. Timothy Nunann, *Carl Schmitt, American Prophet,* HUMANITY (June 2014), http://humanityjournal.org/blog/carl-schmitt-american-prophet/

interests across Latin America.[52] Geographers read him for his keen sense of spatial vision, noting that his "unique 'spatial history' of modernity" and geopolitics has relevance "in light of [the] growing climate crisis."[53] This geographical formulation of international law will prove significant in the Atacama, with its telluric connection to the *ayllus*, as it explains liberalism's inability to close gaps in inequality and neoliberalism's association with extractivism.

Schmitt professed that he should be read as a jurist,[54] ineluctably orienting international law toward the political and spatial. He ascribed "a central place to the geographical and territorial situatedness of law."[55] His spatial vision provided an alternative framework for critiquing international law, which seemingly abides by its own limitations and contradictions involving state centricity. At the interface of international law and geography, Schmittian critique contests liberal idealism and the law and politics of space.

Schmitt's construction of the legal order was personal and land-oriented. However, the normative reshaping of postcolonial Latin America through the importation of the Roman law principle of *uti possidetis* abstractly instrumentalized political power that was removed from telluric underpinnings. *Uti possidetis* accentuated territorial division based on a momentary snapshot of physical or constructive occupation as the metropolitan power was withdrawn. It had little to do with human geography or intrinsic or indigenous connectivity to land. An emergent "statutory state" validated the legal order of newborn republicanism (in Schmittian terms, the problematically translated *Rechtsstaat*, legal state), however it turned the rule of law into "an empty manner of speaking" because the legal rule did not receive "its actual sense through a certain opposition,"[56]

52. See Ana Margheritis & Anthony W. Pereira, *The Neoliberal Turn in Latin America: The Cycle of Ideas and the Search for an Alternative*, 34 LAT. AM. PERS. 25, 32 (2007).

53. Minca & Rowan, *supra* note 29, at 271. *See generally* Claudio Minca & Nick Vaughan-Williams, *Carl Schmitt and the Concept of the Border*, 17 GEOPOLITICS 756–72 (2012); Robert Meyer, Conrad Schetter, & Janosch Prinz, *Spatial Contestation? The Theological Foundations of Carl Schmitt's Spatial Thought*, 43 GEOFORUM 687, 687–96 (2012). Schmitt's spatiality is the subject of an edited collection of essays emerging from the 2009 Annual Meeting of the Association of American Geographers. *See* SPATIALITY, SOVEREIGNTY AND CARL SCHMITT: GEOGRAPHIES OF THE NOMOS xiii (Stephen Legg ed., 2011) (noting the product of the 2009 meeting).

54. Louiza Odysseos & Fabio Petito, *Carl Schmitt*, *in* CRITICAL THEORISTS AND INTERNATIONAL RELATIONS 305, 306 (Jenny Edkins & Nick Vaughan-Williams eds., 2009).

55. WILLIAM E. SCHEUERMAN, CARL SCHMITT: THE END OF LAW 164 (1999).

56. CARL SCHMITT, CONSTITUTIONAL THEORY 181 (Jeffrey Seitzer trans., 2008) [hereinafter SCHMITT, CONSTITUTIONAL THEORY]. Schmitt claimed the term "can stand for as many different concepts as the many institutional arrangements implied by the word

meaning a counterpoint to the concrete situatedness of land appropriation. In his *Verfassungslehre* (1928), one of his major contributions to legal and political theory,[57] Schmitt cautioned against the liberal construction of law as an amalgam of abstract rules.

Uti possidetis represented a "helpless formalism" that designated as law that which resulted from the procedures prescribed for its application.[58] It elevated the application of "formal law," which then appears as an opposition to "material law."[59] It forwarded a normative order without consideration of *nomos*, which Schmitt forewarned led to nihilism.

Steven Ratner noted that the Latin American incorporation of *uti possidetis* beginning in the early nineteenth century fractured almost immediately as a means of setting boundaries for the new republics.[60] The *creoles* class had formed internal political allegiances as opposed to the Iberian *peninsulares*, who for centuries had dominated the political economy of the landscape.[61] Despite its seeming utility, "the precise contours and effects of *uti possidetis* remained unclear,"[62] which led to nineteenth-century political turmoil and war.

All of this was acceptable in Schmittian terms because it took place beyond the European line of amity. Within the bracketed boundaries of his *Jus Publicum Europaeum*, international law's normative decorum prevailed (until the twentieth century); it instantiated an understood practice of peace and normative rulemaking. Beyond the line, continental zones of ambiguity converted bracketed metropolitan international law into a less cogent, not easily convertible[63] colonial engagement with exceptionalism, indeed with a recurrent state of exception that the Italian philosopher Giorgio Agamben would later characterize as a permanent rule of contemporary international relations.[64] European understanding of the line of amity meant that "no peace beyond the line"

Staat." Danilo Zolo, *The Rule of Law: A Critical Reappraisal*, *in* THE RULE OF LAW HISTORY, THEORY AND CRITICISM 3, 5 (Pietro Costa & Danilo Zolo eds., 2007) (quoting Schmitt).

57. *See generally* CARL SCHMITT, CONSTITUTIONAL THEORY, *supra* note 56 (detailing the Weimar constitution).

58. *See id.* at 184.

59. *Id.*

60. Steven R. Ratner, *Drawing a Better Line: Uti Possidetis and the Borders of New States*, 90 AM. J. INT'L L. 590, 593 (1996).

61. *Id.*

62. *Id.* at 594.

63. *See* SCHMITT, NOMOS, *supra* note 21, at 55

64. *See generally* GIORGIO AGAMBEN, STATE OF EXCEPTION (2005) (identifying the state of exception as a product of modernity and as a mid-twentieth-century paradigmatic form of government).

could be guaranteed. The slave trade amounted to the most conspicuous example of the political geography beyond this imaginary zone of (relative) peace,[65] but the widely abused issuance of letters of marque and reprisal, which credentialed seaborne privateers (thinly differentiated from pirates) as lawful and commissioned agents operating under higher authority, also contributed to the permissive aggressions justified by distance from metropolitan rule beyond the line. Although the precise demarcation of this line adhered to a conveniently elusive definition, with egregious violations subject to metropolitan scrutiny in Courts of Prize, it somewhat settled on the Tropic of Cancer,[66] or more informally, around the equator.[67]

The Dynamics of Biogeography

Care must be taken when applying Schmittian spatial analyses to twentieth-century international relations. Lauren Benton generically criticized Schmitt's depiction of imperial zones of exception as an oversimplification.[68] Her reading of imperial history uncovered "variegated spaces" produced by empire, where territorial control could incidentally accompany other pursuits, or unevenly cover space with a patchwork fabric that framed "politically fragmented," "legally differentiated," "irregular, porous, and sometimes undefined borders."[69] Empire produced widely replicated and imperfect geographies—intricate *anomalies* better

---

65. Eliga H. Gould, *Zones of Law, Zones of Violence: The Legal Geography of the British Atlantic, circa 1772*, 60 WM. & MARY Q. 417, 474 (2003). Gould notes the 1772 case of Somerset v. Stewart (20 How. St. Tr. 1, 1772), where Lord Chief Justice Mansfield ruled that a fugitive slave found in England could not forcibly be returned to his master's charge in Jamaica, which was beyond the colonial line of amity. *See id.* at 471–72. England nevertheless tolerated the practice until the Slavery Abolition Act took effect on August 1, 1834.

66. *See* FRANCES GARDINER DAVENPORT, ED., EUROPEAN TREATIES BEARING ON THE HISTORY OF THE UNITED STATES AND ITS DEPENDENCIES TO 1648, at 220 (Frances Gardiner Davenport ed., 1917) (referring to an oral agreement between Philip II and France "to the effect that west of the prime meridian and south of the Tropic of Cancer might should make right, and violence done by either party to the other should not be regarded as in contravention of treaties. Beyond these 'lines of amity' treaties should lose their force. Ships captured there were considered good prize.").

67. LAUREN BENTON, A SEARCH FOR SOVEREIGNTY: LAW AND GEOGRAPHY IN EUROPEAN EMPIRES, 1400–1900, at 114 (2009). *See also* Garrett Mattingly, *No Peace Beyond What Line?* 13 TRANS. ROYAL HIST. SOC'Y 146, 161 (1963) (despite the confusion, Mattingly's historical review concludes: "We can be pretty sure, then, that the 'Line' in question is the Tropic of Cancer").

68. *Id.* at 286.

69. *Id.*

expressed in terms of variation rather than exception.[70] Certainly, *uti possidetis* imaginatively exemplified a Euclidean design, but its application in the Americas and elsewhere created "wormholes" and "contortions" that not only challenged the spatial imagination but, as Benton noted, could not be "conventionally mapped."[71] Although investigating the geography of empire in Southeast Asia, James Scott nevertheless interpreted the long history of state-making as an enterprise affected by the divergent interests of hill peoples, who through geographic displacement created wormholes of governance and culture that disrupted the imperial project.[72]

Schmitt's personal failings have also sounded cautionary concerns. Deplored as the "Crown Jurist" of the Third Reich,[73] Schmitt's association with National Socialism makes him one of the most controversial figures in twentieth-century legal studies.[74] Yet his critique of liberalism and its complicity in the construction of undifferentiated (*raumlose*) universalist values reveals the unreconciled tensions at the base of hemispheric relations.[75] One need not rehabilitate Schmitt from his problematic views to acknowledge that his "prescient and perceptive observations . . . speak directly to the ironies" of the post–Cold War

---

70. *Id.* at 298–99.

71. *Id.* at 287.

72. *See generally* JAMES C. SCOTT, THE ART OF NOT BEING GOVERNED: AN ANARCHIST HISTORY OF UPLAND SOUTHEAST ASIA (2009) (metaphorically referring to highland wormholes, where certain indigenous peoples have resisted or not yet been fully integrated into nation-states). Scott referenced the imaginary highland of Zomia, a concept introduced by Willem van Schendel, *Geographies of Knowing, Geographies of Ignorance: Jumping Scale in Southeast Asia*, 20 ENV'T & PLANNING D: SOC'Y & SPACE 647–68 (2002).

73. *Der Kronjurist des Dritten Reiches. See* REINHARD MEHRING: CARL SCHMITT: A BIOGRAPHY 391 (2014) (quoting Ernst Jünger's 1943 diary entry). Schmitt's public association with the Nazi Party was announced on May 1, 1933, with his inaugural lecture at Cologne University. Schmitt moved to Cologne to teach next to his intellectual adversary, Hans Kelsen, but on his arrival, Kelsen had already been placed "on leave." *See id.* 294–95. Kelsen had voted in favor of Schmitt's appointment to the Cologne law faculty in May 1932, based on Schmitt's undeniable brilliance. OONA A. HATHAWAY & SCOTT J. SHAPIRO, THE INTERNATIONALISTS: HOW A RADICAL PLAN TO OUTLAW WAR REMADE THE WORLD 230–32 (2017). After Kelsen's dismissal, all members of the faculty signed a protest letter, except Schmitt. *Id.* at 233. Schmitt organized the anti-Semitic conference of jurists calling for the elimination of Jewish influences in German law and was detained, interrogated, and released by American authorities who had considered putting him in the docket at Nuremberg. *See* HOOKER, *supra* note 30, at xiii.

74. *See* GROSS, *supra* note 34, at 3 (noting Schmitt's "reputation for brilliance" and calling Schmitt "[p]ossibly the most-discussed German jurist of the twentieth century . . . certainly the most controversial").

75. *See* Carl Schmitt, Großraum *versus Universalism: The International Legal Struggle Over the Monroe Doctrine, in* SPATIALITY, SOVEREIGNTY AND CARL SCHMITT: GEOGRAPHIES OF THE NOMOS 47 (Stephen Legg ed., Matthew Hannah trans., 2011).

world.[76] Indeed, Schmitt's trenchant interest in the idea of *Großraum*[77]—defined as a "great space," but more intended to mean a sphere of influence or geopolitical space[78]—continues to inform critical international legal circles. This spatial mentality would inform the hemispheric transisthmian and Caribbean policy of Theodore Roosevelt and his large policy men—Henry Cabot Lodge, Alfred Thayer Mahan, Leonard Wood, Elihu Root—who turned a stylized tradition of nonentanglement and anticolonialism into a moral and racial rationale for intervention.[79] Schmitt forcefully applied geography to international law, admitting, "as every geographer knows," that cartography, when instrumentalized, can become "highly political."[80] He focused on this point in the context of the Monroe Doctrine in the Western Hemisphere, and as his critics would assert,[81] in association with the virulent darker geography of the Nazi idea of *Lebensraum*.[82]

The dynamics of biogeography conceptually incorporate the idea of

---

76. Michael Heffernan, *Mapping Schmitt*, *in* SPATIALITY, SOVEREIGNTY AND CARL SCHMITT: GEOGRAPHIES OF THE NOMOS 234, 234 (Stephen Legg ed., 2011); *see also* Ernst-Wolfgang Böckenförde, *Carl Schmitt Revisited*, 109 TELOS 81, 83 (1996) (on the separation of Schmitt's personal views from his scholarship and the objectivity gained and imparted, by no means uncritical, in the examination of his political theology as viewed from a distance); Teschke, *supra* note 33, at 61 (on reasons surrounding "a less restrictive rehabilitation" of Schmitt's intellectual thought in the Anglosphere); JAN-WERNER MÜLLER, A DANGEROUS MIND: CARL SCHMITT IN POST-WAR EUROPEAN THOUGHT 2 (2003) (calling Schmitt one of the "most notorious modern intellectuals" and investigating "why his thought has meant *so much* and *so many seemingly contradictory things to so many*" (internal quotations omitted)); CARLO GALLI, JANUS'S GAZE: ESSAYS ON CARL SCHMITT (Adam Sitze ed., Amanda Minervini trans., 2015) (assessing his contributions and faults).

77. *See generally* CARL SCHMITT, VÖLKERRECHTLISCHE GROSSRAUMORDNUNG MIT INTERVENTIONSVERBOT FÜR RAUMFREMDE MÄCHTE: EIN BEITRAG ZUM REICHSBEGRIFF IM VÖLKERRECHT (1939) (postulating a German *Großraum* influence by the Monroe Doctrine and presented in lecture format before the Institute for Politics and International Law at Kiel University).

78. Stuart Elden, *Reading Schmitt Geopolitically: Nomos, Territory and* Großraum, 161 RADICAL PHIL. 18, 19 (2010); *see also* MONTSERRAT HERRERO, THE POLITICAL DISCOURSE OF CARL SCHMITT: A MYSTIC OF ORDER 127 (2015) ("sphere of organization"); HOOKER, *supra* note 30, at 4 (regarding the *Großraumordnung* as "a pluriverse of continental empires").

79. *See* JAY SEXTON, THE MONROE DOCTRINE: EMPIRE AND NATION IN NINETEENTH-CENTURY AMERICA 212–13 (2011).

80. SCHMITT, NOMOS, *supra* note 21, at 88.

81. *Id.*; *see also* HERF, *supra* note 44, at 26 (on the politicization of *Le[b]ensphilosophie*, or the "philosophie of life"); *id.* at 44–46 (on Schmitt's admiration of the authoritarian state and his contributions to reactionary modernism); Richard Wolin, *Carl Schmitt: The Conservative Revolution and the Aesthetics of Horror*, 20 POL. THEORY 424, 424 (1993).

82. *See generally* Trevor J. Barnes & Claudio Minca, *Nazi Spatial Theory: The Dark Geographies of Carl Schmitt and Walter Christaller*, 103 ANNALS ASS'N AM. GEOGRAPHERS 669–87 (2013) (noting that many people contributed to the "geographical vision of Nazism" in addition to the concept of *Lebensraum*, including Schmitt).

nomos. Biogeography has long been understood to combine biological, geographical, and anthropological conditions that shape the spatial needs of human populations.[83] The field developed from the late-nineteenth-century German scholarship of Friedrich Ratzel, who was heavily influenced by Darwin's *On the Origin of Species* (1860),[84] and the earlier, organic structuration of the earth's natural features by geographer Carl Ritter.[85] Swedish constitutional lawyer Rudolf Kjellén—who formalized Ratzel's teachings into the concept of "geopolitics"[86]—and Karl Haushofer[87] profoundly shaped early-twentieth-century conceptions of sovereignty and state formation by systematizing bio-organic attributes of statehood into "a dualistic view of power determined by geographical position."[88] Haushofer deeply mistrusted international law's ability to supplant primordial organicist influences with liberalism's ideological and institutional preference for the League of Nations as a new, institutionalized *Großraumordnung*.[89] Haushofer's *Raum* studies would do virulent disservice to the concept because of his association with biological racism and National Socialism's cooptation of the concept of *Lebensraum* as a justification for territorial aggrandizement.[90] The concept would problematically intrigue Carl Schmitt as a distinctly political idea.[91] Schmitt's lecture on *Großraum*, delivered weeks after the Nazi invasion of Czechoslovakia, contributed to his moniker as *Kronjurist* to the Third Reich.[92] His politicization of *Raum* studies informed his influential attack against liberal cosmopolitanism,[93] which drew interest from

83. C. Abrahamsson, *On the Genealogy of Lebensraum*, 68 GEOGRAPHICA HELVETICA 37, 39 (2013).

84. Friedrich Ratzel, *Über den Lebensraum: Eine biogeographische Skizze*, 21 DIE UMSCHAU 363–67 (1897); FRIEDRICH RATZEL, POLITISCHE GEOGRAPHIE (1897).

85. CARL RITTER, DIE ERDKUNDE IM VERHÄLTNIS ZUR NATUR UND ZURE GESCHICHTE DES MENSCHEN (1817).

86. *See also* Rudolf Kjellén, *Studier ofver Sveriges politiska gränser*, 19 YMER 183, 331 (1899); RUDOLF KJELLÉN, DER STAAT ALS LEBENSFORM (1917).

87. Benno Teschke, *Geopolitics*, 14 HIST. MATERIALISM 327, 327 (2006); KARL HAUSHOFER ET AL., BAUSTEINE ZUR GEOPOLITIK (1928).

88. Teschke, *supra* note 87, at 327.

89. *Id.*

90. The vulgarization of *Raum* studies also had much to do with Haushofer's mentee, Hitler's deputy führer, Rudolf Hess. *See* JOSEPH J. BENDERSKY, CARL SCHMITT: THEORIST FOR THE REICH 252 (1983).

91. *Id.* at 252–53.

92. Charles E. Frye, *Carl Schmitt's Concept of the Political*, 28 J. POL. 818, 818 (1966) (noting Schmitt was "widely known as the Crown Jurist of the Third Reich").

93. *See generally* SCHMITT, NOMOS, *supra* note 21 (explaining the origins of the Eurocentric global order). Schmitt's English-language translator, G. L. Ulmen, and Paul Piccone, the editor of the journal *Telos*, which principally refigured Schmitt as a thinker of

critical legal circles because of his association of economic liberalism with a kind of political authoritarianism.[94] Such criticisms are distinctly reflected in doctrinal presentations of subalternity coming from postcolonial and critical legal hemispheric sectors, whether they are mindful of Schmitt's intellectual penumbra or not. Schmitt's continuing presence in post–*Jus Publicum Europaeum* conversations about the Americas reverberates in these doctrinal discussions, and the topic deeply interested him given his multiple explorations of the long-lasting consequences of the Monroe Doctrine.

Nomos and Ayllus

Unlike Antarctica, the Atacama has a long human history. This region's prehistory traces back more than 10,000 years.[95] Kunza-speaking Atacameña Likan Antai settled from the oases and gorge valleys of the *Altiplano* to the steep slopes of the Andes.[96] Pre-Incan kinship and community associations—*ayllus*[97]—formed nucleated settlements across the central and southern Peruvian Ayacucho area and into the Macha and

great importance to critical studies, noted that the "ecumenical world order" as embodied by the League of Nations and later world order enthusiasts, attempted to deploy a universalist system after World War I that criminalized enemies, making it impossible to recognize the other side as an equal. *See* Paul Piccone & G. L. Ulmen, *Schmitt's "Testament" and the Future of Europe*, TELOS 3, 5 (1990). The destruction of the *Justus Hostis*, the legitimate enemy, destroyed the *Jus Publicum Europaeum's* distinction between just and unjust wars, and replaced its world order with an incoherent series of treaties, war guilt assignment, and reparations, thus destroying the concrete order with incoherence. *Id.* For Piccone's and Ulman's explanation of the need to reread Schmitt, as contained in a special issue of *Telos* devoted to his work, see Paul Piccone & G. L. Ulmen, *Introduction to Carl Schmitt*, TELOS 3,3 (1987).

94. *See* RENATO CRISTI, CARL SCHMITT AND AUTHORITARIAN LIBERALISM (1998); INGEBORG MAUS, BÜRGERLICHE RECHTSTHEORIE UND FASCHISMUS: ZUR SOZIALEN FUNKTION UND AKTUELLEN WIRKUNG DER THEORIE CARL SCHMITT'S (1980).

95. María Soledad Gheggi & Verónica Isabel Williams, *Corrigendum to "New Date on Food Consumption in Pre-Hispanic Population from Northwest Argentina (ca. 1000–1550 A.D.): The Contribution of Carbon and Nitrogen isotopic Composition of Human Bones,"* J. ANTHROPOLOGY 1–13, 3 (2015) (noting northwest Argentina has been occupied since before 10,000 BCE).

96. The Kunza language of the Atacameños exists today only in association with several traditions and fragmentary song texts. Marleen Haboud, *South America: Andean Region*, *in* ATLAS OF THE WORLD'S LANGUAGES IN DANGER 93, 95–102 (3d ed. 2010).

97. Ethnologists and anthropologists struggle with the definition of *ayllu*, alternatively and incompletely associating the concept with communal land, lineage-based community, clans, solidarity-corporate land or lineage, kinship and territorial ties, as well as symbolic social principles or metaphoric association with mountains. *See* JOSEPH W. BASTIEN, MOUNTAIN OF THE CONDOR: METAPHOR AND RITUAL IN THE ANDEAN AYLLU xxiii–xxv (1978).

Potosí regions of Bolivia.[98] Quechua-speaking peoples populated the Ollagüe, Alto Loa, and Tarapacá oases around Antofagasta in what is now Chile.[99] Archeological evidence of sedentary villages dates from 800 BCE.[100] At least four major indigenous peoples inhabited the Atacama region when the Spaniards arrived.[101] Although fragmented, human habitation extended across the desert and central sierra zones, well into the highlands.[102]

American Geographical Society cartographers began charting the Atacama's ancient transportation networks in the 1920s as part of their twenty-five-year comprehensive 1:1 million Map of Hispanic America project (resulting in "the greatest map ever produced of any one area").[103] The dotted pathways across the Atacama left by the ancient indigenous peoples prominently comprise and cover a six-sheet map of the Atacama reproduced by Bowman in his classic 1924 geographic presentation of the Atacama.[104]

The Incan Empire, expanding under Pachacuti (1438–1471) from the imperium's birthplace near Cuzco, Perú, linked these often-warring communities to a proto-viceroyalty-like system of provincial governance,[105] connected by an extensive road system that crisscrossed the Atacama on somewhat east-west axes and stretched in parallel north-south routes from modern day Quito, Ecuador, to Santiago, Chile.[106] This Andean

98. *See* Ricardo A. Godoy, *The Fiscal Role of the Andean Ayllu*, 21 MAN 723–24 (1986); *see also* BAUTISTA SAAVEDRA, EL AYLLU (1903).

99. Chile's Indigenous Peoples, Museo Chileno de arte precolombino, http://www.precolombino.cl/en/culturas-americanas/pueblos-originarios-de-chile/quechua/ (last visited July 26, 2018).

100. ALLEN W. JOHNSON & TIMOTHY EARLE, THE EVOLUTION OF HUMAN SOCIETIES: FROM FORAGING GROUP TO AGRARIAN STATE 315 (2d ed. 2000).

101. The Aymara, Atacameños, Changos, and Diaguita. *See* FRANCAVIGLIA, *supra* note 4, at 66. Francaviglia (referencing anthropologist Anita Carrasco) also noted that the single name for the Atacameños suggests a homology between the name of the indigenous dwellers and the territory, where anthropological evidence suggests that separate groups of peoples may have been lumped into that single cohesive identity. *See id.* at 76.

102. JOHNSON & EARLE, *supra* note 100, at 317.

103. Alastair W. Pearson & Michael Heffernan, *The American Geographical Society's Map of Hispanic America: Million-Scale Mapping Between the Wars*, 61 IMAGO MUNDI 215, 215 (2009).

104. BOWMAN, *supra* note 4, at 10.

105. *See* Terence N. D'Altroy, *Inca Political Organization, Economic Institutions, and Infrastructure*, *in* THE OXFORD HANDBOOK OF THE INCAS 205, 210–11 (Sonia Alconini & R. Alan Covey eds., 2018) (noting that the Incas devised a system of provincial governance that divided their empire into four provinces: Chinchaysuuy in the north, Collasuyu in the south, coastal Condesuyu to the east, which connected to highland Antisuyu in the west).

106. For a cartographic presentation of the Incan road system through the Atacama

road system (*Mapa del Qhapaq Ñan o Camino del Inca*), at its maximum in the fifteenth century, covered 30,000 km and stretched from the coast to an altitude of 6,600 meters.[107] It provided the infrastructural lifeline of the Incan Empire, traversing "mountains, high plains, coastal deserts, and eastern jungles and plains."[108] Two thousand roadside way stations, forts, and supply centers held it together.[109] It took the Cuzco Incas less than 100 years to establish control over this commercial, cultural, economic, and military backbone, and it propelled them to imperial power.

The Incas inherited these routes from areas once controlled by the Chavín, the Wari (Pakaanóva), the Aymara of Tiwanaku, and the Chimú,[110] whose coastal desert capital of Chan Chan had a masterful irrigation system for upward of 60,000 inhabitants, making it the largest such system in pre-Columbian America.[111] The western route followed the Pacific coast, and an inland Andean route skirted the western shore of Lake Titicaca. Control over these routes enabled the Incas to develop "the largest and administratively most complex polity of the prehistoric New World."[112] Their empire incorporated more than 100 ethnic and indigenous communities.[113]

Incaic power in the Atacama region exercised indirect rule and benefitted from adept cooptation of the *ayllu*,[114] "the basic political and social unit of Andean society."[115] Some scholars identify the ancient essence of the *ayllu* in terms of its connectedness to communal land holding,[116] which "quickly became the bedrock of the Andean political

---

Desert and elsewhere, see WALTRAUD Q. MORALES, A BRIEF HISTORY OF BOLIVIA 12 (2d ed. 2010).

107. Qhapaq Ñan, Andean Road System UNESCO, https://whc.unesco.org/en/list/1459

108. D'Altroy, *supra* note 105, at 206 (estimating as well that the road system may have spanned 40,000 to 60,000 km).

109. See *id.*

110. *See The Great Inka Road: Engineering an Empire*, SMITHSONIAN (2016), https://americanindian.si.edu/inkaroad/ancestors/beginningsoftheroad/introduction.html (noting the 14,000-year prehistory of commercial networks that facilitated the rise of the Inca Empire).

111. *See* Bruce Hathaway, *Endangered Site: Chan Chan, Peru*, SMITHSONIAN (March 2009), https://www.smithsonianmag.com/travel/endangered-site-chan-chan-peru-51748031/. *See also* JAMES S. OLSON, THE INDIANS OF CENTRAL AND SOUTH AMERICA: AN ETHNOHISTORICAL DICTIONARY (1991).

112. JOHNSON & EARLE, *supra* note 100, at 315.

113. *Id.*

114. *Id.*

115. JAYME A. SOKOLOW, THE GREAT ENCOUNTER: NATIVE PEOPLES AND EUROPEAN SETTLERS IN THE AMERICAS, 1492–1800, at 15 (2003).

116. WILLIAM H. ISBELL, MUMMIES AND MORTUARY MONUMENTS: A POSTPROCESSUAL PREHISTORY OF CENTRAL ANDEAN SOCIAL ORGANIZATION 13 (1997).

order."[117] Amerindian language terms use locative possessive suffixes to denote place and convey telluric cultural attachment to "my land" and "my soil."[118] Imprecisely translated as "clan," Alan Kolata defined the ancient Andean *ayllu* "as a group of related families that held land in common and traced their descent from a common ancestor."[119] The communal land tenure system precluded the acquisition of "land or water resources as personal property," thus constraining entrepreneurialism and the personal acquisition of water and land rights while "ensur[ing] that the community as a whole would always have enough productive lands to guarantee survival."[120]

Originario populations regard the *ayllu* as "a group of families circumscribed by a territory, united by ties of kinship . . . a common language . . . collective labor, and their own rituals."[121] In this hyperarid region, water, and proximity to it, conditioned settlement structure.[122] It is rooted in "traditional socio-territorial organizational forms dating to pre-Columbian times."[123] Elements of *indigenismo* assert the *ayllu* "as a cornerstone of highland indigeneity" suggestive of "a positive continuation of pre-Hispanic traditions,"[124] and as a counterpoint to land management and neoliberal water agendas that deprive indigenous populations of traditional uses, customs, and resource rights.[125] Notwithstanding social reorganizations under centuries of interceding rule, including the

---

117. PETER GOSE, INVADERS AS ANCESTORS: ON THE INTERCULTURAL MAKING AND UNMAKING OF SPANISH COLONIALISM IN THE ANDES 17 (2008).

118. David J. Robinson, *The Language and Significance of Place in Latin America*, *in* THE POWER OF PLACE: BRINGING TOGETHER GEOGRAPHICAL AND SOCIOLOGICAL IMAGINATIONS 157, 159 (John A. Agnew & James S. Duncan eds., 1989).

119. ALAN L. KOLATA, ANCIENT INCA: CASE STUDIES IN EARLY SOCIETIES 52 (2013). From an anthropological perspective Isbell identified social group organization, corporate management of resources, belief in kinship as an idiom for organization, and, as "the lynchpin of the *ayllu*"—the veneration of the ancestor mummy as the common, putative biological founder of the social group. *See* ISBELL, *supra* note 116, at 286.

120. *Id.* at 53.

121. ROBERT ANDOLINA ET AL., INDIGENOUS DEVELOPMENT IN THE ANDES: CULTURE, POWER, AND TRANSNATIONALISM 101 (2009) (quoting the Federation of Ayllus and Communities of Ingavi Province [Bolivia])

122. Christian Olmos Herrera, *Territory's Fragmentation: The Territory of Aboriginal Communities in the Process of Mining Expansion: The Case of the Atacama Desert, Chile* 5 (2014), DOI: 10.13140/RG.2.1.3899.2484.

123. Thomas Perreault, *Extracting Justice: Natural Gas, Indigenous Mobilization, and the Bolivian State*, *in* THE POLITICS OF RESOURCE EXTRACTION: INDIGENOUS PEOPLES, MULTINATIONAL CORPORATIONS, AND THE STATE 75, 78 (Suzana Sawyer & Edmund Terence Gomez eds., 2012).

124. *Id.* at 56.

125. *Id.* at 132.

Spanish resettlement policy of *reducción*,[126] and the *ayllus*' preservation in areas of Perú and Bolivia, "it is as much the product of interaction with colonial and postcolonial forms of domination, as it is an historical artifact of sociocultural organization,"[127] with explicitly legitimating "claims to territorially based ethnic autonomy."[128]

The Incas did not interrupt the function of the *ayllus*, which acted as an insurance network that allowed indigenous communities to preserve communal land and consociational structure. Rather, the Incas taxed them, and shifted to the *ayllus* the managerial burden of tax collection.[129] Through the labor and tribute exacted, the Incas fortified their conquest of eight to fourteen million people, which anthropologists describe as "one of history's most remarkable events."[130] Over time, approximately ten endogamous *ayllu* kin groups formed, from which ethnic Incas could trace their lineage. Exogamous practices would eventually create greater *ayllu* communities for land distribution and other public purposes.[131] Preservation of the *ayllu* exchange system contributed to the autonomy and long-term survival of the Atacameños.[132]

This indirect independence from Incaic domination contributed as well to the preservation of the multiracial character of the region, which would persist through the period of Iberian colonization. The seclusion of the region further impeded Iberian access and control, facilitating the preservation of multiracial identity. However, colonization eventually created a pigmentocracy across Spain's hemispheric holdings.[133] Spanish rule actively reproduced this "colonial privilege" for Inca elite, owing to the "strong Spanish prejudices that all complex societies contained a

---

126. *Reducción* is the name given to the consolidation attempts of Spain beginning in the 1560s. The Spanish colonial project underwent revision to consolidate dispersed indigenous settlements to replace indirect rule with Spanish fiscal, administrative, and religious organizations. *See* GOSE, *supra* note 117, at 118–19.

127. Perreault, *supra* note 123, at 79.

128. *Id.*

129. *Id.* at 17.

130. *Id.* at 315 (one hundred ethnic groups), 316.

131. Rebecca M. Seaman, *Ayllus*, *in* CONFLICT IN THE EARLY AMERICAS: AN ENCYCLOPEDIA OF THE SPANISH EMPIRE'S AZTEC, INCAN, AND MAYAN CONQUESTS 35 (Rebecca M. Seaman ed., 2013)

132. Godoy, *supra* note 98, at 724.

133. *See* EDWARD TELLES, PIGMENTOCRACIES: ETHNICITY, RACE, AND COLOR IN LATIN AMERICA 1–2 (2014) (noting the persistence of social hierarchies based on race and color among indigenous and Afrodescendants in Latin America and yet the creation of a new ideology of *mestizaje/mestizo* culture); EKKEHARD W. BORNTRÄGER, BORDERS, ETHNICITY, AND NATIONAL SELF-DETERMINATION 41 (1999) (noting widespread miscegenation in Latin America yet problems of ethnic integration).

hereditary estate who rightly enjoyed social preeminence."[134] The ethnoracial complexity of this *castas* line-drawing system marginalized indigenous peoples and sparked a nineteenth-century creole consciousness, which helped to solidify the self-interpreted regional uniqueness of the Americas.[135] It also formed the bases of political disputes among creole elites and spawned indigenous social movements that continue to affect relations in the Andean Cone.[136] This consciousness suggested that Latin American colonialism, harsh to be sure, never "reflect[ed] a binary distinction between dominant and subordinate strata, or between colonizer and colonized, owing to the multiracial hybridity of American societies and the complex networks" formed over vast and remote territories, such as the Atacama.[137]

Spanish Incursions into the Atacama

Spanish conquistadors encountered Mesoamerican transport arteries in the sixteenth century and eventually linked these pathways to southern routes leading into the Atacama.[138] Hernán Cortéz (1484/5–1547) followed the Aztec road from Chalchihuecan (Veracruz, Mexico) in 1519 to conquer Montezuma and the Aztec capital at Tenochtitlán

---

134. David T. Garrett, *Inca Ancestry and Colonial Privilege*, *in* THE OXFORD HANDBOOK OF THE INCAS 759 (Sonia Alconini & R. Alan Covey eds., 2018).

135. Liliana Obregón, *Between Civilisation and Barbarism: Creole Interventions in International Law*, 27 THIRD WORLD Q. 815, 816–17 (2006).

136. *See, e.g.*, Michael Reid, *Forgotten Continent: A History of the New Latin America* 305–7 (2017); Rafael Loayza Bueno & Ajoy Datta, "The Politics of Evo Morales' Rise to Power in Bolivia: The Role of Social Movements and Think Tanks," ODI (2011), https://www.odi.org/sites/odi.org.uk/files/odi-assets/publications-opinion-files/7063.pdf (accessed January 3, 2019); Michael Miller, "The Rise of Evo Morales," web supplement for 8th ed., Brown U. Libr (2014), https://library.brown.edu/create/modernlatinamerica/chapters/chapter-6-the-andes/moments-in-andean-history/the-rise-of-evo-morales/

137. FRANCAVIGLIA, *supra* note 4, at 64 (quoting Cynthia Radding's WANDERING PEOPLES) and 65 (noting historian Claudio Esteva-Fabregat's observation that "the Indians' facility of movement over vast and hostile territories made it practically impossible [for Spain] to subject and control them.").

138. Panama (Darién) served as the initial launching point by ship for the conquest of South America (Francisco Pizarro's first campaign, 1526). Overland connections were made by Pizarro between 1530 and 1535, with specific penetrations into the Atacama by fellow conquistadors Diego de Almagro (1535–1537) and Pedro de Valdivia (1540–1541). For cartographic presentations of these conquests, see JOSÉ MIGUEL OVIEDO, LA EDAD DEL ORO 222 (1986). For a ground-breaking retelling of this history using indigenous Nahuatl-language sources, see CAMILLA TOWNSEND, FIFTH SUN: A NEW HISTORY OF THE AZTECS (2019).

(Mexico City).[139] While subduing the Aztec Empire and peoples of the isthmus, Spanish *encomenderos* and conquistadores, principally Francisco Pizarro (c. 1471–1541), ventured south from Panama,[140] eventually commencing his voyage of conquest in 1530[141] by connecting pre-Hispanic footpaths (*veredas*) and causeways (*calzadas*) to the extensive commercial highways and ports in South America.[142] Pizarro's subordinate and future enemy, Diego de Almagro (1475–1538), followed tributary trails and fortress ruins (*pukarás*) into the Atacama's oasis and mining community of Copiapó in 1534.[143] This was the first European crossing of the Atacama,[144] and Almagro would be the first European to venture into what is now Chile.[145]

Almagro's company found relief from the poisonous insects and reptiles that had tormented its outward journey from Cuzco, but the dry climate took a toll. His expedition had lost most of its llamas in a flash flood while descending from the mountains, and extreme temperature differentials cost his caravan seventy horses in a single night.[146] And yet he noted that the animal carcasses would not decompose.[147] Figures are sketchy regarding the size of Almagro's expedition party, but its descent from the Andes through Tupiza and Salta into the Puna de Atacama may

---

139. *See* Gabrielle G. Palmer, *El Camino Real de Tierra Adentro* 6 SOUTHERN NEW MEXICO HIST. REV. 1, 3 (1999).

140. Francisco Pizarro, commissioned as the *Capitulación de Conquista* (1529), launched a campaign to subdue Atahualpa and the Incan Empire, which he achieved at Cajamarca in 1532 with but 200 volunteers. For general accounts, see STUART STIRLING, PIZARRO, CONQUEROR OF THE INCA (2005); GARCILASO DE LA VEGA, EL INCA, ROYAL COMMENTARIES OF THE INCAS AND GENERAL HISTORY OF PERU, PART TWO (Harold V. Livermore trans., 1966).

141. GOSE, *supra* note 117, at 37.

142. The *Camino Real de Tierra Adentro* advanced northward through a series of towns in Mexico to what is now Sante Fe, New Mexico. It followed trails established by indigenous North American peoples such as the Apache and Chichimecas, and spread in pursuit of silver, which fueled the political economy of Spain's imperium for three centuries. *See generally*, TOMÁS MARTÍNEZ ET AL., EL CAMINO REAL DE TIERRA ADENTRO (2009) (discussing the trail system).

143. Francaviglia, *supra* note 4, at 63; FRÉZIER, A VOYAGE TO THE SOUTH-SEA AND ALONG THE COASTS OF CHILI AND PERU IN THE YEARS 1712, 1713, AND 1714, PARTICULARLY DESCRIBING THE GENIUS AND CONSTITUTION OF THE INHABITANTS, AS WELL . . . , at 141–42 (noting the draw of Copiapós gold, iron, brass, tin, lead, and sulphur mines).

144. PETER BAKEWELL, A HISTORY OF LATIN AMERICA, C. 1450 TO THE PRESENT 117 (2d ed. 2004).

145. OXFORD ATLAS OF EXPLORATION 99 (Foreword by John Hemming, 1997).

146. MICHAEL JACOBS, ANDES 474 (2011).

147. GERARDO LARRAÍN VALDÉS, DIOS, SOL Y ORO: DIEGO DE ALMAGRO Y EL DESCUBRIMIENTO DE CHILE 203 (1987).

have resulted in the loss of 1,600 men.[148] He returned to Cuzco by following the entire western coastal route of the Atacama, not wanting to retrace the horrible outward path he had taken. Juan de Saavedra's (d. 1554) fleet provisioned Almagro's overland return. Saavedra had ventured southward from Arica to establish an entrepôt at the strategic (future Chilean) port of Valparaíso. It would repeatedly come under attack by Francis Drake (1578), John Hawkins (1596), and the Dutchman Olivier Van Noort (1600).[149] Pedro de Valdivia (1497–1553) followed this pathway again in 1539 to establish the port city of Concepción, south of Santiago. Within a short time, Spain had reconnoitered the most difficult stretch of the South American Pacific coast, establishing way stations at Coquimbo, Copiapo, Tarapaca, Arica, and Tacana.[150] Almagro learned through sixteenth-century privation what Bolivia would come to understand in the aftermath of its devastating nineteenth-century defeat in the War of the Pacific—the key to control over the Atacama depended on a seaborne approach.

Dampier's early-seventeenth-century description of the South Sea coast (referred to as "the *Sierra Nuevada de Andes*") noted "that there are no Rivers of note that fall into these Seas." Among the few, small exorheic outlets such as the "Ylo [Ilo] River," "there are but very few of them, for in some places there is not one that comes out into the Sea in 150 or 200 Leagues [517–690 miles]." However, even these were too shallow to navigate, and they often ran dry.[151] Frézier's early-eighteenth-century survey of the Atacama coast noted that between Copiapó and Coquimbo, a distance of 100 leagues, there were but three or four farms; between Copiapó and the Atacama, "the Country is so hideous and desart [sic], that

148. RAYMOND JOHN HOWGEGO, ENCYCLOPEDIA OF EXPLORATION TO 1800, at 34 (2004). Almagro's advance party into the Atacama, under the command of Rodrigo Orgonez, consisted of 570–750 Spanish soldiers and 1,500–12,000 Indians. Almagro's party apparently consisted of 200 Spaniards. *Id.* The expedition included Paulo Túpac, brother of Huáscar, and half-brother of Atahualpa, the last of the Incan emperors. LARRAÍN VALDÉS, *supra* note 147, at 211. Almagro's losses on the return journey up the northern coast of the Atacama "were almost as great." JACOBS, *supra* note 146, at 474.

149. 1 WILLIAM DAMPIER, A NEW VOYAGE ROUND THE WORLD iii (6th ed. corrected, 1717); HOWGEGO, *supra* note 148, at 922. Valparaíso would remain important port for the entire Pacific coast, with substantial penetration by British merchant houses in the financial control of copper mining. *See* John Mayo, *Commerce, Credit and Control in Chilean Copper Mining Before 1880, in* MINERS AND MINING IN THE AMERICAS 33–40 (Thomas Greaves & William Culver eds., 1985) (noting particularly William Gibbs & Co.).

150. *See* MANUEL BALLESTEROS GAIBROIS, HISTORIA DE AMERICA 241–44 (1946) (on La banda meridional de la costa Pacífica).

151. 1 DAMPIER, *supra* note 149, at iii (6th ed. corrected, London: James Knapton, at the Crown in St. Paul's Church-Yard, 1717).

the Mules starve for want of Gras and Water."[152] English sea captains and privateers Edward Cooke and Woodes Rogers reconnoitered the Atacama coastline in the early eighteenth century, paying almost exclusive attention to where mariners could find fresh water.[153] Regarding the Atacama, Darwin wrote, "it was almost a pity to see the sun shining over so useless a country."[154]

The attention paid to locating fresh water sources presented an imperative. Coastal entrepôts afforded strategic way stations that doubled as fortifications to protect sea-lanes and interior transit routes while provisioning connections to the Isthmus of Darién, from which imperial expansion launched up the California coast, and to points westward as well. Renaissance historian C. R. Boxer noted that the lasting maritime connection linking Asia, Europe, Africa, and the Americas came about after the Spanish replicated in clockwise fashion around Patagonia and up the west coast of the Americas the commercial-coastal-port system that the Portuguese had constructed in counterclockwise fashion around the Cape of Good Hope and up the east coast of Africa.[155] Hopscotching around the coastal ports of Africa enabled the Portuguese to locate knowledgeable local mariners who could guide them to the trade winds that would propel them across the Indian Ocean to the fabled Spice Islands of Indonesia, and then into the South China Sea. The Spanish would use Pacific-America coastal ports—Quiaquil [Guayaquil], Truxillo, Lima, Arica, Coquimbo, Govanadore, Valparaíso, and Baldivia[156]—to launch the Spanish galleon exchange of silver bullion for Asian emporia using Manila as the hub in 1571. "Manila was the crucial entrepôt linking substantial, direct, and continuous trade between America and Asia for the first time in human history."[157]

---

152. FRÉZIER, *supra* note 142, at 142.

153. 2 CAPTAIN EDWARD COOKE, A VOYAGE TO THE SOUTH SEA, AND ROUND THE WORLD, PERFORM'D IN THE YEARS 1708, 1709, 1710, AND 1711, at 232 (1712); WOODES ROGERS, A CRUISING VOYAGE ROUND THE WORLD: FIRST TO THE SOUTH-SEA, THENCE TO THE EAST-INDIES, AND HOMEWARDS BY THE CAPE OF GOOD HOPE. BEGUN IN 1708, AND . . . , at 47 (1726).

154. *See* JOHN AARONS & CLAUDIO VITA-FINZI, THE USELESS LAND: A WINTER IN THE ATACAMA DESERT 13–14 (1960) (quoting Darwin).

155. CHARLES R. BOXER, THE PORTUGUESE SEABORNE EMPIRE, 1415–1825, at 17 (1969).

156. HERMAN MOLL, A VIEW OF THE COASTS, COUNTRIES AND ISLANDS WITHIN THE LIMITS OF THE SOUTH-SEA-COMPANY. CONTAINING AN ACCOUNT OF THE DISCOVERIES, SETTLEMENTS . . . 145 (1711).

157. Dennis O. Flynn & Arturo Giráldez, *Latin American Silver and the Early Globalization of World Trade*, *in* NATIONAL IDENTITIES AND SOCIOPOLITICAL CHANGES IN LATIN AMERICA 141 (Mercedes F. Durán-Cogan & Antonio Gómez-Moriana eds., 2001); Dennis O.

To stave off marauding sea plunderers, the Spanish fortified Pacific coast entrepôts. The viceroy of Perú sent Don Pedro Sarmiento (1532–1592) on an expeditionary mission in 1577 to secure the Strait of Magellan to seal off the entire South Sea from foreign intrusion. Sarmiento's personal report to the king of Spain on the need to control this chokepoint resulted in the king's consignment of a fleet of twenty-eight ships with 3,500 men, 500 soldiers, and some additional women to accomplish the mission, which ended badly for Spain. Only 400 men and 30 women made landing.[158] Storms, dissension, and desertion forced Sarmiento back to Spain for more financing, but Sir Walter Raleigh intercepted his voyage and sent him to England as a prisoner; before being captured, however, Sarmiento jettisoned all of his maps and notes regarding the geography he had explored and the colony he had founded.[159] By the time Sarmiento made it back to Spain nine years later—having been imprisoned a second time by Huguenots off the coast of France—Philip II had lost interest in fortifying the strait, and the colonists perished.[160] Arica, another one of these entrepôts—the locus of a key fresh water source[161] and what Dampier and Moll would regard as "a very good Port"[162]—would link the Atacama to global trade and political disputes that would carry into the twenty-first century. It was, and remains, in relative terms, "the best watered site anywhere along this coast between Callao [the port of Lima] and Valparaíso."[163]

Spain's development of this nascent cabotage system and its use of the overland trail network connecting the highlands to the ocean insured that the Atacama Desert would be the subject of multiple rediscoveries over the next five centuries.[164] Bolivia's creole elite understood the

---

Flynn & Arturo Giráldez, *Born with a "Silver Spoon": The Origin of World Trade in 1571*, 6 J. WORLD HIST. 201, 201 (1995).

158. MOLL, *supra* note 156, at 27.

159. ROBERT D. TALBOT, A HISTORY OF THE CHILEAN BOUNDARIES 8–9 (1974).

160. *See id.* at 9.

161. *See* FRÉZIER, *supra* note 142, at 149 (noting a technique of digging for fresh water at low tide, which was potable enough and "kep[t] well at Sea").

162. MOLL, *supra* note 156, at 85 (1711). *See also* 1 DAMPIER, *supra* note 149, at v (referring to Arica, "a strong Town advantageously situated in the hollow of the Elbow, or bending of the *Peruvian* Coast").

163. J. VALERIE FIFER, BOLIVIA: LAND, LOCATION, AND POLITICS SINCE 1825, at 44 (1972).

164. *See* Richard Francaviglia, *Lost in the Atacama: Updates and Corrections*, 50 TERRAE INCOGNITAE 11–14 (2018) (on the multiple rediscoveries and complexities of the Atacama over five centuries). *See* JAIME EYZAGUIRRE, BOLIVIA: AN ISOLATE COUNTRY? 9 (1963) ("The Atacama [D]esert . . . had been an abandoned area for centuries until Chilean explorers . . . began discovering large quantities of natural resources."). BOWMAN, *supra* note 4, at

importance of the sea, and in 1825, shortly after independence, fully expected that Perú (Lower Perú) would cede to it the Pacific coast from Arica southward.[165] The *Libertador,* Simón Bolívar's compatriot, Marshal Antonio José de Sucre (1795–1830), had the Atacama's littoral surveyed in 1825, and reported back to Bolívar that only Arica could functionally serve as a port for Bolivia.[166] Bolívar, committed to upholding the principle of *uti possidetis,* instead designated Cobija as Bolívia's coastal port,[167] a difficult-to-distinguish, water-insufficient bay located 370 miles south of Arica and more than 600 miles from Potosí. United States naval vessels *USS Brandywine* and *USS Falmouth* surveyed the Atacama coast during cruises from 1826 to 1829 and 1831 to 1834, and the ships' officer for both voyages described Cobija as "as barren as can well be imagined . . . not a blade of grass, nor even a cactus to be seen on it . . . [with] a small stream about twenty leagues from it."[168]

Bolívar's adherence to *uti possidetis* fatefully conditioned Andean Cone relations as it deprived Bolivia of its historically most important and direct route to commercial coastal engagement and it politically disrupted ancient pathways of culture and communication. The Audiencia of Lima had functionally recognized Arica's importance to the *Altiplano* as early as 1592 when it decreed "that the *corregidor* [chief administrator] of Arica, even though he be of the district of the Audiencia de Lima, should comply with the orders of the Audiencia de Charcas."[169] To the Ariqueños, Arica "had never been anything more than the port for Upper [Alto] Peru;" its importance since its founding in 1535 dramatically changed in 1546 after the discovery of silver at Potosí. In 1574, the viceroy in Lima designated Arica as the port of Potosí.[170] When the Spanish Crown issued its compendium of laws governing the Americas (*Leyes de las indias,* 1681), the *corregidor* of Arica again was instructed to answer to the Audiencia of Charcas.[171]

---

344 ("It is a striking fact of history that Atacama, extending right along the coast for nine hundred miles, should yet have been crossed by trails and dotted with towns most of which have kept their pioneer quality through four centuries of time." [writing in 1924]).

165. FIFER, *supra* note 163, at 24.

166. *Id.* at 37 (quoting Sucre's letter to Bolívar, January 27, 1826).

167. WALTRAUD Q. MORALES, A BRIEF HISTORY OF BOLIVIA 78 (2d ed. 2003).

168. W. S. W. RUSCHENBERGER, THREE YEARS IN THE PACIFIC: INCLUDING NOTICES OF BRAZIL, CHILE, BOLIVIA, AND PERU 163 ("not a blade of grass . . ."), 164 ("difficult to be found"), 169 ("one hundred and fifty leagues from Chuquisaca [Sucre] . . . ; three hundred from . . . Potosí") (1834).

169. JAIME EYZAGUIRRE, BOLIVIA: AN ISOLATED COUNTRY? 5 (1963).

170. FIFER, *supra* note 163, at 25.

171. 2 RECOPILACIÓN DE LEYES DE LOS REYNOS DE LAS INDIAS Título 15 (1681) ("*Que*

Bolívar preferred to uphold the abstract application of *uti possidetis* and apply it to the highlands because he pledged to respect popular sovereignty. He foresaw emerging rivalries and needed to "placate" postcolonial competition among Upper Perú (Bolivia), Lower Perú (Perú), Colombia, and Río de la Plata.[172] When the viceroyalty of Río de la Plata formed in 1776—in order to quell territorial disputes with Portugal over present-day Uruguay—Upper Perú became part of Río de la Plata, even though it had been nurturing its own highland identity since the creation of the Audiencia of Charcas.[173] Bolívar's independence movement centered on the preservation of the territorial status quo at the inception of the secession movement in 1810, if for no other reason than to keep these disparate and potentially rivalrous factions focused on a common enemy.[174] In a letter to his Sucre, Bolívar's formalistic interpretation of *uti possidetis* required that "[n]either you nor I . . . can violate or disregard what had come to be recognized as a principle of international law in America, namely: that the republican governments are founded within the boundaries of the former viceroyalties, captaincies general, or presidencies, such as Chile. Upper Perú was a dependency of the viceroyalty of [Río de la Plata] . . . [it cannot] lawfully be independent unless a treaty is arranged between the parties concerned. . . ."[175]

Moreover, Bolívar thought an independent Upper Perú geographically remote and unviable and instead felt that it needed to be part of a federation.[176] However, Upper Perú's creole elite anxiously demanded

---

el Corregidor de Arica, aunque sea del distrito de la Audiencia de Lima, cumpla dela de los Charcas" [That the Corregidor of Arica, even though from the district of the Audiencia of Lima, comply with the commandments of Charcas]).

172. Simón Bolívar, *Letter to Sucre, Arequipa, May 15, 1825, in* 2 SELECTED WRITINGS OF BOLIVAR, 1823–1830, at 493 (Harold A. Bierck Jr. ed., Lewis Bertrand trans., 1951). *See also* Simón Bolívar, *Letter to Sucre, Lima, February 21, 1825, in* 2 SELECTED WRITINGS OF BOLIVAR, 1823–1830, at 470 (Harold A. Bierck, Jr. ed., Lewis Bertrand, trans., 1951) (noting that the allowance of breakaway republics to exercise their own sovereignty "will at once incur the disapproval of the Río de la Plata, of Perú, and of Colombia herself").

173. The viceroyalty of the Río de la Plata included Buenos Aires, Paraguay, Tucumán, Potosí, Santa Cruz de la Sierra, Charcas, Mendoza, and San Juan de Pico, which formerly had been dependencies of Chile. *See* ROBERT D. TALBOTT, A HISTORY OF THE CHILEAN BOUNDARIES 14 (1974).

174. *See* GERHARD MASUR, SIMON BOLIVAR 546 (1948).

175. Simón Bolívar, *Letter to Sucre, Lima, February 21, 1825, in* 2 SELECTED WRITINGS OF BOLIVAR, 1823–1830, at 470 (Harold A. Bierck Jr. ed., Lewis Bertrand, trans., 1951).

176. *Id.* at 6. *See also* Simón Bolívar, *Letter to Sucre, Magdalena, May 12, 1826, in* 2 SELECTED WRITINGS OF BOLIVAR, 1823–1830, at 591 (Harold A. Bierck, Jr. ed., Lewis Bertrand trans., 1951) (in discussing the need to "set an example by joining Bolivia and Perú in a federation").

nationhood, not only to secure their interests against the receding void left by the metropolitan power, but to insulate those same interests against emerging threats from Lower Perú and from the Argentine political identity rising from the crumbling viceroyalty of Río de la Plata.[177] Sucre's rout of royalist forces at the decisive battle of Ayacucho (December 1824) led to his famous decree of February 9, 1825, in La Paz's Plaza Murillo, which "unequivocally stated Upper Perú's right to self-determination."[178] This declaration set Bolivia's republican wheels in motion with the formation of a council of delegates. Bolívar grudgingly agreed to this formation, however he "confessed" to Sucre "that I would never have issued this decree" as he was "convinced that everyone will be displeased."[179]

The vast majority of Bolivia's population lived in La Paz, Oruro, Cochabamba, Sucre, and Potosí,[180] locales situated in Bolivia's western highlands. La Paz nested 12,000 feet in the Andes, a month's travel distance to the nearest port city of Arica.[181] Bolivia's internal development, meager as it was, inherited the metropolitan focus on Potosí and its mountain of silver (*Cerro rico*),[182] which made it for two centuries one of the richest cities in the world and the most important holding of the Spanish Empire,[183] save perhaps for Mexico City.[184] The silver strike at Potosí, at altitude of 15,600 feet above sea level, motivated Philip II (1527–1598) to create the Audiencia of Charcas in 1559 at Sucre. The Audiencia of Char-

---

177. See Simon Collier, *Nationality, Nationalism, and Supranationalism in the Writings of Simón Bolívar*, 63 HISP. AM. HIST. REV., 37, 47 (1983).

178. FIFER, *supra* note 163, at 14.

179. Bolívar, *Letter to Sucre, supra* note 172, at 493.

180. WILLIAM F. SATER, ANDEAN TRAGEDY: FIGHTING THE WAR OF THE PACIFIC, 1879–1884, at 12 (2007).

181. *Id.* at 9–10.

182. BARTOLOMÉ ARZÁNS DE ORSÚA Y VELA, TALES OF POTOSÍ xi (ed. & with introduction by R. C. Padden, Frances M. López-Morillas trans., 1975).

183. The motto on the sixteenth-century escutcheon of the city of Potosí reads *Cesaris potential, pro rexis prudential, iste excelsus mons et argenteus, orbem debelare, valent univesisunt* (For the Power of Caesar and for the Prudence of the King, this exalted silver mount was discovered before the whole world). *See Potosí: "Por la Potencia del César y por la Prudencia del Rey,"* LA PATRIA (Aug. 6, 2013), http://www.lapatriaenlinea.com/?nota=152931. An interesting account of the discovery of Potosí and the revenue generated can be found in 2 ANTONIO DE ULLOA, A VOYAGE TO SOUTH AMERICA. DESCRIBING AT LARGE, THE SPANISH CITIES, TOWNS, PROVINCES, &C. ON THAT EXTENSIVE CONTINENT. INTERSPERSED THROUGHOUT . . . , 145–48 (1760). *See also* KRIS LANE, POTOSÍ: THE SILVER CITY THAT CHANGED THE WORLD 8 (2019) (noting that Potosí "produced nearly half the world's silver" in the first century after its discovery).

184. LEWIS HANKE, THE IMPERIAL CITY OF POTOSÍ: AN UNWRITTEN CHAPTER IN THE HISTORY OF SPANISH AMERICA 1–2 (1956).

cas functionally demarcated Bolivia's borders on independence from Spain in 1825.[185] It grew from imperial Spain's fast-formed need to dominate the political landscape that surrounded the remote highland silver lodes that would finance its empire, swiftly focusing "imperial attention upon one of the highest, bleakest and most inaccessible sites in all Latin America."[186] The spatial politics of conquest depended on the formalistic recourse to abstract and poorly defined border demarcations, configured for purposes of resource protection and extraction. The poorly understood formality of land appropriation in the imperial mindset of sixteenth-century Spain would widen during the early stages of the republican era, where *uti possidetis*'s encounter with the dynamics of human geography and biogeographics would take on added complexity.

Bolivia scholar J. Valerie Fifer noted that the Spaniards and their fearsome cavalry never comfortably adapted to the high altitudes of the cordillera mining centers, but geographical circumstance "impaled the administrative machinery of empire upon the highest and most inaccessible regions of the central Andes,"[187] pinning Upper Perú to a geospatial station "weakened by distance." Although the central Andean cordilleras became the financial determinant of Spain's empire, "Spain's authority and prestige in South America" depended on extracting the mountain wealth and transporting it to the "real centers of power," the coastal Pacific ports leading to "the sea lanes of the empire."[188] While Spain's colonial administration maintained "two tenuous links between the Andes and Upper Perú," access to the fluvial highways of the Amazon and Paraguay routeways to the Atlantic Ocean involved a 2,000-mile journey with precipitous overland scalings and risk-filled navigation around or through treacherous rapids, not to mention into the Amazon itself.[189] Any successful portaging of resources across this eastward route invariably involved fractious dealings with the Portuguese. Upper Perú's most realistic pathway to the sea involved a 300-mile trek westward, across "the worst miles of the Atacama desert."[190] For Upper Perú, this meant gaining control over the port of Arica.[191] "Arica was not just *a*

185. *See* FIFER, *supra* note 163, at 6–9.

186. *Id.* at 6.

187. *Id.* at 1–2.

188. *Id.* at 1.

189. *Id.* at 19 ("tenuous links") and 19–21 (Amazon and Paraguay routeways).

190. *Id.* at 22.

191. RONALD BRUCE ST. JOHN, BOUNDARIES, TRADE, AND SEAPORTS: POWER POLITICS IN THE ATACAMA DESERT 3–4 (1992).

port, it was *the* port. . . . the most direct route down to the sea from the Bolivian *Altiplano,* via the Tacna oasis, it continued to handle the bulk of the trade to and from La Paz, Cochabamba and the most densely populated sections of the country."[192] The Bolivian historian Alcides Arguedas noted that Arica was the artery most necessary for the life of the nation.[193]

Bolívar's unyielding defense of *uti possidetis* prompted immediate diplomatic contacts between Upper Perú's *criollos* and Lima, but Lima would not accommodate any proposal to move imperial Spain's line in the Atacama sand. A proposed treaty of November 15, 1826, attempted to achieve the same goal, but Lima refused to sign it. Following Bolivia's 1835 invasion of Perú, Sucre's successor as president of Bolivia, Andrés Santa Cruz (1792–1865), forged a short-lived confederation, which disintegrated when Perú invaded Cobija in 1841, followed by Bolivia's victory at Ingavi, which emboldened it to take Arica, Tacna, Puno, and Moquegua. "It was the first and last time that Bolivia was ever to occupy Arica."[194] However it inaugurated a tortured and lengthy pursuit for Bolivia of a phantom territorial title to counter Bolívar's expedient application of *uti possidetis de jure,* which itself conformed to phantom imperial lines based on the 1559 assignment to the Audiencia of Charcas of administrative control over the mother lode of silver contained in *Cerro rico.*

This abstract consignment of land appropriation depended on the application of the *uti possidetis* norm, which formalistically paid no attention to the surrounding human geography, except to the extent that it attempted to deal with the shadings of *criollo* and *caudillo* pigmentocracy that emerged as quickly in Latin America as metropolitan rule receded. Myriad disputes between Bolivia and its neighbors over successive agreements, over agreements to agree *versus* agreements to negotiate (*pactum de contrahendo; pactum de negotiando*), over the legal (in)significance of restoring Bolivia's claim of a sovereign right to access the Pacific Ocean via Arica, have resulted in major diplomatic disruptions, war, and petitions to international organizations and the World Court for intercession and remediation. Bolivia and Chile have had no formal diplomatic relations since the early 1960s, except between 1975 and 1978 when the Charaña negotiations held out the possibility of a land exchange to end

---

192. FIFER, *supra* note 163, at 25.

193. ALCIDES ARGUEDAS, HISTORIA GENERAL DE BOLIVIA (EL PROCESO DE LA NACIONALIDAD 1809–1921), at 119 (1922) ("*. . . sino porque el Puerto de Arica era considerado como la arteria más necesaria a la vida misma de la nación . . . , es tal 'que arrastrará eternamente a Bolivia a ganar Arica o desaparecer como nación'*").

194. *See id.* at 44–47.

another border dispute caused by the 1962 diversion of the Lauca River.[195] The underrecognized basis for this fracture traces to Bolívar's application of *uti possidetis*, which itself was the product of Philip II's decision to frame imperial policy around the creation of the Audiencia of Charcas in order to protect, administer, and capitalize the fundamental source of colonial power, the silver lode at *Cerro rico*.

195. *See* ULDARICIO FIGUEROA, LA DEMANDA MARITIME BOLIVIANA EN LOS FOROS INTERNACIONALES 117–37 (2007).

FOUR

Guano and Nitrates

In 1861, Spain reconquered Santo Domingo (Hispaniola, now Dominican Republic)—the first European colony in the Americas[1]—and installed the junta royalist, Pedro Santana (1801–1864), as captain general.[2] The annexation ended Santo Domingo's seventeen-year period of self-rule, prompted a counterinsurgency campaign between 1863–1865 (the War of Restoration), and stoked concerns of European irredentism throughout the hemisphere.[3]

In 1862, France invaded Mexico (with the planning and short-lived participation of Spain and Britain), further heightening hemispheric concerns of a return to vassal status. Mired in its own civil war (1861–1865), the United States stood powerless to invoke its Monroe Doctrine (1823), which warned Europeans against recolonizing the Americas.[4] Moreover, the United States Secretary of State, William Henry Seward, pursued a policy of inaction toward the intervention out of concern that condemning France or assistance to Mexico would push the French into an alliance with the Confederacy.[5]

In 1863, a Spanish squadron, sailing as a "scientific commission" yet

1. Harold T. Pinkett, *Efforts to Annex Santo Domingo to the United States, 1866–1871*, 26 J. AF. AM. HIST. 12 (1941).

2. *See* Charles C. Hauch, *Attitudes of Foreign Governments Towards the Spanish Reoccupation of the Dominican Republic*, 27 HISP. AM. HIST. REV. 247 (1947).

3. *See* DAVIS, THE LAST CONQUISTADORES, 22.

4. *See* Hauch, *supra* note 2, at 247. On the Monroe Doctrine, see President's Annual Message, Dec. 2, 1823, Annals of Congress, Senate, 18th Congress, 1st Session, 12–24, *available at Primary Documents in American History, Library of Congress*, https://www.loc.gov/rr/program/bib/ourdocs/monroe.html

5. *See* Kathryn Abbey Hanna, *The Roles of the South in the French Intervention in Mexico*, 20 J. SOUTHERN HIST. 3, 9 (1954).

escorted by two frigates and two heavily armed gunboats, rounded Cape Horn and entered the South Sea (Pacific Ocean).[6] South American republics responded with alarm.[7] In 1864, ships from the squadron appeared off Perú's Atacama coast. Anticipating difficulties with Perú, the Spanish commander carried confidential instructions not to tolerate any slight or defamation.[8] Even by this late date, Spain still had refused to recognize Perú's independence,[9] as it had done with its other former South American colonies. An 1863 incident resulting in two deaths at a hacienda in northern Perú worked by Basques (the Talambo affair) provided the "pretext" to justify Spain's belligerent reaction—the protection of nationals.[10] The Spanish envoy sent to demand satisfaction encountered Perú's counterdemand that talks proceed only after Spain recognized the Peruvian republic. Perú pointed out the absurdity of negotiating with a country that did not recognize it as legally capable of mediating a solution. Spain had to recognize the principle of sovereign equality and engage Perú "on equal footing" before talks could proceed.[11]

To revindicate rights never acknowledged as lost, the Spanish squadron seized the guano islands off the Peruvian Atacama coast and hoisted the Spanish flag.[12] The aggression resulted in the Chincha Islands War (1864–1866), in which Spain bombarded the ports of Valparaíso in Chile and Callao in Perú, and Perú forged a Quadruple Alliance with Bolivia, Ecuador, and Chile to retake the islands.[13] The Chincha Islands War put an end to Spanish revanchism in South America, and Spain would lose its last remaining possession, Cuba, by the end of the century. However,

---

6. DAVIS, THE LAST CONQUISTADORES, 9.

7. *See id.* at 9.

8. *Id.* at 10.

9. Yoer Javier Castaño Pareja, "La Diplomacia Secreta": la participación de Colombia en el conflict entre Perú y España por las islas guaneras," *Historia y sociedad* 24 (2013): 189–214 ("*España no había reconocido la independencia del Perú*").

10. CAPTAIN F. E. CERRUTI, PERU AND SPAIN: BEING A NARRATIVE OF THE EVENTS PRECEDING AND FOLLOWING THE SEIZURE OF THE CHINCHA ISLANDS 6 (London: Williams and Norgate, 1864). *See also* Marco A. Flores Sánchez, *El Incidente de Talambo* 17 (Crónica: 2006) (describing the set of events as a "*pretexto*" for Spanish intervention); DAVID P. WERLICH, PERU: A SHORT HISTORY 91 (1978) ("The murder of two Spanish colonists . . . afforded Madrid a pretext for intervention.").

11. Perú refused to receive the Spanish Commissary because "this would be at variance with the diplomatic rules," but it expressed "readiness to open negotiations on a[n equal] footing." CERRUTI, *supra* note 10, AT 13–14.

12. *See* CERRUTI, *supra* note 10, at 10–11 (reprinting a British eyewitness account).

13. *See* RUTH DEFRIES, THE BIG RATCHET: HOW HUMANITY THRIVES IN THE FACE OF NATURAL CRISIS 90 (2014).

the Chincha Islands War provided a template for territorial enticement involving resource extraction in the Atacama. Spain's attempt to reestablish its foothold in the Americas related as much to controlling emerging resources as it did to restoring national pride; its concentration on the remote Chincha Islands "influenced some of the most powerful currents of modern history."[14]

From 1840 to 1880, valuable guano deposits on the three Chincha Islands, located twelve miles off Perú's Bay of Pisco, generated most of Perú's foreign capital. Over millennia, millions of guanays had flocked annually to the islands to breed and feed. Their rookery created mountains of guano, baked by tropical sun on the bald-pated islands. Demand for the fertilizer peaked during this period, and the service trade, involving "as much as 400,000 tons of this manure, valued at $24 million" annually, shipped around the world.[15] "All told, from 1840–1879, Perú exported an estimated 12.7 million metric tons of guano from its islands with a sale value in the range of £100 to 150 million."[16] At times, "as many as 200 ships lay at anchor at one time off the Chincha Islands, awaiting their turn to be loaded." To meet growing demand, a worldwide search for guano island repositories began in the Caribbean, off the west coast of Australia, and in the Central Pacific,[17] with the aim of breaking the Peruvian monopoly.[18] The global guano rush involved major figures in the American colonization of Hawaii, which also provided indigenous recruits to harvest Central Pacific guano deposits.[19] The United States Navy reconnoitered guano islands sighted by whalers in the Central Pacific and laid claim to any uninhabited guano island. The Guano Islands Act (1856) marked the beginning of the United States's extracontinental expansion. To parry criticism at home and abroad over what appeared to be a project of territorial annexation, Congress added that nothing within the act "shall be construed as obliging the United States to retain possession of the islands, rocks, or keys, after the guano shall have been removed from the same." The ultimate acquisition of territory by formally disclaiming title introduced an unusual *a contrario* defense—an inverted or disguised example

---

14. CUSHMAN, GUANO AND THE OPENING OF THE PACIFIC WORLD: A GLOBAL ECOLOGICAL HISTORY xiv.

15. ARNOLD J. MEAGHER, THE COOLIE TRADE: THE TRAFFIC IN CHINESE LABORERS TO LATIN AMERICA 1847–1874 at 222 (2008).

16. CUSHMAN, *supra* note 14, at 45.

17. *See* CHRISTOPHER R. ROSSI, SOVEREIGNTY AND TERRITORIAL TEMPTATION: THE GROTIAN TENDENCY 156–60 (2017).

18. *See* CUSHMAN, *supra* note 14, at 81.

19. *See id.* at 81–82.

of creeping jurisdiction that predated or perhaps obscured the general periodization of American imperialism as a *fin de siècle* phenomenon.[20] The *a contrario* defense reappeared at the end of the Spanish American War in 1898. As part of rising anti-imperial sentiment, the Teller Amendment prevented the United States from exercising "sovereignty, jurisdiction, or control over [Cuba] except for pacification thereof, and asserts its determination, when that is accomplished, to leave the government and control of the island to its people."[21] Disclaiming sovereignty or control over Cuba, accordingly, needed to be accommodated by the Platt Amendment (1901), which turned Cuba into a United States protectorate. The Article III provision of the Platt Amendment predicated the United States's withdrawal of superintendency over Cuba on the exhaustion of concerns that would conflict with United States hemispheric security interests.[22] The Guano Islands Act nevertheless directly led to the establishment of United States sovereignty over an area in the Pacific more than three times the size of California,[23] one of the earliest chapters in the story of American imperialism.[24]

Collateral industries in Perú developed around the guano trade.[25] They were financed by British and American merchant fleets and supported by 3,000 pickaxing prisoners and indentured African and Chinese laborers.[26] Finance capital fueled the expansion of export commodities related to agriculture and mining and attracted foreign-trading-company establishments, which later would provide credit to develop ports, rail lines, and steam navigation networks along the Atacama and South American Pacific coast. Prior to 1860, Perú did not have a single bank. Ten years later, Lima claimed nine lending institutions.[27]

---

20. *See* Christina Duffy Burnett, *The Edges of Empire and the Limits of Sovereignty: American Guano Islands*, 57 AM. Q. 779, 781 (2005).

21. Joint Resolution [no. 24] for the Recognition of the Independence of the People of Cuba . . . , 30 Stat. 738, Apr. 20, 1898 [Teller Amendment].

22. *See* CHRISTOPHER R. ROSSI, WHIGGISH INTERNATIONAL LAW: ELIHU ROOT, THE MONROE DOCTRINE, AND INTERNATIONAL LAW IN THE AMERICAS 104–05 (2019).

23. *See* ROSSI, *supra* note 17, at 156–60.

24. Burnett, *supra* note 20, at 781.

25. *See* CUSHMAN, *supra* note 14, at 56, 83 (noting the British merchant house, Gibbs & Sons, and the American Guano Company).

26. MEAGHER, *supra* note 15, at 223–24. Each laborer had to fill a quota of digging five tons of guano daily, every day, leading one nineteenth-century observer to claim "[n]o hell has ever been conceived . . . that can be equaled to the . . . damnation of those compelled to labor there." *Id.* at 226—27 (quoting ALEXANDER J. DUFFIELD, PERU IN THE GUANO AGE 77–78 (1877)); CUSHMAN, *supra* note 14, at 55 (noting the Chincha Islands' population at the peak of the guano trade).

27. WERLICH, *supra* note 10, 98–99.

Nitrate discoveries surpassed the importance of the Atacama's guano stores and put the guano trade to an end after 1880. Guano's decline inversely mirrored the rise of nitrate exports,[28] fortuitously located in the same Atacama region. *Originarios* knew of its agricultural potency,[29] but the connection was not as obvious to observers. In 1832, William Ruschenberger, while on shore leave during a naval tour of South America on board the *USS Falmouth*, ventured into the countryside from Pisco. One league (3.4 miles) into the expansive salt flats that surrounded the area, he encountered several men cutting two-foot-long cakes out of the salt beds, six inches into the surface. The area looked like a "frozen lake," however he noted that it was pock-marked with holes filled with reddish ponds of water where the cakes had been removed. "Although almost any amount of salt is obtainable," he noted, "[t]his salt, like all that found along the coast, is so contaminated with nitre, lime, and magnesia, that it is unfit for preserving beef or any kind of meat."[30]

Ruschenberger probably did not understand that the miners were not aiming to extract common table salt (sodium chloride). Rather, they were probably excavating sodium nitrate or saltpeter (*salitre*), condensed in the minerally combinant form of caliche, which was soluble and could be reduced into a potent crystalized agricultural fertilizer. For many years dating from Darwin's 1835 sojourn to the Atacama, scientists puzzled over the accumulation of the Atacama's huge nitrate deposits,[31] given the knowledge that rain easily washed away these surface stores. It is now well settled that climate, tectonics, and the unique conditions of the Atacama's hyperaridity combined to create these massive deposits,[32] bequeathing to the sovereign titleholder a tremendous comparative and financial advantage over an agricultural product (nitrogen) that would dominant an age when most people remained tethered to land and its cultivation. By the mid to late nineteenth century, farming had become increasingly dependent on the mining industry for fertilizer.

---

28. *See* CUSHMAN, *supra* note 14, at 47 (graph).

29. *See* R. A. F. Penrose Jr., *The Nitrate Deposits of Chile*, 18 J. GEO. 2 (1910) ("probably been known from very ancient times").

30. W. S. W. RUSCHENBERGER, THREE YEARS IN THE PACIFIC; INCLUDING NOTICES OF BRAZIL, CHILE, BOLIVIA, AND PERU 355 (1834).

31. *See* George E. Ericksen, *Geology and Origin of the Chilean Nitrate Deposits* (Geological Survey Professional Paper 1188, 1988); J. Seo, *Solving the Mystery of the Atacama Nitrate Deposits: The Use of Stable Oxygen Isotope Analysis and Geochemistry*, 1 J. PURDUE UNDERGRADUATE RESEARCH 38 (2011).

32. *See* Martin Reich & Huiming Gao, *Nitrate Deposits of the Atacama Desert: A Marker of Long-Term Hyperaridity*, 14 ELEMENTS 251 (2018).

The early mining of nitrate would also introduce recurrent problems. The separation of nitrate from caliche required large quantities of water and evaporation tanks. Thousands of mules imported from Argentina portaged the nitrate to the coast, and water would be brought in from the Loa River and the Andes.[33] Government-supported concession agreements allowed duty-free exports, which attracted much-needed foreign capital to finance nitrate extraction, which eventually contributed to rail lines deep into the Atacama. By 1875, more than 400 nitrate enterprises operated in Tarapacá.[34] Nitrate production also required that miners and laborers migrate to the nitrate zones, mostly from Chile's central valley, in a practice referred to throughout Latin America as *enganche*.[35] Chileans quickly overtook the number of Bolivians in mining provinces such as Tarapacá and Antofagasta, launching a de facto Chileanization of the Atacama.

The Tarapacá region of southernmost Perú launched the nitrate trade, which quickly replaced the fast-depleting deposits of guano as the world's fertilizer. In 1866, a major nitrate discovery in Bolivia's Salar del Carmen expanded the trade into Bolivia's Atacama. Two years later Bolivia established the port at Antofagasta to commercialize this trade.[36] The expansion of the nitrate trade southward coincided with a brief period of amity between Bolivia and Chile following the Chincha Islands War. They signed a Mutual Benefits Treaty that divided this contested area of the Atacama at the 24th parallel south. Each republic secured exploitation rights to guano and mineral deposits in a condominium arrangement as between the 23rd and 25th parallels south, and an export duty exemption applied to all products produced between the 24th and 25th degrees of latitude.[37] The formless border in this area and around Mejillones would provide almost a world monopoly on the production of nitrates, demand for which increased due to the production of munitions, explosives, and after Alfred Nobel's 1867 invention, dynamite. World nitrate demand abated only after 1927, when German scientists invented a commercially viable synthetic substitute.[38]

The application of *uti possidetis* never differentiated the territorial

---

33. FIFER, BOLIVIA: LAND, LOCATION, AND POLITICS 56–57.
34. WERLICH, *supra* note 10, at 101.
35. Michael Monteón, *The Enganche in the Chilean Nitrate Sector, 1880–1930*, 6 LAT. AM. PERSPECTIVES 66, 67–68 (1979).
36. FIFER, *supra* note 33, at 57.
37. ROSSI, *supra* note 17, at 254.
38. WILLIAM T. DAUGHERTY, GERMAN CHEMICAL DEVELOPMENTS IN 1927, at 11 (1928).

border in this vastly underpopulated area, because the functional division of Spanish imperial land appropriation schemes never meant to employ *uti possidetis* for such a purpose. Rather, it was imputed to the hemisphere to preserve orderly succession and to promote efficiencies related to the consolidation of new-born republican power. It was a gap-filling technique employed to avoid claims of *res nullius,* or *terra nullius,* which would invite territorial conflicts to politically fill the void regarding ownership over valuable territory, populations, and resources demarcated by the *audiencias,* not over land generically described and "regarded as worthless for colonization," such as the Atacama.[39]

Bolivia's earliest claims to the Atacama extended farther south than the 26 degree parallel—to the Salado River.[40] Spanish colonial maps of the Audiencia of Charcas variously referenced the border along the Salado River or the Copiapó River, and yet both of these rivers were difficult to fix.[41] These claims overlapped with Chile's claim, which gained more immediacy after the 1841 Chilean discovery of guano deposits in the Atacama.[42] Four Chilean constitutions between 1822 and 1833 claimed all Pacific coast territory, but no provision detailed the limits of its northern frontier.[43] "Perú recognized on three occasions (1822, 1823, and 1825) the need to demarcate its boundaries," and formed a congressional boundary commission; overriding territorial uncertainty and a general sense of a lack of need due to the inhospitable terrain, however, precluded any conclusion.[44] Some evidence suggests that the Bolivian claim was retracted to Paposo at the 25th parallel south, which Chile claimed as its coastal frontier town bordering Bolivia from the south.[45] Chile sent warships to the Atacama coast in 1861 to protect citizens; the Bolivian Congress authorized war in 1863, then suspended diplomatic relations in 1864, signaling a move toward open hostilities until Spanish conflict with Perú redirected hemispheric concerns toward a greater threat.[46] Boliv-

---

39. CHARLES EDMOND AKERS, A HISTORY OF SOUTH AMERICA 474 (1930).

40. *See* FIFER, *supra* note 33, at 33 (map).

41. *See* ST. JOHN, BOUNDARIES, TRADE AND SEAPORTS: POWER POLITICS IN THE ATACAMA 3.

42. *See* FIFER, *supra* note 33, at 33; *see also* LUIS BARROS BORGOÑO, THE PROBLEM OF THE PACIFIC AND THE NEW POLICIES OF BOLIVIA 45–55 (1924) (referencing Bolivia's historic title to and possessory occupation of the Atacama).

43. *See* Christopher R. Rossi, *A Case Ill Suited for Judgment: Constructing "A Sovereign Access to the Sea" in the Atacama Desert,* 48 U. MIAMI INTER-AM. L. REV. 28, 56 (2017).

44. *Id.*

45. CLEMENTS R. MARKHAM, THE WAR BETWEEN PERU AND CHILE: 1879–1882, at 83 (1882).

46. AKERS, *supra* note 39 at 475.

ia's northern frontier, although culturally attached to the port of Arica, encountered Peruvian contested claims as far south as the Loa River, as well as a contested claim over the port at Tocopilla, both territories now part of Chile. Before the condominium agreement of 1866, Chile had claimed territory in 1842–1843 up to the port of Mejillones at the 23rd parallel south. The complicated and confusing search for border demarcations redounded to the common observation that there was nothing to dispute until mineral deposits were discovered.[47] Before the introduction of territorial temptations based on resource extraction, imperial documents simply and generically referred to the "vast desert of Atacama" as a logical administrative area of demarcation between *audiencias.*[48] This formless telluric description of separation serviced a completely internal administrative mechanism of land appropriation directed toward fertile or resource-rich areas known to the Spanish Empire and its subaltern administrative agencies. The 400-mile stretch of internal Atacama area, mostly between the 29th and 23rd parallels south, did not even arise as an afterthought with regard to the sovereign intentions of the imperial mindset or to the emerging republican polities of the first half of the nineteenth century, until the mid-nineteenth-century discovery of resources propelled the area to hallmark status in the history of Latin American turmoil. International law's association with the region deeply attaches to disputes over the ownership of these abundant mineral resources, confirming geographer Isaiah Bowman's conclusion that the region "powerfully illuminates" the history if not geography of all of South America.[49]

The War of the Pacific

The brief period of accord between Bolivia and Chile following the defeat of Spain produced the Mutual Benefits Treaty of August 16, 1866. The 25th parallel south set the boundary between the two countries with the proviso that territory between the 23rd and 25th parallels would be administered in common—a condominium arrangement—whereby both governments would share in the exploitation of mineral and guano deposits and the revenue derived therefrom would be divided equally.

---

47. *See* VICTOR ANDRÉS BELAUNDE, NUESTRA CUESTIÓN CON CHILE 10 (1919); MARKHAM, *supra* note 45, at 81.

48. *See* BARROS, *supra* note 42.

49. BOWMAN, DESERT TRAILS OF ATACAMA, at 348.

Bolivia further agreed to traffic resources exclusively through the port of Mejillones on the condition that Chile would appoint its own official to oversee potential problems. This coparcener agreement contained a *jus prohibendi* provision: neither party could trade away its rights in this region to a third party without the express permission of the other party. The merchant houses established in the region were to be remunerated $80,000 by each state, an early foretelling of the perils of rentier status relating to foreign economic penetration and a proto-attempt to assert sovereign control over natural resources.

The agreement began to fall apart almost immediately. Chilean finance and human capital, deficient as it was but not unusual for countries throughout Latin America at this time, nevertheless outweighed Bolivian contributions, which were "wholly non-existent."[50] Bolivia's population base and oligarchic elites remained tethered to highland mining interests, a lasting consequence of Philip II's creation of the Audiencia of Charcas and the drive to exploit the silver mines of *el Cerro rico*.[51] Bolivia did not meet obligations to liquidate the foreign revenue accounts and instead pursued a corrupt Amazon land sale to Brazil, currency devaluations, and abject profiteering owing to a lineage of dictatorial misrule and political instability beginning in 1847.[52] Chilean interests took on the disproportionate responsibility of capitalizing infrastructural projects at the port at Mejillones, and later Antofagasta, fueled by an influx of Chilean laborers.

With rising resentment, both countries sought a diplomatic solution, which resulted in a new treaty signed on August 6, 1874. Chile renounced the condominium arrangement established by the 1866 Mutual Benefits Treaty in exchange for Bolivia's acceptance of terms that froze the export duties on mineral products from the former condominium zone for a period of twenty-five years. Additional guarantees defended Chilean investments and citizens.[53] This export-duty freeze suppressed prices in Europe, much to the discontent of Perú, which maintained full control over nitrate production in its province of Tarapacá. The enmity between Bolivia and Chile gave Perú, which deemed itself militarily strongest among the Andean Cone countries, with a wedge issue. It secured for

---

50. BRUCE W. FARCAU, THE TEN CENTS WAR: CHILE, PERU, AND BOLIVIA IN THE WAR OF THE PACIFIC, 1879–1884, at 21 (2000).

51. *See id.* at 21–22.

52. *See id.* at 22.

53. RONALD BRUCE ST. JOHN, THE BOLIVIA-CHILE-PERU DISPUTE IN THE ATACAMA DESERT 11 (1994).

Bolivia and Perú a "secret" alliance in 1873. An 1877 dispute between Chile and Argentina over Patagonia and guano-ship passage through its disputed maritime strait,[54] another product of *uti possidetis's* application to the cavities of Latin American sovereignty, suggested for Bolivia that Chile had become embroiled in a major foreign policy distraction to its south.

With increasing labor penetration by Chileans into the Atacama, matched by British financial backing, cash-depleted Bolivia abrogated the export-duty agreement. Bolivian general Hilarión Daza's corrupt government levied a ten-cent surcharge on each quintal of nitrate exported by the *Compañía de Salitres y Ferrocarril*, a Chilean-British–owned enterprise.[55] The tax, imposed as the only alternative to expropriation, clearly violated the 1874 agreement. It launched the countries into war on February 10, 1879. Bolivia's severe miscalculation of Chile's military preparedness resulted in devastating consequences for both Bolivia and its ally, Perú, which refused to repudiate its secret alliance.[56] After quickly resolving the maritime strait dispute with Argentina in the far south by allowing joint control over the strait until a comprehensive settlement could be reached, Chile fully engaged the Bolivian abrogation. In response, Chile claimed it would revindicate rights suspended by the 1874 agreement, which Bolivia abrogated; it would revindicate rights suspended by the 1866 treaty, which Bolivia repudiated; it would revindicate rights negotiated by a stillborn 1873 treaty, which Bolivia refused to ratify; and it would protect Chilean investments and citizens and teach the Bolivians a lesson based on national pride.

Ultimately, Chile seized all territory up to the 18th parallel south. It destroyed Perú's navy, on which Bolivia depended,[57] annexed all 400 km of Bolivia's coastline, created a buffer zone from Peruvian territory that included Arica and Tacna, occupied Lima for three years, increased its landmass by one third, and took possession of Atacama resources that would transform its economy and provide the basis for Chile's national wealth up until today. With additional foreign investment, Chile wiped clean its national debt through its control of the nitrate trade; it developed the Atacama ports at Pisagua, Iquique, Tocopilla, Mejillones, Antofagasta, and Taltal, attracting with this development nitrate kings, railroad tycoons, water- and coal-supplying companies, and a degree of

54. WILLIAM F. SATER, CHILE AND THE WAR OF THE PACIFIC 7 (1986).

55. *See id.* at 3.

56. *See id.* at 12.

57. For extensive discussion of the naval engagements and relative fleet strength during the war, see generally *id.*

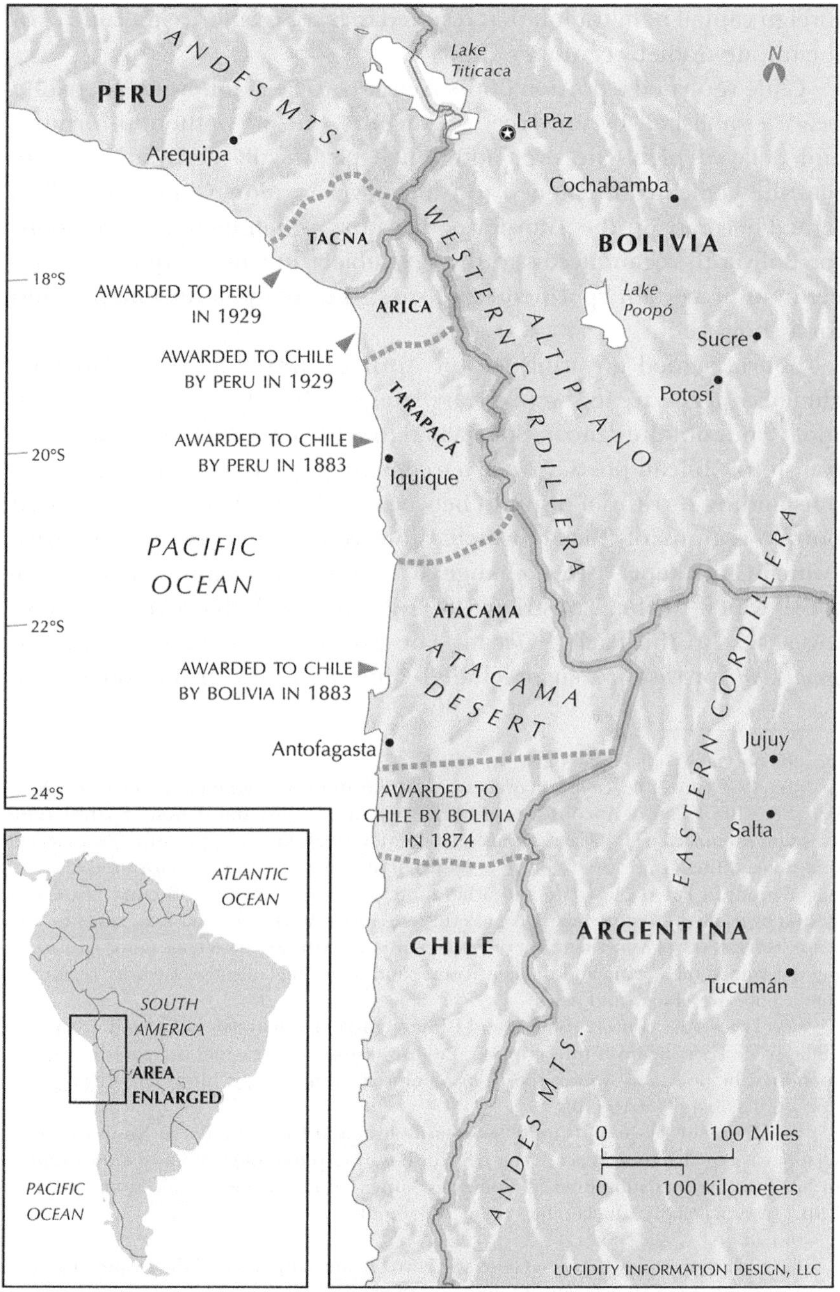

Fig. 4: The Atacama Desert and the territorial repercussions of the War of the Pacific (1879–1884).

foreign capital penetration that resulted in 85 percent foreign control of the nitrate trade by century's end.[58]

Chile returned a portion of the Atacama to Perú following a separate peace established by the Treat of Ancón,[59] but not without a tortured and delayed plebiscite over additional, historically Peruvian territory that the Chileans threatened to Chileanize. In 1895, Chile and Bolivia signed a Treaty on the Transfer of Territory, which included provisions for Bolivia to regain access to the sea subject to Chile acquiring sovereignty over certain specified territories; the treaty never entered into force, however.

Bolivia signed an armistice on April 4, 1884,[60] and formally concluded a peace treaty twenty years later,[61] officially ending the war in 1904,[62] but not the rancor. Bolivia had to settle for a right of commercial transit to Chilean ports. A 1929 agreement (the Treaty of Lima) settled outstanding territorial disputes between Chile and Perú over contested border regions of Tacna (which Chile returned to Peru) and Arica (which Chile kept).[63] In exchange, Chile secured a supplementary protocol, which further constricted Bolivia's national objective of resecuring access to the Pacific Ocean. The protocol contained another *jus prohibendi* provision that precluded Chile and Perú from ever ceding

---

58. *See* FIFER, *supra* note 33, at 74.

59. *See* Treaty of Peace of Ancón between Chile and Peru, signed at Lima on 20 October 1883 (the Treaty of Ancón) (Spanish transcription, English translation); Spanish transcription submitted by Bolivia as Annex 97 to its Memorial, Annex 1, 71, http://www.icj-cij.org/docket/files/153/18616.pdf. The return of this territory involved a tortured series of negotiations, a failed plebiscite and arbitration, and failed attempts to curry favor with Bolivia by trading territory taken from Perú. *See generally* WILLIAM E. SKUBAN, LINES IN THE SAND: NATIONALISM AND IDENTITY ON THE PERUVIAN-CHILEAN FRONTIER (2007) (discussing the War of the Pacific and the controversy and lingering collective memory regarding the dispute over Tacna and Arica).

60. Truce Pact between Bolivia and Chile, signed at Valparaíso on 4 April 1884 (the 1884 Truce Pact) Spanish transcription, English translation, original in Spanish; original submitted by Bolivia as Annex 108 to its Memorial, Annex 2, 77, http://www.icj-cij.org/docket/files/153/18616.pdf

61. Treaty of Peace and Amity between Bolivia and Chile, signed at Santiago on 20 October 1904 (the 1904 Peace Treaty), Spanish transcription, English translation, original in Spanish; original submitted by Bolivia as Annex 100 to its memorial, Annex 10, 137 http://www.icj-cij.org/docket/files/153/18616.pdf

62. *Id.*

63. *See* art. 2, Treaty between Chile and Perú for the Settlement of the Dispute Regarding Tacna and Arica (the Treaty of Lima) and the Supplementary Protocol to the Treaty of Lima, both signed at Lima on 3 June 1929 (entry into force 28 July 1929), original in Spanish, French and English translations, 94 L.N.T.S. 401, Annex 11, 171 http://www.icj-cij.org/docket/files/153/18616.pdf

these territories to any third state without mutual agreement of the two.[64] Bolivia not only lost the war, in defeat it ultimately lost its historical ally.[65] This intertwined and competitive history presents a filter through which overwrought political arguments must be distilled. Bolivia subsequently claimed reliance on declarations attributable to Chile's highest-level representatives granting Bolivia a fully sovereign access to the Pacific Ocean,[66] but these claims were rejected by the International Court of Justice (ICJ).[67] Today, Bolivia maintains a naval fleet of ninety vessels, 4,600 sailors, 2,000 marines, and a naval aviation accompaniment,[68] but the *Armada Boliviana* is consigned to patrol the brown water ports of Lake Titicaca and internal rivers, one of the lingering oddities and ironies of Latin America's long and convoluted encounter with *uti possidetis.*

---

64. *See id.*, art. 1, Supplementary Protocol.

65. *See* DAVID R. MARES, VIOLENT PEACE: MILITARIZED INTERSTATE BARGAINING IN LATIN AMERICA 70 (2001), at 70 (discussing Chile's outmaneuvering of Bolivia by playing Peruvian nationalism off Bolivian aspiration, resulting in Bolivia's loss and Chile's gain of Perú as an important ally).

66. These documents included a 1920 *Acto Protocolizada,* a 1926 memorandum submitted to the United States from the Chilean foreign minister (Matte Memorandum), a 1950 Exchange of Notes, a 1961 hand-delivered memorandum from Chile's ambassador in Bolivia to the Bolivian foreign minister (Trucco Memorandum), the 1975 Charaña Declaration, 1986 communiqués, the 2000 Joint Communiqué (Algarve Declaration), and a 2006 13-Point Agenda. *See* Obligation to Negotiate Access to the Pacific Ocean (Bolivia v. Chile), Judgment 2018 ICJ Rep. ¶ 98—137.

67. *See id.*, ¶ 139. In addition to rejecting the obligatory significance of these bilateral claims, the ICJ rejected Bolivia's claims that Chile had bound itself to return Pacific coastal territory to Bolivia by virtue of unilateral claims. *See id.*, ¶ 147. *See also id.* at ¶ 175 ("The Court . . . is unable to conclude . . . that Chile has "the obligation to negotiate with Bolivia in order to reach an agreement granting Bolivia a fully sovereign access to the Pacific Ocean.").

68. *See* ERIC WERTHEIM, THE NAVAL INSTITUTE GUIDE TO COMBAT FLEETS OF THE WORLD, THEIR SHIPS, AIRCRAFT, AND SYSTEMS 52 (16th ed. 2013).

FIVE

Water

"Silala" is the Bolivian name for waters that Chileans refer to as "Siloli."[1] The waters flow through the Atacama Desert for just eight and one-half kilometers at a rate of 200 liters per second.[2] The waters originate from high-altitude wetlands (*bofedales*) formed by groundwater springs in the Bolivian *Altiplano*,[3] traverse almost four kilometers of Bolivian territory to enter Chile, feed into the San Pedro tributary,[4] then flow into the Loa River's oxbow

1. *See* Cristián le Dantec, *Silala o Siloli*, EL DEMÓCRATA (CHILE) (Apr. 6, 2016). Chile's Foreign Ministry referred to the surface waters as Silala in its application instituting proceedings before the International Court of Justice. *See* República de Chile, Ministerio de Relaciones Exteriores, Application Instituting Proceedings, 6 June 2016, *available at* http://www.24horas.cl/incoming/article2038445.ece/BINARY/DEMANDA%20ANTE%20LA%20HAYA%20EN%20INGL%C3%89S%20-%20ORIGINAL.pdf [hereinafter Chilean Application].

2. *See* Alejandro Zegada, *La disputa sobre el Silala será larga perso no afectará demanda marítima*, EL PAÍS (May 2, 2016), http://elpaisonline.com/index.php/2013-01-15-14-16-26/nacional/item/214229-la-disputa-sobre-el-silala-sera-larga-pero-no-afectara-demanda-maritima ("[E]*s una fuente de agua limpia y fresca, con un caudal de aproximadamente 200 litros por segundo*").

3. B. M. Mulligan & G. E. Eckstein, *The Silala/Siloli Watershed: Dispute Over the Most Vulnerable Basin in South America*, 27 WATER RESOURCES DEVELOPMENT 595, 595 (2011); Gustavo Meza Bórquez, *Chile/Bolivia: ¿Es el río Silala un factor de tensión secundario?* 2 REVISMAR 152, 152 (2014). The Ramsar Convention defines wetlands as "areas of marsh, fen, peatland or water, whether natural or artificial, permanent or temporary, with water that is static or flowing, fresh, brackish or salt, including areas of marine water the depth of which at low tide does not exceed six metres." Convention on Wetlands of International Importance Especially as Waterfowl Habitat art. 1, Feb. 2, 1971, 996 U.N.T.S. 245 [Ramsar Convention].

4. *See* Press Release (Unofficial), Chile Institutes Proceedings against Bolivia with Regard to a Dispute Concerning the Status and Use of the Waters of the Silala, No. 2016/16 (June 6, 2016), http://www.icj-cij.org/docket/files/162/19018.pdf (hereinafter ICJ Press Release No. 2016/16). The tributary is alternatively referred to as San Pedro de Inacaliri or Inacaliri. *Id.*

before emptying into the Pacific Ocean.[5] The Loa River is the only exorheic (allowing outflow) basin in a region synonymous with scarcity.[6]

Forty percent of the world's population share the transboundary waters of the 264 largest river basins in the world.[7] These basins cover more than 45 percent of the earth's land surface.[8] However, in this remote region of the world, where the nearest Bolivian community of Alota is seventy kilometers away and outside of the Silala/Siloli watershed,[9] only a handful of soldiers and stray llamas draw from its headwaters.[10]

Chile and Bolivia dispute more than the name of this watershed; they dispute ownership of its waters. In the age of climate change, where increasing demand for freshwater resources threaten many of the great hydrographic ecosystems in the world,[11] the dispute over the tiny and remote Silala/Siloli basin reinforces the importance of fresh water[12] while making these waters, according to the United Nations, "one of the most hydropolitically vulnerable basins in the world."[13]

---

5. *See* Ronald Bruce St. John, *Andean Water Wars: The Silala Case*, COUNCIL ON HEMISPHERIC AFF. (Aug. 5, 2019), http://www.coha.org/andean-water-wars-the-silala-case/

6. MULLIGAN & ECKSTEIN, *supra* note 3, at 596; *see also* Douglas Aitken et al., *Water Scarcity and the Impact of the Mining and Agricultural Sectors in Chile*, 8 SUSTAINABILITY 128 (2016) (noting that Chile contains some of the driest areas in the world, particularly the arid climactic northern regions of Atacama, Antofagasta, Tarapacá, and Arica and Parinacota); *see also* Jessica Budds, *Water Rights, Mining and Indigenous Groups in Chile's Atacama*, *in* OUT OF THE MAINSTREAM: WATER RIGHTS, POLITICS AND IDENTITY 197, 204 (Rutgerd Boelens et al. eds., 2010) (discussing water-scarcity issues in the central Atacama and the Loa River basin). Farther to the south, the Copiapó River egresses into the Pacific Ocean.

7. Joseph W. Dellapenna, *The Customary International Law of Transboundary Fresh Waters*, 3/4 INT'L. J. GLOBAL ENVTL. ISSUES 264, 265 (2001). The United Nations lists 276 transboundary river basins in the world along with 200 transboundary aquifers. *See* U.N. WATER, TRANSBOUNDARY WATERS (2013), http://www.unwater.org/fileadmin/user_upload/unwater_new/docs/transboundary_waters.pdf

8. BJØRN-OLIVER MAGSIG, INTERNATIONAL WATER LAW AND THE QUEST FOR COMMON SECURITY 6 (2015).

9. *See* MULLIGAN & ECKSTEIN, *supra* note 3, at 597.

10. Jacob Klein, *Eight Kilometers of Petty Diplomacy*, BOLIVIANEXPRESS (Aug. 28, 2016), http://www.bolivianexpress.org/blog/posts/eight-kilometres-of-petty-diplomacy

11. *See, e.g.*, Achille Mbembe, *At the Edge of the World: Boundaries, Territoriality, and Sovereignty in Africa*, 12 PUB. CULTURE 259, 272–73 (Steven Rendall trans., 2000) (referencing degradations to the Great Lakes region of Africa); *see also* WHITE & CASE, LLP, INTERNATIONAL WATERS: REVIEW OF LEGAL AND INSTITUTIONAL FRAMEWORKS (2011), *available at* http://iwlearn.net/iw-projects/3340/reports/international-waters-review-of-legal-and-institutional-frameworks (reviewing management schemes for notable basins and water frameworks).

12. For an assessment of the magnitude of the global freshwater crisis, see THE GLOBAL WATER CRISIS: ADDRESSING AN URGENT SECURITY ISSUE (Harriet Bigas et al. eds., 2012).

13. United Nations Envtl. Program, Hydropolitical Vulnerability and Resilience along

Fig. 5: The Lithium Triangle, salt flats, and disputed waters of the Silala/Siloli in the Atacama Desert.

During Bolivia's annual Day of the Sea (*Día del Mar*) observation on March 23, 2016, which commemorates Bolivia's loss of its coastline and adjacent territory due to the War of the Pacific, then-president Evo Morales vowed to take Bolivia's claim of sovereign ownership over the Silala/Siloli to the ICJ.[14] He accused Chile of robbery and unilateral use of the waters.[15] The Bolivian government put a $1 billion price tag on the historical debt owed to it by Chile in recompense.[16] Previous bilateral attempts to arrive at a formula for pro-rated use, including a seventeen-article agreement on water rights in 2009, never advanced beyond a discussion stage.[17] In response to allegations of a Chilean military base

---

International Waters: Latin America and the Caribbean, United Nations Environment Program 65 (2007).

14. Observatorio Boliviano de Opinión Pública, *Discurso de Evo Morales en el Día del Mar 2016*, YOUTUBE (Mar. 23, 2016), https://www.youtube.com/watch?v=dmYM6DEB9FE. For a partial transcription, see María Paz Núñez, *Evo Morales conmemoria Día de Mar y anuncia studio de "alternativas jurídicas" por aguas del Silala*, LA TERCERA (Chile) (Mar. 23, 2016), http://www.latercera.com/noticia/politica/2016/03/674-673521-9-evo-morales-conmemora-dia-del-mar-y-anuncia-estudio-de-alternativas-juridicas.shtml (Morales indicated that "'*resulta imprescindible que resolvamos los demás temas pendientes de la agenda bilateral como el relative al uso y aprovechamiento unilateral de Chile de las aguas de los manantiales del Silala. Cada día' Chile se aprovecha illegal y arteramente de ese recurso natual sin compensar este acto abusive que vulnera nuestro patrimonio, 'los resultados que hemos alcanzado ante la Corte Internacional de Justicia demuestran que Bolivia está preparado para efectuar la defense legal de nuestros derechos, contamos con un equipo nacional e internacional altamente especializado para asumir este y cualquier otro hito jurídico en la defense del pueblo boliviano, he instruido a Diremar* [Bolivia's Strategic Directorate for the Revindication of Maritime Claims] *que estudie las alternativas jurídicas' para asumir la defense de nuestras aguas del Silala ante las instancias jurídicas competentes.*'").

15. Raquel García, *Chile demanda a Bolivia ante La Haya por el río Silala: Gobierno chileno dijo que el país no se podía quedar pasivo frente a la reiterada insistencia de Bolivia "de desconocer sus derechos" en el río Silala*, PANAMPOST (June 7, 2016), http://es.panampost.com/raquel-garcia/2016/06/06/chile-demanda-a-bolivia-ante-la-haya-por-el-rio-silala/ (quoting Morales's charges that Chile's use of the waters are "unilateral e ilícito" and constitute "un robo").

16. Bolivia's Congress calculated that Chile owed $900 million and $1billion for past use and future consideration of the resources of the Silala. *Compare* Randy Woods, *Ductec Concession Under Review*, BNAMERICAS (Mar. 20, 2003), http://www.bnamericas.com/en/news/privatization/Ductec_concession_under_review; ($900 million), *with* Klein, *supra* note 10 (estimating $1 billion).

17. Klein, *supra* note 10; *see also* FERNANDO HORMAZÁBAL DÍAZ, EL LIBRO BLANCO DE CHILE: EL PROBLEMA MARÍTIMO BOLIVIANO 454–55 (2005) ("[E]*ste grupo mixto a la fecha no se ha constituido*"). This specific riparian issue and water resource issues generally are included in the so-called 13-Point Agenda (point seven) introduced by Bolivia and Chile in 2006. The agenda, now stalled, presented a road map of bilateral issues for discussion to improve relations. *See generally* Pablo Cádiz, *¿Qué es la agenda de los 13 puntos que Chile y Bolivia buscan retomar?* LA TERCERA (Jan. 29, 2015), http://www.latercera.com/noticia/politica/2015/01/674-614769-9-que-es-la-agenda-de-los-13-puntos-que-chile-y-bolivia-buscan-retomar.shtml (listing the thirteen points, including point seven: *Silala y recursos*

within fifteen kilometers of the Silala/Siloli, itself a response to claims of a nearby Bolivian military camp,[18] President Morales impaneled a Council to Defend the Waters of the Silala to prepare for proceedings.[19] Chile responded by filing suit first,[20] claiming it can no longer allow Bolivia to use international law and its institutions as vehicles for "political harassment."[21]

The dispute over the waters of the Silala/Siloli must be viewed against the evolving backdrop of international law's spatial orientation. The dispute also highlights the coming crisis of transboundary freshwater resources in an age of global climate change,[22] even among the most water-rich countries in the world.[23] This dispute extends the persistent and contested sovereignty claims over the Atacama Desert, which frame the national identities of these two rivals and amplify their foreign policy rhetoric.[24]

Bolivia and Chile remain caught up in a grievance involving Bolivia's landlocked status and Bolivia's forestalled attempt to compel Chile to

---

hídricos). In 1997 and more recently, Chile offered to purchase fifty percent of the water produced on the Bolivian side at a flow rate of 100 Lt/sec but negotiations stalled as well. *See* Fernando Urquidi Barrau, *Water Resources in Bolivia: A Strategic Viewpoint of the Issues Associated with Transboundary Waters, in* DIAGNOSIS OF WATER IN THE AMERICAS: INTERAMERICAN NETWORK OF ACADEMIES OF SCIENCES 91, 115 (Blanca Jiménez-Cisneros & José Galizia-Tundisi eds., 2013)

18. *See* Daniel Ramos & Anthony Esposito, *Bolivia's Morales Accuses Chile of Setting Up Military Base Near Border,* REUTERS (May 8, 2016), http://www.reuters.com/article/us-bolivia-chile-border-idUSKCN0XZ0QF (noting mutual claims that Chile and Bolivia have militarized the border over the Silala/Siloli water dispute).

19. Sabrina Martín, *Evo Morales crea Consejo que defender las aguas del Silala,* PANAM POST (May 11, 2016), http://es.panampost.com/sabrina-martin/2016/05/11/evo-morales-crea-consejo-que-defendera-las-aguas-del-silala/ (reporting on Bolivia's preliminary actions anticipating the initiation of proceedings and the preceding tensions caused by the establishment of a Chilean military base in the vicinity of the source waters).

20. *See* Laura Iesue, *Beating Bolivia to the Punch? Chile Takes the Silala River Dispute to the International Court of Justice,* COUNCIL ON HEMISPHERIC AFFAIRS (June 7, 2016) (questioning whether Chile's quick response was a political stunt to boost all-time-low approval ratings of Chilean president Michele Bachelet while catching Bolivia off guard).

21. *See* García, *supra* note 15 (quoting Chilean Chancellor Herald Muñoz: "*Chile no puede permitir que Bolivia siga intentando instrumentalizar el derecho internacional y sus instituciones como vehículo de hostigamiento político.*").

22. *See generally* Michael Kidd & Loretta Feris, *Introduction: Water and the Law—Towards Sustainability, in* WATER AND THE LAW: TOWARDS SUSTAINABILITY 1–9 (Michael Kidd et al. eds., 2014) (noting various reports proclaiming fresh water as the environmental crisis of the twenty-first century).

23. *See Total Renewable Water Resources,* WORLD FACTBOOK (2016), https://www.cia.gov/library/publications/the-world-factbook/fields/2201.html (listing Bolivia and Chile among the most water-rich countries in the world).

24. *See infra* text accompanying nn. 86–94.

return land Bolivia lost in war. The return of this land would satisfy Bolivia's national objective of securing a sovereign corridor to the Pacific Ocean. However, such a conveyance would reconfigure the well-established geography and history of modern Chile and revitalize, at least partially, sixteenth-century border demarcations vaguely charted by Spain's imperial viceroyalty system.[25] Such imprecise demarcations in the nineteenth century contributed to the outbreak of the War of the Pacific,[26] and continue to vex foreign relations in Central and South America well into the twenty-first century.

The transboundary status of this freshwater resource and the disputed riparian question in this microcosm present serious unanswered questions of international law. However, the deep and dramatic political subtext may have more control over the outcome in terms of reaching a peaceful and mutually beneficial settlement. The politics of memory and culture—together with the politics of forgetfulness—reconstruct imaginaries and uphold performance traditions. They have a bearing on the collective identities, sociopolitical interactions, and public rituals of these two rivals.[27] Framing this discussion by borrowing from Erving Goffman's sociological metaphor of dramaturgy metaphorically links the parties and their performative behaviors to multilayered audiences and stages that are behind the drapes of the public dispute.

The Source of the Riparian Dispute

Amid a foreign currency crisis in 1908,[28] authorities in the Bolivian Prefecture of Potosí granted a Chilean-owned railroad company, the *Ferro-*

---

25. David R. Mares insightfully noted that "[o]ne reason why Latin American international politics appears so geared to legal argumentation is because most states have numerous colonial documents supporting expansive claims over territory." DAVID R. MARES, VIOLENT PEACE: MILITARIZED INTERSTATE BARGAINING IN LATIN AMERICA 30 (2001).

26. *See* BRUCE W. FARCAU, THE TEN CENTS WAR: CHILE, PERU, AND BOLIVIA IN THE WAR OF THE PACIFIC, 1879–1884, at 32 (2000).

27. *See generally* DIANA TAYLOR & SARAH J. TOWNSEND, EDS., STAGES OF CONFLICT: A CRITICAL ANTHOLOGY OF LATIN AMERICAN THEATER AND PERFORMANCE (2008) (exploring hemispheric themes of performance practice in the shaping and contesting collective identities in Latin America); ALICIA DEL CAMPO, TEATRALIDADES DE LA MEMORIA: RITUALES DE RECONCILIACIÓN EN EL CHILE DE LA TRANSICIÓN (exploring "la teatralidad política del funeral official de Salvador Allende" and "la teatralidad beatífica: Jaime Guzmán, cordero sacrificial de la reconciliación nacional").

28. *See generally* Mario Napoleón Pacheco Torrico, *The Foundation of the Central Bank of Bolivia (1929–1932)*, 2 REVISTA DE HUMANIDADES Y CIENCIAS SOCIALES (ST. CRUZ SIERRA) 133 (Jeremy Jordan trans., 2006) (noting the foreign-exchange crisis, recession, and collapse in Bolivian tin prices in 1908–1909).

carril de Antofagasta a Bolivia, use of the Silala/Siloli waters to run steam-engine boilers to extract nitrate from mining operations.[29] The company owed its origins to the *Sociedad Exploradora del Distrito de Atacama,*[30] a Bolivian concern formed in the 1860s to exploit the nitrate deposits.[31] To raise capital, the Bolivians turned in 1872 first to Melbourne Clarke & Co. and then to William Gibbs & Co., a British company with a dominant advantage in nitrate mining in the Peruvian province of Tarapacá.[32] Concessions granted to the company allowed duty-free exports of products through Antofagasta and duty-free imports of goods or machinery needed to construct the rail line.[33] The location of Antofagasta as the coastal terminus attracted Chilean interest. In 1878, Chileans outnumbered Bolivians in the town by a ratio of more than six to one, Antofagasta's "municipal functionaries were all Chilean," and by terms of the 1874 Mutual Benefits Treaty, Bolivia could not levy any new duties.[34] By the late 1870s, these circumstances attracted substantial investment from Chileans. The company's principal shareholder was Chilean, and stockholders included nine past or future Chilean ministers and members of congress, including the foreign minister and a future president.[35] Although the waters of this basin once indisputably belonged to Bolivia, the War of the Pacific retracted Bolivia's border to this area, which once again has produced territorial dispute.

To collect water for use by the company's steam locomotives and mining operations high in the *Altiplano* between Antofagasta and the Bolivian city of Oruro, the company negotiated a concession contract from Bolivia that allowed it to tap into the waters of the Silala/Siloli. Pursuant

---

29. Urquidi, *supra* note 17, at 113 (referencing Public Document No. 48, Sept. 23, 1908). Another claim asserts that Chileans diverted the water as early as 1868 in conjunction with transporting silver from the Potosí region. *See* Zegada, *supra* note 2 (referencing the research of Antonio Bazoberry Quiroga).

30. *Estación de Ferrocarril de Antofagasta a Bolivia,* CONSEJO DE MONUMENTOS NACIONALES DE CHILE, https://www.monumentos.gob.cl/monumentos/monumentos-historicos/estacion-ferrocarril-antofagasta-bolivia (last visited Aug. 22, 2019).

31. John Mayo, *A "Company" War? The Antofagasta Nitrate Company and the Outbreak of the War of the Pacific,* 28 BOLETIN DE ESTUDIOS LATINOAMERICANOS Y DEL CARIBE 3, 4 (1980).

32. *Id.* at 4–5.

33. *See id.* at 5.

34. *Id.* at 6.

35. *Id. See also* Luis Ortega, *Nitrates, Chilean Entrepreneurs and the Origins of the War of the Pacific,* 16 J. LAT. AM. STUD. 337–80 (1984) (detailing the incorporation of the nitrate territories as an important factor prompting the war). For a general history of the rail line and the politics involving Bolivia, Chile, and the influence of foreign capital, see HAROLD BLAKEMORE, FROM THE PACIFIC TO LA PAZ: THE ANTOFAGASTA (CHILE) AND BOLIVIA RAILWAY COMPANY 1888–1988 (1990).

to that agreement, the company constructed open stone channels, a south canal and a north canal, to feed into a principal canal, and elsewhere blasted out rock to create reservoirs.[36] Bolivia claims that, if undisturbed, the Silala marshes would pool in place amid the seventy springs arising exclusively in Bolivia, subject only to evaporation.[37] Bolivia further notes that if the Silala were an international river, the Chilean company would not have needed to petition for access to the headwaters or to expend considerable funds to channelize and redirect their flow.[38] Chile claims the canal work "merely augment[ed]" the Siloli's natural flow along the course of its original channel,[39] and that the river emanates from groundwater springs fed by an aquifer that straddles the border between the two countries.[40] Little else is known about the relationship between the surface water and the groundwater, or indeed, about this transboundary aquifer and watershed (the Ollagüe-Pastos Grandes).[41] Generally, international water law has only recently turned

---

36. Urquidi, *supra* note 17, at 113 (stone channels); NELLIE BURNHAM ALLEN, SOUTH AMERICA 275 (1918) (created reservoirs).

37. *See* Leo Robles Belmar, *Chile prefiere perder una batalla,* LATINOAMÉRICA PIENSA (June 28, 2016), http://latinoamericapiensa.com/politica/3629-batalla-por-el-silala-a (quoting Bolivian Foreign Ministry Vice Chancellor Juan Carlos Alurralde); *see also* Urquidi, *supra* note 17, at 113. According to Mulligan & Eckstein, more than seventy small-volume groundwater springs have been identified in Bolivian territory discharging from fractures of volcanic deposits dating to the Miocene age, with evidence of glacial melt replenishment. Mulligan & Eckstein, *supra* note 3, at 596. A leading Bolivian authority rejects any hydrological connection between the waters of the Silala and Chile. *See* ANTONIO BAZOBERRY Q., EL MITO DEL SILALA 21 (2002) (*"Por investigaciones de mapas cartográficos y estudios sobre recursos hidráulicos internacionales, se puede afirmar que en la region del Quetena y a lo largo de la cordillera Occidental [Bolivia] no existe una interconexión hidrológica que se extienda hasta el nuevo territorio chileno."*).

38. *See* Robles *supra* note 37 (quoting Bolivian Foreign Ministry Vice Chancellor Juan Carlos Alurralde: *"Se estima que la compañía gastó alrededor de 5 millones de dólares, lo cual es mucho dinero para esos años, los que se invirtieron en construir canales, redes de drenaje, ampliar obras colectoras, incluso para dinamitar los manantiales y así aumentar el caudal y forzar artificialmente el flujo de agua hacia Chile."*).

39. Gabriel Eckstein, *The Silala Basin: One of the Most Hydropolitically Vulnerable Basins in the World,* INTERNATIONAL WATER LAW PROJECT BLOG (2011), http://www.internationalwaterlaw.org/blog/2011/10/27/the-silala-basin-one-of-the-most-hydropolitically-vulnerable-basins-in-the-world/

40. *See* Chilean Application, *supra* note 1 (referencing groundwater springs emanating from the Orientales and Cajones Ravines).

41. Mulligan & Eckstein, *supra* note 3, at 596. Hydrologists regard groundwater as the part of subterranean zones of saturation, as opposed to subterranean zones of aeration. Not all water underground is groundwater, but wide-ranging subterranean conditions of soil porosity and permeability can make distinctions between groundwater and surface water difficult to determine. *See* Joseph W. Dellapenna, *A Primer on Groundwater Law,* 49 IDAHO L. REV. 265, 265 (2012–2013) (quoting the views of hydrologist Harold Thomas).

attention to problems of transboundary groundwater,[42] with "continuing disconnects between water science and water law."[43] Notable law-making initiatives involving transboundary aquifers include the Genevese aquifer along the French-Swiss border (2008),[44] and less formal consultative arrangements involving the Hueco Bolson aquifer straddling the Mexico–United States border (1999), the Abbotsford-Sumas aquifer between the United States and Canada (1996), the Nubian Sandstone and Northwestern Sahara aquifers in North Africa (2002), the Iullemeden Aquifer System in West Africa (2009), and the Guarani aquifer in South America (2010). However, this law remains "in an early stage of development."[45]

Geological, topographical, and historical evidence suggests that the Silala/Siloli springs flowed overland from Bolivia to Chile before canalization, and there is evidence of deep alluvial cross-border erosion, indicating a natural topographical water flow.[46] The hydrological gradient slopes from east (Bolivia) to west (Chile).[47] A 1904 frontier map details evidence of the existence of a river.[48] However, that flow may be intermit-

---

42. Gabriel E. Eckstein, *Managing Buried Treasure across Frontiers: The International Law of Transboundary Aquifers*, 36 WATER INTERNATIONAL 573, 573 (2011); Adrien Bodart, *Transboundary Groundwater Management: Comparison between International Law Codification and EU Water Policy*, *in* WATER AND THE LAW: TOWARDS SUSTAINABILITY 108, 108–9 (Michael Kidd et al. eds., 2014).

43. Dellapenna, *supra* note 41, at 268.

44. Convention relative à la protection, à l'utilisation, à la réalimenation et au suivi de la nappe souterraine franco-suisse du Genevois, signed between France (the Community of the Annemassienne Region, the Community of the Genevois Rural Districts, and the Rural District of Viry) and Switzerland (the Republic and Canton of Geneva), signed on 18 December 2007, coming into effect on 1 January 2008, *available at* https://www.ge.ch/legislation/accords/doc/3038.pdf

45. Eckstein, *supra* note 42, at 574.

46. *See* Mulligan & Eckstein, *supra* note 3, at 597.

47. Urquidi, *supra* note 17, at 113.

48. *See* Tratado de Paz y Amistad Celebrado Entre El Gobierno de Bolivia y el de Chile el 20 De Octubre de 1904, Republica de Bolivia, Ministerio de Relaciones Exteriores y Culto, http://www.diremar.gob.bo/sites/default/files/1904.pdf (noting that the map does not identify the river by name but marks the existence of a river at the location in question); *see also* Meza Bórquez, *supra* note 3, at 155. Marshall noted the map's sole reference to the Cerrito Silala, but concludes that it denotes not a river but a point of reference for demarcation. Dena Marshall, *Por qué el Silala está en disputa?* EL DIARIO (Bol.) (June 12, 2016), http://m.eldiario.net/?n=33&a=2016&m=06&d=12. Chilean arguments point to additional maps (Mapa de las Cordilleras, 1884; Mapa Geográfico y Corográfico de Boliva, 1890) "demonstrating" that the Río Cajón (the Silala/Siloli's original name) originated in Bolivia and flowed into Chile. *See* Javier Neira R., *Las claves para entender la demanda de Chile contra Bolivia ante La Haya por el río Silala*, EMOL (June 11, 2016), http://www.emol.com/

tent rather than perennial,[49] a finding that adds confusion to the legal status of the waters.[50]

Fundamentally, this dispute reduces to a question: is the Silala/Siloli a river?[51] If it is a river—or transboundary watercourse in modern legal parlance—international conventional and customary law require equitable utilization of the water, which would provide Chile, as the lower riparian, rights of reasonable access and use.[52] If it is not a river, the surface water belongs to Bolivia. Because the legal term "watercourse" more broadly incorporates groundwater basins that cross borders and feed the surface waters in one or more states, the question of the hydrological connection of the Silala/Siloli to the Ollagüe-Pastos Grandes fossil aquifer may present an important consideration if true.[53] Fossil aquifers are nonrenewable, and it also has been suggested that their management in Latin America requires prioritized attention because in many instances they are the only source of fresh water available to service long-term use and vital human needs.[54] If this aquifer straddles the border, and if it

---

noticias/Nacional/2016/06/11/807231/Las-claves-para-entender-la-demanda-de-Chile-contra-Bolivia-ante-La-Haya-por-el-rio-Silala.html

49. Eckstein, *supra* note 39 (noting, "to the extent that the flow of the pre-canalized Silala was intermittent rather than perennial, applicability of international norms also may be tenuous").

50. Mulligan & Eckstein, *supra* note 3, at 603 (arguing "[w]here a stream fails to flow for natural reasons, as an intermittent stream is wont to do," the absence of state practice suggests the customary application of international water law norms is "at best, unresolved").

51. *See* García, *supra* note 15 (quoting Chilean Chancellor Herald Muñoz's objective for the lawsuit): *El ministro Muñoz afirmó que el objetivo del recurso es "que se determine que el Silala es un río internacional y por lo tanto, Chile tiene derechos sobre las aguas de este curso de aguas internacionales."*

52. *See* Margaret J. Vick, *The Law of International Waters: Reasonable Utilization*, 12 CHI.-KENT J. INT'L & COMP. L. 143, 143–44 (2012) (referencing the principal's development from immemorial as codified in the 1997 Watercourses Convention).

53. *See* Dena Marshall, *¿Qué leyes internacionales aplican a la cuestión del Silala?* ECONOMÍABOLIVIA (June 14, 2016), http://www.economiabolivia.net/2016/06/14/que-leyes-internacionales-aplican-a-la-cuestion-del-silala/. UNESCO describes what little is known about the aquifer as located in the "fragile ecosystem" of the Cordillera Occidental de los Andes; it estimates its extent at 4,350 km^2, and says it may or may not be confined to "tertiary fractured rocks and quaternary sediments." *See* ATLAS OF TRANSBOUNDARY AQUIFERS: GLOBAL MAPS, REGIONAL COOPERATION AND LOCAL INVENTORIES, UNESCO-IHP ISARM PROGRAMME 149 (2009), http://unesdoc.unesco.org/images/0019/001921/192145e.pdf

54. Pilar Carolina Villar, *International Cooperation on Transboundary Aquifers in South America and the Guarani Aquifer Case*, 59 REV. BRAS. POLIT. INT. 1, 6 (2016). A joint UNESCO-Organization of American States report describes the Ollagüe-Pastos Grandes aquifer as immeasurably important to the region. *See* UNESCO & ORGANIZACIÓN DE ESTADOS AMERICA-

feeds the Silala/Siloli, it would be difficult to craft a satisfactory unilateral solution to the dispute.

In 1997, the Bolivian government "reversed and annulled" the 1908 concession, claiming the waters long had been used without payment for purposes beyond the scope of the original concession.[55] The railroad had replaced its steam engines with diesel locomotives in 1961, but by that time Chile long had put to other uses the commingled waters of the Loa.[56] Moreover, Chile privatized the water sector of its economy, decentralizing official uses and control over the resource by treating it as a private property right rather than a public good.[57] This permissive policy of water commodification occurred during the military dictatorship of General Augusto Pinochet (1973–1990),[58] in line with free-market teachings of Chicago School economists.[59] The economic externalities of trading away water rights have adversely affected quality of life among many small Atacama communities, but have promoted efficiencies in large-scale industrial uses.[60] Chile's privatized system achieves near-universal coverage of safe drinking water and sanitation services in urban areas,[61] but generates criticism over the laissez-faire role of government except as a defender of supply.[62] Today, the Loa meets the industrial and potable needs of the cities of Antofagasta and Calama, as well as towns such as Sierra Gorda and Baquedano.[63] It also serves as the water intake for

---

NOS, SISTEMAS ACUÍFEROS TRANSFRONTERIZOS EN LAS AMÉRICAS: EVALUACIÓN PRELIMINAR 132 (2007).

55. Chilean Application, *supra* note 1, ¶ 23.

56. Meza Bórquez, *supra* note 3, at 154.

57. *See generally* Manuel Prieto, *Privatizing Water in the Chilean Andes: The Case of Las Vegas de Chiu-Chiu*, 35 MOUNTAIN RES. & DEV. 220 (2015) (detailing effects of changes to Chile's water code in 1981 that implemented a laissez-faire and uniform system of water management designed to distribute water according to its highest economic value); VICTOR POCHAT, WATER AGENDA FOR SOUTH AMERICA: CHALLENGES, VISION AND STRATEGY 23 (2015) (noting Chile's tradable water rights in Chile).

58. Madeline Baer, *Private Water, Public Good: Water Privatization and State Capacity in Chile*, 49 ST. COMP. INT'L DEV. 141, 147 (2014).

59. *Id.*

60. *See* Alexei Barrionuevo, *Chilean Town Withers in Free Market for Water*, NEW YORK TIMES (Mar. 14, 2009), http://www.nytimes.com/2009/03/15/world/americas/15chile.html?_r=0

61. Baer, *supra* note 58, at 142.

62. *See id.* Boer has questioned whether Chile's privatized water system comports with broader standards of human rights as opposed to meeting minimum standards of access, quality, and affordability.

63. *See* Press Release, *supra* note 4; Meza Bórquez *supra* note 3, at 155 (indicating 1,200 persons depended on the water in Sierra Gorda and Baquedano).

Chile's Chuquicamata mine,[64] one of the largest open-pit copper mines in the world.[65] Copper mining is a water-intensive industry[66] and a tremendous wealth generator for Chile.[67] Chile's decision to force this litigation puts these commercial interests at risk. Its logic has been questioned,[68] but the decision to proceed underscores deeply embedded political calculations. Chile has claimed these uses of the Loa for more than a century, but with increasingly disturbing environmental consequences for the water quality of the Loa and the diminishing volume of its basin.[69]

---

64. Meza Bórquez, *supra* note 3, at 155 (quoting Molina, whose study indicates the Silala represents slightly more than 14 percent of the Chuquicamata water intake needs). Meza Bórquez concludes that the Silala is not essential to maintain the mining operation (due to alternative sources) or the population of Antogagasta ("*se estima que el aporte hídrico del río Silala no es esencial para la División Chuquicamata de CODELCO o la población de Antofagasta*"), but it does create "*un problema de principios*" that does not allow Chile to countenance any questioning of its use. *Id.* at 156 (quoting the Chilean Director of Borders and Boundaries, Maria Teresa Infante).

65. *Top 10 Deep Open-Pit Mines,* MINING TECHNOLOGY.COM (Sept. 27, 2013), http://www.mining-technology.com/features/feature-top-ten-deepest-open pit-mines-world/ (noting its dimensions: 4.3 kilometers long, 3 kilometers wide, and more than 850 meters deep, making it the second-deepest open-pit mine in the world).

66. Historically, copper mining is more dependent on water intake than other mining enterprises. ORVILLE D. MUSSEY, WATER REQUIREMENTS OF THE COPPER INDUSTRY 181 (1961). Most of Chile's copper mines are located in the Atacama region, where water consumption projections are increasing dramatically. *See Chile Copper Mine Water Use Seen Rising Rapidly in Next Decade,* REUTERS (Jan. 13, 2015), http://www.reuters.com/article/us-chile-copper-water-idUSKBN0KM1VG20150113. The Chuquicamata mine requires twelve cubic meters of water per second. Budds, *supra* note 6, at 204.

67. Chile leads the world in copper production. It produces more than one-third of the world's output; it accounts for over 40 percent of the country's exports and is Chile's main source of income; Chile also has the largest copper reserves. Cecilia Jamasmie, *Chile the Largest Copper Producer and the Country with the Biggest Reserves—USGS,* MINING.COM (Feb. 20, 2012), http://www.mining.com/chile-the-largest-copper-producer-and-the-country-with-the-biggest-reserves-usgs/ (referencing U.S. Geological Survey statistics). Bolivia claims that Chile has reaped almost $1 trillion in revenue since the dispute over sovereignty began in 1879. *Lo que gana Chile y pierde Bolivia por no tener acceso al mar,* CORREO DEL SUR (May 6, 2015), http://correodelsur.com/politica/20150506_lo-que-gana-chile-y-pierde-bolivia-por-no-tener-acceso-al-mar-.html ("*. . . , el canciller boliviano David Choquehuanca aseguró que la mayor riqueza de Chile es el cobre, por el que habría recibido más de 900.000 millones de dólares desde la adhesión del territorio del desierto de Atacama que hasta 1879 pertenecía a Bolivia, publicó ABI.*").

68. *See* Robles, *supra* note 37 (posing the proposition that it would be easier for Chile to pay for the water rather than jeopardize the operation of an important component of its mining economy).

69. *See* Leslie Rae Wilson, "Determination of Trace Element Provenance, Rio Loa Basin, Northern Chile" (Graduate thesis, Department of Chemistry, Western Carolina University, July 2011), https://libres.uncg.edu/ir/wcu/f/WilsonLR2011.pdf (detailing industrial contaminants affecting the aquatic biota of the Río Loa basin).

After revoking the concession, Bolivia awarded a $47 million contract to a Bolivian company, DUCTEC SRL, and undertook a feasibility study to develop a hydroelectric plant on the Silala/Siloli.[70] Chile viewed this as a provocation, and a bilateral working group was formed to head off a coming dispute, but failed to achieve an equitable solution in 2001.[71] In 2003, Bolivia rescinded its contract with DUCTEC on the grounds of nonperformance; DUCTEC had been unable to collect any money from *Ferrocarril de Antofagasta a Bolivia* or the Chilean state-owned National Copper Corporation that had converted the original use of the water for more modern purposes.[72] In 2006, Bolivia's Loa Infantry Regiment set up a garrison near the source waters. Chile called the establishment of the military installation a provocation; Bolivia claimed that border security is an unassailable sovereign right.[73]

A Deep History of Tension

Tensions between these two countries run deep, and the Silala/Siloli dispute cannot be viewed as isolated from this history.[74] Chile's and Bolivia's poor neighborly relations date to Spain's early-nineteenth-century retreat from the New World. Bolivia was the last of Spain's American continental possessions to achieve independence (1825), and it emerged from colonization with the weakest economic and political

70. Mulligan & Eckstein, *supra* note 3, at 598 (calling the award to DUCTEL SRL "potentially provocative"). The Silala/Siloli's water flow was found to be too low to sustain profitable power use. *See* Klein, *supra* note 10. The company then attempted to charge Chile's copper-producing company at the Chuquicamata mine (CODELCO) for the unauthorized use of the waters, but no payment has been made. *Id.*

71. Meza Bórquez, *supra* note 3, at 154 (referencing Homazábal).

72. *See* St. John, *supra* note 5.

73. *Bolivia tiene base military a menos de dos kilómetros de frontera con Chile*, CAMBIO21 (May 10, 2016), http://www.cambio21.cl/cambio21/stat/movil/articulo.html?ts=20160510092047; Imágenes muestran que Bolivia cuenta con una base military a 1,4 kilómetros del Silala, emol.Nacional (Chile), http://www.emol.com/noticias/Nacional/2016/05/10/801984/Imagenes-muestran-que-Bolivia-cuenta-con-una-base-militar-a-14-kilometros-del-Silala.html (quoting Chilean ambassador Gabriel Gaspar's skepticism of Bolivia's rationale and Bolivian president Morales's explanation: "*Esta presencia de las Fuerzas Armadas en el Silala no es ninguna provocación, no es ninguna agresión a ningún país. Cualquier Estado, cualquier nación, tiene la obligación de sentar soberanía en las fronteras.*").

74. *See* Laura Iesue, *Tensions Rise between Chile and Bolivia Over the Perceived State of the Former's Military Base Near the Silala River*, COUNCIL ON HEMISPHERIC AFFAIRS (May 23, 2016), http://www.coha.org/tensions-rise-between-chile-and-bolivia-over-the-perceived-state-of-the-formers-military-base-near-the-silala-river/ (noting the connection, particularly in Bolivia, between this dispute and Bolivia's "loss of access to the Pacific Ocean in the War of the Pacific").

institutions.[75] Chile was on the periphery of Spain's New World empire,[76] but its human geography was far more homogeneous than Bolivia's and its natural geography was more amenable to infrastructural development, particularly railroad construction and sea transport.[77] Chile's geography facilitated industrialization and migration north through the establishment of coastal entrepôts that bypassed inhospitable land routes throughout the Atacama. The Chileanization of the Atacama occurred in part because Chile used the sea as a highway north. It supplied needed and initially welcomed laborers for unpopulated stretches of the Bolivian littoral, stretches rich in resources awaiting excavation. With its few population centers located high on the *Altiplano*, Bolivia maintained waning control over its littoral by means of one month's travel down the deep rifts of the *cordilleras* of the *Altiplano* and across the Atacama.[78] Chile's geographic situation also attracted infusions of British capital,[79] which accelerated infrastructural development. Chile's postcolonial political trajectory, turbulent like all former Spanish New World political histories, nevertheless promoted a more rapid consolidation of power, and it would soon challenge the crown jewel of Spain's New World imperium: Peru.[80] In the 1830s, Chile successfully disrupted the establishment of a Peruvian-Bolivian Confederation,[81] underscoring sensitive balance-of-power considerations that continue to beset the regional politics of the Andean Cone.[82]

---

75. *See* FARCAU, *supra* note 26, at 20–22 (2000) (discussing Bolivia's geographic, economic, and political challenges postindependence).

76. CHRISTON I. ARCHER, *Enlightenment, Governance, and Reform in Spain and Its Empire, 1759–1808*, at 221–22 (2008) (book review) (quoting Parquette and listing Chile as part of the "imperial periphery").

77. *See generally* Alberto A. Zalles, *Bolivia y Chile: los imperativos de una nueva época*, NUEVA SOCIEDAD 34 (2007) (discussing divergent social and geographical factors shaping development paths of Bolivia and Chile).

78. *See* SATER, ANDEAN TRAGEDY 9–10 and 11–12 (discussing topographic and demographic challenges to administering the Atacama).

79. *See* JOHN MAYO & SIMON COLLIER, MINING IN CHILE'S NORTE CHICO: JOURNALS OF CHARLES LAMBERT, 1825–1830, at 2 (1998) (noting more than forty British-organized mining companies as early as the 1820s); J. FRED RIPPY, BRITISH INVESTMENTS IN LATIN AMERICA, 1822–1949: A CASE STUDY IN OPERATIONS OF PRIVATE ENTERPRISE IN RETARDED REGIONS 133–41 (1966) (detailing British concessionaires in Chile's railway, telegraph, and nitrate industries). *See generally* JOHN MAYO, BRITISH MERCHANTS AND CHILEAN DEVELOPMENT, 1851–1886 (1987) (discussing British financial interests in Chile).

80. *See* Christopher R. Rossi, *A Case Ill Suited for Judgment: Constructing "A Sovereign Access to the Sea" in the Atacama Desert*, 48 INTER-AM. L. REV. 28, 53 (2017) (noting the importance of Perú and New Granada).

81. *See* WILLIAM F. SATER, CHILE AND THE WAR OF THE PACIFIC 2 (1986).

82. Mares contends that the forestalled confederation appeared poised to create the

Enmity between Bolivia and Chile erupted with the War of the Pacific, but the origins of this war remain in dispute. Historian J. R. Brown attributed it to Chile's "imperialistic policy in Atacama."[83] James G. Blaine, the United States Secretary of State, claimed it was due to British meddling.[84] The Latin Americanist John Mayo blamed the "feckless, reckless and foolhardy" Bolivian government, which "lit the fuse that ignited the conflagration."[85] All perspectives converge on the point that the conflict was decades in the making, exacerbated by Bolivia's compromised geographic position and Chile's migratory expansion into the Atacama, that it was motivated in part by control over resources, and that its consequences were disastrous.

Psychological Effects of the War of the Pacific and Goffmanian Metaphor

Few references to the foreign relations between Chile and Bolivia overlook the psychological impact of the War to the Pacific.[86] Protean nuances of animus, conceptualized in terms of a Mediterranean emotivism (*emotivismo*),[87] revindication (*reivindicacionismo*),[88] and a mutual cul-

most powerful union in the region; Bolivia's status as the poorest state in Latin America (along with Paraguay) reflects today Chile's interruption of the regional distribution of power presented by the Peru-Bolivia confederation of 1836–1839. MARES, *supra* note 25, at 35. *See also id.* at 32 (listing the participants in the dispute as Chile [Argentina] v. Perú and Bolivia). Even among the historical allies, Perú and Bolivia, Rodríquez emphasized the famous phrase of Ulloa: "*. . . sería exagerado decir que esas relaciones han sido de mala vecindad, pero quizás sería más exagerado aún decir que han sido de buena vecindad.*" JOSÉ RODRÍGUEZ ELIZONDO, HISTORIA DE DOS DEMANDAS: PERÚ Y BOLIVIA CONTRA CHILE 183 (2014).

83. J. R. Brown, *The Frustration of Chile's Nitrate Imperialism*, 32 PACIFIC HIST. REV. 384 (1963).

84. *See* DAVID HEALY, JAMES G. BLAINE AND LATIN AMERICA 63 (2001) (quoting Blaine): "It is a perfect mistake to speak of this as a Chilean war on Peru. It is an English war on Peru, with Chile as the instrument. . . . Chile would never have gone into this war one inch but for her backing by English capital, and there was never anything played out so boldly in the world as when they came to divide the loot and the spoils."

85. Mayo, *supra* note 31, at 10, 11.

86. *See* G. Van Der Ree, *Chile's (Inter) National Identities: Framing the Relations with Bolivia and Peru*, 29 BULL. LAT. AM. RES. 208, 209 (2010) (noting the crucial role the War of the Pacific has played in constructing national identities of the countries); Leonardo Jeffs Castro, *Las relaciones chileno-bolivianas: aproximación histórica y desafíos*, VI CONGRESO DE RELACIONES INTERNACIONALES 1, 1 (Nov. 21–23, 2012) (noting that the rupture in diplomatic relations between the two countries stems from "*la pérdida de Bolivia de su cualidad marítima.*"); Leslie E. Wehner, *Developing Mutual Trust: The Othering Process Between Bolivia and Chile*, 36 CANADIAN J. LAT. AM. & CARIB. STUD. 109, 109 (2011) (linking the mutual hostility and lack of trust between Bolivia and Chile to the War of the Pacific).

87. Sergio González Miranda & Cristián Ovando Santana, *"Emotivistas" bolivianos en la relación diplomática entre Bolivia y Chile en torno a la mediterraneidad*, 183 ESTUDIOS INTERNACIONALES 39–65 (2016). http://www.revistaei.uchile.cl/index.php/REI/article/viewFile/39880/41450

88. *Id.*

ture of enmity,[89] now characterize treatments of their discursive relationship. In part, this hostility has been associated with the larger regional security concerns of Latin America and the *problématique* of its colonial history, its proximity to the hegemonic pulls and pushes of the United States, and its highly stratified domestic social structure.[90] A Latin American interstate culture of rivalry has developed. It affects national identities and serves performative functions to satisfy internal politics.[91] Militarized bargaining postures have been viewed as forms of officially sanctioned military violence, but not with war as the intended result.[92] In symbolic and sociological ways, and distinct from alternative pragmatic or integrationist themes,[93] Bolivian-Chilean relations fit into this pattern as much as those of neighboring states anywhere else in Latin America. These relations rise to a level of Goffmanian metaphor.[94]

The Importance of Metaphors and International Law

Metaphors are familiar forms of word play.[95] They "require that we see what is in front of us as different from what it at first seemed to be."[96] If employed fittingly,[97] metaphors present things in a better light by "giving

---

89. *See* Wehner, *supra* note 86, at 110 (discussing Bolivia's and Chile's mutual culture of enmity).

90. *See* MARES, *supra* note 25, at 28–32.

91. *See generally* Cameron Thies, *The Construction of a Latin American Interstate Culture of Rivalry*, 34 INTERNATIONAL INTERACTIONS 231 (2008) (analyzing rival relationships and role identities in Latin America).

92. *See* MARES, *supra* note 25, at 7 (2001) (discussing the concept of violent peace).

93. GONZÁLEZ MIRANDA & OVANDO SANTANA, *supra* note 87, at 44 (distinguishing *emotivista* explanations from "*otras posiciones como las pragmáticas or practicistas e integracionistas*").

94. Erving Goffman adapted sociological inquiry to phenomena of social interaction, concentrating on public and private (or intersubjective) beliefs and face-to-face encounters that conceal and reveal the social utility of hostility and adversarial relations. Dramaturgy and theatrical performance were common vehicles through which Goffman investigated the symbols of social interaction. *See, e.g.*, ERVING GOFFMAN, THE PRESENTATION OF SELF IN EVERYDAY LIFE (1959) (deriving frameworks of sociological inquiry from principles of dramaturgy, presentation, communication, and the art of impression); ERVING GOFFMAN, ENCOUNTERS (1961) (on the dynamics of personal communication); ERVING GOFFMAN, INTERACTION RITUALS (1967) (exploring face-work as a ritual element of social interaction); ERVING GOFFMAN, STRATEGIC INTERACTION (1969) (developing ideas of expression games and strategic interactions).

95. MICHAEL P. MARKS, THE PRISON AS METAPHOR: RE-IMAGINING INTERNATIONAL RELATIONS 15 (2004) (noting, as borrowed from literature and poetry, that metaphors are used to persuade and further knowledge).

96. MICHAEL DAVIS, ARISTOTLE'S POETICS: THE POETRY OF PHILOSOPHY 123 (1992).

97. *See* Nicholas Onuf, *Polemics: Fitting Metaphors—The Case of the European Union*, 18 PERSPECTIVES 63, 63 (2010) (quoting ARISTOTLE'S *Rhetoric*: "[M]etaphors, like epithets, must be fitting, which means they must fairly correspond to the thing signified."); *see also* NANCY FRASER, SCALES OF JUSTICE: REIMAGINING POLITICAL SPACE IN A GLOBALIZING WORLD 4–5, and ch. 2 (2009) (noting that powerful images of political space, such as the Westphalian map, are losing hold and may no longer be fitting).

the thing a name that belongs to something else;"[98] they are "devices for 'seeing something in terms of something else.'"[99]

Metaphors are embedded and familiar in the analytic language of international law, so "sedimented" and commonplace as to appear to be nothing more than expressions of common sense.[100] Realist and positivist literature have long employed metaphors of anarchy, order, balance, structure, or levels to represent the international system.[101] Extended metaphors of the body, the person, and even mythical biblical monsters—among the most influential, the *Leviathan*[102]—have represented images of the state. These representations invite literal linguistic or human-like assessments of a system's or state's health, intentions, capabilities, and limitations. Liberal metaphors often reference regimes or the incentivizing imagery of the market system to underscore a pervasive rationality of accord and mutuality of interest.[103] Metaphors function as an editorial embellishment, as when a picture is framed.[104] And here, Goffman's metaphor of dramaturgy appropriately informs theoretical commentaries about this dispute—where the disputants are conceptualized as "per-

---

98. ARISTOTLE, ON THE ART OF POETRY: THE POETICS 71–72 (Ingram Bywater trans., 1920).

99. Petr Drulák, *Motion, Container and Equilibrium: Metaphors in the Discourse about European Integration*, EUR. J. INT'L REL. 499, 502 (2006) (internal references omitted).

100. *Id.*

101. *See, e.g.*, ROBERT E. OSGOOD & ROBERT W. TUCKER, FORCE, ORDER, AND JUSTICE (1967); HEDLEY BULL, THE ANARCHICAL SOCIETY (1977); on levels, for example, see KENNETH WALTZ, MAN, THE STATE, AND WAR (1959); J. David Singer, *The Level-of-Analysis Problem in International Relations*, 14 WORLD POL. 77–92 (1961); *see also* R. B. J. WALKER, INSIDE/OUTSIDE: INTERNATIONAL RELATIONS AS POLITICAL THEORY (1993) (discussing the metaphorical language of international relations theory from an inside/outside [domestic/international] perspective). For a more general discussion of levels, see Nicholas Onuf, *Levels*, 1 EUR. J. INT'L REL. 35–58 (1995). *See generally* MICHAEL P. MARKS, METAPHORS IN INTERNATIONAL RELATIONS THEORY (2011) (highlighting the general importance of metaphors in international relations discourse).

102. *See* THOMAS HOBBES, LEVIATHAN OR THE MATTER, FORME AND POWER OF A COMMONWEALTH ECCLESIASTICALL AND CIVILL (1651) (referencing the Book of Job, 41:24, on the copperplate artistic representation of the Leviathan as sovereign). *See generally* Carl Schmitt, THE LEVIATHAN IN THE STATE THEORY OF THOMAS HOBBES: MEANING AND FAILURE OF A POLITICAL SYMBOL (1938) (discussing biblical metaphoric images of the state in Hobbes's LEVIATHAN).

103. *See* MARKS, *supra* note 95, at 36–42 (on liberal/rational metaphors). *See also* Roderick A. Macdonald, *Metaphors of Multiplicity: Civil Society, Regimes and Legal Pluralism*, 15 ARIZ. J. INT'L & COMP. L. 69–91 (1988) (investigating legal metaphors of multiplicity and pluralism).

104. JUDITH BUTLER, FRAMES OF WAR: WHEN IS LIFE GRIEVABLE? 8 (2010).

formers engaged in manipulative presentations of self,"[105] framed and constrained by a script written by the War of the Pacific many years ago.

Dramaturgy

Dramatization affects legal presentation; indeed "judicial proceedings are a *source* of drama."[106] The very name and backdrop of the Peace Palace at The Hague intentionally dramatized the aura of international law.[107] However, dramatizations also take symbolic forms that stray from evocations of majesty. They can be intentional, yet disingenuous or unrealistic. Goffman developed schemata to explain the background for understanding events shaped by agency, as opposed to nature, that describe the "guided doings" (deeds, not mere events) and social frameworks of opposing parties.[108] He construed underlying aspects of behavior as deeply symbolic, although not perceived as necessarily central or obvious.[109] Symbolic interactions attain information intended to control the behavior of others and to maintain or conform perceptions of self.[110]

---

105. Frank Schimmelfennig, *Goffman Meets IR: Dramaturgical Action in International Community*, 12 INT'L REV. SOC. 417, 417 (2002) (adapting Goffman's frame analysis to international relations theory); *see also* André Nollkaemper, *Framing Elephant Extinction*, 3 ESIL REFLECTIONS (2014), http://www.esil-sedi.eu/sites/default/files/ESIL%20Reflection%20-%20Nollkaemper.pdf (adapting interpretations of frame analysis to international law).

106. Milner S. Ball, *The Play's the Thing: An Unscientific Reflection on Courts Under the Rubric of Theater*, 28 STAN. L. REV. 81, 82 (1975).

107. The Peace Palace's granite, sandstone, and red-brick façade, with its "imposing roof of greyish slate," rising clock tower, and interior ornamental "Woodwork, stained-glass, mosaics, tapestries and art objects," was designed in a predominantly neo-Renaissance style and placed in a seven-hectare park by Louis Coordonnier to "evoke justice and peace" and "reflect the diversity of the world's cultures." *Practical Information*, INT'L COURT OF JUSTICE, http://www.icj-cij.org/information/index.php?p1=7. Indeed, the intention of Scottish-American industrialist Andrew Carnegie, who in 1903 made a lavish $1.5 million gift to build the edifice, was the creation of a "Temple of Peace." *See* Randall Lesaffer, *The Temple of Peace: The Hague Peace Conferences, Andrew Carnegie and the Building of the Peace Palace (1898–1913)*, Tilburg Law School Legal Studies Research Paper Series No. 024/2013, at 2, 40 (2013) (noting Carnegie's gift and details regarding the construction of the building).

108. *See generally* ERVING GOFFMAN, FRAME ANALYSIS: AN ESSAY ON THE ORGANIZATION OF EXPERIENCE (1986) [hereinafter GOFFMAN, FRAME ANALYSIS] (discussing the proposition that meanings in everyday life are projections of the ways in which they are framed).

109. *See id.* at 569.

110. *See generally*, GOFFMAN, INTERACTION RITUAL, *supra* note 94, ch. 2 (discussing face-work, and the maintenance of verbal and nonverbal cues and acts to maintain established lines and ritual elements of social encounter).

They are "diffusely located in the flow of events."[111] Goffman often referenced the voluble characteristics of the actor on stage, who would emote "before a much larger number of people than would witness these outpourings in ordinary life."[112] Goffman's acting metaphor implied actions directed toward an external audience, to which Chile and Bolivia play in forums such as the United Nations or the Organization of American States. However, dramaturgy also references internal audiences, as noted by the favored theatrical technic of the play-within-the-play.[113] Internal audiences can become a key domestic determinant of foreign policy,[114] as has been noted by observers of this never-ending conflict.[115] The dramaturgy of the stage, reframed as a contested arena, informs the rationality and timing of legal proceedings[116]—where international law serves as the structural mannequin for counternarratives, dressed up as ideational orthodoxies of otherness.[117] This symbolic interaction has a function; it cues internal audiences when to applaud or how to react.

Taking pages from absurdist theater as well, Bolivia's and Chile's legal performances are not intended for resolution.[118] They are calibrated to

---

111. *Id.* at 7.

112. GOFFMANN, FRAME ANALYSIS, *supra* note 108, at 570.

113. The technique of staging a play within a play is common among playwrights. *See, e.g.*, WILLIAM SHAKESPEARE, A MIDSUMMER NIGHT'S DREAM, TWELFTH NIGHT, and HAMLET; THOMAS KYD, THE SPANISH TRAGEDY; ANTON CHEKHOV, THE SEAGULL; BERTOLT BRECHT, THE CAUCASIAN CHALK CIRCLE. It is also found in other art forms, such as opera. *See, e.g.*, RUGGERO LEONCAVALLO, I PAGLIACCI.

114. For seminal studies on domestic determinants of foreign policy and conflict, see OLE R. HOLSTI, PUBLIC OPINION AND AMERICAN FOREIGN POLICY (1996), and Jack S. Levy, *Domestic Politics and War*, 18 J. INTERDISCIPLINARY HIST. 653–73 (1988). *See also* Christopher Sprecher & Karl DeRouen Jr., *The Domestic Determinants of Foreign Policy Behavior in Middle Eastern Enduring Rivals, 1948–1998*, 1 FOR. POL. ANALYSIS 121–41 (2005) (arguing that rivalry-related issues tend to dominate foreign policy agendas).

115. *See, e.g.*, Pablo Jofré Leal, *A Never-Ending Conflict. Bolivia's Access to the Sea (Part II)*, THE DAWN (Mar. 28, 216), http://www.thedawn-news.org/2016/04/14/a-never-ending-conflict-bolivias-access-to-the-sea-part-ii/ (discussing Chile's and Bolivia's portrayals of the dispute as means to distract attention from internal problems, including Bolivian president Morales's defeat on a constitutional reform measure and mounting opposition from traditional left-wing and peasant union supporters, and Chilean president Michelle Bachelet's low approval ratings—the lowest in history—and government credibility crises).

116. *See* Iesue, *supra* note 20 (arguing that Chile beat Bolivia to the punch by filing first the Silala River dispute with the ICJ).

117. Wehner, *supra* note 86, at 115.

118. *See, e.g.*, EUGÈNE IONESCO, THE LESSON (1951) (an archetypical example of the theater of the absurd resulting not in resolution but in an ending taking the viewer back to the beginning).

preserve flexibility and promote paralegal or illusory outcomes.[119] In another dispute between these countries, recently decided by the ICJ,[120] the parties had not asked the Court to determine whether Chile must cede territory to Bolivia, thus securing for Bolivia a sovereign access to the sea, but whether Chile broke its promise to either reach such a future agreement or to enter into good-faith negotiations that possibly would produce such a future agreement.[121] This case involved "obligations arising from" oblique distinctions between *pacta de contrahendo* versus *pacta de negotiando*.[122] While a *pactum de contrahendo* obligates parties to conclude a future agreement, a *pactum de negotiando* obligates parties to enter into future negotiations but does not "[bind] the parties to arrive at an agreement,"[123] and neither instrument actually presents a resolution to a dispute. Indeed, Bolivia claimed "the specific modalities of sovereign access are not matters for the Court, but, rather, are matters for future agreement."[124] Interestingly, and despite the name of the case which framed the dispute in terms of the expression "sovereign access to

---

119. *See, e.g.*, Richard Baxter, *International Law in Her Infinite Variety*, 29 INT'L & COMP. L.Q. 549, 552 (1980) (calling such pledges "empty" and "rhetorical").

120. Obligation to Negotiate Access to the Pacific Ocean (Bol. v. Chile), Judgment, 2018 I.C.J. 1 (Oct. 1, 2018).

121. *See* Obligation to Negotiate Access to the Pacific Ocean (Bol. V. Chile), Application Insituting Proceedings, 2013 I.C.J. 10 (Apr. 24, 2013), ¶ 1 ("The present Application concerns the dispute between [Bolivia and Chile] relating to Chile's obligation to negotiate . . . with Bolivia in order to reach an agreement granting Bolivia a fully sovereign access to the Pacific Ocean.").

122. *See* Obligation to Negotiate Access to the Pacific Ocean (Bol. V. Chile), Preliminary Objection, Verbatim Record, CR 2015/21, ¶ 6, at 32 (May 8, 2015, 3 PM), http://www.icj-cij.org/docket/files/153/18648.pdt (Mr. Akhayan).

123. *See* Hisashi Owada, *Pactum de Contrahendo, Pactum de Negotiando, in* MAX PLANCK ENCYCLOPEDIA OF PUBLIC INT'L L. 18–19 (2008); *see also* Antonio Cassese, *The Israel-PLO Agreement and Self-Determination*, 4 EUR. J. INT'L L. 564, 566–68 (1993) (distinguishing *pacta de contrahendo* from the "more tenuous" *pacta de negotiando*). In the North Sea Continental Shelf Cases, the ICJ (citing the P.C.I.J.'s Advisory Opinion in the case of Railway Traffic between Lithuania and Poland) recognized that "the obligation [to negotiate] was 'not only to enter into negotiations but also to pursue them as far as possible with a view to concluding agreements,' even if an obligation to negotiate did not imply an obligation to reach agreement." North Sea Continental Shelf Cases (F.R.G. v. Den.; F.R.G. v. Neth.), Judgment, 1969 I.C.J. 3, ¶ 87 (Feb. 20).

124. Obligation to Negotiate Access to the Pacific Ocean (Bolivia v. Chile) Preliminary Objection, ¶ 30 (Sept. 24, 2015); *see also* Obligation to Negotiate Access to the Pacific Ocean (Bol. v. Chile), Written Reply of Bolivia to the Question Put by Judge Owada at the Public Sitting Held on the afternoon of 8 May 2015, 13 May 2015, at 2 http://www.icj-cij.org/docket/index.php?p1=3&p2=3&k=f3&case=153&code=bch&p3=10 ("Bolivia reiterates once more that its case on the merits is not about the precise modalities or specific content of sovereign access to the sea . . . . only that . . . such sovereign access may be achieved by a modality to be specified by a future agreement among the parties.").

the sea," Judge Hisashi Owada asked the parties to define the meaning of that phrase.[125] For him, the fundamental nomenclature encapsulating the case was itself a stylization: "This is not a term of art in general international law," he said.[126]

Bolivia's and Chile's ICJ water disputes presented a question about Bolivia's right to cut off Chile's access to sweet water, and Chile's right to cut off negotiations over Bolivia's access to blue water.[127] A tit-for-tat quality has attached to these proceedings,[128] but this may present complications. International courts abjure opening their doors to performance; merely abiding by the formalities of dispute settlement or orchestrations of legal language and process is not sufficient proof of good-faith intentions to resolve disputes.[129] As handed down from the practice of Roman law *praetors* (magistrates), decision-makers resist drawing from deep cisterns of equitable remedies to provide relief to complainants who do not come before them with clean hands or good intentions.[130] This basis for denying relief has been found particularly applicable in matters involving transboundary (pollution) issues,[131] where the principle of equitable utilization is a cornerstone of customary transboundary water law.[132]

---

125. Obligation to Negotiate Access to the Pacific Ocean (Bol. v. Chile), Preliminary Objection, International Court of Justice CR 2015/21, 38–39 (question of Judge Owada), http://www.icj-cij.org/docket/files/153/18648.pdf

126. *Id.*

127. *See* Obligation to Negotiate Access to the Pacific Ocean (Bol. v. Chile), Application Instituting Proceedings 10 (Apr. 24, 2013), http://www.icj-cij.org/docket/files/153/17338.pdf; Press Release (Unofficial), International Court of Justice, Bolivia Institutes Proceedings Against Chile with Regard to a Dispute Concerning the Obligation of Chile to Negotiate the "Sovereign Access of Bolivia to the Pacific Ocean," No. 2013/11 (Apr. 24, 2013), http://www.icj-cij.org/docket/files/153/17340.pdf [hereinafter ICJ Press Release No. 2013/11].

128. *See, e.g.*, Walter Guevara Anaya, *Chile Over-reacts to Bolivian Alleged Legal Frivolity*, MEDIUM (May 5, 2016), https://medium.com/@walter.guevara.anaya/chile-over-reacts-to-bolivian-alleged-legal-frivolity-93e904efbd1f#.ftt8ljtc5 (referencing Bolivian president Evo Morales's pledge to take the Silala case to the ICJ followed by Chilean President Michelle Bachelet's response of a counter complaint).

129. *See* North Sea Continental Shelf Cases, Judgment, 1969 I.C.J. 3, at ¶ 85 (requiring that parties "are under an obligation so to conduct themselves that the negotiations are meaningful").

130. *The Highwayman's Case*, 9 L. Q. REV. 197, 198 (1893) (denying relief to highway robbers disputing division of their ill-gotten gains). *See generally* Zechariah Chafee Jr., *Coming into Equity with Clean Hands*, 47 MICH. L. R. 877–906 (1949) (discussing the history of the maxim with reference mostly to common law).

131. *See* Thomas W. Merrill, *Golden Rules for Transboundary Pollution*, 46 DUKE L. J. 931, 936 (1997).

132. *See, e.g.*, International Law Association, Helsinki Rules on the Uses of the Waters of International Rivers, ch. 2, August 1966, *available at* http://www.internationalwaterlaw.org/documents/intldocs/Helsinki_Rules_with_comments.pdf (on equitable utilization of

However, complaints arise that the Silala/Siloli dispute has, like an earlier *gas por mar* dispute,[133] been manufactured as a secondary tension to secure for Bolivia a bargaining chip over Chile's control of its coast.[134] Chile's discursive references to the war have been interpreted as manipulations "to shape and enhance" Chilean identity.[135] "The art of acting is always Janus-faced," and elements of comedy and tragedy transpose as symbolic theater masks of Chilean-Bolivian relations.[136] A definitive adjudication of Bolivia's and Chile's historical animus may hinge on the Court's ultimate determination that international law requires more than the element of play-acting cultivated by the performing arts.[137]

Ceremonial Profanations and Legal Vandalism

Perhaps a ceremonial process of contestation, with international law as the backdrop, now serves for Bolivia and Chile as *the* multi-act play. With little prospect of a *denouement* or appearance of a *deus ex machina* to end

---

the waters of an international drainage basin) [hereinafter Helsinki Rules]); *see also* Patricia Wouters, *International Law—Facilitating Transboundary Water Cooperation*, GLOBAL WATER PARTNERSHIP TEC BACKGROUND PAPERS, NO. 17, 16 (2013) (identifying "equitable and reasonable use" as the most important rule of customary international law on watercourses); Alistair Rieu-Clarke et al., *Transboundary Water Governance and Climate Change Adaptation: International Law, Policy Guidelines, and Best Practice Application*, United Nations World Water Assessment Programme Technical Paper 33 (2015) (claiming "[t]he principle of equitable and reasonable utilization" is the "cornerstone of customary international water law").

133. In the early 2000s, Bolivia and Chile held secret negotiations on exporting Bolivian gas to Mexico through a Chilean port. News of the negotiations leaked to the public and severely complicated both countries' internal politics, perhaps more in Bolivia because the deal suggested the expiry of Bolivia's historical claim of re-establishing a sovereign access to the sea. Bolivian gas was then linked to negotiations for an outlet to the sea with Chile (the *gas por mar* debate). *See* Wehner, *supra* note 86, at 111; *see also* Pascale Bonnefoy, *Gas por mar*, 45 ESTUDIOS INTERNACIONALES 15, 18–19 (2013).

134. Meza Bórquez, *supra* note 3, at 153 (noting that the dispute has elements that constitute "*un 'Factor de Tensión Secundario', que puedan ser manipulados por el Gobierno boliviano para una maniobra de crisis o como una potencial herramienta de negociación.*").

135. Wehner, *supra* note 86, at 114 (citing Hernán Cuevas, *Narrating National Unity and Facing the Enemy: Fantasies and Traumas of Chilean Identity* [ISA Annual Convention Paper, 2008]).

136. ROBERT WILLOUGHBY CORRIGAN & JAMES L. ROSENBERG, THE CONTEXT AND CRAFT OF DRAMA: CRITICAL ESSAYS ON THE NATURE OF DRAMA AND THEATRE 348 (1964).

137. *See* North Sea Continental Shelf Cases, Judgment, 1969 I.C.J. 3, ¶ 85 ("[T]he parties are under an obligation to enter into negotiations with a view to arriving at an agreement, and not merely to go through a formal process of negotiation."); *see also* Gabčíkovo-Nagymaros Project (Hung./Slovk.), Judgment, 1997 I.C.J. 7, ¶ 141 (Sept. 25) (noting that "the [parties] are under an obligation so to conduct themselves that the negotiations are meaningful , which will not be the case when either of them insists upon its own position without contemplating any modification of it").

the bickering over the War of the Pacific, there is no call to draw down the final curtain. Goffman envisioned a need for ceremonial profanations, spite actions of law, which generate interaction rituals formed in face-to-face encounters as expressions of vendetta and victimology—or what he likened to a form of vandalism.[138] Slights, gestures, and posturing—perceived and intended indignities beyond formal interaction—set the theatrical stage that fuels a diplomatic rupture of relations and also implicates another transboundary water dispute between the two countries—the Lauca River dispute in 1962.[139] The dispute, involving an "insignificant" and "minor" watercourse, "gravely strained" relations between Chile and Bolivia and compromised the effectiveness of the OAS.[140]

In the Lauca River dispute, Chile diverted waters originating in the Chilean Andes but feeding into Bolivia's Lake Coipasa; this diversion was to irrigate the Azapa Valley in Chile's northern province of Arica.[141] Territory formerly belonging to Perú was offered to Bolivia as part of an exchange for unassailable Chilean control of the upper waters of the Río Lauca.[142] Bolivia (and Perú) regarded the offer as illusory because it amounted to an attempt by Chile to pay off a dispute using territory taken from Perú.[143] Chile had attempted the same idea of a land swap before.[144] Nothing would be gained for Bolivia by allowing Chile to remove itself from the controversy by inserting Perú in Chile's stead.[145]

---

138. GOFFMAN, INTERACTION RITUALS, *supra* note 94, at 86n25.

139. *See id.* at 2 (discussing verbal statements and positionings of face-to-face interaction).

140. Robert D. Tomasek, *The Chilean-Bolivian Lauca River Dispute and the O.A.S.*, 9 J. INTER-AM. STUD. 351, 351 (1967).

141. *See* Terence R. Lee, *The Management of Shared Water Resources in Latin American*, 35 NAT. RESOURCES J. 542, 545 (1995) (noting that the dispute originated with plans in 1939 and that Chile's diversion was based on a joint commission's report of no damage to Bolivian interests); Martin Ira Glassner, *The Río Lauca: Dispute Over an International River*, 60 AM. GEO. SOC. 197–207 (1970); Tomasek, *supra* note 140, at 351–66 (discussing the development of the dispute and the serious problems caused notwithstanding the river's relatively minor potential).

142. Dennis R. Gordon, *The Question of the Pacific: Current Perspectives on a Long-Standing Dispute*, 141 WORLD AFF. 321, 328 (1975) (noting Chile's offer of former Peruvian territory to secure "exclusive and unassailable access to the Río Lauca").

143. *See id.* at 329 (noting "the Chilean president could not be so naïve as to assume his proposal would be greeted with open arms either in Perú or Bolivia").

144. *See* SATER, CHILE AND THE WAR OF THE PACIFIC, *supra* note 81, at 224 (discussing a proposal to break a deadlock over a promised plebiscite dealing with Tacna and Arica territories).

145. Although the idea appealed to Chile to "force Perú to pay Chile's obligations," Santiago's plan hinged on Perú's willingness to yield its claim over the northern border.

While Bolivia was made to suffer the consequences of the *jus prohibendi* agreement negotiated by more-powerful Chile and Perú in the 1929 Treaty of Lima, Bolivia had little ability to substantiate a similar accord by beggaring the interests of much-more-powerful Perú.[146] Instead, Bolivia sought assistance from the OAS.[147] Chile initially agreed to adjudicate the question before the ICJ,[148] but the dispute never made it that far. Both countries severed diplomatic relations, and except for a brief rapprochement between 1975 and 1978 (the Charaña negotiations), the two countries maintain only consular relations.[149] In the *other* case presented to the ICJ, Bolivia instituted proceedings against Chile in April 2013.[150] Without defining the specific modalities guaranteeing it a right of sovereign access,[151] Bolivia asserted that its sovereign entitlement derived "from Chile's own unilateral declarations or its repeated agreements with Bolivia to negotiate sovereign access."[152] In the meantime, however, Chile and Perú adjudicated before the ICJ yet another sovereign question over the seaward projection of border at the terminal point of their land boundary.[153] This dispute involved Perú's grievance stemming from its defeat in the War of the Pacific and Chile's twentieth-century maritime delimitation proclamation, which severely cut off Perú's claim.[154]

"[U]ntil Perú yielded on the north, the Moneda [Chile's seat of power] could not reach an agreement with La Paz." *Id.*

146. *See* Daniel Flemes & Michael Radsek, *Creating Multilevel Security Governance in South America* 5, 11 Ger. Inst. Glob. & Area Studies Working Paper No. 117 (2009) (noting complicated trilateral relations among Chile, Bolivia, and Peru).

147. *See* ULDARICIO FIGUEROA PIA, LA DEMANDA MARÍTIMA BOLIVIANA EN LOS FOROS INTERNACIONALES 83, 88–94 (2007) (discussing generally the suspension of diplomatic relations caused by the Río Lauca dispute and specifically Bolivia's demands before the O.A.S.).

148. Lee, *supra* note 141, at 545.

149. *Chile-Foreign Relations*, GLOBALSECURITY.ORG (July 21, 2016), https://www.globalsecurity.org/military/world/chile/forrel.htm (noting that the countries severed diplomatic ties in 1978 and maintain only consular relations).

150. ICJ Press Release No. 2013/11, *supra* note 127, at 1.

151. *See* Obligation to Negotiate Access, Preliminary Objection, *supra* note 124, ¶ 30.

152. *See Bolivia's Comments on Chile's Reply to Judge Owada's Question*, ESTADO PLURINACIONAL DE BOLIVIA, EMBAJADA LA HAYA—PAÍSES BAJOS, ¶ 4, http://www.icj-cij.org/docket/files/153/18664.pdf

153. *See* Maritime Dispute (Perú v. Chile), Judgment, 2014 I.C.J. 3 (Jan. 27).

154. The terminal point of Perú's and Chile's land boundary, a point called Concordia, had been established by the 1929 Treaty of Lima. *Id.* ¶ 1. In 1947, both countries unilaterally proclaimed maritime rights extending 200 nautical miles from their coasts. *Id.* ¶ 19. Perú maintained that no agreed-upon maritime boundary existed with Chile and that Chile's delimitation severely cut off Perú's entitlement to a full 200-nautical-mile maritime extension; Chile claimed that the subsequent Santiago Declaration established the maritime border along the latitude passing through Concordia. *Id.* ¶¶ 22–23.

The resolution of this case raised an absurd prospect: even if Bolivia secured its long-sought littoral, there is no more sea remaining for Bolivia to reclaim now that Perú and Chile have adjudicated a demarcation between their adjoining territorial seas.

The Evolution of Transboundary Freshwater Law

Despite the complications associated with an increasing number of intractable border complaints between the two countries, the Silala/Siloli dispute raises important issues of international riparian law. International law supports the resolution of these questions within a framework of mutual respect, if not equality, and equitable utilization—a framework that rejects spite applications and ceremonial profanations of law. However, before the law can identify a resolution, certain questions must be answered and certain issues resolved. Foremost among these issues is the deceptively simple question: what is a watercourse?

Evolution of the International Law Defining Watercourse

The United Nations originally took up this question in 1959 but encountered problems and soon determined that it was unnecessary to first define the term. [155] It concentrated instead on preliminary studies on the utilization of international rivers.[156] In 1970, the General Assembly charged the International Law Commission (ILC) with the tasks of codifying the law on nonnavigational uses of international watercourses.[157] After more than two decades of study, the ILC adopted a first set of draft articles in 1991.[158] The ILC then submitted a revised draft to the General Assembly's Sixth (Legal) Committee in 1994.[159] Convening as a Working Group of the Whole, the Sixth (Legal) Committee worked with member states and specialized agencies to revise the Draft Articles.[160] After almost

---

155. *See* G.A. Res. 1401 (XIV) (Nov. 21, 1959).

156. *See* Stephen C. McCaffrey, *Convention on the Law of the Non-Navigational Uses of International Watercourses, Introductory Note,* United Nations Audiovisual Library of International Law 1 (1988), *available at* http://legal.un.org/avl/pdf/ha/clnuiw/clnuiw_e.pdf (referring to the decision by the ILC in 1976 to temporarily set aside the attempt to define the term "international watercourse").

157. *See* G.A. Res. 2669 (XXV) (Dec. 8, 1970).

158. *See Draft Articles on the law of the Non-Navigational Uses of International Watercourses,* U.N. Doc. No. A/CN.4/L.458, 1991 Y. B. INT'L L. COMM'N 140, http://legal.un.org/ilc/documentation/english/a_cn4_l458.pdf

159. *See* McCaffrey, *supra* note 155, at 1–2.

160. *See id.* at 2.

forty years of work, the General Assembly adopted the United Nations Convention on the Law of the Non-Navigational Uses of International Watercourses (UN Watercourses Convention) on May 21, 1997.[161] However, it took seventeen additional years for the treaty to obtain the requisite number of signatures to come into effect (on August 17, 2014), a delay caused by problems reconciling equitable utilization (art. 5) and preserving the integrity of watercourses (art. 7).[162]

The Watercourses Convention

According to the Watercourses Convention,[163] a watercourse is "a system of surface waters and groundwaters constituting by virtue of their physical relationship a unitary whole and normally flowing into a common terminus." An international watercourse "means a watercourse, parts of which are situated in different States."[164]

In the Atacama example, the two countries are not parties to the treaty but appear to embrace its application as a matter of customary international law.[165] Neither country disputes the constitutive compo-

161. *See* G.A. Res. 51/229 (July 8, 1997). For a detailed accounts of its legislative history, see Stephen C. McCaffrey, *The 1997 U.N. Watercourses Convention: Retrospect and Prospect*, 21 PAC. MCGEORGE GLOBAL BUS. & DEV. L. J. 165, 167 (2008). The definition of a "watercourse" had been on the agenda of the ILC alone for twenty-six years and involved thirteen reports and five special rapporteurs. *See* Ruth Lapidoth, *Dispute Settlement Under the 1997 Convention on the Law of the Non-Navigational Uses of International Watercourses, in* INTERNATIONAL LAW ACROSS THE SPECTRUM OF CONFLICT: ESSAYS IN HONOR OF PROFESSOR L. C. GREEN ON THE OCCASION OF HIS EIGHTIETH BIRTHDAY 231, 231 (Michael N. Schmitt ed., 2000).

162. *See generally* Alistair Rieu-Clarke & Flavia Rocha Loures, *Still Not in Force: Should States Support the 1997 UN Watercourses Convention?*, 18 REV. OF EUR. COMMUNITY & INT'L L. 185, 185–97 (2009) (reviewing problems associated with bringing the convention into force); Patricia Wouters, *The Legal Response to International Water Conflicts: The UN Watercourses Convention and Beyond*, 42 GER. Y. B. INT'L L. 293–336 (1999) (discussing conflicts-of-uses and water scarcity within the context of the convention).

163. Convention on the Law of the Non-Navigational Uses of International Watercourses, May 21, 1997, 36 I.L.M. 700.

164. *See id.* at arts. 2(a) and (b). For commentary, see ATTILA TANZI & MAURIZIO ARCARI, THE UNITED NATIONS CONVENTION ON THE LAW OF INTERNATIONAL WATERCOURSES: A FRAMEWORK FOR SHARING (2001); Patricia Wouters, *The International Law on Watercourses: New Dimensions, in* III COLLECTED COURSES OF THE XIAMEN ACADEMY OF INTERNATIONAL LAW 347 (2011).

165. Chile requested the Court to declare that the Silala/Siloli is an international watercourse and to adjudge the applicability of customary international law to the Silala/Siloli River system. *See* Application Instituting Proceedings, Dispute Over the Status and Use of the Waters of the Silala (Chile v. Bol), ¶¶ 4, 40, 42 (June 6, 2016), *available at* http://www.icj-cij.org/docket/files/162/19020.pdf; *see also* ICJ Press Release No. 2016/16, *supra* note 4, at 1.

nents of a watercourse at this juncture; they dispute the factual predicate as to whether the waters of the Silala/Siloli by virtue of their physical relationship constitute a unitary whole that would normally flow across a border to the common terminus.[166] Bolivia insists the Silala has been artificially diverted into the Loa by the creation of a drainage network.[167] Chile claims the Siloli is a river and that it has an equitable right to the waters.[168] Regardless of the Silala/Siloli's status as an international watercourse or a diverted spring, the Silala/Siloli remains Bolivia's sole psychological finger-link to the Pacific Ocean,[169] a wishful servitude restoring blue-water access to its landlocked naval fleet.[170]

A Clash of Interests: Sovereignty versus Watercourse Integrity

Worldwide, disputes over nonnavigational uses of freshwater resources have increased since the nineteenth century and commonly juxtapose the sovereignty claims of the uppermost riparian against lower riparian concerns about protecting the integrity of the watercourse.[171] Customary international law is particularly influential in this realm, as two-thirds of the world's transboundary watercourses are not covered by international agreements.[172] Existing legal instruments have been described as "frag-

---

166. For Chile's perspective on the rivers system constituting a unitary whole, see *id.* Bolivia, by implication, embraces the definition of an international watercourse to deny the international character of the Silala/Siloli. *See Discurso de Evo Morales, supra* note 14.

167. *See Discurso de Evo Morales, supra* note 14 (calling the diversion illegal, sly, abusive, arbitrary, and harmful). *See generally* Wilson Mercado Vargas, *Aguas Internacionales y el Aprovechamiento Boliviano,* MONOGRAFIAS.COM, http://www.monografias.com/trabajos87/aguas-internacionales-aprovechamiento-boliviano/aguas-internacionales-aprovechamiento-boliviano.shtml (discussing the dispute within the context of other transboundary water issues facing Bolivia).

168. *See* Chilean Application, *supra* note 1, at ¶ 44 ("There can be no doubt that the Silala River is an international watercourse under customary law"); *see also id.* ¶ 50 ("Chile is entitled to the equitable and reasonable use of the waters of the Silala River system in accordance with customary international law.").

169. See Hugo Llanos Mansilla, *El Caso Del Río Silala o Siloli Diferendo Chileno-Boliviano,* 21 AHLADI 339, 339 (2013).

170. The Bolivian Navy (Armada Boliviana) is staffed by 6,659 personnel. Its fleet is relegated to the brown-water ports of Lake Titicaca, various internal river patrols, and, by agreement with Perú, in 2010, a small Pacific Ocean port in Perú near Ilo. For statistical information about the Bolivian fleet and staff, see STEPHEN SAUNDERS HIS JANE'S FIGHTING SHIPS 2014–2015, at 68–69 (116th rev. ed. 2014).

171. Dellapenna, *supra* note 7, at 269.

172. *See* Patricia Wouters, *"Dynamic Cooperation"—The Evolution of Transboundary Water Cooperation, in* WATER AND THE LAW: TOWARDS SUSTAINABILITY 13, 63 Michael Kidd et al. eds. (2014) [hereinafter Wouters, *"Dynamic Cooperation"*].

mented," [173] with multiple new emphases,[174] such as environmental and human-rights dimensions that already have an impact on discussions of the Silala/Siloli.[175] However, the customary development of transboundary water law has also had a fitful history.

The Doctrine of International Servitude

Historically, servitudes arose when the territory of one state was made to serve the interests of another state, based on the Roman law theory that the servitude "ran with the land."[176] Owners and all successors in title to the servient land were subject to its burdens, while owners and successors of the dominant land could claim its benefits.[177] Established authorities first located customary authority in the doctrine of international servitude, which created special titles established not by right but by use.[178] However, this doctrine has been described as "warped" by historical treatments, first in the private law of the Romans, then in the quasi-autonomous but semifeudal *jus publicum* of the sixteenth and seventeenth centuries, and then with the maturation of the *jus gentium* in the eighteenth century.[179] The doctrine entered the twentieth century "sadly shattered,"[180] construed more as a moral obligation than a legal classification.[181] However, it bears clear association with the common-law doctrine of easement and with

---

173. Irina Zodrow, *International Aspects of Water Law Reforms, in* WATER LAW FOR THE TWENTY-FIRST CENTURY: NATIONAL AND INTERNATIONAL ASPECTS OF WATER LAW REFORM IN INDIA 36, 37 (Philippe Cullet et al. eds., 2010).

174. *See id.* at 43–57 (adding environmental, economic, human rights, conflict, and governance dimensions).

175. *See id.*

176. PETER MALANCZUK, AKEHURST'S MODERN INTRODUCTION TO INTERNATIONAL LAW 158–59 (7th rev. ed. 1997) (citing in part Ulrich Fastenrath, *Servitudes,* 10 ENCYCLOPEDIA OF PUBLIC INTERNATIONAL LAW 389–92 [R. Bernhardt ed., 1987]).

177. *Id.* at 159.

178. *See* J. L. KLUBER, 1 DROIT DES GENS MODERNE DE L'ERUOPE §§ 139, 218–19 (1819) (applying principles of strict construction to its establishment); A. G. HEFFTER, LE DROIT INTERNATIONAL PUBLIC DE L'EUROPE §§ 43, 98–102 (J. Bergson trans., 1857) (noting servitude's derivation from immemorial usage); and JOHANN CASPAR BLUNTSCHLI, LE DROIT INTERNATIONAL CODIFIÉ 212 (1895) (noting *"[l]es servitutes juris gentium, ou servitudes internationals, n'existent jamais de plein droit; il faut toujours qu'elles soient constituée par acte special"*).

179. Pitman B. Potter, *The Doctrine of Servitudes in International Law,* 9 AM. J. INT'L L. 627, 627 (1915).

180. *Id.*

181. *See id.* at 631 (attributing servitude's decomposition of legal status to incongruities between natural and conventional expressions of servitude).

right of way, notwithstanding criticisms of servitude's status as an anachronism.[182]

A servitude created obligations to minimize invasion or injury.[183] In riparian law it developed into the obligation of every country to receive (as the servient) streams that naturally flow into it from other (dominant) countries.[184] The servient could not obstruct the flow or cause the water to back up over the border from which it came.[185] Dominant countries also had servient obligations, because they could not alter the watercourse or direct its egress haphazardly (or intentionally) elsewhere onto the territory of the servient. Servitudes developed as "essentially negative" and passive obligations; they worked to restrain and refrain jurisdictional acts.[186] History records a progressive and more formalized movement in the law toward recognition of hydrological interconnectedness,[187] but competing theories brought into conflict principles of sovereignty and state responsibility.

The Absolute View: The Harmon Doctrine

In 1895 United States attorney general Judson Harmon articulated an absolute theory of sovereignty over international rivers.[188] His opinion,

182. On the general and close relationship between easements and servitudes, see EMORY WASHBURN, A TREATISE ON THE AMERICAN LAW OF EASEMENTS AND SERVITUDES 5 (3d ed. 1873) (noting indiscriminate usages of the terms at common law but generally applying easements to rights enjoyed and servitudes to burdens imposed). *See also* MALANCZUK, *supra* note 176, at 159 (noting that "many writers criticize [the] use [of servitudes] in international law, on the grounds that so-called international servitudes are not subjects to the same rules as servitudes in Roman law").

183. Ulrich Fastenrath, *Servitudes*, 10 ENCYCLOPEDIA OF PUBLIC INTERNATIONAL LAW 389–92 (1987).

184. *See generally* HEFFTER, *supra* note 178, §§ 43, 98 ("*Elles portent le nom de servitudes publiques naturelles [servitutes juris gentium necessariae]. Au nombre de ces servitudes naturelles on comprend, par exemple, l'obligation de recevoir lex equx qui déoulent naturellement d'un territoire limitrophe.*").

185. *See* ROBERT PHILLIMORE, COMMENTARIES UPON INTERNATIONAL LAW 389 (3d ed. 1879) ("Thus a state is bound to receive the waters which *naturally* flow within its boundaries from a conterminous state. This obligation belongs to the class of '*servitutes* juris gentium *naturales*.'").

186. Potter, *supra* note 179, at 628–29.

187. *See* CHRISTINA LEB, COOPERATION IN THE LAW OF TRANSBOUNDARY WATER RESOURCES 42 (2013) (discussing the historical evolution over hydrologic interconnectedness).

188. *See* written opinion of Judson Hudson, *Treaty of Guadalupe Hidalgo—International Law, in* 21 Official Opinions of the Attorney-General of the United States Advising the President and Heads of Departments in relation to their Official Duties 274–83 (E. C. Brandenburg ed., 1898) [hereinafter Harmon Doctrine].

known eponymously as the Harmon Doctrine, grew from a dispute with Mexico over "a great many" irrigation trenches dug by Colorado and New Mexico farmers on the upper Rio Grande and its affluents.[189] A crisis ensued for 20,000 Mexican border inhabitants around El Paso del Norte in 1894 when the river ran dry.[190] Mexican authorities claimed violation of the governing treaty, the 1848 Treaty of Guadalupe Hidalgo,[191] which prohibited "any work that may impede or interrupt, in whole or in part, the exercise of" navigation rights.[192] Harmon replied that the operative provision of the treaty governed only navigation rights on the river "free and common to the navigation of both countries," and not the upper, nonnavigable tributaries "far above the head of navigation."[193] According to Harmon, Mexico was complaining about a remote and indirect diminution of the servitude but dressing up the complaint as a deprivation of a prior enjoyment.[194] Harmon opined: "The fact that there is not enough water in the Rio Grande for the use of the inhabitants of both countries for irrigation purposes does not give Mexico the right to subject the United States to the burden of arresting its development."[195]

The Harmon Doctrine, labeled "perhaps the most notorious theory in all of international natural resources law," [196] would have allowed a complete diversion of use for an upper riparian under the theory that "[t]he jurisdiction of the nation within its own territory, is necessarily exclusive and absolute; it is susceptible of no limitation, not imposed by

---

189. *Id.* at 276.

190. See David J. Lazerwitz, *The Flow of International Water Law: The International Law Commission's Law of the Non-Navigational Uses of International Watercourses*, 1 IND. J. GLOBAL L. STUD. 247, 250 (1993) (discussing Harmon's view of riparian disputes as political, not legal).

191. Treaty of Peace, Friendship, Limits, and Settlement Between the United States of America and the United Mexican States Concluded at Guadalupe Hidalgo, Mex.-U.S., Feb. 2, 1848, *available at* http://www.loc.gov/rr/hispanic/ghtreaty/

192. *See* Harmon Doctrine, *supra* note 188, at 277 (referencing the treaty's key provision, art. VII).

193. *Id.* at 277–78 (specifically noting these headwaters were "wholly within the United States").

194. *See id.* at 280–81.

195. *Id.* at 274. *See also id.* at 281 ("So it is evident that what is really contended for is a servitude which makes the lower country dominant and subjects the upper country to the burden of arresting its development and denying to its inhabitants the use of a provision which nature has supplied entirely within its own territory.").

196. Stephen C. McCaffrey, *The Harmon Doctrine One Hundred Years Later: Buried, Not Praised*, 36 NATURAL RESOURCES J. 965, 965 (1996) (discussing the Harmon Doctrine and concluding that the United States never construed it as part of international law).

itself."[197] A countertheory—the theory of absolute territorial integrity—presented mirror-image advantage to the lower riparian, which awarded "a right of veto to downstream states" over any interruption of a river's natural flow.[198] The Harmon Doctrine was so questionable that the United States never put it into practice,[199] and its mirror image, despite some minimal support in practice and among publicists, never took hold either.[200] A finding that the waters of the Silala/Siloli constitute a river would put Bolivia in the difficult position of defending the statist and discredited Harmon Doctrine. A Chilean defense of the absolute territorial integrity argument would be equally anachronistic. The trend of general international law has moved away from absolutist standards and toward negotiated solutions.

The Restrictive Theory of Prior Rights

Theories of riparian uses of waterways sometime depended on the establishment of prior rights, which presented a restrictive theory of allocation that neutralized the upstream or downstream position of the riparian by basing entitlement on first user.[201] Water-use practices in the United States tended to embrace prior appropriation standards.[202] This practice was uniform throughout the American West with the development of mining camps,[203] and subordinated junior appropriators to the superior as measured by the first-in-time rule.[204] James Kent (1763–1847), in his *Commentar-*

197. 21 Official Opinions of the Attorney-General of the United States Advising the President and Heads of Departments in relation to their Official Duties 281–82 (E. C. Brandenburg ed., 1898).

198. NAHID ISLAM, THE LAW OF NON-NAVIGATIONAL USES OF INTERNATIONAL WATERCOURSES: OPTIONS FOR REGIONAL REGIME-BUILDING IN ASIA 106 (2010); *see, e.g.*, Gabčíkovo-Nagymaros Project (Hung./Slovk.), Judgment, 1997 I.C.J. 7 (Sept. 25) (argument of Hungary vis-à-vis Slovakia).

199. McCaffrey, *supra* note 196, at 965. The United States and Mexico negotiated by treaty a solution in 1906. *See* Convention between the United States and Mexico Concerning the Equitable Distribution of Waters of the Rio Grande for Irrigation Purposes, Mex.–U.S., May 21, 1906, *available at* http://www.ibwc.state.gov/files/1906conv.pdf

200. ISLAM, *supra* note 198, at 106.

201. *See* Lazerwitz, *supra* note 190, at 250 (discussing the restrictive principle of prior allocation).

202. *See* A. Dan Tarlock, *The Future of Prior Appropriation in the New West*, 41 NAT. RES. J. 769, 769 (2001) (calling it "the primary institution for the development and use of" water in the West).

203. *See* Charles F. Wilkinson, *Aldo Leopold and Western Water Law: Thinking Perpendicular to the Prior Appropriation Doctrine*, 24 LAND & WATER L. REV. 1, 6 (1989) (discussing the origins of prior appropriation and the water needs of mining camps).

204. *See* Richard C. Ausness, *Water Use Permits in a Riparian State: Problems and Proposals*,

ies, contemplated a collision between prior-use and absolute-sovereignty standards, hewing to a qualified middle line by the 1830s:

> No proprietor has a right to use [running waters] to the prejudice of other proprietors, above or below him, unless he has a prior right to divert it, or a title to some exclusive enjoyment;" . . . "the law requires of the party, by or over whose land a stream passes, is, that he should use the water in a reasonable manner, and so as not to destroy, or render useless, or materially diminish, or affect the application of the water by the proprietors below on the stream. He must not shut the gates of his dams and detain the water unreasonably, or let it off in unusual quantities, to the annoyance of his neighbor.[205]

In the early twentieth century, the prior appropriation standard ceded influence to third-party and public interests involving unused waters.[206] International arbitral practice also reinforced this juridical movement toward a middle ground with repudiations of the absolute standard. In the *Trail Smelter Arbitration* (1941), the Tribunal found that "no State has the right to use or permit the use of its territory in such a manner as to cause injury . . . in or to the territory of another." [207] In the *Island of Palmas Case* (1928), a "corollary" to territorial sovereignty imposed the duty "to protect within the territory the rights of other states."[208] And in the *Lac Lanoux Arbitration* (1957),[209] which most directly dealt with transboundary freshwater resources,[210] territorial sovereignty imparted a presumption: it must bend before all international obligations, whatever their source, but only for such obligations.[211]

---

66 KY. L. J. 191, 194 (1977–1978) (distinguishing prior appropriation in the western United States from riparianism in most of the eastern United States); *see also* World Water Forum, *Water in the U.S. American West: 150 Years of Adaptive Strategies* 15 (March 2012) (discussing the customary evolution the American West's "first in time, first in right" prior appropriation rule).

205. JAMES KENT, 3 COMMENTARIES ON AMERICAN LAW 439–40 (3d ed. 1836).

206. Tarlock, *supra* note 202, at 770.

207. *See* Trail Smelter Case (U.S. v. Can.), 3 R.I.A.A. 1905–82 (1941) ("[N]o State has the right to use or permit the use of its territory in such a manner as to cause injury . . . in or to the territory of another.").

208. Island of Palmas Case (Neth. v. U.S.), 2 R.I.A.A. 829 (1928) (holding that the principle of territorial sovereignty contained as a corollary the duty "to protect within the territory the rights of other states").

209. Affaire du Lac Lanoux (Fr. v. Spain), 12 R.I.A.A. 281–317 (1957).

210. *See* LEB, *supra* note 187, at 46 (noting the transboundary freshwater implications of this case).

211. Affaire du Lac Lanoux, *supra* note 209, at 301 ("La souveraineté territorial joue

General international law derived from this award the duty of riparian states of an international watercourse to conduct in good faith consultations and negotiations aimed at peaceful settlement.[212] The period marked a transition in riparian law from the classical constructions of a statist view to the more contemporary period denoted by cooperation, coordination, and community participation.[213] As the Tribunal recognized in the *Lac Lanoux Arbitration*, "states are today perfectly conscious of the importance of the conflicting interests . . . and of the necessity to reconcile them by mutual concessions."[214]

Rise of Equitable Use and Mutual Accord: A Community of Interest?

International organizations and soft law associations played a "central role" in the development of freshwater law.[215] The 1992 Dublin Statement on Water and Sustainable Development established a participatory approach and efficient and equitable use as important components of two of its four guiding principles.[216] The emphasis on mutual accord was noted by the International Law Association (ILA), a body of experts constituted to study, clarify, and develop public and private international law.[217] In 1966, it undertook a study of the customary international law of transboundary water resources,[218] and ultimately it produced the Hel-

---

à la manière d'une présomption. Elle doit fléchir devant toutes les obligations internationals, quelle qu'en soit la source, mais elle ne fléchit que devant ells.").

212. J. G. LAMMERS, POLLUTION OF INTERNATIONAL WATERCOURSES: A SEARCH FOR SUBSTANTIVE RULES AND PRINCIPLES OF LAW 517 (1984). *Cf.* NICO SCHRIJVER, SOVEREIGNTY OVER NATURAL RESOURCES: BALANCING RIGHTS AND DUTIES 238 (1997) (noting the obligation to provide information and to consult in planning and carrying out the project).

213. ISLAM, *supra* note 198, at 100 (2010).

214. Affaire du Lac Lanoux, *supra* note 209, at 308 ("*En realité, les Etats ont aujourd'hui parfaitement conscience de l'importance des intérêts contradictoires, que met en cause l'utilisation industrielle des fleuves internationaux, et de la nécessité de les concilier les uns avec les autres par des concessions mutuelles.*").

215. *See* Zodrow, *supra* note 173, at 40.

216. *See* Principle 2 and Principle 4, Dublin Statement on Water and Sustainable Development, International Conference on Water and the Environment, 31 January 1992, *available at* http://www.wmo.int/pages/prog/hwrp/documents/english/icwedece.html#p2 (recommending that water development and management should be based on a participatory approach and that water should be recognized as an economic good and managed to achieve efficient and equitable use). The two other guiding principles of the Dublin Statement involved the central role of women as providers and users of water (Principle 3) and the recognition of water as an economic good (Principle 4). *Id.*

217. *See generally* INTERNATIONAL LAW ASSOCIATION, http://www.ila-hq.org/index.cfm

218. *See* Dellapenna, *supra* note 7, at 273. Earlier twentieth-century attempts to codify this law included the Institute of International Law's Madrid Resolution on International

sinki Rules on the Uses of the Waters of International Rivers.[219] The ILA's Helsinki Rules treated international drainage basins as indivisible hydrologic units—incorporating "the phrase 'equitable utilization' to express the rule of restricted sovereignty as applied to fresh waters."[220] These characterizations reduced distinctions between legal regimes of groundwater and surface water, suggesting that the standard of equitable utilization should apply to surface and subsurface sources straddling borders.[221] The application of the same legal standard made sense because such ground and surface waters represented the same body of water "moving in differing stages of the hydrologic cycle, and what is today one will tomorrow be the other."[222] The principle was incorporated into the International Law Commission's (ILC) draft articles on transboundary aquifers.[223]

Regulations Regarding the Use of International Watercourses for Purposes Other than Navigation (1911) and its Salzburg Resolution on Utilization of Non-Maritime International Waters (Except for Navigation) (1961), but the Helsinki Rules was the most substantively ambitious and covered uses other than those related to navigation. *See* Stephen C. McCaffrey, *The Codification of Universal Norms: A Means to Promote Cooperation and Equity?*, *in* INTERNATIONAL LAW AND FRESHWATER: THE MULTIPLE CHALLENGES 125, 127 (Laurence Boisson de Chazournes et al. eds., 2013).

219. *See generally* The Helsinki Rules, *supra* note 132 (presenting general rules applicable to the use of the waters of an international drainage basin except as may be provided otherwise by convention, agreement, or binding custom).

220. Dellapenna, *supra* note 7, at 273.

221. *See id.* at 274.

222. *Id.* at 274; *see also* Helsinki Rules arts. X and XIII, cmts, *supra* note 132 (commenting on the community-of-interests standard attaching to equitable utilization of international drainage basins and equal rights relating to navigable rivers). The ILC draft articles have influenced a number of cooperative agreements, including the Agreement on the Cooperation for the Sustainable Development of the Mekong River Basin, 5 April 1995, *available at* http://www.mrcmekong.org/assets/Publications/policies/agreement-Apr95.pdf; the Treaty Between His Majesty's Government of Nepal and the Government of India Concerning the Integrated Development of the Mahakali Barrage Including Sarada Barrage, Tanakpur Barrage and Pancheshwar Project, 12 February1996, *available at* http://www.internationalwaterlaw.org/documents/regionaldocs/Mahakali_Treaty-1996.pdf; the Treaty between the Government of the Republic of India and the Government of the People's Republic of Bangladesh on Sharing of the Ganga/Ganges Waters at Farakka, 12 December 1996, *available at* http://www.ssvk.org/koshi/reports/treaty_on_farakka_india_bangladesh_4_ganga_river_water.pdf; the 1994 Agreement between the Government of the People's Republic of China and the Government of Mongolia on the Protection and Utilization of Transboundary Waters, 29 April, 1994, *available at* http://faolex.fao.org/cgi-bin/faolex.exe?rec_id=012938&database=FAOLEX&search_type=link&table=result&lang=eng&format_name=@ERALL; and the Agreement between Syria and Lebanon for the sharing of the Great Southern River basin waters and the building of a joint dam on it, 20 April 2002, *available at* http://faolex.fao.org/cgi-bin/faolex.exe?rec_id=027944&database=faolex&search_type=link&table=result&lang=eng&format_name=@ERALL

223. *See* Int'l Law Commission, Draft Articles on the Law of Transboundary Aquifers,

The movement toward a more unified understanding of groundwater and surface water first developed from transboundary surface water concerns, but those concerns soon focused attention on varying uses of surface water. The hallmark case setting this movement into motion was the *River Oder Case* (1929).[224] Here, the Permanent Court of International Justice (PCIJ) introduced a "new approach" to navigable international watercourses by acknowledging the legal partnership that such watercourses formed between riparians. That partnership required cooperation[225] and the application of an equitable principle, the community of interest standard.[226] This standard optimized economic uses of an entire river basin while limiting a state's sovereignty by imposing reciprocal limitations on the sovereignty of other states sharing the same basin.[227] The PCIJ concluded that this community of interest "becomes the basis of a common legal right, the essential features of which are the perfect equality of all riparian States in the use of the whole course of the river and the exclusion of any preferential privilege of any one riparian State in relation to the others."[228]

By 1933, the Montevideo Declaration reflected this standard of equality by establishing the principle of prior notice to other interested states regarding plans to harness or alter the use of an international river "which may prove injurious."[229] The PCIJ extended this idea of recipro-

---

art. 4 (2008) *available at* http://legal.un.org/ilc/texts/instruments/english/draft_articles/8_5_2008.pdf. For a history of the ILC's involvement with transboundary aquifers, see generally Chusei Yamada, *Codification of the Law of Transboundary Aquifers (Groundwaters) by the United Nations*, 36 WATER INTERNATIONAL 557–65 (2011).

224. Territorial Jurisdiction of the International Commission of the River Oder (U.K. v. Pol.), Judgment, 1929 P.C.I.J. (ser. A) No. 23, at 5 (Sept. 10) [hereinafter River Oder Case]; *see also* EDUARDO JIMENEZ DE ARECHAGA, II CURSO DE DERECHO INTERNACIONAL PÚBLICO 494–95 (1961) (discussing the River Oder Case and its formal consecration of the community of interests [*comunidad de derechos*] standard).

225. *See* LEB, *supra* note 187, at 53 (noting that the community of interest standard evokes the necessity of cooperation).

226. Lilian del Castillo-Laborde, *Case Law on International Watercourses, in* THE EVOLUTION OF THE LAW AND POLITICS OF WATER, 319–20 (Joseph W. Dellapenna & Joyeeta Gupta eds., 2008).

227. *See* Habtamu Alebachew, *International Legal Perspectives on the Utilization of Transboundary Rivers: The Case of the Ethiopian Renaissance (Nile) Dam*, in WATER AND THE LAW: TOWARDS SUSTAINABILITY 66, 76–77 (Michael Kidd et al. eds., 2014).

228. River Oder Case, 1929 P.C.I.J. (ser. A) No. 23, at 27.

229. *See* Declaration of the Seventh International Conference on the Industrial and Agricultural Use of International Rivers, art. 2, adopted at Montevideo on Dec. 24, 1933, *in* 28 AM. J. INT'L L., SUPP. 59–60 (1934). For commentary, see LAMMERS, *supra* note 212, at 291 ("By making the utilization of the waters dependent on the consent of the other riparian States . . . the Declaration . . . actually confers a veto right on those other States and hence must be deemed to embody the principle of absolute territorial integrity.").

cal responsibility to a circumstance involving alteration of the flow of international watercourses in the famous case *Diversion of Water from the River Meuse* (1937).[230] Notwithstanding an 1863 treaty that permanently regulated the Meuse River's flow through Belgium and its debouching in the Netherlands,[231] both countries subsequently and unilaterally modified the treaty's terms by constructing canals that altered the river's flow.[232] The Netherlands sought injunctive relief from Belgium's actions, but the Court sidestepped its claim[233] (and Belgium's counterclaim that the Netherlands' prior actions forced Belgium's hand[234]), holding that neither party had violated the objects and purposes of the 1863 treaty.[235] Instead, it applied the principle of equality, which resulted in a future and negotiated settlement between the parties.[236] In his famous individual opinion,[237] Judge Manley O. Hudson addressed more forthrightly what the equitable understanding of equality implies: "[W]here two parties have assumed an identical or a reciprocal obligation, one party which is engaged in a continuing non-performance of that obligation should not be permitted to take advantage of a similar non-performance of that obligation by the other party."[238] Hudson's individual opinion essentially recalled the Roman law maxim that both parties had violated the "clean hands" doctrine (*inadimplenti non est adimplendum*; he who fails to fulfill his part of an agreement cannot enforce that bargain against the other party).[239]

The disputants might pause to reflect on the *Meuse Case* and on Judge

230. The Diversion of the Water from the Meuse, P.C.I.J. (ser. A/B) No. 70, at 4.

231. Traité du 12 Mai 1863 Portant Règlement du Régimes des Prises d'eau à la Meuse, 1937 P.C.I.J. (ser. C) No. 81, at 15–18 (June 28), *available at* http://www.icj-cij.org/pcij/serie_C/C_81/C81_03_Prises_d_eau_a_la_Meuse_Pieces_procedure_ecrite.pdf

232. The Netherlands claimed Belgium's construction of the Albert Canal violated the treaty; Belgium counterclaimed that the Netherlands had done the same with the construction of the Juliana Canal and Borgharen barrage. *See* Diversion of the Water from the Meuse, 1937 P.C.I.J. (ser. A/B) No. 70, at 5, 14.

233. *Id.* at 32.

234. *See id.*

235. *See id.* at 23.

236. *See* del Castillo-Laborde, *supra* note 226, at 323.

237. *See* The Diversion of Water from the Meuse, 1937 P.C.I.J. (ser.A/B) No. 70, at 73–80 (J. Hudson, individual opinion) (developing, inter alia, the principle of equity and its relation to the sources of international law).

238. *Id.* at 77 (J. Hudson, individual opinion)

239. L.F.E. Goldie, *Equity and the International Management of Transboundary Resources*, 25 NAT. RESOURCES J. 665, 668 (1985); *see also* CHRISTOPHER R. ROSSI, EQUITY AND INTERNATIONAL LAW: A LEGAL REALIST APPROACH TO INTERNATIONAL DECISIONMAKING 161 (1993) (discussing the offensiveness of one party benefitting from its own illegal action and the *inadimplenti non est adimplendum* principle's close association with the *ex injuria jus non oritur* principle).

Hudson's much-discussed individual opinion. Although it is clear that, except for their purported embrace of customary law, Bolivia and Chile have not assumed reciprocal obligations, this finding may change if they are found to share an aquifer or a river. As a measure of judicial decision-making, however, the penchant of the ICJ to impose a condition of equality between the parties, and to require a mutually negotiated equitable accord, should not be overlooked. This penchant is particularly relevant when the parties' mutual behaviors involve actions motivated by ceremonial discord or pretext.

The status of the community of interest standard in general international law remains a subject of dispute.[240] Doctrinal treatments vary regarding conclusions about its maturation into a workable principle,[241] as opposed to an aspirational norm.[242] Its treatment in case law is strengthening, but also marked by notable ambivalence. For example, in the Central American dispute called the *Gulf of Fonseca Case* (1992), the ICJ Chamber concluded that the existence of a community of interest among Honduras, El Salvador, and Nicaragua was "not open to doubt" with regard to sovereignty over the waters of the Gulf of Fonseca.[243] The Chamber deemed a condominium or shared sovereignty arrangement involving Fonseca's waters "almost an ideal juridical embodiment of the community of interest's requirement of perfect equality of user."[244] How-

---

240. *See supra* notes 234–36.

241. *See* BELA VITÁNYI, THE INTERNATIONAL REGIME OF RIVER NAVIGATION 56 (1980) (affirming the historical legal status of the "community of riparians" standard from the 1815 Act of the Congress of Vienna); LAMMERS, *supra* note 212, at 506 (affirming the community of interest standard from a review of the practice of states dating to the Congress of Vienna); *see also* Wouters, *"Dynamic Cooperation," supra* note 172, at 62–65 (discussing the emergence of dynamic cooperation as a norm of integrated water resource management).

242. STEPHEN C. MCCAFFREY, THE LAW OF INTERNATIONAL WATERCOURSES: NON-NAVIGATIONAL USES, 167–71 (2001) (noting that a community of interest falls far short of co-ownership in the absence of an agreement making it so); A. TANZI & M. ARCARI, THE UNITED NATIONS CONVENTION ON THE LAW OF INTERNATIONAL WATERCOURSES: A FRAMEWORK FOR SHARING 21 (2001) (amplifying the voluntary nature of the community of interest); Lucius Caflisch, *Règles générales du droit des cours d'eaux internationaux,* 219 RECUEIL DES COURS 9, 59–61 (1989) (*"Mais les régimes dont il s'agit, s'ils vont relativement loin dans les limitations dont ils assortissent la souveraineté territorial des Etats, n'ont pas une force d'intégration suffisante pour transformer les cours d'eau don't ils'agit et leurs ressources naturalles en un 'patrimoine commun' des Etats concernés, avec tout ce que ce concept peut comporter."*); *see* LEB, *supra* note 187, at 56 (concluding that the status of the community of interest standard as a distinct legal theory remains to be seen).

243. Land, Island and Maritime Frontier Dispute (El Sal./Hond.: Nicar. intervening), Judgment, 1992 I.C.J. 351, ¶ 407 (Sept. 11) [hereinafter Gulf of Fonseca Case].

244. *Id.*

ever, the Chamber's conclusion that the Gulf of Fonseca constituted an historic bay[245]—indeed, an enclosed "pluri-State historic bay"—shared by the three littorals and not subject to delimitation[246] proved problematic. Not only did the dissent question the idea of a pluri-state bay, claiming it was as a legal invention,[247] but Honduras was in enough doubt of the standard to claim it *required* a delimitation of the waters,[248] precisely the opposite application that the Chamber asserted.

The standard gained prominence in the ICJ's decision in the *Pulp Mills Case* (2010), where the Court held that a treaty-based commission (*CARU: Comisión Administradora del Río Uruguay*/Administrative Commission of the River Uruguay) "established a real community of interests and rights in the management of the River Uruguay and in the protection of its environment."[249] The limited application of the community of interest standard nevertheless mandated that the commission "devise the necessary means to promote the equitable utilization of the river."[250] As held in the *Gabčíkovo-Nagymaros Project Case* (1997), the unilateral diversion of a shared resource would deprive the other riparian of "its right to an equitable and reasonable share of the natural resource" and violate respect for proportionality (as implied by equality), "which is required by international law."[251]

Although not in effect at the time, the Court took notice of the Watercourses Convention, which it claimed strengthened the development of the community of interest standard for nonnavigational uses.[252] The community of interest standard and the principle of equitable utilization have been incorporated into the Cooperative Framework Agreement of

---

245. *Id.* ¶ 432.

246. *Id.* ¶¶ 395, 412.

247. Gulf of Fonseca Case, 1992 I.C.J. 351, 733, ¶¶ 2, 24 (J. Oda, dissenting opinion) (arguing that a historic pluri-state bay has "*no* existence as a *legal* institution" and that "there did not and still does not (or, even cannot) exist any such legal concept as a 'pluri-State bay'").

248. *See id.* ¶ 372 ("Honduras argues that within the Gulf there is a community of interests which . . . necessitates a judicial delimitation."); *id.* ¶ 408 (noting Honduras's argument that a community of interest standard is not the same as a "*communauté de patrimoines*, in the waters").

249. Pulp Mills on the River Uruguay (Arg. v. Uru.), Judgment, 2010 I.C.J. 14, ¶ 281 (Apr. 20).

250. *Id.* ¶ 266. Specifically, Uruguay was found to have breached its procedural obligations. *See id.* ¶ 282.

251. Gabčíkova-Nagymaros Project (Hung. v. Slovk.), Judgment, 1997 I.C.J. 7, ¶ 851 (Sept. 25).

252. *Id.*

the 1999 Nile Basin Initiative,[253] but the references also generated disputes regarding water security and current uses.[254] Other references can be found in the 2002 Senegal River Water Charter[255] and the 2003 Protocol for Sustainable Development Lake Victoria Basin.[256] Within the Southern African Development Community (SADC), the community of interest standard was included in the 1995 Protocol on Shared Water Course Systems in the SADC Region, but later retracted.[257] Canvassing the development of the international law on watercourses, Lucius Caflisch cast doubt on the establishment of an integral theory, arguing that a set of principles more equitable but less simple and certain seems to now operate.[258]

However, in the Atacama region, an integral application may apply in the case involving the Silala/Siloli waters. Chile's confrontational initiation of proceedings against Bolivia presents interesting avenues for the ICJ to pursue, and possibly upsetting outcomes for the parties should integrationist perspectives of customary freshwater law prevail. Although much discussion about the establishment of a community of interest derives from a specific conventional foundation, the ICJ Chamber noted in the *Gulf of Fonseca Case* that an earlier court, the Central American Court of Justice, had located a community of interest among Honduras, El Salvador, and Nicaragua (which was "not open to doubt") within the imperial and uninterrupted 300-year administrative rule of Spanish vice-

---

253. *See* Agreement on the Nile River Basin Cooperative Framework, art. 3(4), (9) *opened for signature* May 14, 2010, *available at* http://www.nilebasin.org/images/docs/CFA%20-%20English%20%20FrenchVersion.pdf. Ethiopia, Tanzania, Uganda, and Rwanda signed the agreement on May 14, 2010, joined later by Kenya and Burundi. *See* Salman M. A. Salman, *The Nile Basin Cooperative Framework Agreement: A Peacefully Unfolding African Spring?* 38 WATER INT'L 17, 20–21 (2013).

254. Mwangi S. Kimenyi & John Mukum Mbaku, *The Limits of the New "Nile Agreement,"* BROOKINGS (Apr. 28, 2015), *available at* https://www.brookings.edu/blog/africa-in-focus/2015/04/28/the-limits-of-the-new-nile-agreement/ (noting opposition principally from Egypt and Sudan).

255. *See* Organisation pour la Mise en Valeur Du Fleuve Sénégal, Charte des Eaux du Fleuve Sénégal, pmbl., May 28, 2002, O.M.V.S., *available at* http://lafrique.free.fr/traites/omvs_200205.pdf (referencing *la communauté des intérêts entre les Etats riverains du Fleuve Sénégal*) [Senegal River Water Charter].

256. *See* Protocol for Sustainable Development of Lake Victoria Basin, art. 4(2)(k), November 29, 2003, *available at* http://www.internationalwaterlaw.org/documents/regionaldocs/Lake_Victoria_Basin_2003.pdf (affirming the community of interests as a guiding principle in the management of the resources of the basin).

257. LEB, *supra* note 187, at 55.

258. *See* Lucius Caflisch, *The Law of International Watercourses: Achievements and Challenges, in* INTERNATIONAL LAW AND FRESHWATER: THE MULTIPLE CHALLENGES 24 (Laurence Boisson de Chazournes et al. eds., 2013).

royaties.[259] That same system created the viceroyalty of Perú, which contained both Bolivia (known as Alto Perú) and Chile.[260] Interestingly, the Chamber extended the community of interest standard in the *Gulf of Fonseca Case* to cover a condominium arrangement,[261] which essentially mandated that the coparceners cohabitate the space and craft through negotiated undertakings a managerial system. The rationale proffered by the Chamber clearly preferenced a pragmatic solution. Divisions of "narrow waters" and historic bays "into separate and unqualified sovereignties" present "great practical difficulties,"[262] as might the division of rivers and aquifers.

However, returning to the Atacama dispute, the Goffmanian drama between Bolivia and Chile raises concerns about the practical difficulties associated with a negotiated settlement. The most obvious difficulty is the broader play-within-this-play to negotiate a settlement—the parties' willingness to continue their verbalisms staged to refight the War of the Pacific.

Conclusion

Pragmatic considerations of codependency mark the evolving customary and conventional law on fresh water. Yet difficulties associated with this case relate to poorly understood *effectivités* relating to the basin itself. Customary and conventional application of international water law depends on whether the Silala/Siloli conforms to the common evidence of a transboundary watercourse. The canalization of the flow represents either an adulteration of its natural course that does not cross the boundary (Bolivia's argument), which remains unaffected by any incidental runoff through marginally or undefined channels, or the augmentation of a natural servitude that preexisted the Bolivian-Chilean border across which it now flows (Chile's argument). Either argument is plausible but may give way to the emerging possibility that the hydrological basin commingles groundwater and surface water-regimes, much as the human geography and *ayllus* have historically done.

Evidence of intermittent flow adds to the complexity, but might be

---

259. Gulf of Fonseca Case (El Sal./Hond.: Nicar. Intervening), Judgment, 1992 I.C.J. 351, ¶ 407 (Sept. 11).

260. ST. JOHN, BOUNDARIES, TRADE, AND SEAPORTS: POWER POLITICS IN THE ATACAMA DESERT 1.

261. Gulf of Fonseca Case, 1992 I.C.J. 351, ¶ 418.

262. *Id.* ¶ 407.

better understood by consulting the scientific studies in the region.[263] Moreover, the possibility of one (or more[264]) transboundary aquifer(s) further complicate(s) legal analysis. Transboundary aquifers have been largely ignored in terms of legal significance and are increasingly the "source of friction among overlying riparians."[265] Geological and hydrological evidence suggests that the waters flowed before canalization, and substantially enough to carve alluvial erosion patterns on the terrain—indicating a natural riparian condition. The increasingly understood relationship between groundwater and surface water systems suggests a need for a more holistic treatment of watercourse systems, as reflected in emerging state practice and by recognition of the disconnect between water science and water law.

The above observations notwithstanding, both countries have forestalled efforts to shine more scientific light onto the hydrological relationship between the underground and surface systems, because their Goffmanian penchant is not to resolve the dispute at all, but rather to use it as a ceremonial profanation to emboss each other's national and domestic narratives of victimization. Their entrenched emotivism has propelled them toward litigation without first having secured factual assurances of what hydrological *effectivités* await scientific investigation. Ceding sovereign interests over the waters, from Bolivia's perspective, would tacitly affirm Chile's consolidation of power over the Atacama and its littoral. Recognizing wholly or in part Bolivia's claims, from Chile's perspective, would animate demands for damages and injunctive relief, and give Bolivia a bargaining chip to use toward its consuming interest in reestablishing itself as a coastal state. Chile's water privatization policy and cooptation of use by mining concerns may prompt additional water-security, pollution, and human rights concerns regardless of the outcome.[266]

---

263. The surfacing of underground water, depositing in its eventual retreat a thick crust of mineral and salt, is an obvious feature of the Atacama, contributing to the San Pedro de Atacama region's nomination as a UNESCO World Heritage site. *See* Convention Concerning the Protection of the World Cultural and Natural Heritage, Nov. 16, 1972, *available at* http://whc.unesco.org/archive/convention-en.pdf; UNESCO World Heritage Convention Description, San Pedro de Atacama, *available at* http://whc.unesco.org/en/tentativelists/1191/

264. *See* Marshall, *¿Por qué el Silala está en disputa?*, *supra* note 48 (noting cartographic information presented at the 4th World Water Forum [2006] identifying possibly two aquifers side by side)

265. Eckstein, *supra* note 42, at 574.

266. *See generally* Inga Winkler, *The Human Right to Sanitation*, 37 U. PA. J. INT'L L. 1331–1406 (2016); Sharmila L. Murthy, *The Human Right(s) to Water and Sanitation: History,*

International rivers can be catalytic agents of cooperation on multiple riparian levels; they may also enable integration and pragmatic "cross-border cooperation beyond the river."[267] However, "international rivers, without exception, create some degree of tension among the societies that they bind."[268] The parties have sought recourse to international law as a construct of ceremonial profanation—a pretext for legal vandalism that instantiates vilification of the other for domestic political purposes. International law exists to facilitate peaceful settlement of disputes.[269] However, if Bolivia and Chile expect a judgment that quiets title to these waters, they should expect a solution that squarely burdens them to end their voluble symbolic interactions and parochial displays of legal vandalism. The solution to this case will probably involve the elusive but evolving transboundary requirement of an equitable and negotiated settlement, as opposed to a world-weary casting call to restage, yet again, the War of the Pacific.

Meaning, and the Controversy over Privatization, 31 BERKELEY J. INT'L L. 89–147 (2013) (addressing privatization of sanitation services in Bolivia and Chile).

267. Claudia Sadoff & David Grey, *Beyond the River: The Benefits of Cooperation on International Rivers*, 4 WATER POLICY 389, 399 (2002).

268. *Id.* at 391.

269. *See* J. G. Collier, *The International Court of Justice and the Peaceful Settlement of Disputes*, *in* FIFTY YEARS OF THE INTERNATIONAL COURT OF JUSTICE 364, 364 (Vaughan Lowe & Malgosia Fitzmaurice eds., 1996) ("[T]he pacific settlement of disputes is the function of the [I.C.J.].").

SIX

Lithium

Gigantic salt flats spread across the high altitude *puna* of the Atacama Desert.[1] They intersperse bunch grass and vegetation patterns stretching to the gorge valleys and *precordillera* of the Andes Mountains. Beneath them rest huge deposits of lithium, a metal of immense importance to medicine,[2] industry,[3] the information age,[4] and increasingly, electric and hybrid vehicles.[5] A triangular region of the Atacama overlaying the borderlands of Chile, Argentina, and Bolivia contains the world's largest and

1. Geographers struggle to define the parameters of the Atacama Desert, sometimes differentiating subregions of lower elevation coastal desert, generally devoid of vegetation, from higher-elevation, less-barren *puna* stretches. *Puna* are sometimes differentiated from *pampa*, which are "fairly flat interior lands" and may, as in Argentina, support grasslands. RICHARD V. FRANCAVIGLIA, IMAGINING THE ATACAMA DESERT: A FIVE-HUNDRED-YEAR JOURNEY OF DISCOVERY 15 (2018). Francaviglia noted "that even today there is not complete agreement on what the term Atacama Desert signifies": "just an array of perceptions that have varied through time." *Id.* 19–20. Geographer Isaiah Bowman's classic account of the region, DESERT TRAILS OF ATACAMA (1924), borrowed from the American Geographical Society's six-sheet map series to locate the region between 18° and 28° south latitude (approximately from Tacna, Perú, to Copiapó, Chile) to 64° meridian west. *Id.* at 10 (including northern Chile, northwestern Argentina, and southwestern Bolivia).

2. *See generally* Michael Bauer, *70 Years of Research and 50 Years of Lithium Clinics: From Serendipity to Gold Standard in Mood Disorders*, 51 PHARMACOPSYCHIATRY 173 (2018) (noting lithium's many clinical uses as the "aspirin of psychiatry").

3. *See, e.g.*, *Lithium: What Role Is Tesla Playing in the Demand for This Precious Metal? The Ultimate Guide*, COMMODITY.COM, https://commodity.com/precious-metals/lithium/ (charting demand for lithium's multiple industrial uses) (last updated Aug. 16, 2019).

4. *See, e.g.*, Amit Katwala, *The Explosive Race to Totally Reinvent the Smartphone Battery*, WIRED (July 30, 2018), https://www.wired.co.uk/article/smartphone-battery-life-lithium-ion-future (noting the portable electronic information industry dependence on lithium-ion batteries).

5. *See generally* Xin Fang & Huisheng Peng, *A Revolution in Electrodes: Recent Progress in Rechargeable Lithium-Sulfur Batteries*, 11 SMALL 1488 (2014) (on progress in lithium-sulfur rechargeable battery technology involving electric vehicles and portable devices).

highest-quality proven reserves.[6] This region—the Lithium Triangle—includes Chile's *Salinas de Pedernales, Maricunga,* and *Atacama;* Argentina's *Salinas de Olaroz, Guayatayoc, Cauchari,* and *Salinas Grandes*; and Bolivia's *Salar de Uyuni.* Bolivia's *Salar de Uyuni* alone, at an elevation of 3,656 meters (11,995 feet), contains 50 to 70 percent of the world's lithium reserves.[7] These projections translate to nine million tons of untapped lithium reserves in Bolivia, with Argentina and Chile harboring over eight million tons[8] [see fig. 5].

Lithium production in the salt flats of the Atacama will probably soon surge,[9] with demand increasing by perhaps 650 percent by 2027.[10] But at what cost? To date, the global market remains tightly controlled, because only an oligopolistic handful of concessionaires engage in lithium production in the triangle.[11] Australia presents the only other formidable

---

6. Dennis Nguyen, *The White Gold Rush: A Battle for Supremacy in the Lithium Triangle*, ECONOMIST (June 15, 2017), https://www.economist.com/the-americas/2017/06/15/a-battle-for-supremacy-in-the-lithium-triangle [hereinafter Nguyen, *The White Gold Rush*].

7. *Lithium Mining in Bolivia*, LITHIUMMINE.COM (2018), http://www.lithiummine.com/lithium-mining-in-bolivia

8. Talib Visram, *Why Chile Is Leading South America in Lithium Production*, CNN BUSINESS (Aug. 15, 2018), https://money.cnn.com/2018/08/15/news/world/lithium-chile-bolivia/index.html; Maximiliano Proaño, *Lithium in Bolivia: Beyond Extractivism*, GLOBAL ENERGIEWENDE (Jan. 22, 2019), https://energytransition.org/2019/01/bolivia-beyond-extractivism/

9. *See* William Wilkes, *Surging Demand for Lithium Spurs Interest in European Mines*, WALL ST. J. (Apr. 13, 2018) (charting the global demand for lithium carbonate and estimating the lithium-ion battery market to surpass $90 billion by 2025); Axel Anlauf, *¿Secar la tierra para sacar litio? Conflictos socio-ambientales en la minería del litio*, *in* ABC DEL LITIO SUDAMERICANO: SOBERANÍA, AMBIENTE, TECNOLOGÍA E INDUSTRIA 171 (Federico Nacif & Miguel Lacabana eds., 2015) ("*Grandes expectativas están asociadas con la minería del litio en Sudamérica ya que se proyecta una demanda creciente por la industria electronica y automotriz.*").

10. Proaño, *supra* note 8.

11. Principal concessionaires include Chile's state enterprise, SQM (*Sociedad Química y Minera de Chile S.A.*), the US conglomerates Albemarle and FMC Corporation, and China's Tiangi. *See Chasing Lithium in Bolivia, Argentina and Chile*, FLEETEUROPE (June 25, 2018), https://www.fleeteurope.com/en/technology-and-innovation/global/features/chasing-lithium-bolivia-argentina-and-chile. Bolivia's state-run company, YLB (*Yacimientos de Litios Bolivianos*), formed in 2017, produces merely 10 tons per month, while Chile and Argentina produce 70,000 and 30,000 tons per year, respectively. Alexandra Alper, *Bolivia Seeks Investors to Power Up Lagging Lithium Output*, REUTERS (Dec. 27, 2017), https://www.reuters.com/article/us-bolivia-lithium-analysis/bolivia-seeks-investors-to-power-up-lagging-lithium-output-idUSKBN1EL1JB. In December 2018, YLB announced a joint venture with ACI Systems, a privately owned German company, to develop lithium production in the Uyuni salt flat. *See* Michael Nienaber, *Germany Secures Access to Vast Lithium Deposit in Bolivia*, REUTERS (Dec. 12, 2018), https://www.reuters.com/article/us-germany-bolivia-lithium/germany-secures-access-to-vast-lithium-deposit-in-bolivia-idUSKBN1OB206

challenge to South American lithium production. In its thinly populated western Pilbara region, home for centuries to Aborigines, mining operations already produce more than half of the world's lithium, and production is ramping up.[12] However, the Atacama Desert has a unique comparative advantage.

Lithium is derived from pulverizing pegmatites rich in the mineral,[13] or by leaching the mineral from mined chloride salts through a saturation and evaporation process employing brine pools.[14] Crushing stone to obtain lithium, as is done in Australia, is more costly than obtaining concentrated supplies through the natural, evaporative process cheaply available in the hyper-arid Atacama Desert.[15] Like most if not all mining operations, however, lithium extraction comes with a high ecological price. It uses water intensively.[16] Mining operations, generally, can use in one day what a family would use in twenty-two years.[17] These operations prefer to access surface freshwater. Groundwater exploitation requires costly deep-well drilling, which often captures water too saline for direct application.[18] The effects of more than 650 mining operations in the Atacama region, especially around Calama and other areas east of

---

12. *See* Darren Gray, *Australia Tipped to Soon Produce More than Half of the World's Lithium*, SUNDAY MORNING HERALD (Apr. 29, 2018), https://www.smh.com.au/business/companies/australia-tipped-to-soon-produce-more-than-half-of-the-world-s-lithium-20180427-p4zc5h.html (noting Pilbara Minerals' Pilgangoora mine, one of the world's leading lithium production and processing plants).

13. Pegmatites are coarse-grained igneous rocks of mineralogical composition. *See Pegmatite*, SANDATLAS, https://www.sandatlas.org/pegmatite/ (last visited Sept. 27, 2018).

14. *See* Pratima Meshram et al., *Extraction of Lithium from Primary and Secondary Sources by Pre-Treatment, Leaching and Separation: A Comprehensive Review*, 150 HYDROMETALLURY 192, 193 (2014), at 193. Saline groundwater enriched in dissolved lithium, pumped to the surface and stored in closed basins (artificial ponds), concentrates with evaporation, and within months to a year, yields lithium carbonate and lithium metal.

15. *See* Jonathan Gilbert, *Argentina Is Set to Become a Lithium Superpower, But There's One Big Problem*, FINANCIAL POST (Dec. 28, 2017), https://business.financialpost.com/commodities/mining/argentina-is-set-on-becoming-a-lithium-superpower-but-theres-one-big-problem (noting the more cost-effective means of extracting lithium though evaporation).

16. *See Lithium Mining and Environmental Impact*, LITHIUMMINECOM (2018), http://www.lithiummine.com/lithium-mining-and-environmental-impact

17. John Vidal, *As Water Scarcity Deepens Across Latin America, Political Instability Grows*, THE GUARDIAN (Mar. 1, 2107), https://www.theguardian.com/global-development-professionals-network/2017/mar/01/water-scarcity-latin-america-political-instability (quoting Universidad San Francisco de Quito/Amherst College professor Manuela Picq).

18. Jessica Budds, *Water Rights, Mining and Indigenous Groups in Chile's Atacama*, in OUT OF THE MAINSTREAM 204 (Rutgerd Boelens et al. eds., 2010) (noting as well that Chile's Chuquicamata open-pit copper mine in the Atacama requires twelve cubic meters of water per second).

Antofagasta, have severely taxed the surface and groundwater supply, drying it up as far north the Atacama's Loa River before it reaches the sea. The result has been severe, depopulating Atacameño villages and fostering territorial disputes among indigenous and mining communities, "especially over the lithium-rich brine that makes up 40 percent of the world's production."[19]

Securing water rights to support mining operations in the Lithium Triangle focuses on the same state policies that historically have given preference to economic interests over humanistic visions of topophilia[20] and alternative forms of sovereignty promoted as indigenous autonomy.[21] Although the continent of South America holds the world's largest supply of freshwater outside Antarctica, allocation and infrastructure issues beset water access and quality;[22] water privatization policies have resulted in concentrated ownership among industrialists and transnational corporations. Neoliberal policy prescriptions sought to remedy flawed, statist policies of import substitution. As a "politically guided intensification of market rule and commodification," they gained prominence in the 1980s,[23] and contributed to consolidated water holdings until recent constitutional changes began to instantiate greater governmental control over water issues.[24] However, a continental movement away from neoliberalism's embedded appeal to market self-regulation

---

19. Alonso Barros, *Water Justice, Mining, and the Fetish Form of Law in the Atacama Desert*, *in* A SENSE OF JUSTICE: LEGAL KNOWLEDGE AND LIVED EXPERIENCE IN LATIN AMERICA 170, 173 (Sandra Brunnegger & Karen Ann Faulk eds., 2016).

20. *See* YI-FU TUAN, TOPOPHILIA: A STUDY OF ENVIRONMENTAL PERCEPTION, ATTITUDES AND VALUES 4 (1990) (1974) (defining topophilia as "the affective bond between people and place or setting"); PATRICIA URTEAGA & RUTGERD BOELENS EDS., DERECHOS COLECTIVOS Y POLÍTICAS HÍDRICAS EN LA REGION ANDINA (Patricia Urteaga & Rutgerd Boelens eds., 2006) (on challenges to local populations and hydric resources of Andean water-management schemes).

21. *See generally* Nancy Postero & Nicole Fabricant, *Indigenous Sovereignty and the New Developmentalism in Plurinational Bolivia*, 19 ANTHROPOLOGICAL THEORY 95–119 (2019) (on the promotion across Latin America of indigenous visions of self-governance within multiple meanings of sovereignty).

22. *Brazil, Colombia and Peru Are Among the Countries of the World with the Most Water*, WORLD BANK (Mar. 10, 2015), http://www.worldbank.org/en/news/feature/2015/03/10/brasil-colombia-peru-paises-mas-agua-tienen-en-el-mundo (noting Latin America has the world's largest supply of fresh water).

23. Neil Brenner et al., *Variegated Neoliberalization: Geographies, Modalities, Pathways*, 10 GLOBAL NETWORKS 182, 184 (2010).

24. *See* Leila M. Harris & María Cecilia Roa-García, *Recent Waves of Water Governance: Constitutional Reform and Resistance to Neoliberalization in Latin America (1990–2012)*, 50 GEOFORUM 20, 20 (2013) (noting constitutional and water-governance shifts in Uruguay, Ecuador, Bolivia, and Colombia).

remains a "considerable challenge,"[25] considering neoliberalism's migration into Latin American landscapes of civil society and cultural rights.[26]

Neoliberalism's migration into cultural discourse has been controversial. Walter Benn Michaels has argued that neoliberalism's interplay with the globalized economy has blunted criticism, redescribing economic and structural inequality as compatible cultural differences.[27] In Latin America, neoliberalism's cross-cutting consequence has affirmed a limited degree of indigenous cultural rights and the rhetoric of multiculturalism while simultaneously supporting wholesale economic marginalization.[28]

Neoliberalism's water privatization effects have been profound. In Ecuador, for instance, the wealthiest 1 percent owns approximately 64 percent of the country's fresh water,[29] an extreme mark of concentrated ownership that has sparked confrontations in Ecuador and similar protests across the continent.[30] In 1996, Argentine provincial authorities in Tucumán province unilaterally rescinded a French concession contract securing water privatization efforts due to massive rate hikes, quality issues, and ensuing social unrest.[31] The dispute created the longest-running arbitration of its time for the International Center for Settle-

25. *Id.* at 25.

26. Charles R. Hale, *Neoliberal Multiculturalism: The Remaking of Cultural Rights and Racial Dominance in Central America*, 28 POL. & LEGAL. ANTHROPOLOGY REV. 10 (2005) (discussing neoliberalism's unexpected effects beyond economic reforms).

27. *See* WALTER BENN MICHAELS, THE TROUBLE WITH DIVERSITY: HOW WE LEARNED TO LOVE IDENTITY AND IGNORE INEQUALITY 144, 161–62 (2006).

28. *See* Hale, *supra* note 26, at 10–28.

29. *See* Vidal, *supra* note 17 (quoting Universidad San Francisco de Quito/Amherst College professor Manuela Picq).

30. *See* Kimberly Brown, *Ecuador's Indigenous March Over 600km to Demand an End to Mining*, AL JAZEERA (Nov. 14, 2018), https://www.aljazeera.com/news/2018/11/ecuador-indigenous-march-600km-demand-mining-181115011033618.html (on protests against mining encroachments and indigenous territory). *See generally* OUT OF THE MAINSTREAM: WATER RIGHTS, POLITICS AND IDENTITY (Rutgerg Boelens et al. eds., 2010) (examining multiscale struggles on redistribution of water in South America); Robert Glennon, *Water Scarcity, Marketing, and Privatization*, 83 TEX. L. REV. 1873, 1890 (2005) (noting widespread continental water demonstrations).

31. The dispute resulted in a tortured series of arbitrations beginning in December 1996 and ending in August 2010 involving the Aguas del Aconquija concession. It included two annulment decisions, an award of damages totaling $105 million plus interest, and multiple challenges to the integrity to the arbitral proceedings. *See* Compañía de Aguas del Aconquija S.A. y Vivendi Universal S.A. c. La República Argentina (Caso CIADI No. ARB/97/3 [Aug. 10, 2010]), https://www.italaw.com/sites/default/files/case-documents/ita0222.pdf. For a synopsis of the case and its history, see Lise Johnson & Fiona Marshall, *Vivendi v. Argentina*, INVESTMENT TREATY NEWS (Oct. 18, 2018), https://www.iisd.org/itn/2018/10/18/vivendi-v-argentina/

ment of Investment Disputes (ICSID) tribunal.[32] Persistent protests in Argentina's dry region of La Rioja periodically erupt over the protection of mountain streams from mining encroachment.[33] In 2018, indigenous communities of the *Salinas Grandes* in Jujuy province protested lithium mining's threat to livelihood and water supply—concerns that Amnesty International concluded went unheard by Argentina's government.[34] The Mapuche, Chile's largest indigenous population, contest hydroelectric damming of the San Pedro River Valley,[35] a sacred domain identified as an energy source in Chile's Energy 2050 national initiative.[36] Tens of thousands of protesters in Cochabamba, Bolivia, organized against a transnational consortium's privatization of the city's water services in 2000, launching Bolivian president Evo Morales's national political career and "the first large-scale rejection of water privatization in Latin

---

32. *See* Malissa Khumprakob, *The Vivendi-Argentina Water Dispute: ICSID Creates New Arbitration Tribunal to Hear the Longest Running Case on its Docket*, 5 SUSTAINABLE DEV. L. & POL. 68 (2005).

33. *See* Marcela Valente, *Environment-Argentina: Scarce Water Threatened by Gold Mine*, IPS (Aug. 25, 2008), http://www.ipsnews.net/2008/08/environment-argentina-scarce-water-threatened-by-gold-mine/; Jorge Daniel Taillant, *Argentine Police Fire at Peaceful Protesters Against Mining Operations*, CHRE (Oct. 16, 2015), http:/center-hre.org/argentine-police-fire-at-peaceful-protesters-against-mining-operations/

34. *See Argentina: Amnesty International Calls on President Macri to Address Key Human Rights Issues*, AMNESTY INT'L (Apr. 12, 2018), https://www.amnesty.org/en/latest/news/2018/04/argentina-amnistia-internacional-pide-al-presidente-macri-que-aborde-cuestiones-clave-de-derechos-humanos/ (on Secretary General Salil Shetty's visit to the Atacama).

35. Heather Brady, *Native Community Fights to Defend Their Sacred River from Dam*, NAT. GEO. (July 27, 2018), https://www.nationalgeographic.com/culture/2018/07/sacred-san-pedro-river-dam-mapuche-chile/. Hydroelectric development in the 1990s of another sacred Mapuche waterway, the 240-mile Biobío River, Chile's second longest, resulted in dislocations of Mapuche and Pehuenche populations, who had inhabited adjacent ancestral lands for centuries. Animating indigenous concerns are outstanding promises of remuneration yet to be fulfilled. Max Radwin, *Chile's Mapuche-Pehuenche: 10 Years After Relocation*, AL JAZEERA (Jan. 31, 2016) https://www.aljazeera.com/indepth/features/2016/01/chile-mapuche-pehuenche-10-years-relocation-160127111719637.html; Gerardo Azócar et al, *Conflicts for Control of Mapuche-Pehuenche Land and Natural Resources in the Biobío Highlands*, Chile, 4 J. LAT. AM. GEO. 57 (2005) (noting the nonprotection of indigenous rights in view of Chilean governmental land-ownership policies).

36. *See Energía 2050*, POLÍTICA ENERGÉTICA DE CHILE, MINISTERIO DE ENERGÍA 2050 (2016), http://www.energia2050.cl/en/; Jens Benöhr & Patrick J. Lynch, *Should Rivers Have Rights? A Growing Movement Says It's About Time*, YALE ENV'T 360 (Aug. 14, 2018), https://e360.yale.edu/features/should-rivers-have-rights-a-growing-movement-says-its-about-time. For an involved history of conflicts between the Mapuche and the Chilean state, see DIANE HAUGHNEY, NEOLIBERAL ECONOMICS, DEMOCRATIC TRANSITION, AND MAPUCHE DEMANDS FOR RIGHTS IN CHILE (2006).

America."[37] The ICJ is currently adjudicating a dispute between Chile and Bolivia over an Atacama watercourse that debouches into the Pacific Ocean.[38] Water grabs, privatized wetland enclosures, and watercourse diversions to fuel agribusiness and energy demands regularly feed these continent-wide confrontations.[39] The nascent turn toward lithium production in the Atacama already adds to these water privatization tensions. It will increasingly challenge the adequacy of national schemes to confront the coming water crises[40] and reinforce water and sanitation access issues as international human rights concerns.[41]

As much as coming questions about water management frame the general and regional history of international law in the Americas, neoliberalism's codependent relationship with international law itself should also be a focus. Neoliberalism's interaction with international law in Latin America, wide-ranging as it has been, informs the development of national schemes and in important historical ways conditions policy prescriptions and orientations toward international law. A subtext of rivalry involving Argentina, Bolivia, and Chile[42] presents generally divergent yet

---

37. Madeline Baer, *The Global Water Crisis, Privatization, and the Bolivian Water War, in* WATER, PLACE, & EQUITY 195, 195 (John M. Whiteley et al. eds., 2008).

38. Dispute over the Status and Use of the Waters of the Silala (Chile v. Bolivia), Application Instituting Proceedings, filed June 6, 2016, https://www.icj-cij.org/files/case-related/162/162-20160606-APP-01-00-EN.pdf. *See generally* Christopher R. Rossi, *The Transboundary Dispute Over the Waters of the Silala/Siloli: Legal Vandalism and Goffmanian Metaphor*, 53 STAN. J. INT'L L. 55 (2017) (discussing the question of whether the water of the Silala/Siloli forms a natural transboundary watercourse that flows from Bolivia to Chile as a servitude, or an adulterated canalization and water theft by Chile of water that would normally spring from and pool exclusively in Bolivia).

39. *See* Alejandro Camargo, *The Water Grab That Powers Predatory Development*, NACLA (Dec. 4, 2014), https://nacla.org/blog/2014/12/04/water-grab-powers-predatory-development (highlighting water-grabbing tensions in Latin America).

40. *See* Dave Sherwood & Fabian Cambero, *In Chilean Desert, Global Thirst for Lithium Is Fueling a "Water War,"* CHANNEL NEWSASIA (Aug. 29, 2018), https://www.channelnewsasia.com/news/asia/in-chilean-desert—global-thirst-for-lithium-is-fuelling-a—water-war—10664366 (noting increasing demands for water by local indigenous groups, regional mining companies and newcomers to the region).

41. *See* Sara Larrain, *Human Rights and Market Rules in Chile's Water Conflicts: A Call for Structural Changes in Water Policy*, 5 ENV'T JUST. 82, 82–83 (2012) (noting that progressive concentration of water ownership in Chile has undermined human rights and has "resulted in serious water access problems"). The problem is worldwide. In 2015, 663 million people (80 percent from rural areas) lacked basic access to safe water. *See* PAUL HUTCHINGS ET AL., COMMUNITY MANAGEMENT OF RURAL WATER SUPPLY: CASE STUDIES OF SUCCESS FROM INDIA 8 (2017) (referencing WHO and UNICEF).

42. *See, e.g.*, Leslie Wehner, *From Rivalry to Mutual Trust: The Othering Process Between Bolivia and Chile*, GIGA WORKING PAPER No. 135 (May 2010) (noting Bolivia's and Chile's mutual construction of the other as a threat); KRISTINA MANI, DEMOCRATIZATION AND MILITARY TRANSFORMATION IN ARGENTINA AND CHILE: RETHINKING RIVALRY 2 (2011) (noting

occasionally convergent extraction pathways, which contribute to regional conflict and competition[43] while exposing disparate approaches to international law. Nevertheless, all three countries envision lithium extraction as a central avenue for development.[44]

Most natural resources in Chile and Argentina are privately owned. However, the two countries view lithium as a strategic resource subject to both state regulation and robust exploitation.[45] Bolivia's government asserts state ownership over all natural resources,[46] and views extraction measures with greater circumspection than do Chile and Argentina.[47]

---

a long history of more than two dozen unresolved territorial disputes between Argentina and Chile and the Beagle Channel conflict that brought the countries to the brink of war in 1978); CARLOS A. PARODI, THE POLITICS OF SOUTH AMERICAN BOUNDARIES 17–21 (2002) (surveying boundary conflicts, *inter alia*, between Argentina/Chile, and Bolivia/Chile).

43. Competition over natural gas accentuates this point. Bolivian gas exports to heavily-dependent Brazil and Argentina create dependencies that lead each country to search for diversification and alternatives. All of Bolivia's natural gas exports go to Brazil and Argentina; simmering enmity with neighboring Chile over a border dispute stemming from Bolivia's massive defeat in the War of the Pacific (1879–1884) prevents diplomatic and economic relations with Chile. *See South America and the Energy Merry-Go-Round*, STRATFOR WORLDVIEW (Sept. 28, 2017), https://worldview.stratfor.com/article/south-america-and-energy-merry-go-round. Bolivia has pursued greater Chilean port access at Arica, Chile (as opposed to the much smaller port of Ilo, Peru), for purposes of worldwide distribution, a negotiation point well understood by Chile. Brazil has signaled an end to its state-owned oil company's (Petrobras) monopoly over Bolivian gas imports to stimulate private energy distributorships in Brazil. Chile and Argentina have opened talks about establishing natural gas swaps to circumvent Bolivia's unreliable winter deliveries, while Argentina and Brazil discuss investment and partnerships with Bolivia to harness Bolivia's underdeveloped electricity sector. *See Old Rivalries Still Simmer Between Bolivia and Chile*, STRATFOR WORLDVIEW (July 24, 2017), https://worldview.stratfor.com/article/old-rivalries-still-simmer-between-bolivia-and-chile

44. *See* Lorenzo Pellegrini, *Imaginaries of Development through Extraction: The "History of Bolivian Petroleum" and the Present View of the Future*, 90 GEOFORUM 130, 139 (2018) (noting models of development through extraction "in the same vein" in Chile, Argentina, Bolivia [and Mexico]).

45. *See* Javiera Barandiarán, *Lithium and Development Imaginaries in Chile, Argentina and Bolivia*, 113 WORLD DEV. 381, 381 (2018) (noting some similarities in Argentina's and Chile's lithium policies vis-à-vis Bolivia). *See also* Pia Marchegiani et al., *Indigenous Peoples' Rights to Natural Resources in Argentina: The Challenges of Impact Assessment, Consent and Fair and Equitable Benefit-Sharing in Cases of Lithium Mining* 4 (Benelex Working Paper No. 19, 2018) (noting Argentina's 2011 declaration of lithium as a strategic national resource in line with provincial and federal authority).

46. Specifically, Bolivia's state-owned enterprise, Corporación Miner de Bolivia (Coimbol) currently manages Bolivia's eighteen mining projects, including lithium exploration in the Uyuni salt flat. *See Lithium Supply in Bolivia*, LITHIUM TODAY (2017), http://lithium.today/lithium-supply-by-countries/lithium-supply-bolivia/

47. *See* Clayton Mendonça Cunha Filho & Rodrigo Santaella Gonçalves, *The National Development Plan as a Political Economic Strategy in Evo Morales's Bolivia: Accomplishments and Limitations*, 37 L. AM. PERSPECTIVES 177, 183–84 (2010) (noting Bolivia's circumspect

This circumspection reflects Bolivia's geographic station[48] and "moral landscape," which incorporates "a social terrain pregnant with cultural meanings and social imaginaries;"[49] it also affects Bolivia's standing in the Lithium Triangle.

In 2017, a Bolivian pilot project in the *Salar de Uyuni* produced 250 tons of lithium, "less than two percent of Chilean production."[50] Bolivia's extraction policy conflicts with stakeholder positions, adding complexity and uncertainty to future actions.[51] Bolivia's state enterprise, Yacimientos de Litio Bolivianos (YLB), signed a concession agreement for lithium extraction with a German company (ACI) in December 2018.[52] The agreement attempts to shore up skeptical investor confidence, given Bolivia's reputation as a difficult place to do business.[53] Previous conces-

---

embrace of the neo-developmentalist framework based on the Morales administration's 2007 National Development Plan, which asserts state control over strategic sectors and makes the state "the protagonist in development"). For a comparative analysis of state regulations regarding extractive industries, see FOREIGN INVESTMENT IN SOUTH AMERICA: A COMPREHENSIVE GUIDE TO INFRASTRUCTURE AND THE LEGAL ENVIRONMENT (Ricardo Barreto Ferreira da Silva & Paulo Marcos Rodrigues Brancher eds., 2018).

48. *See* Carlos D. Mesa Gisbert, *Bolivia: autonomías y pluralism politico: Un modelo condicionado por el horizonte indígena, in* DESCENTRALIZACIÓN Y DEMOCRATIZACIÓN EN BOLIVIA: LA HISTORIA DEL ESTADO DÉBIL, LA SOCIEDAD REBELLED Y EL ANHELO DE DEMOCRACIA 43, 47 (Moira Zuazo et al. eds., 2012) ("*Los problemas de frontera traducidos en varias guerras internacionales y la imposibilidad de mantener la heredad con la que nacimos en 1825, demostraron la gran dificultad del ejericico de su soberanía geográfica y demográfica efectivas.*"). *See also* WALTRAUD Q. MORALES, A BRIEF HISTORY OF BOLIVIA xxxi (2d ed. 2010) (noting the country's "inward-looking orientation" due to its history and landlocked geography).

49. Anna C. Revette, *This Time It's Different: Lithium Extraction, Cultural Politics and Development in Bolivia*, 38 THIRD WORLD Q. 149, 150 (2017).

50. Proaño, *supra* note 8.

51. *See* Barandiarán, *supra* note 45, at 382.

52. *Germany Shores Up Lithium Supply with Landmark Bolivia Deal*, DW (Dec. 12, 2018), https://www.dw.com/cda/en/germany-shores-up-lithium-supply-with-landmark-bolivia-deal/a-46708512

53. Bolivia's treatment of foreign capital is governed by Investment Promotion *Ley* N° 516. Net foreign investment inflows to Bolivia declined from over $1 billion USD in the 1990s to −$223 million in 2005, "with investors leaving the country for fear of renationalizations." After a period of reinvestment, Bolivian president Morales renationalized major industries such as oil and gas, energy, mining, and telecommunications, and in 2007 Bolivia withdrew from the ISCSID, claiming it was biased toward investors. *See Opening the Door to Foreign Investment? An Analysis of Bolivia's New Investment Promotion Law*, INV. TREATY NEWS (Aug. 11, 2014), https://www.iisd.org/itn/2014/08/11/opening-the-door-to-foreign-investment-an-analysis-of-bolivias-new-investment-promotion-law/. Chile's legal framework (*Ley* N° 20,848/2015) promotes foreign investment and is "usually perceived as one of the main causes for Chile's economic stability and growth." FERREIRA DA SILVA & RODRIGUES BRANCHER *supra* note 47, at 173. Argentina's foreign investment law (*Ley* N° 21,382) "[a]s a general rule . . . provides for equal treatment for local and foreign investments." *Id.* at 7.

sion negotiations with Japanese conglomerates Mitsubishi and Sumitomo, South Korea's Posco company, and France's Eramet enterprise produced stillborn results.[54] Posco and Eramet, frustrated by Bolivia's strictures, moved their operations to Argentina.[55] The Japanese concerns noted the ease with which they could follow suit.[56]

The unfolding prospect of a white gold rush for lithium raises longstanding historical tensions dating from the colonial period. It implicates conflicting national narratives over Atacama territory between Bolivia and Chile that began as early as 1836.[57] The conflict ultimately resulted in the War of the Pacific while also provoking contested claims between Chile and Argentina over large portions of Patagonia.[58] It displays miscible remnants of patrimonialism and *caudillismo*, which personalize informal sources of power in Latin America and complicate market reforms.[59] It harbors racial shadings connected to Argentina's Iberian heritage, and the homogeneity of Chilean elites in relation to Chile's own and to Bolivia's mestizo and indigenous populations.[60] And it reflects elements of the "resource curse" thesis, where suspicions of global engagement within resource-rich countries provoke insularity, inculcate a rentier mentality, impede cross-sector development, and benefit vested interests.[61]

---

54. *See* Laura Millan Lombrana, *Bolivia's Almost Impossible Lithium Dream*, BLOOMBERG (Dec. 3, 2018), https://www.bloomberg.com/news/features/2018-12-03/bolivia-s-almost-impossible-lithium-dream (on failed Japanese and South Korean negotiations); *Lithium Supply in Bolivia*, *supra* note 46 (on failed South Korean and French negotiations).

55. *See Lithium Supply in Bolivia*, *supra* note 46.

56. Rebecca Hollender & Jim Shultz, BOLIVIA AND ITS LITHIUM: CAN THE "GOLD OF THE 21st CENTURY" HELP LIFT A NATION OUT OF POVERTY? 22 (2010) (noting that Japanese executives "made it clear that Bolivia is not the only game in town").

57. Internal opposition to the Peru-Bolivian Confederation created in 1836 resulted in major territorial disputes and armed conflict over ownership of the Atacama Desert in 1841. *See* ST. JOHN, THE BOLIVIA-CHILE-PERU DISPUTE IN THE ATACAMA DESERT 3.

58. Jerónimo Ríos Sierra, *La compleja relación de Perú, Bolivia y Chile, una herencia de la Guerra del Pacífico*, ESGLOBAL (Oct. 3, 2018), https://www.esglobal.org/la-compleja-relacion-de-peru-bolivia-y-chile-una-herencia-de-la-guerra-del-pacifico/

59. *See* Judith Teichman, *Merging the Modern and the Traditional: Market Reform in Chile and Argentina*, 37 COMP. POL. 23, 23–24 (2004) (discussing distinct features of Latin American history).

60. *See* Nancy Postero et al., *Introduction: The Politics of Identity in Neoliberal Chile*, 13 L. AM. & CARIB. ETHNIC STUD. 203, 204 (2018) (noting Chile's much smaller population of indigenous people and Chile's "pervasive ethnocentric belief in national homogeneity that deems the indigenous population as irrelevant or non-existent"). It should be noted that the Bolivian definition of *mestizo* more closely identifies with indigenous heritage and in this sense "differs considerably from the more general meaning of this term for most Latin Americans." HERBERT S. KLEIN, A CONCISE HISTORY OF BOLIVIA x (2d ed. 2011).

61. *See* R. M. Auty, *Industrial Policy, Sectoral Maturation, and Postwar Economic Growth in*

Intermixed in this history is neoliberalism's nuanced interaction with international law. Neoliberalism is a "constitutive element" of national identity politics in Latin America, embraced in Chile,[62] contested in Bolivia,[63] and questioned in Argentina.[64] These receptions express differences in investment policies that combine with indigenous and human rights concerns, and they condition regional orientations toward international law.

Capitalizing lithium extraction in the Atacama sets the competing investment landscapes of Lithium Triangle countries against each other. Technological mining practices demand skilled human capital. Chile and Argentina rank among the top education-nurturers in Latin America; Bolivia ranks near the bottom.[65] The resource-rich bazaar of investment opportunity pressures national schemes to balance production and skilled labor requirements against the allure of neighboring investment environments, in addition to raising myriad human rights considerations. Lithium production poses competing referenda on neoliberalism's approach to resource management and exploitation—variations on themes well recorded in international law's intimate encounter with colonialism.[66]

The interplay of international legal, political, and economic interests

Brazil: The Resource Curse Thesis, 71 ECON. GEO. 257, 258 (1995) (referring to the resource curse as "the process by which a bountiful natural resource endowment proves a handicap to development rather than an blessing").

62. G. Van Der Ree, *Chile's (Inter)National Identities: Framing the Relations with Bolivia and Peru*, 29 BULL. L. AM. RES. 208, 212 (2010).

63. *See* Pía Riggirozzi, *Social Policy in Post-Neo-liberal Latin America: The Cases of Argentina, Venezuela and Bolivia*, 53 DEV. 70, 71 (noting the rejection of the neoliberal governance project in Bolivia [and Argentina] in the early 2000s).

64. Tomás Undurraga, *Neoliberalism in Argentina and Chile: Common Antecedents, Divergent Paths*, 23 REVISTA DE SOCIOLOGIA E POLÍTICA 11, 12 (2015) (noting capitalist commonalities between the neoliberal trajectories of Chile and Argentina and Argentina's severe scrutiny of such policies much earlier than Chile).

65. *See Global Human Capital Report 2017: Preparing People for the Future of Work*, WORLD ECON. F. (2017), at 8, https://www.insidehighered.com/sites/default/server_files/files/WEF_Global_Human_Capital_Report_2017.pdf (ranking Argentina 56th, Chile 65th, and Bolivia 123rd of 130 countries in the "know-how" subindex). Chile, in particular, produced an unusually high number of professionals versed in socioeconomic appraisal of investment projects and capital budgeting. *See* Ernesto R. Fontaine, *Project Evaluation Training and Public Investment in Chile*, 87 AM. ECON. REV. 63, 63 (1997).

66. *See* DAVID HARVEY, NEOLIBERALISM 19 (2005) (interpreting neoliberalism as a *utopian* project of reorganized capitalism or as a *political* project for reinforced capital accumulation); Hans Achterhuis et al., *Water Property Relations and Modern Policy Regimes: Neoliberal Utopia and the Disempowerment of Collective Action*, *in* OUT OF THE MAINSTREAM, 27, 29 (Rutgerd Boelens et al. eds., 2010) (on neoliberalism's utopian dreams and dystopian nightmares).

makes the Lithium Triangle a contested geography for international law, which has informed the development of domestic economic orientations in the region, layering complexity onto resource-management decisions that otherwise would be viewed exclusively and incompletely within domestic frameworks.

This chapter contextualizes these challenges by exploring the near history of resource exploitation, with some unavoidable references to deeper historical problems. Extraction policies create discord among countries that in many ways anticipate a need to create a regional management scheme.[67] These policies drive the double movement of marketization that generates calls for social protection against the very same dialectical forces that drive the process of marketization.[68]

In the Andean Cone, neoliberalism and international law co-constitute as forces, although they play out differently across the region. They have produced *histories* of international legal and economic interaction. These histories complicate consonant extraction policies in the lithium-laced underground of the Atacama's High Desert plains. Indeed, the pursuit of the Atacama's white gold foretells of accelerations in production cycles that already prompt scholars to caution about an even-more-impending conflict to come over blue gold—the catchphrase for diminishing freshwater resources in a water-thirsty world.[69]

One should expect a continuation of international law's complicated encounter with neoliberalism as freshwater scarcity widens into a major

---

67. *See* Danilo José Dalio, *The Vargas Administration and the Proposal of the ABC Pact: The Place of Peronist Argentina in Brazilian Foreign Policy*, 38 CONTEXTO INTERNACIONAL 731 (2016) (reviewing regional integration schemes involving Argentina, Brazil, and Chile dating from 1908 and invigorated in the 1950s); Jorge Heine, *Regional Integration and Political Cooperation in Latin America*, 47 L. AM. RES. REV. 209 (2012) (reviewing literature on fitful attempts to integrate Latin American economies starting with the 1960 Latin American Free Market Association, the 1969 Andean Pact, Mercosur as launched with the 1991 Asunción Treaty, and more).

68. *See generally* KARL POLANYI, THE GREAT TRANSFORMATION (1944) (discussing the full costs of the material achievements of the neoliberal order). Latin American critiques of neoliberalism have rediscovered Polanyi's thesis of the social counterbalances needed to the impaired self-regulation of markets. *See, e.g.*, Geoff Goodwin, *Rethinking the Double Movement: Expanding the Frontiers of Polanyian Analysis in the Global South*, 49 DEV. & CHANGE 1268 (2018); Ronaldo Munck, *Karl Polanyi for Latin America: Markets, Society and Development*, 36 CAN. J. DEV. STUD. 425 (2015); Eduardo Silva, *Exchange Rising? Karl Polanyi and Contentious Politics in Contemporary Latin America*, 54 LAT. AM. POL. & SOC. 1 (2012).

69. *See* MAUDE BARLOW & TONY CLARKE, BLUE GOLD: THE BATTLE AGAINST CORPORATE THEFT OF THE WORLD'S WATER (2017); BRAHMA CHELLANEY, WATER: ASIA'S NEW BATTLEGROUND 1 (2011) (predicting that water scarcity will become Asia's defining crisis by midcentury).

hemispheric conflict.[70] Much of the conversation moves in the direction of postneoliberalism,[71] or neoextractivism—the countervailing left-leaning responses in, for instance, Ecuador under Correa and Moreno, Colombia under Santos, Venezuela under Chávez and Maduro, Argentina under the Kirchners, and until recently, Bolivia under Morales.[72] Our focus here tethers this conversation to international law, expanding it emphasis from the scattered debris fields of international political economy, development economics, and critical social theory. Neoliberalism's structural impress appears as a policy revenant to haunt redemocratized statecraft initiatives that seek to reframe the politics, practices, and history of extraction in the Lithium Triangle.

Competing Perspectives

Lithium production in the Atacama contrasts the unreconciled global engagement policies of rivals, principally Chile and Bolivia, along with Argentina's recent assertive attempts to attract capital inflow to exploit its lithium holdings. Chile's free-market philosophy, informed by waves of Latin American economists and technopols trained in the *laissez faire* approach to economics taught at the University of Chicago and other North American universities,[73] contrasts with *dependencia* theory and the

70. *See* Joseph B. Treaster, *First Take: The Struggle for Clean Drinking Water in Latin America*, REVISTA: HARVARD REV. L. AM. (2013), https://revista.drclas.harvard.edu/book/struggle-clean-drinking-water-latin-america (projecting increasing freshwater scarcity across Latin America due to climate change, poverty, agribusiness, and more).

71. Defined as "an evolving attempt to develop political economies that are attuned to the social responsibilities of the state whilst remaining responsive to the demands of 'positioning' nation economics in a rapidly changing global political economy." Jean Grugel & Pía Riggirozzi, *Post-neoliberalism in Latin America: Rebuilding and Reclaiming the State after Crisis*, 43 DEV. & CHANGE 1, 4 (2012).

72. *See* Liisa L. North & Ricardo Grinspun, *Neo-extractivism and the New Latin American Developmentalism: The Missing Piece of Rural Transformation*, 37 THIRD WORLD Q. 1,482, 1,484 (2016) (noting that the "twenty-first century progressive or left-leaning regimes are in fact pursuing new developmentalist policies"); Alberto Acosta, *Extractivism and Neoextractivism: Two Sides of the Same Curse*, *in* BEYOND DEVELOPMENT: ALTERNATIVE VISIONS FROM LATIN AMERICA 61, 72 (Miriam Lang & Dunia Mokrani eds., 2013) (framing the neoextractivist debate as part of a contemporary version of developmentalism in South America maintained under a new culture and political hybridity); Richard Clayton Doughman, *Might the Keys to Peace Open the Doors to Extractivism? Reflections on Colombia's Post-Conflict Extractive Economy*, *in* HANDBOOK ON RESEARCH ON TRANSITIONAL JUSTICE AND PEACE BUILDING IN TURBULENT REGIONS 444–70 (Fredy Cante & Hartmut Quehl eds., 2015) (discussing the neo-extractivist movement in Colombia and in the Andean Cone).

73. *See* DANIEL YERGIN & JOSEPH STANISLAW, THE COMMANDING HEIGHTS: THE BATTLE BETWEEN GOVERNMENT AND THE MARKETPLACE THAT IS REMAKING THE MODERN WORLD 237 (1998).

indigenous politics embraced by Bolivia under the more circumspect socialist stewardship of its first indigenous president, Juan Evo Morales. Chile's encounter with neoliberalism has had an extraordinary influence on hemispheric international law, on models of domestic resource allocation, and on international economic integration and its legal constructs.

Although interpreted variously in liberal, Marxist, and world systems theories,[74] *dependencia* theory explains problems of economic underdevelopment in terms of external political, economic, and cultural influences on national development policies.[75] Morales's political rhetoric and identity politics aligned him with anti-imperialist class struggle, even though structural practicalities resulted in overt collaborations with agro-export elites.[76] Under Morales, who was overthrown by a combination of forces following contested election results in October 2019, Bolivia rationalized state dominance in economic matters and demoted market rules to government administration, which contrasted markedly with the more free-market orientation of Chile and Argentina. His party, now headed by his former economics minister, Luis Arce, won a landslide electoral victory in 2020, indicating the continuation of Bolivia's profound ideological split beyond the power of Morales's personality. In Argentina, nationalist principles, framed in terms of *Peronismo,* a politically motivated expression of clientelism and traditionalism in reaction to modernity,[77] have long attached to its model of global engagement.[78] Argentina's emerging foreign direct investment policy under conservative president Mauricio Macri represented a substantial deviation from the prior nationalist policies of Cristina Fernández de Kirchner (term of

---

74. Vincent Ferraro, *Dependency Theory: An Introduction, in* THE DEVELOPMENT ECONOMICS READER 58, 59 (Giorgio Secondi ed., 2008) (associating Raul Prebisch, Andre Gunder Frank, and Immanuel Wallerstein with liberal, Marxist, and world systems interpretations of *dependencia* theory, respectively).

75. *See id.* at 59 (quoting Osvaldo Sunkel, National Development Policy and External Dependence in Latin America, 6 J. DEV. STUD. 23 [1969]).

76. Benjamin Kohl & Linda Farthing, *Material Constraints to Popular Imaginaries: The Extractive Economy and Resource Nationalism in Bolivia,* 31 POL. GEO. 31 (2012) (on structural constraints conditioning Bolivia's extractive economy); James Petras, *Evo Morales' Pursuit of "Normal Capitalism,"* 42 ECON & POL. WEEKLY 2155 (2007) (noting multinational dependencies affecting change in Bolivia); Diego Andreucci, *Resources, Regulation and the State: Struggles over Gas Extraction and Passive Revolution in Evo Morales's Bolivia,* 61 POL. GEO. 170 (2017) (on statist and structural constraints on Morales's agenda).

77. *See generally* JAVIER AUYERO, LA POLÍTICA DE LOS POBRES: LAS PRÁCTICAS CLIENTELISTAS DEL PERONISMO (2001) (highlighting, as well, Peronism's popularity among the urban poor).

78. *See* Julio A. Fernández, *The Nationalism Syndrome in Argentina,* 8 J. INTER-AM. STUD. 551–64, 560 (1966) (remarking on the lessons of *Peronismo*).

office: 2007–2015),[79] and it posed an economic threat to nascent Chilean and Bolivian lithium industries.[80] Unlike Chile's, Argentina's encounter with authoritarianism (March 1976–December 1983) produced international humiliation (with the military's defeat by Great Britain in the Falkland/Malvinas Islands War) and economic ruin, and yet its tenure was neither as systemic nor as enduring as Chile's encounter, although it was much more brutal in terms of extrajudicial killings.[81] Argentina's return to democracy shortly thereafter met with periods of hyperinflation (1989–1990) and currency devaluation (2001–2002), which greatly affected confidence in neoliberal reforms,[82] fomenting Argentina's international standing as "supremely enigmatic."[83]

The triangulated interplay of Chicago-style economists, *dependencia* theory, and authoritarianism, each set against a common 300-year colonial heritage, shapes the dynamics of the Lithium Triangle. It creates a substratum of encodings that informs the vocabulary of international law, highlight divergent approaches to resource extraction, and inevitably encounter historical tensions that continue to abridge human factors of geography.

Chile's Economic Transition and "Lost Decade"

Chile's market orientation regarding its natural resources formed under a succession of regimes dating to the 1973 military junta of General Augusto Pinochet (1915–2006), and more recently under the democratic governance of former president Michelle Bachelet (terms of office: 2006–2010, 2014–2018) and most recently president Sebastián Piñera (2018–). Chile's dramatic embrace of free-market principles, ushered in during an eco-

---

79. *See* Nguyen, *The White Gold Rush*, *supra* note 6 (noting the business-unfriendly investment climate in Argentina under Fernández de Kirchner).

80. *See* Laura Millan Lombrana & Jonathan Gilbert, *High Risk–High Reward Lithium Bet Drives Argentina Mining Surge*, BLOOMBERG (Dec. 5, 2018), https://www.bloomberg.com/news/articles/2018-12-05/high-risk-high-reward-lithium-bet-drives-argentina-mining-surge (noting Argentina's promarket agenda under Macri).

81. Between 3,000 and 5,000 Chileans died or disappeared as a result of Chile's period of political repression (1973–1989); the ratio of Chileans tried in military courts to those killed extrajudicially was 1.5:1. Between 20,000 and 30,000 Argentines died or disappeared during Argentina's period of political repression (1976–1983); the ratio of Argentines tried in military courts to those killed extrajudicially was 1:71. ANTHONY W. PEREIRA, POLITICAL (IN)JUSTICE, AUTHORITARIANISM AND THE RULE OF LAW IN BRAZIL, CHILE, AND ARGENTINA 21 (2005).

82. *See* ALEJANDRO GRIMSON & GABRIEL KESSLER, ON ARGENTINA AND THE SOUTHERN CONE: NEOLIBERALISM AND NATIONAL IMAGINATIONS 79 (hyperinflation), 3 (crisis of 2001–2002).

83. MARGUERITE FEITLOWITZ: A LEXICON OF TERROR: ARGENTINA AND THE LEGACIES OF TORTURE 4 (2011).

nomic turn toward "shock therapy" in the 1970s, marked the first attempt to systemically implement neoliberalism's program.[84] It penetrated more deeply, quickly, and thoroughly in Chile than elsewhere in the world.[85] It produced startling yet controversial export-based results, ultimately achieving expression in structural reforms introduced during the 1980s that have been described as an "authentic capitalist revolution."[86] Most dramatically, in 1980 Chile constitutionally construed water rights as an individual right, not as a public good.[87] This revision followed from Pinochet's rejection of the 1967 Agrarian Reform Law.[88] This confirmation of private title to expropriated land in turn necessitated a rejection of statist regulatory controls over water.[89] Chile's authoritarian government then implemented a Water Code in 1981[90] and Mining and Electricity Codes in 1982—both of which gave preference to privatized rights[91] and underscored the commanding importance of agribusiness, energy pursuits, and copper mining in the Atacama Desert.[92] Chile dominates world copper production,[93] which remains Chile's principal source of wealth.[94]

---

84. Postero et al., *supra* note 60, at 208 (calling Chile's "shock doctrine" the "forerunner of neoliberalism").

85. MARCUS TAYLOR, FROM PINOCHET TO THE "THIRD WAY": NEOLIBERALISM AND SOCIAL TRANSFORMATION IN CHILE 1 (2006).

86. Leslie Parraguez Sanchez, "The Chilean Student Movement: A Family Matter. The Intimate and Conflicting Construction of Revolution in a Post Dictatorial Country" 22 (2016) (Dissertation, Loyola University, Chicago, 2016) (citing Ricardo Ffrench-Davis, Javier Martínez & Alvaro Díaz, and Marcus Taylor).

87. *See* Artículo 19, Constitución Política de la República de Chile de 1980, Decreto Ley N° 3.464 [Constitution] Aug. 8, 1980, art 19 (n° 21) (Chile) (granting all persons *El derecho a desarrollar cualquier actividad económica que no sea contraria a la moral, al orden público o a la seguridad nacional, respetando las normas legales que la regulen*). For a comprehensive study on the history of water law in Chile, see generally CARL J. BAUER, SIREN SONG: CHILEAN WATER LAW AS A MODEL FOR INTERNATIONAL REFORM (2004).

88. The 1967 Water Code was repealed in 1979. *See* Budds, *supra* note 18, at 200.

89. *Id.* at 199, 200.

90. Codigo de Aguas, Decreto con Fuerza de Ley 1122, 29 agusto 1981.

91. According to the current 1981 water rights regulation, "ownership and use of water is held and exercised independently of the land where it is located. Water remains in the public domain, but the owners of water rights have an indefinite right that can be freely transferred to third parties." FERREIRA DA SILVA & RODRIGUES BRANCHER, *supra* note 47, at 191.

92. *See* Larrain, *supra* note 41, at 83. The Atacama is home to some of the largest copper mines in the world, including Escondida, Collahuasi, Chuquicamata, and Radomiro Tomic. *See* INTERNATIONAL COPPER STUDY GROUP, WORLD COPPER FACTBOOK 2017, 15 (2017), http://www.icsg.org/index.php/component/jdownloads/finish/170/2462. For a discussion of privatization efforts affecting other sectors, such as agriculture, forestry, fishing, telecommunications, transportation, and government services, see HERNÁN BÜCHI, THE ECONOMIC TRANSFORMATION OF CHILE: A PERSONAL ACCOUNT ch. 4 (2010).

93. *See With Lithium Demand Rising, Chile Reins in Water Usage*, REUTERS (Aug. 29, 2018), https://www.pri.org/stories/2018-08-29/lithium-demand-rising-chile-reins-water-usage

94. Cecelia Jamasmie, *Chile the Largest Copper Producer and the Country with the Biggest*

The dramatic pendulum swing from long-standing regulatory control over a public good to a market-based allocation was "unprecedented both in Chile and in other countries."[95] It marked the apex of neoliberalism's arc of influence[96]at the end of the twentieth century, public utilities still supplied over 90 percent of the world's water.[97] Chile's bold turn toward private administration initiated a global trend that "has not gone unopposed,"[98] but the neoliberal commodification of fresh water reserves found international support among institutions such as the World Bank, the International Monetary Fund, and regional development banks.[99]

For the better part of the twentieth century, Chile pursued the economic policies of an entrepreneurial state, transposing from the oligarchic agrarian-based *latifundia* or estate system of the nineteenth century into a more diverse economy of smallholders (*minifundistas*), with a burgeoning middle class forming in urban centers.[100] The *latifundia* system descended from Spanish colonial practices, which granted huge swaths of territory to *ecomenderos*, who paid tribute to the crown and employed indigenous labor to work the land. Latifundia owners were defined as holders of title to more than 5,000 hectares (12,355 acres) into the mid-1930s.[101] State-owned enterprises and holding companies dominated the development of a national industrial policy based on price, wage, and interest-rate controls, extensive trade protection measures, and rent-seeking regulations.[102] These policies solidified operations of the state at

---

Reserves—USGS, MINING.COM (Feb. 20, 2012), MINING.COM, http://www.mining.com/chile-the-largest-copper-producer-and-the-country-with-the-biggest-reserves-usgs/

95. Carl J. Bauer, *In the Image of the Market: The Chilean Model of Water Resources Management*, 3 INT'L J. WATER 146, 150 (2005).

96. *See* Budds, *supra* note 1818, at 200 (noting the 1981 Water Code passed "at a time when neoliberalism was at its most ascendant").

97. *See* Violeta Petrova, *At the Frontiers of the Rush for Blue Gold: Water Privatization and the Human Right to Water*, 31 BROOK. J. INT'L L. 577 (2006) (noting as well that around 90 percent of the developing world's investment in water management stemmed from public financing).

98. *Id.* at 578.

99. On World Bank and institutional-lending-agency support for water privatization, see Thomas Coleman, *Who Owns the Water? An Analysis of Water Conflicts in Latin America and Modern Water Law*, 12 INTERSECTIONS 4 (2012); Tanya Kapoor, Note, *Is Successful Water Privatization a Pipe Dream? An Analysis of Three Global Case Studies*, 40 YALE J. INT'L L. 157, 158 (2015); Baer, *supra* note 37, at 199, 205–12.

100. PATRICIO MELLER, THE UNIDAD POPULAR AND THE PINOCHET DICTATORSHIP: A POLITICAL ECONOMY ANALYSIS 1–5 (Tim Ennis trans., 2000).

101. Donald McConnell, *The Chilean Nitrate Industry*, 43 J. POL. ECON. 506, 506 (1935).

102. *See* Ronald J. Gilson & Curtis J. Milhaupt, *Economically Benevolent Dictators: Lessons for Developing Democracies*, 59 AM. J. COMP. L. 227, 250 (2011) (discussing the Chilean economy from the Great Depression to the coup that brought Pinochet to power).

its core and among its key, strategic sectors. When the military seized power in 1973 from the democratically elected socialist government of Salvador Allende (*Unidad Popular*, 1970–1973),[103] "Chile was one of the most closed and heavily regulated economies in the world."[104] Into the early 1980s, the military regime "pursued a 'foundational' transformation of Chilean politics and society, and a consequent radical transformation of Chile's economy."[105]

Described now as a part of Latin America's "Lost Decade,"[106] during the 1980s problems of debt, inflation, and political and military ruptures associated with severe structural adjustment and stabilization policies dominated the country and region.[107] Inadequate regulation led to a major banking crisis in 1981, where, under the leadership of Hernán Büchi, major liquidations and the rewriting of bad loans to the Central Bank resulted in a $26 billion foreign currency borrowing initiative for a country with a gross domestic product of $75 billion.[108] Negative annual growth persistently accompanied neoliberal reforms until the mid-1980s.[109] However, during the 1990s, Chile's output growth entered posi-

---

103. Allende came to power in a split election with but 36.3 percent of the popular vote. *See* ANDRÉS SOLIMANO, CHILE AND THE NEOLIBERAL TRAP: THE POST-PINOCHET ERA 20 (2012).

104. *See* Gilson & Milhaupt, *supra* note 102, at 251.

105. Esteban Jadresic & Roberto Zahler, "Chile's Rapid Growth in the 1990s: Good Policies, Good Luck, or Political Change," 7 IMF Working Paper WP/00/153 (Oct. 2000).

106. Raphael Bergoeing et al., *A Decade Lost and Found: Mexico and Chile in the 1980s*, 5 REV. OF ECON. DYNAMICS 166, 167 (2002) (describing much of Latin America in the 1980s); Roberto Bouzas & Jaime Ros, *The North-South Variety of Economic Integration: Issues and Prospects for Latin America, in* ECONOMIC INTEGRATION IN THE WESTERN HEMISPHERE 1, 3 (Roberto Bouzas & Jaime Ros eds., 1994).

107. *See* Ernesto Talvi, *Thirty-Five Years of Recurring Financial Crises in Latin America: Toward a New (and Better) Paradigm?* BROOKINGS (June 4, 2005), https://www.brookings.edu/opinions/thirty-five-years-of-recurring-financial-crises-in-latin-america-toward-a-new-and-better-paradigm/ (on the collapse of international capital flow to Latin America during the lost decade of the 1980s); A DECADE OF LIGHT AND SHADOW: LATIN AMERICA AND THE CARIBBEAN IN THE 1990S 19 (José Antonio Ocampo & Juan Martin eds., 2003); Margaret Daly Hayes, *The U.S. and Latin America: A Lost Decade?* 68 FOR. AFF. 180 (1988/1989) (noting minimal GDP growth in Latin America in the 1980s, despite population increases). As an indication of the economic turmoil, Chile went through six finance/treasury ministers between March 1982 and February 1985. *See* HERNÁN BÜCHI, THE ECONOMIC TRANSFORMATION OF CHILE: A PERSONAL ACCOUNT 21 (2010) (listing de Castro, de la Cuadra, Lüders, Cáceres, Escobar, and himself).

108. *See* SALVATORE BIZZARRO, HISTORICAL DICTIONARY OF CHILE 73–74 (3d ed. 2005).

109. Chile experienced negative annual grown as a percentage of GDP in 1972 (-3.44%), 1973 (-7.8%), 1974 (-1.51%), 1975 (-15.14%), 1982 (16.15%), 1983 (-5.68%), and 1985 (-1.09%). JUAN BRAUN ET AL., ECONOMÍA CHILENA 1810–1995: ESTADÍSTICAS HISTÓRICAS 25–26 (2000).

tive territory, averaging 7 percent per year, more than double the average growth observed in Chile in the previous three decades, and the highest in Latin America.[110]

Chile's "miraculous" turnaround generated supporters and skeptics.[111] Defenders of the Pinochet regime attributed these economic advances to market liberalizations and reforms that produced Chile's "peaceful, gradual, and constitutional . . . return to democratic rule in 1990."[112] Skeptics pointed to the end of Chile's restive political rule under Pinochet and the political transition away from authoritarianism.[113] Others noted massive restructuring of international credit markets, such as the Baker and Brady Plans, which mixed debt forgiveness with lower interest rates to renew capital flows to the region.[114] Even here, the complexity of sustained and coordinated international management suggested that dismantling state-owned enterprises overly affected needed public-sector functions, contributing to persistent tensions regarding regulatory administration and oversight.[115] Central to this concern was the marketization of water rights, which ultimately allowed municipalities and even individuals to trade away water

---

110. Jadresic & Zahler, *supra* note 105, at 3.

111. For a favorable review of Chile's economic turn from important mainstream economists, *see, e.g.*, THE CHILEAN ECONOMY: POLICY LESSONS AND CHALLENGES (Barry P. Bosworth et al. eds., 1994). For a critique of the free-market epithet attaching to Chilean structural transformation policies that involved heavy subsidies and government intervention, see CHILE'S FREE-MARKET MIRACLE: A SECOND LOOK (Joseph Collins & John Lear eds., 1995). For a critique locating success in Chile's communitarian social structure more than in dictates of neoliberalism, see Michel Duquette, *The Chilean Economic Miracle Revisited*, 27 J. SOC.-ECON. 299 (1998).

112. José Piñera, *Latin America: A Way out* 22 CATO J. 409–16, 410 (2003).

113. Raúl Labán & Felipe Larraín, *Continuity, Change, and the Political Economy of Transition in Chile*, *in* REFORM, RECOVERY, AND GROWTH: LATIN AMERICA AND THE MIDDLE EAST 115–48 (Rudiger Dornbusch & Sebastian Edwards, eds. 1995).

114. The 1985 Baker Plan identified fifteen middle-income debtor countries (ten in Central and Latin America) and focused on growth stimuli that provided debt relief through liberalized structural reforms matched by World Bank and private bank aid. *Id.* The Brady Plan, introduced in March 1989, more specifically addressed the 1982 debt crisis in Latin America that cast major shadows on the creditworthiness of Mexico, Argentina, Costa Rica, Venezuela, Ecuador, Brazil, the Dominican Republic, and various other debtor countries around the globe that could not service payments held primarily by US banks. *See generally* Manuel Monteagudo, *The Debt Problem: The Baker Plan and the Brady Initiative: A Latin American Perspective*, 28 INT'L LAWYER 59–81 (1994) (discussing US plans to restructure international debt problems); *The Brady Plan*, EMTA, https://www.emta.org/template.aspx?id=35 (last visited Aug. 31, 2018). Chile was the first country to apply the Baker Plan even before it translated into the Brady Plan. *See* BÜCHI, *supra* note 92, at 169.

115. *See* OCAMPO & MARTIN, *supra* note 107, at 19.

rights—an allowance that severely dehydrated remote areas,[116] diminished communal safeguards, and supplanted the political economy of extraction based on humanized forms of terracing and irrigation with concentrated industrial development schemes among indigenous highland communities.[117]

The Chicago Boys

Interpreted historically, Chile's transition to a market-based economy took a consequential turn in 1955. Persistent inflation, averaging around 80 percent per year during the 1950s administration of Carlos Ibáñez del Campo (1952–1958), had produced a politically unpopular and short-lived proto-shock-treatment template for major structural adjustment.[118] At around this time, an agreement emerged between the Pontifical Catholic University of Chile, the University of Chicago, and the Ford Foundation (promoted by Albion Patterson at the Administration for International Cooperation, the predecessor to the US Agency for International Development),[119] to establish an education exchange program—the *Proyecto Chile*.[120] This project secured until 1964 graduate study scholarships for Chilean economic students at the University of Chicago.[121]

---

116. *See* Budds, *supra* note 18, at 199 (on the social impact and challenges facing Atacameño indigenous groups and the conversion of water rights into tradable private property); BAUER, *supra* note 87, at 132 (noting deficiencies in water management adversely affecting peasants and poor farmers).

117. Paul H. Gelles, *Cultural Identity and Indigenous Water Rights in the Andean Highlands, in* OUT OF THE MAINSTREAM 119, 127–29 (Rutgerd Boelens et al. eds., 2010); Budds, *supra* note 18, at 208 (noting forced migrations involving Atacameño communities due to mineral extraction and surface water reductions).

118. The Klein-Saks Mission program, which was abandoned within six months. *See generally* Rolf Lüders, *La Misión Klein-Saks, los Chicago Boys y la Política Económica*, INSTITUTO DE ECONOMÍA, DOCUMENTO DE TRABAJO N° 411, at 1 (2012) (discussing the use of the consulting firm by the del Campo regime to implement an anti-inflationary program), http://economia.uc.cl/docs/dt_411.pdf

119. *See* Luis Portillo, *Chicago Boys*, HISTORIA CULTURAL (Mar. 12, 2013), https://www.historiacultural.com/2013/03/chicago-boys-economia-chile.html

120. *See* Soffa Correa, *Algunos antecedents historicos del proyecto neoliberal en Chile (1955–1958)*, 6 OPCIONES 106, 117 (1985) (referencing the formal establishment of the project in March 1956).

121. MILTON & ROSE D. FRIEDMAN, TWO LUCKY PEOPLE: MEMOIRS 397 (1998) (hereinafter FRIEDMAN & FRIEDMAN). Notable other students, such as 1989 presidential candidate Hernán Büchi, who attended Columbia, and future governor of the Central Bank of Chile Vittorio Corvo, who attended Harvard, are commonly regarded as part of the Chicago School cohort. As Büchi explained, in reference to himself but as an attribute attaching to others, as well: "Although by education I did not strictly fit the 'Chicago Boy' profile, I never felt like an outsider." BÜCHI, *supra* note 92, at 11.

The Pontifical Catholic University nested a conservative-liberal student sentiment organized by the future Chilean senator, Jaime Guzmán (1946–1991).[122] It would grow into the *Gremialista* movement,[123] which resisted inclusive Christian Democratic university reforms[124] and sought to promote a corporatist, conservative Catholic agenda that would mute the discretionary political powers of the state and exclude such inclusive expressions at the level of university education.[125] Many of the Chicago Boys began as *Gremialistas*,[126] and their segue into the University of Chicago's economics department traversed an important point of contact. The department had already secured its standing as one of the first autonomous graduate programs in the nation. With that autonomy, it became a leading voice in shaping public policy in a university devoted at its inception to graduate study.[127] Under the tutelage of its free-market enthusiasts, primarily Arnold Harberger,[128] but also Milton Friedman,[129]

---

122. Guzmán founded the conservative Independent Democratic Union party and supported Pinochet's regime. He was assassinated in 1991, during the formative stage of Chile's return to democratic rule. *See* Patrick J. McDonnell & Jorge Poblete, *Chile's Path from Dictatorship to Democracy was Uneasy and Marked by Bloodshed*, L.A. TIMES (MAR. 18, 2018)

123. RENATO CRISTI, PENSAMIENTO POLÍTICO DE JAIME GUZMÁN: AUTORIDAD Y LIBERTAD 9 (2000).

124. *See* JAIME RETAMAL SALAZAR, NOS SIGUEN PEGANDO ABAJO: JAIME GUZMÁN, DICTADURA, CONCERTACIÓN Y ALIANZA: 40 AÑOS DE EDUCACIÓN DE MERCADO 29–30 (discussing Guzmán's views on the "*Teoría sobre la Universidad*" and controversies regarding "*la Universidad para Todos.*"); Parraguez Sanchez, *supra* note 86 (on the Pinochet government's pervasive neoliberalization of higher education in Chile and its depoliticizing effects, followed by the formation of reform in postdictatorial Chile).

125. Karin Fischer, *The Influence of Neoliberals in Chile Before, During, and After Pinochet*, 305, 312, *in* THE ROAD FROM MONT PÈLERIN: THE MAKING OF THE NEOLIBERAL THOUGHT COLLECTIVE (Philip Mirowski & Dieter Plehwe ed., 2009).

126. Victor Muñoz Tamayo, *Chile es bandera y juventud. Efebolatría y gremialism durante la primera etapa de la dictadura de Pinochet (1973–1979)*, 54 HISTÓRIA CRÍTICA 195, 207 (2014); Carlos Huneeus, *Technocrats and Politicians in an Authoritarian Regime. The "ODEPLAN Boys" and the "Gremialists" in Pinochet's Chile*, 32, J. L. AM. STUD. 461, 501 (2010).

127. *See* LANNY EBENSTEIN, CHICAGONOMICS: THE EVOLUTION OF CHICAGO FREE MARKET ECONOMICS 27 (2015).

128. *See* ASCANIO CAVALLO ET AL., LA HISTORIA OCULTA DEL REGIMEN MILITARY: MEMORIA DE UNA ÉPOCA 1973–1988, 104–5 (2012) (noting Harberger's connection with De Castro).

129. Friedman was awarded the 1976 Nobel Prize in Economic Sciences. *See Press Release*, THE NOBEL PRIZE (Oct. 14, 1976), https://www.nobelprize.org/prizes/economic-sciences/1976/press-release/

Larry Sjaastad,[130] and Robert Fogel,[131] an array of Chilean economists cycled through the program. Prominent students included Luis Arturo Fuenzalida, Ernesto Fontaine, Miguel Kast, Alberto Valdés, Pedro Jeftanovic, Sergio de Castro, Rolf Lüders, and José Piñera. More than sixty Chilean economists had pursued graduate degrees at the University of Chicago by 1964,[132] and forty more by 1970.[133]

On return to their homeland, they profoundly influenced Chile's economic course.[134] The so-called "Chicago Boys," between twenty-six

---

130. Sjaastad was a leading economic authority on Latin American trade and public finance. His 1961 doctoral dissertation at the University of Chicago focused on human capital theory, the social and personal rewards of knowledge transmission, and the analytics of migration decisions. University of Chicago Nobel Laureate (Economics) Robert Lucas acclaimed his dissertation as exemplary, and it was regarded as "legendary" in the university's Department of Economics. William Harms, *Larry Sjaastad, Scholar of International Economics, 1934–2012*, UCHICAGO NEWS (May 9, 2012), https://news.uchicago.edu/story/larry-sjaastad-scholar-international-economics-1934-2012. Sjaastad reworked the dissertation and published it as *The Costs and Returns of Human Migration*, 70 J. POL. ECON. 80 (1962).

131. *See* Sarah Gold, *Interview with an Ex-Minister of State: Rolf Lüders*, BUTLER SCHOL. J. (May 9, 2017), http://butlerscholarlyjournal.com/2017/05/09/interview-with-an-ex-minister-of-state-rolf-luders/ (noting that Fogel served as Lüders's PhD dissertation advisor). Fogel was a corecipient of the Nobel Prize for Economics in 1993.

132. Gilson & Milhaupt, *supra* note 102, at 253n83. Funding for the *Proyecto Chile* ended in 1964, however additional resources sustained recruitment beyond this period. *See* Glen Biglaiser, *The Internationalization of Chicago's Economics in Latin America*, 50 ECON. DEV. & CUL. CHANGE 269, 275 (2002).

133. JOHAN VAN OVERTVELDT, THE CHICAGO SCHOOL: HOW THE UNIVERSITY OF CHICAGO ASSEMBLED THE THINKERS WHO REVOLUTIONIZED ECONOMICS AND BUSINESS 349 (2008). Between 1962 and 1965 a similar program developed with the National University of Cuyo in Mendoza, Argentina. Twenty-four Argentine students studied at the University of Chicago under this program. *See* JUAN GABRIEL VALDÉS, PINOCHET'S ECONOMISTS: THE CHICAGO SCHOOL IN CHILE 182 (1995). *See also* Biglaiser, *supra* note 132, at 277–79 (noting the extension of *Proyecto Chile* to Argentine students studying in Chicago and at the Universidad de Cuyo and the Universidad de Tucumán, as well as the 1978 establishment of the Centro de Estudios Macroeconómicos de Argentina by former Chicago students).

134. Other notable Chicago Boys included Jorge Cauas (Ministro de Hacienda, 1975–1977), Pablo Barahona (Ministro de Economía, 1976–1979), Juan Carlos Méndez (Director de Presupuestos, 1975–1981), Sergio de la Cuadra (Ministro de Hacienda, 1982–1983), Miguel Kast (Ministro de Planificación, 1978–1980), Martín Costabal (Director de Presupuestos, 1987–1989), Juan Ariztía Matte (Superintendente del Sistema Privado de Pensiones, 1980–1990), María Teresa Infante (Ministra de Trabajo 1988–1990), Joaquín Lavín (Ministro de Educación, 2010–2011, Ministro de Planificación 2011–), Cristián Larroulet (Ministro de la Secretaría General de la Presidencia [SEGPRES], 2010–), and Juan Andrés Fontaine (Ministro de Economía, 2010–2011). Other Latin American economists associated with the Chicago Boys include Francisco Gil Díaz, Fernando Sánchez Ugarte, and Carlos Isoard y Viesca (Mexico); Adolfo Diz and Roque Benjamín Fernández (Argen-

and thirty-five years of age,[135] drafted a 189-page roadmap for Chile's economic recovery—nicknamed, due to its heft, *El Ladrillo* (The Brick).[136] Former conservative Chilean president, Jorge Alessandri (1958–1964), considered but then rejected its early policy prescriptions during his 1970 bid to regain the presidency against Allende.[137] However, *El Ladrillo* resurfaced as an economic action program two years after Pinochet's September 1973 *coup d'état* against the Allende government. By this time, the junta's head of the economic ministry, Admiral José Toribio Merino,[138] recognized that the junta's money-printing response to depleted foreign reserves and falling GDP had inadvertently created a monetary disaster. Bereft of solutions and wary of spiraling, destabilizing inflation,[139] the junta turned national economic management over to the Chicago Boys.[140] The junta's relinquishment of control over the economy to technopols uprooted imaginaries of the hierarchical military mindset and to this day remains one of the more surprising elements of Latin American encounters with authoritarianism.

El Ladrillo's ten principal authors were Chicago Boys,[141] and many of

tina); and Carlos Alfredo Rodríguez, Fernando de Santibáñes, and Ricardo López Murphy (Argentina). *See* Portillo, *supra* note 119.

135. Büchi, *supra* note 92, at 10.

136. *See* Jorge Rojas, *El Ladrillo de Sergio De Castro*, THE CLINIC (Apr. 7, 2015), http://www.theclinic.cl/2015/04/07/el-ladrillo-de-sergio-de-castro/ (interviewing De Castro, who had recently recovered the original notes for *El Ladrillo* that recorded meetings with Roberto Kelly and Chilean economics doctoral students at Chicago, including José Toribio Merion, Pablo Barahona, and Álvaro Bardon).

137. *See Chile's Chicago Boys and Latin America's Other Market Reformers*, HOOVER INST. (Apr. 26, 2011), https://www.hoover.org/news/chiles-chicago-boys-and-latin-americas-other-market-reformers

138. PHIL O'BRIEN & JACKIE RODDICK, CHILE: THE PINOCHET DECADE: THE RISE AND FALL OF THE CHICAGO BOYS 46 (1983).

139. *See* Valerie Brender, *Economic Transformations in Chile: The Formation of the Chicago Boys*, 55(1) AM. ECON. 111, 120 (Spring 2010); VAN OVERTVELDT, *supra* note 133, at 350. The Allende government had established fixed prices on more than 3,000 goods, prompting food shortages and rampant black marketeering; import tariffs averaged 105 percent on more than 5,000 goods, effectively sealing off most foreign trade; the government had taken over hundreds of companies, and most were operating at substantial losses; the government financed its 55 percent fiscal deficit by printing money, generating inflation that exceeded 1,000 percent. Claudia Rosett, *Looking Back on Chile: 1973–1984*, NAT. REV. 25, 26 (June 1, 1984).

140. *See* DOMINIQUE HACHETTE & ROLF LÜDERS, PRIVATIZATION IN CHILE: AN ECONOMIC APPRAISAL 167 (1993) ("Pinochet strongly supported [privatization] . . . . After the 1983 reversals, he was willing not only to reprivatize . . . but also to decisively deepen the process by privatizing public utilities . . . . The head of the economic team, unconditionally supported by the so-called Chicago Boys, was firmly behind the privatization policies."); Rosett, *supra* note 139, at 26.

141. *See* CHILE'S CHICAGO BOYS AND LATIN AMERICA'S OTHER MARKET REFORMERS, *supra* note 137.

them came to occupy important academic and government posts in Chile's authoritarian regime. They formed an epistemic community[142] denominated in the language of free-market enterprise and "incremented annually by new generations of economists graduating from Chilean universities. They shared the same technical language, a rationalistic approach to problem solving and the eagerness to contribute, through their efforts, to creating a prosperous, fair and free society."[143] Although "highly cohesive . . . with strong bonds of loyalty born of a common educational experience and fervently held convictions on the desirability of market reforms," they were a product of "their increasingly polarized social and political climate," making them distinct from their Chicago tutors.[144]

This point may have escaped group detection. In his personal account of the economic transformation of Chile, written in view of Pinochet's reign of impunity, Chicago Boy sympathizer Hernán Büchi nevertheless puzzled over Chileans' strange unawareness of the economic leap in progress created by the Chicago Boys and their genuine disposition to service that the military "steered . . . toward an unexpected future of reconciliation and prosperity."[145] Their rise also challenged established

142. Epistemic communities focus on the role and influence of knowledge-based experts on complex matters of international decision-making, such as in the field of political economy. Such a community has a belief system that reflects a shared set of values for social action, a shared set of causal connections framing their domain, a shared understanding of intersubjective criteria that weigh the importance of knowledge accumulation, and a shared set of common practices associated with the problems addressed by their professional competencies. *See* Peter M. Haas, *Introduction: Epistemic Communities and International Policy Coordination*, 46 INT'L ORG. 3 (1992).

143. VALDÉS, *supra* note 133, at 18 (quoting Rolf Lüders). *But see* ORLANDO LETELIER, CHILE: ECONOMIC "FREEDOM" AND POLITICAL REPRESSION 6 (Washington, DC: Institute for Policy Studies, 1976) (alleging that the Chicago Boys were "[d]eeply involved in the preparation of the *coup*" and that they "convinced the generals that they were prepared to supplement the brutality, which the military possessed, with the intellectual assets it lacked"). Letelier served as Allende's ambassador to the United States. He was assassinated in Washington, DC, three years after the *coup* by a car bomb allegedly planted by the Chilean secret police. *See* Missy Ryan, *CIA Found "Convincing Evidence" Chilean Dictator Was Behind 1976 D.C. Attack*, WASH. POST (Sept. 23, 2016), https://www.washingtonpost.com/news/checkpoint/wp/2016/09/23/cia-found-convincing-evidence-chilean-dictator-was-behind-1976-washington-d-c-attack/?utm_term=.456eefaab9c9 (According to the CIA document: "A review of our files on the Letelier assassination has provided what we regard as convincing evidence that President Pinochet personally ordered his intelligence chief to carry out the murder."). In June 1999, the United States released approximately 20,000 pages of classified material detailing widespread human rights abuses by the Pinochet regime. For more on the declassified collection, see Sean D. Murphy, *U.S. Assistance Regarding Information on Former Chilean President Pinochet*, 94 AM. J. INT'L L. 368 (2000).

144. Teichman, *supra* note 59, at 27.

145. BÜCHI, *supra* note 92, at 11 (noting as a non-Chicago graduate his intellectual

Keynesian orthodoxies and sectarian interests among Chile's elite business community, which had been "invested in the existing national-developmentalist form of capital accumulation."[146]

Arnold Harberger regarded Sergio de Castro as the leader of the group's first generation.[147] De Castro served as Pinochet's minister of finance (1977–1982),[148] as did Lüders and Büchi.[149] José Piñera, who helped privatize Chile's pension system, became Pinochet's labor and social security minister (1978–1980) and secretary of mining (1980–1981).[150] Kast directed the National Planning Office (ODEPLAN, 1978) and served as labor minister (1980) and governor of the Central Bank (1982). Roberto Kelly directed ODEPLAN,[151] which played a major role in developing procedures to improve public investment.[152] In 1962, Sjaastad created a parallel training program for Argentine students at the Universidad Nacional de Cuyo, financed through the Kennedy administration's Alliance for Progress program.[153] Chicago Boy affiliates

---

attachment to Chicago-styled economics as well the military's "decisive and fundamental service to the country . . . which changed Chile's history for the better").

146. TAYLOR, *supra* note 85, at 51.

147. VAN OVERTVELDT, *supra* note 133, at 350 (quoting Harberger). De Castro had been the long-time dean of the Catholic University economics faculty and as finance minister was regarded as "far and away the most powerful . . . the country has ever had." RICARDO LAGOS, THE SOUTHERN TIGER: CHILE'S FIGHT FOR A DEMOCRATIC AND PROSPEROUS FUTURE 41 (2012).

148. *Chile's Chicago Boys and Latin America's Other Market Reformers, supra* note 137.

149. Lüders served as finance minister and economic minister between 1982–1983, following the banking crisis of 1981, and otherwise has maintained since 1971 an academic career on the economics faculty of the Pontificia Universidad Católica de Chile. *See Curriculum Vitae, Rolf Lüders Schwarzenberg,* http://economia.uc.cl/wp-content/uploads/2015/01/cv_rluders-2009.pdf. Büchi served as finance [treasury] minister between 1985 and 1989. He also served as superintendent of banks and financial institutions (1984–1985), national planning minister (1983–1984), and undersecretary for economy (1979–1980) and health (1980–1983). He ran for president in 1989. *See* BÜCHI, *supra* note 92, at 2; Silvia Santacruz, *A Latin America Miracle,* FORBES (Mar. 17, 2010), https://www.forbes.com/2010/03/16/latin-america-hernan-buchi-opinions-book-review-silvia-santacruz.html#1d285d1128fe

150. *See José Piñera,* JOSÉ PIÑERA, http://www.josepinera.org/josepinera/jp_jp_cv.htm (last visited Mar. 4, 3019); *José Piñera,* CATO INSTITUTE, https://www.cato.org/people/jose-pinera (last visited Mar. 4, 2019).

151. *See* GUY SORMAN, CHEERS FOR CHILE'S CHICAGO BOYS: MILTON FRIEDMANESQUE REFORMS HELPED CREATE SOUTH AMERICA'S MOST PROSPEROUS NATION, CJ (2008), https://www.city-journal.org/html/cheers-chile%E2%80%99s-chicago-boys-13073.html

152. Fontaine, *supra* note 65, at 64 (discussing ODEPLAN).

153. *Larry A. Sjaastad Fund Will Support Graduate Fellowships,* Kenneth C. Griffin Department of Economics, University of Chicago (Nov. 13, 2017), https://economics.uchicago.edu/blog/larry-sjaastad-fund-will-support-graduate-fellowships (recapping his career and announcing graduate fellowship in memory of Professor Sjaastad).

spread across Latin America,[154] including Colombia, Panama, Ecuador, and Bolivia. Indeed, Chile's neoliberal imprint stood behind Bolivia's 1985 New Economic Policy, ushered in by another Chicago Boy, Bolivian president Gonzalo "Goni" Sánchez de Lozada's 1993 *Plan de Todos.*[155] This privatization plan contributed to subsequent president Banzer's 1999 Law 2029, which commodified public water, impaired water management rights in rural communities, and launched the Cochabamba protests.[156]

The Chicago Boys' managerial acumen ranks as a *pharmakon*—vilified as a poison and lauded as a remedy.[157] As technopols, they entered government with an economic focus, and were professedly unaware of the

---

154. *See generally* Biglaiser, *supra* note 132 (noting neoliberalism's reception, spread, and varying degrees of embrace in Latin America while focusing on Argentina, Chile, and Uruguay).

155. Gonzalo Sánchez de Lozada, a staunch advocate of aggressive structural adjustment, was the architect of Bolivia's "shock therapy" program. He was elected to Bolivia's Congress in 1979, served as Chile's minister of planning in 1985, and was elected president in 1993. He received his 1951 PhD from the University of Chicago (in philosophy and literature, not economics). For exceptional achievement over an entire career, he received the university's 2001Alumni Medal. *See Two Exceptional Graduates Honored at Reunion*, 93 U. CHI. MAG. (Aug. 2001), https://magazine.uchicago.edu/0108/class-notes/newsmaker.html. Lozada also founded Bolivia's largest private mining company. *See* Julie Deardorff, *Bolivian President More Comfortable Playing Soccer Than Watching*, CHI. TRIB. (June 16, 1994), https://www.chicagotribune.com/news/ct-xpm-1994-06-16-9406160054-story.html. In April 2018, Lozada and his former defense minister, residents of the US, were found guilty in Federal District Court in Fort Lauderdale of extrajudicial killings and crimes against humanity involving indigenous Aymara communities under the Alien Tort Statute and Torture Victim Protection Act. The case marked the first time in US history that a former head of state faced accusers in a US human rights proceeding. *See* Gonzalo Sánchez de Lozada Sánchez Bustamante, et al., v. Elroy Rojas Mamani, et al. (11 cir.) (awarding plaintiffs $10 million in compensatory damages). The jury verdict was overturned on May 30, 2018, on grounds of insufficient evidence to support the verdict. The 11th Circuit Appeals Court reversed that ruling but remanded the case for further evidentiary considerations. *See* Carwil Bjork-James, *US Court Revives Case Against Gonzalo Sánchez de Lozada, Widens Accountability for Extrajudicial Killings*, Carwil Without Borders (Aug. 5, 2020), https://woborders.blog/2020/08/05/court-revives-goni-case/.

156. *See* Coleman, *supra* note 99, at 10. For more on the *pharmakon*, see Jacques Derrida, *"Plato's Pharmacy," in* DISSEMINATION 63, 70 (Jacques Derrida & Barbara Johnson trans., 1981) (referencing Plato's dialogue *Phaedrus*, where Socrates notes the *pharmakon* "acts as both remedy and poison").

157. *See, e.g.*, Jacob G. Hornberger, *Pinochet's Chicago Boys Versus Freedom*, FFF (Feb. 1, 2018), https://www.fff.org/explore-freedom/article/pinochets-chicago-boys-versus-freedom/ (deriding their service to a brutal dictatorship); Bret Stephens, *Opinion: How Milton Friedman Saved Chile*, WSJ Opinion (Mar. 1, 2010), https://www.wsj.com/articles/SB10001424052748703411304575093572032665414 (associating Chicago Boys reforms with Chile's prosperity).

regime's brutality.[158] For his mentorship of Chicago Boys, and his six-day visit to Chile in 1975[159] (which included a forty-five-minute private session with Pinochet and fellow junta members),[160] Friedman received intense moral criticism.[161] In his memoir, he wrote, "That six day visit plus my prior role as a professor turned out to have consequences that we never anticipated and that we had to deal with for the next decade."[162] In response to criticisms, he provided a pharmacological explanation reduced to an economic antidote: rendering technical economic advice to end an inflation plague differed not at all from offering medical advice to end a medical plague.[163]

The technocratic exposition of domestic economic fixes to endemic

---

158. *See* Greg Grandin, *The United States Didn't Just Help Topple Allende—We Trained the Economists, Too*, NATION (Nov. 16, 2015), https://www.thenation.com/article/the-united-states-didnt-just-help-topple-allende-we-trained-the-economists-too/. (noting denials of Pinochet's brutality by de Castro). *But see* Orlando Letelier, *Economic Freedom's' [sic] Awful Toll: The "Chicago Boys" in Chile*, THE NATION, Aug. 28, 1976 (warning in 1976 that the Pinochet regime was "torturing, jailing and persecuting all its critics"). Letelier was assassinated by car bomb on Scott Circle in Washington DC, twenty-four days after his article appeared in THE NATION. Ronnie Moffitt, a US citizen, also died in the blast, and her husband was injured. *See Orlando Letelier: Dead by Whose Hand?* THE NATION, OCT. 2, 1976. A 1987 CIA special intelligence assessment, released in September 2016, concluded that Pinochet "personally ordered his intelligence chief to . . . murder [Letelier]." *See CIA: "Pinochet Personally Ordered" Letelier Bombing*, NAT. SEC. ARCHIVE (Sept. 23, 2016), https://nsarchive.gwu.edu/briefing-book/chile/2016-09-23/cia-pinochet-personally-ordered-letelier-bombing. Targeted assassinations of key exiled dissidents, including Chile's former chief of the army, General Carlos Prats, and former Christian Democrat vice president, Bernardo Leighton, formed part of an international covert operation named Operation Condor. *See* LAGOS, *supra* note 147, 41–42.

159. *See* FRIEDMAN & FRIEDMAN, *supra* note 121, 591–602 (1998) (reprinting Nobel laureate and anonymous professorial condemnations, along with Friedman's defenses of his trip to Chile and debated association with Chile's authoritarian regime and economic policies).

160. *See id.* at 601 ("meeting with General Pinochet and his fellow junta members").

161. *See id.* at 591–602 [Appendix A] (reprinting notable letters of protest). Hayek also visited Chile during Pinochet's rule, generating similar controversy regarding his "perceived failure to speak out against human rights abuses." Bruce Caldwell & Leonidas Montes, *Friedrich Hayek and His Visits to Chile*, 28 REV. AUSTRIAN ECON. 261, 263 (2015). He met privately with Pinochet for twenty minutes in November 1977, and returned in 1981 as the honorary president of the newly formed *Centro de Estudios Públicos*. *See id.* at 261 (Pinochet meetings), 262 (*Centro de Estudios Públicos*). Hayek's less-than-technical approach to economics, and departmental opposition to private-source funding for a position in the department, kept him off the economics faculty at the University of Chicago. *See* ALAN EBENSTEIN, FRIEDRICH HAYEK: A BIOGRAPHY 175 (2001). Instead, he served as professor of social and moral science in the University of Chicago's Committee on Social Thought from 1950 to 1962. He received the Nobel Prize for Economics in 1974.

162. FRIEDMAN & FRIEDMAN, *supra* note 121, at 400 (1998).

163. *See id.* at 596 (letter in response to concerns of the Citizens' Committee on Human Rights and Foreign Policy).

development problems in Chile reinforced a division in hemispheric history that presents opposing views of international law in the hemisphere. Borne out of a common revolutionary tradition, as against a hemispheric backdrop of metropolitan rule and colonization, diffuse sentiments of common cause held out the long-sought prospect of some sort of federated hemispheric union—a promise of establishing an America for Americans, with "immensely growing commercial . . . connections."[164] Seen in deeper historical context, the idea stood behind South America's great *Libertador*, Simón Bolívar's (1783–1830) call for the 1826 Congress of Panama. Such sentiments were welcomed by early-nineteenth-century politicians in the United States, notably mirroring statesman Henry Clay's (1777–1852) call for an "American system,"[165] and Secretary of State James Blaine's (1830–1893) idea of an International Union of American Republics.[166] It took active form in the fitful history and imperfect amalgam of the Federation of the Center of America and the Pan-American movement.[167] And it counted among its doctrinal expositors regional integrationists such as Jesús María Yepes,[168] José Matos,[169] F. J. Urrutia,[170] Albert Guani,[171] and most influentially, Alejandro Álvarez, who promoted in the first part of the twentieth century the idea of an American International Law, a theoretically distinct and substantively

164. John Q. Adams, *Special Message, March 15, 1826*, *in* 2 ADDRESSES AND MESSAGES OF THE PRESIDENTS OF THE UNITED STATES, INAUGURAL, ANNUAL, AND SPECIAL, FROM 1789 TO 1851, at 632, 639 (1853).

165. ROBERT V. REMINI, HENRY CLAY: STATESMAN FOR THE UNION 174 (1991) (quoting Clay).

166. *See generally* A. Curtis Wilgus, *James G. Blaine and the Pan American Movement*, 5 HISP. AM. HIST. REV. 662 (1922) (discussing Blaine's attempts to form closer Pan-American relations). While the antecedents to the inter-American system date to the Congress of Panama, the decision to convene periodically did not arise until the proposal to constitute the International Union of American Republics, which first met in Washington, DC, in October 1889. *See Our History*, OAS, http://www.oas.org/en/about/our_history.asp (last visited May 10, 2019).

167. *See* A GUIDE TO THE UNITED STATES' HISTORY OF RECOGNITION, DIPLOMATIC, AND CONSULAR RELATIONS, BY COUNTRY, SINCE 1776: CENTRAL AMERICAN FEDERATION, ST. DEPT. OFF. HIST., https://history.state.gov/countries/central-american-federation (noting the diplomatic recognition by the United States of the Federation of Central American States on August 4, 1824).

168. *See generally* J. M. Yepes, *La contribution de l'Amérique latine au développement du droit international public et privé*, 32 RECUEIL DES COURS 691 (1930) (presenting the Colombian jurist's lectures on notable public and private international law contributions of Latin America before the Académie de Droit International).

169. José Matos, *L'Amérique et la Société des Nations*, 28 RECUEIL DES COURS 1 (1929).

170. F. J. Urrutia, *La codification du droit international en Amérique*, 22 RECUEIL DES COURS 81, 85–89 (1928).

171. Albert Guani, *La solidarité international dans l'Amérique Latine*, 8 RECUEIL DES COURS 203 (1925).

mature counterbalance to Anglo-Saxon and continental Old World expressions.[172]

However, Chile's neoliberal action plan also stood apart from another integrationist scheme that began to emphasize an emergent Latin American, as opposed to a Pan-American, sense of economic and political solidarity. Latin Americanism emerged from a deeply circumspect nineteenth-century regard for the hegemonic foreign-policy intentions of the United States, which had weaponized the defensive construct of its Monroe Doctrine (1823) with the annexation of Texas (1845), the Mexican-American War (1846–1848), and an assortment of turn-of-the-century interventions and power plays in the Caribbean and Central America over future control of the Panama Canal.[173]

In the mid to late twentieth century, the Chicago Boys structurally reformed Chile's economy through multiple periods of economic shock treatment.[174] Their imprint reached to the 1981 Water Code and 1980 Constitution, both currently in force.[175] Their legacy continues to be questioned. One critic identified their "technocratic prerogatives" as a form of revolutionary (as opposed to reactionary) vanguardism that radically transformed the material and ideological orientation of the Chilean state in ways that to this day promote Chile's "extraordinary levels of inequality."[176] More neutrally, they may be seen as catalytic. In a term

---

172. CHRISTOPHER R. ROSSI, WHIGGISH INTERNATIONAL LAW: ELIHU ROOT, THE MONROE DOCTRINE, AND INTERNATIONAL LAW IN THE AMERICAS 93 (2019). *See generally* JUAN PABLO SCARFI, THE HIDDEN HISTORY OF INTERNATIONAL LAW IN THE AMERICAS: EMPIRE AND LEGAL NETWORKS (2017).

173. *See, e.g.*, El Salvador v. Nicaragua, CACJ, Judgment (Mar. 9, 1917), *reprinted in* 11 AM. J. INT'L L. 674–730 (1917) (on El Salvador's successful complaint against Nicaragua's attempt to lease a naval station to the United States in the Gulf of Fonseca); Manley O. Hudson, *The Central American Court of Justice*, 26 AM. J. INT'L L. 759, 775–77 (1932) (summarizing the case).

174. Collins and Lear counted two periods, from 1975 to 1981 and 1985 to 1990. *See* COLLINS & LEAR, *supra* note 111, at 51. Alejandro Foxley counted four periods of economic adjustment (deregulation, 1973–1975; shock, 1975–1976; curbing expectations, 1976–1979; and monetarism 1979). *See* ALEJANDRO FOXLEY, LATIN AMERICAN EXPERIMENTS IN NEOCONSERVATIVE ECONOMICS 49–61 (1983). *Cf.* SEBASTIAN EDWARDS & ALEJANDRA COX EDWARDS, MONETARISM AND LIBERALIZATION: THE CHILEAN EXPERIMENT 17 (1987) (four phases). Friedman paid a six-day visit to Chile, meeting with Pinochet for forty-five minutes. He later wrote, "I believe that the 'Chicago Boys' had already reached the conclusion that a shock treatment was required to end the inflation" and that Pinochet "was sympathetically attracted to the idea" but concerned about the unemployment effects. FRIEDMAN & FRIEDMAN, *supra* note 121, at 399.

175. ANNA BERTI SUMAN, THE HUMAN RIGHT TO WATER IN LATIN AMERICA: CHALLENGES TO IMPLEMENTATION AND CONTRIBUTION TO THE CONCEPT 76 (2018).

176. Timothy David Clark, *Rethinking Chile's "Chicago Boys": Neoliberal Technocrats or*

reclaimed from antiquity by Friedrich Hayek, the Chicago Boys harnessed the disparate constructs of Chile's *catallaxy* ("a network of many interlaced economies"[177]) and transformed them into a market society,[178] with intentional perturbations to the system.

The 1981 recasting of Chile's education system "as a new private market" accelerated neoliberalism's colonization of higher education by its Chicago-styled crusaders.[179] This structural reorientation regenerated neoliberalism's ethos among Chile's academic progeny. It has come to reflect a justificatory retrospective gloss as to how Chile implemented neoliberal reforms,[180] and it helps to explain how four successive social democratic administrations (the multiparty *Concertación*) maintained and extended the neoliberal model in the post-Pinochet era.[181] A similar argument has been made about Chile's consolidated juridical alignment with authoritarianism, noting a degree of institutional integration that "moderates political oppression by allowing for its judicialization."[182]

Büchi equated the logic of Allende's socialist platform with the "loathsome monopolistic privileges" it "denounced and sought to dismantle,"[183]

Revolutionary Vanguard? 38 THIRD WORLD Q. 1,350 ("technocratic prerogatives"), 1,360 ("extraordinary levels of inequality") (2017). Chile's richest 5 percent has an estimated income 830 times greater than the poorest 5 percent. *See* Barros, *supra* note 19, at 174. In 2017, the number of Latin Americans living in poverty reached 30.2 percent of the population (184 million), "of whom 62 million live in extreme poverty" (10.2 percent of the population). *See* ECLAC (Jan. 15, 2019), https://www.cepal.org/en/pressreleases/poverty-latin-america-remained-steady-2017-extreme-poverty-increased-highest-level

177. Hayek found the term *economy* misleading. Common usages associated the term with a "unified plan" among competing ends. However, "[t]he market order serves no such single order of ends." A social or national economy is not a single economy, "but a network of many interlaced economies." Furthermore, "the cosmos of the market neither is nor could be governed by such a single scale of ends; it serves the multiplicity of separate and incommensurable ends of all its separate members." Due to widespread confusion about the word *economy*, Hayek employed his own idiom to describe "the special kind of spontaneous order produced by the market." Derived from the Greek verb *katallattein*, meaning "to exchange" but also "to admit into the community," he referred to this creative disunited operation of the market as *catallaxy*. 2 F. A. HAYEK LAW, LEGISLATION AND LIBERTY 107–9 (1976).

178. *See* Clark, *supra* note 176, at 1,354.

179. Undurraga, *supra* note 64, at 18.

180. *See* LESSIE JO FRAZIER, SALT IN THE SAND: MEMORY, VIOLENCE, AND THE NATION-STATE IN CHILE, 1890 TO THE PRESENT 245 (2007) (noting that "The Chilean story has been used to support the conclusion that state violence is regrettable but ultimately justifiable if the end result is a market-driven economy.").

181. *See* ANDRÉS SOLIMANO, CHILE AND THE NEOLIBERAL TRAP: THE POST-PINOCHET ERA 9 (2012) (analyzing Chile's post-Pinochet political economy).

182. PEREIRA, *supra* note 81, at 13 (2005).

183. BÜCHI, *supra* note 92, at 3.

which necessarily had to be supplanted as it represented the "simple façade" of a socialist market bureaucracy "to reap personal or group advantages."[184] He claimed it met its match with the tenacious Pinochet, who "dared to challenge voguish myths and put the country's economic transformation into effect."[185] Lüders did not think such shock therapy could endure absent an authoritarian state. He and another Chicago Boy, Dominique Hachette, more strongly suggested that Chile's massive dislocations caused by system-wide privatization "probably required an authoritarian regime."[186] De Castro retrospectively noted the unavoidable pain of such corrective measures.[187] Friedman predicted that such measures "almost invariably" cause recession.[188] One of Pinochet's most vocal critics, Orlando Letelier (1932–1976), four months before his assassination by Pinochet's security forces on Embassy Row in Washington, D.C., abjectly noted that the reforms required a "system of institutionalized brutality" involving the "drastic control and suppression of every form of meaningful dissent."[189]

Through a strategy of "creative destruction" the coercive deployment of macroeconomic policies obliterated the political structure and sustaining social relations of the Allende government, and ushered in the dramatic social transformation of the Chilean state.[190] Having become a juggernaut, it could not but have had a profound effect on the development of international law in the Americas, with its emotionally loaded and historically construed emphases on freedoms of trade, navigation, commerce, and integrationist sentiments dating from the advent of republicanism in the early Americas. Chile's economic miracle, beholden to the strong arm of authoritarian impunity, permeated social, educational, and religious strata[191] with powers no democracy could assert and influences that hemispheric international law could not resist.

In Chile, the contraposition of economic ideologies could not have

---

184. *Id.*

185. *Id.* at 9.

186. DOMINIQUE HACHETTE & ROLF LÜDERS, PRIVATIZATION IN CHILE: AN ECONOMIC APPRAISAL, *supra* note 140, at 176.

187. Grandin, *supra* note 158 (quoting Lüders and de Castro and noting, additionally, that "a number of Chicago Boys were members of *Opus Dei*, right-wing Catholics [who] saw no contradiction between [market supremacy] and submission to authoritarian order").

188. FRIEDMAN & FRIEDMAN, *supra* note 121, at 405.

189. Letelier, *Economic Freedom's' [sic] Awful Toll*, *supra* note 158.

190. TAYLOR, *supra* note 85, at 53.

191. *See* Paul E. Sigmund, *Revolution, Counterrevolution, and the Catholic Church in Chile*, 483 ANNALS OF AM. ACAD. POL & SOC. SCI. 25, 32–33 (1986) (on the Chilean Catholic church's pledge of cooperation with the Pinochet junta).

been more opposite or immediate.[192] The economists lifted wage and price controls, liberalized financial markets, privatized state-owned enterprises, reformed the tax system, restructured foreign investments, reduced trade protections, privatized the social security system, and created an independent central bank.[193] Between 1975 and 1989, Chile "sold off government ownership in 160 corporations, 16 banks, and over 2,600 agroindustrial plants, mines, and real estate holdings, in addition to returning property expropriated by the Allende government."[194] Interestingly, even during the period of authoritarian-based privatization, Pinochet's junta excluded the bulk of copper production from its list of privatized concessions and structural adjustment plans,[195] which it viewed as inextricably connected to domestic and national security.[196] Neoliberalism in Chile transformed the taxonomy of government and governmentality. In doing so, it impacted the state's construction of international law from a distance. [197]

---

192. VALDÉS, *supra* note 133, at 7; RICARDO FFRENCH-DAVIS, ECONOMIC REFORMS IN CHILE: FROM DICTATORSHIP TO DEMOCRACY 53 (2010) (calling Chile's unilateral import liberalization post-1973 "unprecedented in modern economic history"). *See also* REFORMAS, CRECIMIENTO Y POLÍTICAS SOCIALES EN CHILE DESDE 1973 (Ricardo Ffrench-Davis & Barbara Stallings eds., 2001) (presenting essays on Chile's economic liberalization following the military *coup d'état*).

193. Gilson & Milhaupt, *supra* note 102, at 227 (quoting ESTEBAN JADRESIC & ROBERTO ZAHLER, CHILE'S RAPID GROWTH IN THE 1990S: GOOD POLICIES, GOOD LUCK, OR POLITICAL CHANGE? 5 [IMF Working Paper 00/153, 2000]).

194. COLLINS & LEAR, *supra* note 111, at 49.

195. Chile had nationalized copper mines in 1971 and had solidified state ownership under Art. 17 of the Chilean Constitution. To provide foreign investors with credible assurances that future mining rights would be secure without modifying the nationalization clause, a delicate reinterpretation over six extended sessions arrived at a means of providing "juridical security without amending the constitution." ROBERT BARROS, CONSTITUTIONALISM AND DICTATORSHIP: PINOCHET, THE JUNTA, AND THE 1980 CONSTITUTION 105–6 (2002). *See also* Caldwell & Montes, *supra* note 161, at 272n37 (noting that Chile's CODELCO remained state-owned for "strategic" reasons); Juan Agustin Allende, *Historical Constraints to Privatization: The Case of the Nationalized Chilean Copper Industry*, STUD. IN COMP. INT'L DEV. 55, 56 (1988) (on the Pinochet government's bureaucratic-authoritarian need to control the Chilean National Copper Corporation [CODELCO], notwithstanding an ideological orientation toward privatization). By 2012, "no more than one-third of the copper industry [was] still state-owned." ANDRÉAS SOLIMANO, CHILE AND THE NEOLIBERAL TRAP: THE POST-PINOCHET ERA 5 (2012). Proposals to cut public spending have brought new attention on the call to privatize Chile's public copper company. *See* Laura Millan Lombrana, CODELCO UNION LEADERS FEARS PRIVATIZATION BY NEW CHILE PRESIDENT (Mar. 2,2018),Mining.com,http://www.mining.com/web/codelco-union-leader-fears-privatization-new-chile-president/

196. *See* BÜCHI, *supra* note 92, at 64–65.

197. *See* Undurraga, *supra* note 64, at 16 (referencing Foucault's idea of governmentality, or the art of government, broadly considered).

The Chicago Boys structurally reformed Chile's economy through multiple periods of economic shock treatment.[198] The aggressive privatization of public utilities in Chile, particularly its public water system,[199] laid the basis for emerging concerns about human rights and indigenous access to water.[200] Legislative enactments classifying lithium as a "strategic" material (due to its application in nuclear energy production) dampen the prospect that Chile will seek to replicate such a divestiture of state control over lithium production in the desert's fragile ecosystem.[201] Increasingly in Chile, neoliberalism's engagement with the environment and human geography suggests it is ripe for recalibration. Environmental consequences, democratic governance, and interest-group politics, together with possible restrictions to *campesinos'* and indigenous peoples' access to water, may contribute to a more-regulated lithium extraction policy for Chile.[202]

Bolivia and Dependency Theory: The Antipode

The Chicago School stood in stark contrast to the development economics championed by Argentine economist Raúl Prebisch (1901–1986).[203] Prebisch served as first executive secretary of the Economic Commission for Latin America of the United Nations from 1948–1962 and as founding secretary-general of the United Nations Conference on Trade and

---

198. Collins and Lear counted two periods, from 1975 to 1981 and 1985 to 1990. *See* COLLINS & LEAR, *supra* note 111, at 51. Alejandro Foxley counted four periods of economic adjustment (deregulation, 1973–1975; shock, 1975–1976; curbing expectations, 1976–1979; monetarism, 1979). *See* ALEJANDRO FOXLEY, LATIN AMERICAN EXPERIMENTS IN NEO-CONSERVATIVE ECONOMICS 49–61 (1983). *Cf.* SEBASTIAN EDWARDS & ALEJANDRA COX EDWARDS, MONETARISM AND LIBERALIZATION: THE CHILEAN EXPERIMENT 17 (1987) (four phases).

199. Gustavo Anríquez & Oscar Melo, *The Socio-Economic Context of Chilean Water Consumption and Water Markets Growth: 1985–2015*, *in* WATER POLICY IN CHILE 53, 54 (Guillermo Donoso ed., 2018).

200. *See* Chile, Ley Indigena N° 19.253.5, Octubre 5, 1993 (acknowledging indigenous communities as an essential part of the Chilean nation).

201. *See* Nguyen, *The White Gold Rush*, *supra* note 6.

202. In 2014, Chilean president Bachelet created a presidential delegate position for water resources (*Delegado Presidencial para los Recursos Hídricos*), affirming creation of regulations "*que aseguren el uso prioritario del agua para fines sociales.*" *See Gobierno nombra a Reinaldo Ruiz como nuevo delegado presidencial para los recursos hídricos*, FEDEFRUTA (Oct. 1, 2019), http://fedefruta.cl/gobierno-nombra-a-reinaldo-ruiz-como-nuevo-delegado-presidencial-para-los-recursos-hidricos/

203. *See* VALDÉS, *supra* note 133, at 181; EDGAR J. DOSMAN, THE LIFE AND TIMES OF RAÚL PREBISCH, 1901–1986, at 5 (2008).

Development.[204] Inspired by the Harrod-Domar model,[205] he and German-British economist Hans W. Singer propounded in the 1940s a theory of international trade that contrasted the interests of commodity producers, generally situated in countries at the periphery of world capitalism, and manufacturers, generally situated in countries comprising the core of world capitalism. The Singer-Prebisch model "postulated that, absent regulatory intervention, the terms of trade between primary (commodity) producers and manufacturers deteriorate over time." [206] This theory, suggestive of neoliberal structural *maladjustment*, holds that concentrated efforts to capitalize and increase commodity production (located generally in developing countries) create downward pressure and diminishing returns on commodity prices in relation to the value-added price of goods reaped by manufacturers using the commodity (who are located generally in developed countries).[207]

To rebalance the scales of world trade, they promoted technology transfer, regulatory intervention, import tariffs, import substitution, and invigorated means to enhance productive capacities through trade protectionism, capital controls, and self-sufficiency throughout the developing world.[208] Their means for escaping structural underdevelopment and poverty ultimately depended on efforts to reframe international economic law. Notable and contentious international legal outgrowths of *dependencia* theory, not exclusively applicable to Latin American history but certainly connected to it,[209] included expression of the New

---

204. *See* Caldwell & Montes, *supra* note 161, at 265n12 and accompanying text (referring to Prebisch as the main intellectual behind ECLA's influence, noting as well his contribution to the import-substitution model of dependency theory [the Singer-Prebisch model]). For more on Prebisch's significance, see generally EDGAR J. DOSMAN, THE LIFE AND TIMES OF RAUL PREBISCH, 1901–1986 (2008). In 1967 ECLA was renamed the Economic Commission for Latin America and the Caribbean (ECLAC).

205. The Harrod-Domar model is an amalgam of neo-Keynesian growth projections relating to the field of development economics. It emphasizes the importance of savings and investment as the key features of economic growth, and suggests that there is no natural reason for economies to produce balanced growth. *See generally* R. F. Harrod, *An Essay in Dynamic Theory*, 49 ECON. J. 14 (1939) (discussing the preliminary outlines of his "dynamic" theory); Evsey D. Domar, *Capital Expansion, Rate of Growth, and Employment*, 14 ECONOMETRICA 137 (1946) (discussing the relationship between capital accumulation and employment).

206. Nils Gilman, *The New International Economic Order: A Reintroduction*, 6 HUMANITY 1, 3 (2015).

207. *See* José Antonio Ocampo & María Angela Parra, *The Commodity Terms of Trade and Their Strategic Implications for Development*, *in* GLOBALIZATION UNDER HEGEMONY: THE CHANGING WORLD ECONOMY 164, 164 (Jomo K.S., 2006).

208. *See id. See also* VAN OVERTVELDT, *supra* note 133, at 347.

209. *See* Frank Griffith Dawson, *Contributions of Lesser Developed Nations to International*

International Economic Order,[210] promotion of permanent sovereignty over natural resources,[211] formulation of the Charter of Economic Rights and Duties and extension of national jurisdiction to regulate foreign investment in conformity with national objectives,[212] abrogation of the "prompt, adequate, and effective" standard of remuneration for foreign wealth deprivations,[213] establishment of the Group of 77 (G-77),[214] and articulation of the wide range of distributive justice concerns framing the so-called North-South debate.[215]

Dependencia teachings influenced Latin American approaches to international law from the 1940s to the 1980s, and informed the development of the international law of development.[216] Chicago School advo-

---

Law: The Latin American Experience, 13 CASE W. RES. J. INT'L L. 37 (1981) (noting that many proclamations of the NIEO crystallized the aspirations of Latin America).

210. *See* KOEN BYTTEBIER, TOWARDS A NEW INTERNATIONAL MONETARY ORDER (2017)

211. A/Res/ 1803 (XVIII) (Dec. 14, 1962). For background, see Stephen M. Schwebel, *The Story of the U.N.'s Declaration on Permanent Sovereignty over Natural Resources* 49 A.B.A. J. 463 (1963).

212. A/Res/29/3281 (Dec. 12, 1974) (especially Art. 2). For background, see Karol N. Gees, *Permanent Sovereignty Over Natural Resources: An Analytical Review of the United Nations Declaration and Its Genesis*, 13 INT'L & COMP. L.Q. 398 (1964).

213. The so-called Cordell Hull standard, expressive of the orthodox positon regarding the standard of remuneration for foreign wealth deprivations. *See* BILATERAL INVESTMENT TREATIES 1995–2006: TRENDS IN INVESTMENT RULEMAKING 48n76, and accompanying text (UNCTAD, 2007); 6 HUMANITY (2015) (presenting essays re-examining the salience of the NIEO); Frank G. Dawson & Burns H. Weston, *"Prompt, Adequate and Effective": A Universal Standard of Compensation?* 30 FORDHAM L. REV. 723, 733—34 (1962). For general review, see ROLAND KLÄGER, "FAIR AND EQUITABLE TREATMENT" IN INTERNATIONAL INVESTMENT LAW (2011).

214. G-77 formed in 1964 as a coalition of seventy-seven developing countries oriented around the establishment of a new division of labor to render consonant the framework of international trade with the needs of accelerated development. It developed specific and general trade policy issues and a permanent institutional structure at its first ministerial meeting with the issuance of the Charter of Algiers and its Programme of Action. *See* Charter of Algiers (Oct. 10–25, 1967), http://www.g77.org/doc/algier~1.htm. The group now claims 134 member states. *See The Member States of the Group of 77*, GROUP OF 77, http://www.g77.org/doc/members.html (last visited Feb. 21, 2019).

215. *See generally* JEFFREY A. HART & JOAN EDELMAN SPERO, THE POLITICS OF INTERNATIONAL ECONOMIC RELATIONS ch. 5 (5th ed. 2013) ("The North-South System and the Possibility of Change"); Charles Carter, *The North-South Debate*, 10 POL. STUD., 51 (2007) (discussing the need to give more scholarly research to the conventional wisdom that asserts an economic and social divide between the North and the South in the context of the United Kingdom); *see, e.g.*, Michael W. Doyle, *Stalemate in the North-South Debate: Strategies and the New International Economic Order*, 35 WORLD POL. 426 (1983) (reviewing earlier literature on the North-South debate).

216. *See* DANIEL YERGIN & JOSEPH STANISLAW, THE COMMANDING HEIGHTS: THE BATTLE

cates rejected Prebisch's structuralist orientation, deeming it populist and undesirable in terms of its reliance on state intervention.[217]

Although waning in influence, *dependencia* theory receives revitalized expression in academia[218] and in Bolivia (and notably Venezuela, as well), where the counterpoising developmental expression of international economic law continues to centrally inform a critique of the neoliberal model.[219] The argument here is that *dependencia's* somewhat indirect emphasis on extractivism, which focused on price inequalities associated with terms of trade and an assumed binary relationship between core and periphery, have reformulated under the banner of neoextractivism. This reformulation has created a new commodities consensus that more explicitly recognizes Latin America's "indisputable comparative advantages for economic growth" while identifying "new asymmetries" that accompany if not exacerbate continental inequalities.[220] These asymmetries find broader expression in burgeoning postcolonial international legal scholarship, growing at the Helsinki School under Martti Koskenniemi, in the Melbourne School under Anne Orford, in New Stream and Critical Legal Studies, and with TWAIL (Third World Approaches to International Law) and NAIL (New Approaches to International Law) movements.[221] And yet the co-constitutive effect of international law and

BETWEEN GOVERNMENT AND THE MARKETPLACE THAT IS REMAKING THE MODERN WORLD 234 (1998).

217. James H. Street, *Raúl Prebisch, 1901–1986: An Appreciation*, 21 J. ECON. ISSUES 649, 655 (1987).

218. Christy Thornton, *A Mexican International Economic Order? Tracing the Hidden Roots of the Charter of Economic Rights and Duties of States*, 9 HUMANITY 389, 408 (2018) (noting "the NIEO has been subject to renewed study"); Congyan Cai, *New Great Powers and International Law in the 21st Century*, 24 EUR. J. INT'L L. 755, 777 (2013) (noting that attempts to regulate transnational corporations more effectively through investment treaties suggest "that many claims of developing states in the NIEO movement . . . are largely justified."); Ruth Gordon, *The Dawn of a New, New International Economic Order?*, 72 L. & CONTEMP. PROBS 131, 132 (2009) (on potentials for a new NIEO following global economic problems in light of the 2008 banking crisis).

219. Venezuela's implosion under the successive and increasingly authoritarian regimes of Hugo Chávez and Nicolás Maduro has metastasized into a politically charged convergence of major power interests, with foreboding signs of coming conflict. *See* Press Statement of Michael R. Pompeo, Secretary of State, Recognition of Juan Guaido as Venezuela's Interim President by Several European Countries, US Dept. State (Feb. 4, 2019), https://www.state.gov/secretary/remarks/2019/02/288744.htm (announcing individual EU member state support for US recognition of a rival Venezuelan government).

220. Maristella Svampa, *The "Commodities Consensus" and Valuation Languages in Latin America*, 2 ALTERNAUTAS 45, 46 (2015).

221. Emergent and extant counterapproaches to established paradigmatic formula-

neoliberalism necessarily intrudes on the analytics of development, resulting in a limitation of exploitation options outside the ambit of neoliberal expectation in the aftermath of *dependencia's* demise.

Bolivia's Alternative View of Extractivism

If Chile's national embrace of neoliberal precepts owes its origins to the infusion of technocratic system-shocks supported by a legal cohabitation with authoritarianism, Bolivia's orientation toward extractivism traces to a national loss of spatial identity precipitated by nineteenth-century international interferences.

Bolivia remains South America's poorest country. [222] Its geography and remote distance from capital concentrations contributed to its impoverished status, making it also the last Latin American country to attain independence from imperial rule. Social and political unrest disrupted economic development and impeded state formation, over time producing weak structures of government and regulation. Poverty and geography combined to diminish the efficacy of Bolivia's already enfeebled bureaucratic class, inviting perceived intrusions from *compradores*, middlemen, and foreign financial meddlers. In the twentieth century, social movements, draped in nationalist master frames involving resource extraction, have achieved "inordinate symbolic potency," overturning governments in 1952, 2003, and 2005.[223] Notwithstanding periods of considerable misrule, Bolivia's political and international legal cultures remain wedded to the idea of external victimization by parties.

Lingering Effects of Bolivia's Postcolonial Encounter

The nineteenth-century War of the Pacific deeply affected Bolivia's international legal outlook, particularly in terms of perpetuating its rivalry

---

tions of international law can be found, as examples, in ANDERA BIANCHI ED., INTERNATIONAL LAW THEORIES (2016); ANNE ORFORD ED., INTERNATIONAL LAW AND ITS OTHERS (2006); Makau Mutua, *What Is TWAIL?*, 94 AM. SOC'Y INT'L L. PROC. 31 (2000); and NEW APPROACHES TO INTERNATIONAL LAW: THE EUROPEAN AND AMERICAN EXPERIENCES (José Maria Beneyto & David Kennedy eds., 2013).

222. *See GDP Per Capita (Current US$)*, WORLD BANK (2019), https://data.worldbank.org/indicator/NY.GDP.PCAP.CD?locations=ZJ-CL (ranking Bolivia's GDP last among South American countries [at $3,394] and fourth-poorest in the hemisphere [ahead of Honduras, Nicaragua, and Haiti]).

223. Kohl & Farthing, *supra* note 76, at 225; KLEIN, *supra* note 60, at xiii (noting that Bolivia's political evolution and mass popular movements sharply diverge from more common Latin American patterns).

with Chile and fomenting suspicions over North American and European imperial economic penetrations.[224] Putting aside the military and diplomatic miscalculations on the part of Bolivia and Perú that led to that war, it would grow in the twentieth century into deep reservations about the neoliberal model and its embedded representation in international law. Bolivia today still regards neoliberalism's antecedents as a major cause of the war, where the extractivist interests of British financiers and foreign capital harnessed Chileans as belligerent proxies against the combined, weaker interests of Perú and Bolivia.[225]

This history is more involved than a specific encounter with Chile. Spain's accelerating loss of control over its New World empire after 1810 threatened more immediate consequences affecting the orderly emergence of a new American system. Britain's taking of Trinidad (1797) and then Menorca in the Mediterranean (1798) foretold Spain's maritime weakness. Spain's secret retrocession of the Louisiana Territory to France (the Treaty of San Ildefonso, 1800[226]) signaled its imperial overextension and interest in consolidating hemispheric holdings. Maritime defeat at the Battle of Trafalgar (1805) and France's shocking invasion of Portugal (1807) and Spain (1808)—resulting in Napoleon's placement of his brother on the Castilian throne—underscored Spain's internal fragility, which turned Iberia into a battlefield.[227] This turmoil spurred tendentious thoughts of secession across Latin America. Emerging American republics relied on international law's efficient and adaptable ordering principle, *uti possidetis*, to close New World border gaps and forestall emerging territorial disputes caused by Spain's imperial implosion. The gains and costs of *uti possidetis* reverberate today. Bolivia's complicated geographic position resulted in additional defeats, making it a "prisoner of geography and a victim of historical adversity."[228] Bolivia has warred with all of its neighbors over resources and borders. Notable engagements included the Acre War with Brazil (1899–1903), for control over rubber and oil resources, and the Chaco War with Paraguay (1932–1935),

224. *See* Leslie E. Wehner, *Developing Mutual Trust: The Othering Process Between Bolivia and Chile*, 36 CANADIAN J. LAT. AM. & CARIB STUD. 109, 110 (2011) (discussing a culture of enmity tracing to the War of the Pacific [Nitrate War]).

225. *See supra*, ch. 2 text accompanying n. 41.

226. *See* Treaty of San Ildefonso (Oct. 1, 1800), AVALON PROJECT, http://avalon.law.yale.edu/19th_century/ildefens.asp

227. PAUL KENNEDY, THE RISE AND FALL OF THE GREAT POWERS: ECONOMIC CHANGE AND MILITARY CONFLICT FROM 1500 TO 2000, at 134 (1987).

228. *See* MORALES, *supra* note 48, at xxvii; JAMES DUNKERLEY, BOLIVIA: REVOLUTION AND THE POWER OF HISTORY IN THE PRESENT 2 (2007) (suggesting geographical determinism).

involving oil fields again and Bolivia's furtive attempt to restore national pride by gaining access to the Atlantic Ocean.[229] The lingering effects of *uti possidetis* have precipitated additional Andean violence elsewhere. Perú has disputed land claims against Bolivia and Ecuador. Brazil and the United Provinces of the Río de la Plata (the future Argentina) warred for five years over poorly defined borders of the Eastern Bank (Banda Orientale) during the transition from the colonial period.[230] Argentina and Chile sought papal mediation over the Southern Cone of Patagonia's Tierra del Fuego (Beagle Channel).[231] Border disputes from Central and South American continue to populate the docket of the International Court of Justice.[232] The entire region reflects the application of *uti possidetis*, which ironically purported to quiet title to border disputes in the wake of receding imperial rule.

However, a history of external encounters has created a sort of Potosí syndrome, where a succession of Iberian imperialists, Anglo neocolonialists, and extractivist applications over the mineral wealth of what was Kollasuyo, then Charcas, then Alto Peru, produced in Bolivia a "disavowal of modernity" and neoliberal Enlightenment principles as "expressed through a kind of retentive mercantilism or telluric protectionism."[233] Historian Kris Lane viewed the tortured history of

229. WALTRAUD QUEISER MORALES, BOLIVIA: LAND OF STRUGGLE 55 (1992).

230. *See generally* BRIAN VALE, A WAR BETWIXT ENGLISHMEN: BRAZIL AGAINST ARGENTINA ON THE RIVER PLATE 1825–1830 (2000) (the Cisplatine War) (detailing the failings of *uti possidetis* and the dispute over what would become Uruguay); Aldo Janotti, *Historigrafia Brasileira e Teoria da Fronteira Natural*, 51 REVISTA DE HISTÓRIA 239 (1975) (discussing the disagreement over using the Prata River as the border demarcation between Argentina and Brazil, which contributed to the war's initiation).

231. *See generally* James L. Garrett, *The Beagle Channel: Confrontation and Negotiation in the Southern Cone*, 27(3) J. INTERAMERICAN STUD. & WORLD AFFS. 81–109 (1985) (discussing the mediation of the dispute).

232. The ICJ Registry lists one pending case between Bolivia and Chile, one recently concluded; two disputes between Nicaragua and Colombia, and Guyana's appeal against a boundary award involving Venezuela. *See Pending Cases*, INT'L CT JUST., https://www.icj-cij.org/en/pending-cases (last visited Oct. 2, 2020). *See also* Case Concerning a Boundary Dispute between Argentina and Chile Concerning the Delimitation of the Frontier Line between Boundary Post 62 and Mount Fitzroy XXII RIAA 3–149 (1994) (border dispute in Patagonia between Argentina and Chile).

233. DUNKERLEY, *supra* note 228, at 3. The "syndrome" derives from the motto on the sixteenth-century escutcheon of the city of Potosí—marking this city on Bolivia's high plain as the envy of the world and the source of Spain's imperial wealth. The rank of "Imperial Villa," so named by the fifth viceroy of Perú, Francisco Toledo in 1575, elevated the city to world class status, with an extensive and segmented class structure and significant population base. *See Potosí: "Por la Potencia del César y por la Prudencia del Rey,"* LA PATRIA (Aug. 6, 2013), http://www.lapatriaenlinea.com/?nota=152931

Bolivia and the millions of lives consumed by five centuries of colonial extraction of the resources of *Cerro rico* and its surroundings as an ambivalent "exemplum" of a rich historical legacy cast into sharp relief against the "many paradoxes of global modernity."[234] These legacies cast deep Bolivian suspicions over liberal constructions of international law.

Bolivia's Fitful Relation to Neoliberalism

Bolivia's economic development reflected this "unusual degree of national control over its own resources,"[235] although its trajectory in natural-resource-led development has been uneven.[236] Bolivia ushered in a series of neoliberal economic reforms shortly after its 1982 return to democratic rule. Bolivia accepted loan guarantees from the IMF and World Bank in exchange for a dramatic downscaling of its public sector, including the privatization of major industries.[237] In 1996, Bolivia privatized its oil and gas industries.[238] Its state-owned petroleum enterprise (YPFB) subdivided into three companies and 50 percent shares were auctioned off, ending up under the control of Enron, Shell, and Repsol YPF.[239] Taxation rates on the energy sector were reduced to 18 percent from 50 percent, with international companies taking possession of the hydrocarbons extracted, except for an amount reserved for domestic consumption. Bolivia's Banzer government (term of office: 1997–2001) then privatized water in major Bolivian cities,[240] divesting the public util-

234. LANE, POTOSÍ 182.

235. KLEIN, *supra* note 60, at xiv.

236. *See* Brent Z. Kaup, *A Neoliberal Nationalization? The Constraints on Natural-Gas-Led Development in Bolivia*, 37 L. AM. PERSP. 123, 125 (2010) (noting Bolivia's attempt to recapture control over primary commodity production following a period of market liberalization).

237. *See Bolivia: Decreto Supremo N° 21060, 29 de Agosto de 1985*, Lexivox https://www.lexivox.org/norms/BO-DS-21060.html (pegging the Bolivian boliviano to the US dollar, reducing public-sector outlays and subsidies, eliminating quotas and tariffs in exchange for the temporary suspension of foreign debt payment and IMF credit); Isabella M. Radhuber, *Indigenous Struggles for a Plurinational State: An Analysis of Indigenous Rights and Competences in Bolivia*, J. LAT. AM. GEO. 167, 172 (2012).

238. *Ley de Hidrocarburos, Ley N° 1689, Ley de 30 de Abril de 1996, Congreso Nacional de Bolivia* [Hydrocarbons Law No. 1689], *available at* https://digitalrepository.unm.edu/cgi/viewcontent.cgi?article=1255&context=la_energy_policies (establishing the fundamental principles and norms governing Bolivia's hydrocarbon sector).

239. BRENT Z. KAUP, MARKET JUSTICE: POLITICAL ECONOMIC STRUGGLE IN BOLIVIA 76 (2013).

240. *Ley de Agua Potable y Alcantarillado Sanitario, Ley N° 2029 del 29 de Octubre de 1999*, Congreso Nacional de Bolivia, *available at* http://extwprlegs1.fao.org/docs/html/bol26680.htm (establishing rules regulating the provision and use of potable water and

ity to transnational corporations.[241] Shortly after 2000, these measures had created multidimensional social unrest among indigenous populations and labor groups.[242] A social movement among Bolivian coca leaf growers (*cocaleros*) formed in response to government market liberalization and privatization initiatives,[243] followed by the so-called Water War (*Guerra del Agua*) in Chochabamba (2000), Bolivia's third-largest city,[244] the violent Gas War protest in the indigenous city of El Alto (2003),[245] and the October Agenda, the series of stipulations in 2003 that forced the resignation of Bolivian president Gonzalo Sánchez de Lozada and ended Bolivia's neoliberal embrace.[246]

This disillusionment with neoliberalism resulted in the *campesino* and indigenous movement that produced Morales's election (2006) and his MAS (*Movimiento al Socialismo*) party's turn to a form of indigenous

---

procedures for granting concessions and licenses for the provision of such services). In effect, the legislation forced "other private entities, individuals, cooperatives, and communities" to enter into private contracts with the concessionaire for access to water. Coleman, *supra* note 99, at 10. Banzer first came to power as the result of a *coup d'état.* He was overthrown in 1978 but was elected to the presidency from 1997 to 2001.

241. MORALES, *supra* note 48, at 236; Coleman, *supra* note 99, at 10.

242. *See* Sharmila L. Murthy, *The Human Right(s) to Water and Sanitation: History, Meaning and the Controversy Over Privatization*, 31 BERKELEY. J. INT'L L. 89, 97 (2013) (discussing the Cochabamba protests); *Timeline: Chochabamba Water Revolt*, FRONTLINEWORLD (June 2012), http://www.pbs.org/frontlineworld/stories/bolivia/timeline.html (detailing IMF and World Bank loans of 1998 and 1999 conditioned on Bolivia's acceptance of structural reforms to sell off public enterprises, end water subsidies, and privatize water systems, including the Cochabamba water service).

243. *See* Eric Toussaint, *Bolivia: avances sobre los bienes communes y la reforma constitutional*, CADTM (Feb. 3, 2008) http://www.cadtm.org/Bolivia-avances-sobre-los-bienes (last accessed Sept. 24, 2018). A majority of the *cocaleros* were Quechua or Aymara migrants connected to indigenous communities where the growing of coca was a long-standing practice.

244. A series of public demonstrations against the divestiture of control over water service by Bolivia's SEMAPA municipal water authority for Cochabamba to a transnational consortium of private British and American companies operating under the name *Aquas del Tunari. See generally* Willem Assies, *David versus Goliath in Cochabamba: Water Rights, Neoliberalism, and the Revival of Social Protest in Bolivia*, 30 LATIN AM. PERSP. 14–36 (2003) (discussing the labor violence that ultimately forced the transnational consortium out of Cochabamba).

245. A forestalled effort using British and American petroleum-company capital to create a Pacific pipeline through Chile to access Bolivian hydrocarbon reserves. Protests resulted in the deaths of sixty citizens in clashes with government forces.

246. Lozada was a Chicago Boy, and subscribed to shock therapy free-market reforms, although his 1951 doctorate was in philosophy and literature. He also founded Bolivia's largest private mining company. *See* Julie Deardorff, *Bolivian President More Comfortable Playing Soccer Than Watching*, CHI. TRIB. (June 16, 1994), https://www.chicagotribune.com/news/ct-xpm-1994-06-16-9406160054-story.html.

nationalism predicated on decolonization.[247] Securing social-movement support enabled Morales to build on constitutional reforms in the early 1990s (for example, Ley de Participación) that decentralized national political party power and governance and strengthened municipal autonomy and local-level control.[248] On his hundredth day in office, Morales undertook measures to nationalize oil and natural gas production,[249] restructure the Bolivian constitution to allow for directly representation, and define for Bolivia a plurinational state of indigenous peoples with thirty-six official languages.[250] His turn toward rentier plurinationalism gained strong support from mestizo and indigenous communities, and resulted in an income stream to fund macroeconomic wealth redistribution,[251] but his policies evoked negative reactions from foreign investors, principally from Brazil, Spain, and Argentina,[252] and substantial questions about whether Bolivia can develop lithium-mining operations without substantially ceding control of them.

Argentina and Neoliberalism

Despite commonalities with Chile in terms of free-market reforms undertaken by authoritarian regimes, the neoliberal trajectories in Chile and Argentina diverged.[253] Pinochet's authoritarianism achieved more concentrated market transformations due to numerous factors, including media influences (principally the newspaper and radio complex, *El Mecurio*), the *Gremialista* impact on higher education, and the absence of Peronist-style networks, which in Argentina eroded technocratic, market-friendly policies and centered power among the poor.[254] The Argentine

247. *See* Nancy Postero, *Morales's MAS Government: Building Indigenous Popular Hegemony in Bolivia*, 37 L. AM. PERSP. 18, 19 (2010); Thomas Perreault, *From the Guerra Del Agua to the Guerra Del Gas: Resource Governance, Neoliberalism and Popular Protest in Bolivia*, 38 ANTIPODE 150, 153 (2006) (on Bolivia's popular rejection of neoliberal reforms and its re-scaling of resource governance); DONNA LEE VAN COTT, FROM MOVEMENTS TO PARTIES IN LATIN AMERICA: THE EVOLUTION OF ETHNIC POLITICS 58 (2005) (associating the coca growers movement with indigenous resistance to the Bolivian state and US imperialism).

248. MORALES, *supra* note 48, at 243–44.

249. Morales's actions repealed the Hydrocarbons Law. No. 1689 (1996).

250. Radhuber, *supra* note 237, at 171.

251. Christopher W. Euans, "Bolivia's 'Left Turn' Toward Rentier Plurinationalism and Its Effects on Ethnic Tensions and Solidarity" 3–4 (thesis, Naval Postgraduate School, June 2016).

252. Carin Zissis, *Bolivia's Nationalization of Oil and Gas*, COUNCIL ON FOREIGN REL. (May 12, 2006), https://www.cfr.org/backgrounder/bolivias-nationalization-oil-and-gas

253. Undurraga, *supra* note 64, at 11.

254. *See generally* Undurraga, *supra* note 64. Additionally, "full-scale economics train-

junta's loss of credibility following the humiliating Malvinas defeat and subsequent explosion of public debt and inflation "destroyed not only the reputation of the military but also that of liberal market reform."[255] Unable to advance its own terms of transition to democracy, the junta ceded agenda-setting authority to forces inhabiting Argentina's civil society, creating political space for the expression of social resistance.[256] These sectors precipitated "an unusually high level of human rights innovation and protagonism,"[257] shaping Argentine social movements at domestic and international levels.[258]

Efforts to reestablish neoliberalism resurfaced under Carlos Menem's presidency (term of office: 1989–1999).[259] In concert with the so-called Washington Consensus,[260] which articulated "ten neoliberal commandments,"[261] Menem confronted a convertibility crisis and accelerating devaluation of the peso by implementing with "unusual speed and thoroughness"[262] economic prescriptions that privatized the bulk of Argentina's state enterprises.[263] Decentralized constitutional reforms

---

ing did not begin in Argentina until the late 1950s," and structuralist views identified with Prebisch tended to prevail over neoliberal approaches. Biglaiser, *supra* note 132, at 277–78.

255. *Id.* at 19.

256. *See* ALISON BRYSK, THE POLITICS OF HUMAN RIGHTS IN ARGENTINA: PROTEST, CHANGE, AND DEMOCRATIZATION 21–22 (on the emergence in Argentina of collective action and a "culture of resistance.").

257. Kathryn Sikkink, *From Pariah State to Global Protagonist: Argentina and the Struggle for International Human Rights*, 50 L. AM. POL. & SOC'Y 1, 2 (2008).

258. *Id.* at 3; Richard Stahler-Sholk & Harry E. Vanden, *A Second Look at Latin American Social Movements: Globalizing Resistance to the Neoliberal Paradigm*, 38 L. AM. PERSP. 5, 6 (2011) (reviewing the role of Latin American social movements domestically and in terms of transnational developments); Edward C. Epstein, *The Piquetero Movement of Greater Buenos Aires: Working Class Protest During the Current Argentine Crisis*, 28 CAN. J. L. AM. & CARIBBEAN. STUD. 11, 12 (2003) (on the rise of the *piquetero* [picketer] movement in Argentina).

259. *See* KAREN ANN FAULK, IN THE WAKE OF NEOLIBERALISM: CITIZENSHIP AND HUMAN RIGHTS IN ARGENTINA 76 (2013) (noting neoliberalism's embrace following the hyperinflationary spirals that had plagued the Alfonsín regime [1983–1989]).

260. The Washington Consensus policy prescriptions included fiscal discipline; redirected public spending; tax, interest rate, and exchange rate reform; trade liberalization; foreign direct investment promotion; state enterprise privatization; deregulation; and enhanced property rights. For more, see John Williamson, *What Washington Means by Policy Reform*, *in* LATIN AMERICAN ADJUSTMENT: HOW MUCH HAS HAPPENED? ch. 2 (John Williamson ed., 1990).

261. Laura Macdonald & Arne Ruckert, *Post-Neoliberalism in the Americas: An Introduction*, *in* POST-NEOLIBERALISM IN THE AMERICAS 1, 3 (Laura Macdonald & Arne Ruckert eds., 2009).

262. Teichman, *supra* note 59, at 31.

263. Miguel Teubal, *Rise and Collapse of Neoliberalism in Argentina: The Role of Economic Groups* 20 J. DEV. SOC., 173, 181 (2004). Argentina sold off $31 billion worth of public

granted provinces original dominion over natural resources existing in their territory.[264] However, an agroindustrial and finance concentration exposed Argentina's manufacturing sector to pressures of globalization,[265] ushering in, between 1989 and 2002, the worst economic crisis in the country's history. Hyperinflation spawned recession followed by depression, leading ultimately to the largest debt default of any country ever.[266] The disarticulation of Argentina's industrial sector continues to render its economy susceptible to agricultural price fluctuations and vicissitudes associated with primary commodity exports.

President Mauricio Macri's agenda in 2020, complicated by a legislative plurality of seats in both houses of Argentina's legislature, was to reestablish policies that to create an attractive a foreign investment climate, with lithium exploitation at the forefront of extraction policy. Macri's market-friendly government eliminated the export tax on mineral products and relaxed repatriation of profits to overseas headquarters, creating a new and more congenial atmosphere for transnational corporations than decades of Peronista rule ever allowed.[267] Although confronting acute conditions of financial insecurity and a deeply divided electorate that again brought Peronistas back into power in late 2019,[268] Argentina's ambition is to secure as much as 45 percent of the global lithium market, a substantial increase from its already-impactful 16 percent market share.[269]

---

enterprises between 1991 and 1998. *See* Paul Cooney, *Argentina's Quarter Century Experiment with Neoliberalism: From Dictatorship to Depression*, 11 REV. ECON. CONTEMP. 7, 18 (2007).

264. Artícolo 124, Constitucion de la Naciona Argentina, Ley N° 24.430 (Diciembre 15 de 1994) ("Corresponde a las provincias el dominio originario de los recursos naturales exístentes en su territorio").

265. Cooney, *supra* note 263, at 9, 17.

266. *Id.* at 9.

267. Juliana Castilla, *Argentina Seeks to Overtake Chile in South America Lithium Race*, REUTERS (Nov. 13, 2017), https://uk.reuters.com/article/uk-argentina-mining-lithium/argentina-seeks-to-overtake-chile-in-south-america-lithium-race-idUKKBN1DD2IP

268. The Argentine economy experienced massive dislocations between 1998 and 2002 but recovered after debt restructuring by 2005. Macri's market-friendly government came to power in 2015 with confident international expectations of maintaining stability through measured peso devaluations. This belief rapidly collapsed in view of concerns that the strengthening dollar would cause massive inflationary pressure and difficulty with debt management given a $50 billion International Monetary Fund loan and Macri's unexpected bid to secure emergency release of some of that loan. *See* Luc Cohen, *Argentina's Economic Crisis Explained in Five Charts*, REUTERS (Aug. 28, 2018), https://www.reuters.com/article/us-argentina-economy/argentinas-economic-crisis-explained-in-five-charts-idUSKCN1LD1S7. Argentina's Peronists defeated Macri in 2019, with former president Cristina Fernandez de Kirchner running as vice president alongside President Alberto Fernandez.

269. Gilbert, *supra* note 15 (noting Argentina's primary deficiency in human capital).

Argentina is the only country in the triangle to permit exploitation of lithium freely through concessions, a policy introduced by Macri in 2015.[270] Since 2016, the lithium sector has received nearly $2 billion in foreign investment, with 53 feasibility studies underway, covering a total of 876,000 hectares in northwest Argentina.[271] More than simply a return to state management, the challenges of Argentina's growth and management strategy must incorporate a market locus while balancing social needs and demands that respond to local traditions and communities and a history of energized social movements.[272] Argentina's return to refashioned neoliberalism has only incompletely balanced these concerns against the suspicions of its antiglobalists, which again have moved Latin America's third-largest economy toward the left. Broader consideration of emerging water and sanitation concerns in pursuit of lithium extraction creates an as-yet unreconciled ambivalence for Argentina and its oscillating encounter with neoliberalism in the Lithium Triangle.

Conclusion

Throughout the Lithium Triangle, the politics of memory and authoritarianism compete to shape visions of the redemocratized public sphere. Social forces are entangled in the debate, creating "a pluralistic but tension-ridden public agenda."[273] Country-specific encounters with international law and its neoliberal emphases create hemispheric histories that influence extraction policies in the Lithium Triangle.

While scholars debate neoliberalism's transformative change in the Americas, pathways toward post-neoliberal politics will probably include socially interventionist and ameliorative alternatives to the shock therapies introduced by the Chicago Boys and subsequently forwarded by the structural adjustment prescriptions of the Washington Consensus.[274] Assessments differ as to whether these pathways will amount to minor

---

270. Sabrina Roth, *Communities Challenge Lithium Production in Argentina*, DIÁLOGO CHINO (Mar. 12, 2019), https://dialogochino.net/24736-communities-challenge-lithium-production-in-argentina/

271. Daniel Gutman, *Argentina Pursues the Lithium Dream*, IPS (Jan. 11, 2018), http://www.ipsnews.net/2018/01/argentina-pursues-lithium-dream/

272. Grugel & Riggirozzi, *supra* note 71, at 3.

273. *See* Luis Roniger & Mario Sznajder, *The Legacy of Human-Rights Violations in the Southern Cone: Argentina, Chile, and Uruguay* 184 (1999).

274. *See* Laura Macdonald & Arne Ruckert, *Afterward: Post-Neoliberal Politics and Pathways*, *in* POST-NEOLIBERALISM IN THE AMERICAS 246 (Laura Macdonald & Arne Ruckert eds., 2009).

tinkerings with the neoliberal model,[275] or broad reformations of extraction policies that include human rights and human geographic considerations.

An important explanation for the overall continuity of neoliberal extraction policies in the Atacama, however, underscores forum-shopping investor incentives that complicate the capital-seeking economies of the region. Argentina's and Chile's investment climates, matched by internal human capital capacities, make the development of lithium brine assets much more likely than it is in Bolivia. In effect, Bolivia's reliance on the "double movement" of marketization stimulates state interventions against the same investment forces relied on to capitalize its lithium industry. Bolivia's post-neoliberal extraction policy appears to be caught between sentiments of victimization and disavowal of foreign intrusion—a historically derived Potosí syndrome—on the one hand, and on the other hand, efforts to free its plurinational state from the resource trap that instantiates a rentier mentality. The co-constitutive forces of international law and neoliberalism perpetuate Bolivia's stasis, making it codependent on extraction policies developing amid its Andean neighbors. Bolivia's compromised placement between the double movement of marketization makes it a policy-taker, not policy-maker, in the unfolding triangulated dynamics of extraction politics in the Atacama.

Argentina also appears to be caught between co-constitutive forces of international law and neoliberalism. In Argentina, the subordination to the provinces of federal control over mineral deposits has increased its business-friendly reputation while strengthening aggressive foreign investment initiatives. However, a rising rejection of extensive market deregulation appears to signify recognition of neoliberalism's limitations. This rejection, fomented by populist protest and left-of-center social movements, stems in part from civil society responses to authoritarian rule, suspicions of transnationalism, and an emboldened sense of citizenship and human rights concerns connected to the Lithium Triangle's emerging water and human geographic considerations. Argentina's ambivalence marks the persistent disconnect between the state and *populi.* Official attempts to establish an atmosphere conducive to foreign direct investment encounter robust social countermovements in response to the tradition of corruption and authoritarian misrule.

---

275. Paul Alexander Haslam, *Is There a Post-Neoliberal Policy Toward Foreign Direct Investment in Argentina and Chile?, in* POST-NEOLIBERALISM IN THE AMERICAS 131 (Laura Macdonald & Arne Ruckert eds., 2009).

What might the future hold? Perhaps neoliberalism's and international law's association with plunder extractivism will yield new development strategies that accommodate sustainable "middle road" environmental alternatives. These imaginaries would still capture income associated with increasing demand for minerals such as lithium,[276] while balancing concerns for topophilia, indigenous populations, and hyperarid environmental conditions.

Election of Chile's postauthoritarian *Concertación* governments stimulated thoughts of a major shift toward these policy directions. However, policy continuities seemed to endure, notwithstanding an end to impunity.[277] The resilience of neoliberalism's postauthoritarian reign highlighted the depth to which Chicago-style economics penetrated the catallaxy of Chile's interlaced economies. Here, extractivism, water rights, and human rights conformed to the market ethos of Chicago-style teachings. Here, tertiary education stymied universalizing reforms, invigorating the concept of the education citadel populated by epistemic communities of foreign-trained and self-replicating technopols. Here, compliant ecclesiastical and bureaucratic institutions facilitated a paradoxical model of public administration, which allowed military men trained in regimental hierarchy to engage coercive power while divesting control over the economy. And here, Chile's neoliberal ideology most effectively permeated hemispheric international law as the antipode to *dependencia*, which it roundly defeated.

Neoliberalism forged a space between self-reliant Latin Americanism and integrationist Pan-Americanism. This new space imported and absorbed the generative ethos of market capitalism while clinically disaggregating the authoritarian influences relied on to promote market capitalism's development and exportation. The palliative aspects of neoliberalism *qua pharmakon* overshadowed the poisonous side effects of shock therapy, which could only be controlled by forcibly strapping Chilean society to the Procrustean gurney of impunity.

While not an exemplary pathway for development, forces internal to Chile's postauthoritarian rule may now provide counterbalances to neoliberalism's application in the resource-rich Lithium Triangle. While other scenarios are possible, it appears certain that neoliberalism's trans-

---

276. On the growing prioritization of environmental concerns and mining interests, see Robin Broad & Julia Fischer-Mackey, *From Extractivism Towards Buen Vivir: Mining Policy as an Indicator of a New Development Paradigm Prioritising the Environment*, 38 THIRD WORLD Q. 1327 (2017).

277. *See* TAYLOR, *supra* note 85, at 99.

formative hold on Chile will drive regional responses to mineral development in the high-altitude plains of the Atacama.

Lithium, as much as it is a metal for the future, is a metaphor for the sustaining and central influence of neoliberal extraction policy in the Andean Cone. It harbors the history and counterpoising demands of industry and human geography, revealing once again in an area perceived as remote and removed that the Atacama Desert is a central contested space in the coming history of international law in the Americas.

SEVEN

The Spatial Turn, Extractivism, and Remoteness

Neoliberalism and international law co-constitute within the history of the Atacama Desert. They inhabit a world of remoteness and contribute to a process of marketization that propels adoption of economic liberalization principles that at the same time conflict with, destabilize, or challenge public security. This interaction breeds a kind of misunderstood ambivalence that generally marks international law's engagement with the Americas. This double pull of marketization and international law creates a security dilemma in terms of international law's interface with domestic policy objectives. It pressures historically based associational schemes of the *ayllus*, the communal land- and lineage-based exchange and security system of the indigenous Andean peoples. It adds pressure to growing inequities relating to water and sanitation use and intensifies criticisms relating to domestic distribution relating to these public goods. And it makes poignant the *pharmakon*-like costs and benefits of globalized engagement among Andean Cone countries, where curative pursuits, poorly administered by weak states, often incubate prodromal maladies.

If remoteness is a metaconcept, it has substantive effects. Remote areas of the world contain hidden background norms, which more than passively act on international law's development or reception.[1] International law's spatial turn helps to identify the process by which these norms emerge. Interactions with the geographic and temporal environment help to shape and frame the normative content of the interna-

1. *See* Yishai Blank & Issi Rosen-Zvi, *The Spatial Turn in Legal Theory*, 10 HAGAR: STUDIES IN CULTURE, POLITY AND IDENTITIES 39, 51 (2010) (identifying the role of critical legal geography in exposing hidden background norms that construct space).

tional legal rules that give expression to the landscape. International law's engagement in the Atacama teaches us that the intersubjectivities of time and space complicate and impact the Eurocentric rational-choice construct of international law. Social and spatial structures inhabiting areas perceived as remote affect the formation and application of international law. They simultaneously evidence international law's formation at the periphery as they frame the periphery.

The double pull of extraction policy and international law in the Atacama reveals the complexity of this relationship. It gives rise to the emerging and incongruent attribute of neoliberal multiculturalism,[2] which embraces a language of cultural regard and yet offsets that rhetoric with policy decisions that impede sovereign control over natural resources. The "paradox of simultaneous cultural affirmation and economic marginalization" supports a discursive state interest in human rights that practically conflicts with indigenous empowerment.[3] The spatial geography of neoliberalism instantiates a language of international legal progressivity that seemingly has outdistanced its chief critic, the NIEO movement,[4] but it inadequately addresses problems of inequality. It accounts for the simultaneous construction of pluralistic and solidaristic pathways of development in the Americas. It also complicates rhetorical references to plurinationalism, which still must operate within the outer reaches of neoliberalism.

The NIEO attempted to rebalance structural inequities relating to extraction policy and national sovereignty; it attempted to rebalance terms of trade and fictions of Most Favored Nation status (now unhelpfully rephrased as normal trade relations); and it attempted to reach into and rebalance private international law's transnational presence in corporate, quasipublic concession engagements with domestic economies and the public international legal edifice that gave transnational expression to them.[5] However, its absolute economic sovereignty stance

2. *See generally* Charles R. Hale, *Does Multiculturalism Menace? Governance, Cultural Rights and the Politics of Identity in Guatemala*, 34 J. LAT. AM. STUD. 485–524 (2002) (challenging the assumption that underlying principles of state-endorsed multiculturalism conflict with neoliberal political and economic policies).

3. *Id.* at 493.

4. The NIEO informal last "hurrah" has been associated with the publication of THE CHALLENGE TO THE SOUTH: THE REPORT OF THE SOUTH COMMISSION (1990). Branislav Gosovic, *The Resurgence of South-South Cooperation*, 37 THIRD WORLD Q. 733, 734 (2016).

5. *See generally* Antony Anghie, *Legal Aspects of the New International Economic Order*, 6 HUMANITY 145–58 (2015) (discussing the legal context contributing toward the drive to establish the New International Economic Order).

conflicted with neoliberalism's emphasis on transnational economic interdependence.[6]

Although the NIEO ultimately failed to recast the international law of foreign wealth deprivation, its political significance admits to something more than the phantom twitches of an amputated limb.[7] Its historiographic periodization, between ECLA's birth in 1946 and informal death with the 1982 Latin American debt crisis,[8] did not supplant neoliberalism's policies of structural adjustment with a more broadly construed Third World right of development. Neoliberalism's enduring penetration into the geospace of the Global South may yet create emerging markets beyond the dramatic rise of the BRIC countries.[9] However, it remains connected to incongruities of neoliberalism's unfulfilled encounter with human and indigenous rights.

Formative presentations of the NIEO movement adopted a geo-framework bounded by a Tordesillas-like simplicity, systematically and geographically segmenting the world into two sectors, the rich North and the poor South.[10] The NIEO's origins grew out of Latin America, beginning with Raúl Prebisch's stewardship of the Economic Commission for Latin America in the late 1940s. It spread to the Asian-African Bandung Conference in 1955, and then to the United Nations Conference on Trade and Development, again under Prebisch's secretary-generalship in the 1960s. It congealed as a voting bloc in the United Nations General Assembly with the establishment of the Group of 77, an amalgam of poor southern states and states associated with the Nonaligned Movement. Nils Gilman noted the important but underacknowledged afterlife of the NIEO—an increase in global GDP for emerging markets to 40 percent of world GDP.[11] The binary contraposition of core and periphery, as represented by the North-South engagement with international law, never appropri-

6. Nils Gilman, *The New International Economic Order: A Reintroduction*, 6 HUMANITY 1, 5 (2015).

7. *See id.* at 9 (contesting the ignominious failure of the NIEO project).

8. *See id.* at 8 (referring to the 1982 bail out of indebted Latin American countries as "[t]he final dagger" of the NIEO's bid to reframe global economic governance).

9. *See* Li Xing, *Understanding the Hegemony and the Dialectics of the Emerging World Order*, in THE BRICS AND BEYOND: THE INTERNATIONAL POLITICAL ECONOMY OF THE EMERGENCE OF A NEW WORLD ORDER 1, 12 (Li Xing ed., 2014).

10. *See, e.g.*, ROGER D. HANSEN, BEYOND THE NORTH-SOUTH STALEMATE (1979).

11. Gilman, *supra* note 6, at 10 (borrowing the phrase from Jennifer Wenzel). He noted that the Global North's production of world GDP fell from 80 percent (from the time of the 1974 Global South declaration of its Charter of Economic Rights and Duties of States) to 57 percent. *Id.*

ately reflected the complexity of the relationship or the interplay within it.

This study of remoteness in the Atacama reveals that the NIEO's legacy in the Americas is not as moribund as it seems, and neoliberalism's impress in the Americas is not as well received as the casualness of the NIEO's obituary and periodization would suggest. However, a convergence of fitful economic growth and weak political institutions continues to stand behind the "social malaise" of Latin American countries generally and Andean countries specifically.[12] Without capital investment, the Andean Cone region will continue to struggle with "underlying social problems, different in each society but all too similar at many levels of analysis."[13] The allure of globalization also exposes these economies "to the vicissitudes of international financial markets," where the need to attract and retain capital results in "competitive bidding."[14] Metrics relied on by the Global Competitive Index indicate substantial divergence among Andean Cone countries in terms of global competitiveness.[15] Identifying the most conducive economic environment for investment leverages concessions or creates competitions among Andean Cone countries and results in a climate of international capital forum-shopping protected by the pro-investment structure of international economic law. Balancing a Hobson's choice of plunder extractivism on the one hand, with transnational isolation on the other, contributes to stylized and simplistic either/or characterizations of the problem. Oscillating waves of neoliberal engagement, bounded by the parameters or nodal inflection points of Chicago-school economics and *dependencia* theory, result in globalized intrusions of deregulation that contrast a desire for foreign capital infusions with loss-of-sovereignty concerns.

12. Riordan Roett, *Conclusion: The Andean Crisis in Context, in* THE ANDES IN FOCUS: SECURITY, DEMOCRACY & ECONOMIC REFORM 191 (Russell Crandall, Guadalupe Paz, & Riordan Roett eds., 2005).

13. *Id.*

14. Kurt Weyland, *Neoliberalism and Democracy in Latin America: A Mixed Record,* 46 LAT. AM. POL. & SOC. 135, 144 (2004).

15. The twelve pillars of competitiveness compiled by the World Economic Forum Global Competitiveness Index include measurements of institutional strength, infrastructure, macroeconomic environment, health and primary education, higher education and training, goods market efficiency, labor market efficiency, financial market development, technological readiness, market size, business sophistication, and innovation. Andean Community countries ranked as follows: Chile 33, Colombia 66, Peru 72, Argentina 92, Ecuador 97, Bolivia 121, and Venezuela 127, of 151 countries covered for sampling data collected between 2007 and 2017. *See Global Competitiveness Index,* WORLD BANK (2017), https://tcdata360.worldbank.org/indicators/gci?country=BRA&indicator=632&viz=line_chart&years=2007

This balancing act has left its greatest impact on Bolivia's engagement with international law, although iterations of the antiglobalization story abound throughout the southern continent, especially in Ecuador, Venezuela, and Peru. Bolivia's major populations centers, concentrated in the distant highland regions, developed from the colonial focus on the Audiencia de Charcas and its mother lode of silver. The structural configuration of its colonial contours laid bare its remote access to its littoral zone, which attracted an influx of foreign labor and capital when a succession of mineral temptations and resources were found in the Atacama, making it ripe for annexation. The political demarcation of the colonial frontier in no way contemplated the impact on human geography,[16] and in unanticipated ways launched its own dynamic. A similar circumstance occurred with the 1825 Mexican colonization laws.[17] These laws encouraged Anglo Americans to settle the "unoccupied" Coahuila and Tejas territories as a buffer against European encroachment and rising Native American discontent. Within five years, having failed first to counter, then to ban, the onslaught of new immigration,[18] the frontier immigrants warred against the Mexican government, taking the territory of Tejas and establishing the Republic of Texas in 1836.

More meaningful than the faint cartographic imaginaries of colonial line-drawing is the actual process of land appropriation, division, and cultivation that breeds the spatial consciousness of secession. The *nomos* of Spanish land configuration in the New World depended on a presumptive and fictively unchallengeable universalism—a process that was as dispossessive of indigenous interests as it was oblivious to a concept of the political. Indeed, indigenous populations of the Americas "played no significant role in fixing the international boundaries that divide the two continents today."[19] However discounted, human geography and the spatial politics of memory have had and continue to have an effect on the development of international law in the Americas.

Bolivia's engagement with the structure of modern international economic organization bears the psychological imprint of its structural seclusion notwithstanding attempts in the 1980s to open up its economy

16. VICTOR PRESCOTT & GILLIAN D. TRIGGS, INTERNATIONAL FRONTIERS AND BOUNDARIES: LAW, POLITICS AND GEOGRAPHY 30 (2008).

17. *Colonization Law of Coahuila and Texas* (March 24, 1825), 1 GAMMEL'S LAWS OF TEXAS 1822–1905, 40ff. (1906).

18. *See* Josefina Zoraida Vázquez, *The Colonization and Loss of Texas: A Mexican Perspective*, *in* MYTHS, MISDEEDS, AND MISUNDERSTANDINGS: THE ROOTS OF CONFLICT IN U.S.-MEXICAN RELATIONS 47, 61 (Jaime E. Rodríguez O. & Kathryn Vincent eds., 1997).

19. PRESCOTT & TRIGGS, *supra* note 16, at 261.

through resource deregulation. The experience of neoliberalism's shock therapy resulted in the domestic turbulence of the oil and gas wars between 2000 and 2005 and provoked a retrenchment and governmental consolidation of the natural-gas industry in 2006. It revealed the rise of remote resource extraction as a spur for mobilization politics.

Although long characterized as a "beggar on a throne of gold," Bolivia's modern encounter with neoliberalism and extractivism has been closely associated with the rise of resource nationalism, a phenomenon whereby countries rich in natural resources nevertheless devolve into a condition of economic dependency and peripheralization.[20] Its modern manifestation in Bolivia assigns an important role to the foreign oil companies in prompting the Chaco War (1932–1935), which resulted in Bolivia's loss of most of the disputed oil-rich area to Paraguay.

The war itself presented something of an odd twentieth-century mirror image to the nitrate war in the Atacama. Spain had parceled out the Gran Chaco (technically, the Chaco-Boreal[21]) to the Audiencia of Charcas, notwithstanding the absence of interest among the Spanish *Altiplano* successors to the remote region save for control over the navigable Paraguay River.[22] The Bolivian *caudillos*, by virtue of *uti possidetis*, asserted *de jure* title to this ill-defined, remote, and arid spatial imaginary that otherwise contained indigenous people (the Guaraní) and Paraguayan cattle settlers. Paraguay asserted *de facto* control over the area given its nearby settlements; Bolivia's nearest settlements were hundreds of kilometers away.[23] In a serious and early indictment of the historical *effectivités* or factual circumstances on which colonial line-drawing sometimes depends, the League of Nations' Report of the Chaco Commission concluded:

> This was the definite beginning of the controversy concerning legal titles, the scope of the rule of the *uti possidetis* of 1810 in American law, the interpretation of the Acts of the Spanish Crown before that date, the narrations of the expeditions of the conquistadors, the evidence

20. *See generally* KEVIN A. YOUNG, BLOOD OF THE EARTH: RESOURCE NATIONALISM, REVOLUTION, AND EMPIRE IN BOLIVIA (2017) (discussing Bolivia's historical struggle for control over its natural resources in the context of the 1952 Bolivian revolution and the middle-class reform party that led it, the Movimiento Nacionalista Revolucionario).

21. The war was fought over the Chaco Boreal, the area north of the Pilcomayo River, as distinguished from the Chaco Central and the Chaco Austral.

22. *See* BRUCE W. FARCAU, THE CHACO WAR: BOLIVIA AND PARAGUAY, 1932–1935, at 6 (1996).

23. *Id.* at 8.

> of explorers and that furnished by geographical maps. The dispute has never ceased since then. It has only become more and more bitter . . . This battle of historians and jurists, convinced of the justice of their own cause and of the adversary's bad faith, has helped to create the noxious atmosphere surrounding the dispute.[24]

In 1928, the United States–owned Standard Oil Company struck oil in the western region of Chaco.[25] Bolivia's interest in the region intensified immediately. The oil-exploitation prospect linked with Bolivia's longstanding interest in gaining pelagic access to global commerce. When the Treaty of Lima (1929) settled the Tacna and Arica dispute between Perú and Chile, a festering remnant of the War of the Pacific, Bolivia's only remaining hope of regaining sovereign access to the sea meant turning eastward toward the Paraguay River. The Paraguay River merges with the Paraná River and then the Uruguay River to debouch into the Atlantic Ocean. This winding riparian pathway to blue water made more imperative the control over the Chaco oil fields. Bolivia's defeat in the war, which is sometimes described as a proxy war involving competing oil interests of foreign concessionaires,[26] Royal Dutch Shell and Standard Oil, prompted a pattern of nationalistic and authoritarian retrenchment, beginning with José David Toro's 1937 nationalization of Standard Oil Company's holdings in Bolivia (the first of many Latin American nationalizations), the tin-mining-industry takeover in 1952, and more oil nationalizations in 1969 following the reopening of the oil sector with Bolivia's 1955 petroleum code. The cross-cutting interests of resource nationalists reveal populist sentiments and multiclass coalitions—urban and labor groups, grassroots and worker associations, intellectuals, and a spectrum of political ideologies—that congeal around state control over natural resources.[27]

These resource nationalists and populists reemerged during the troubled period of Bolivia's engagement with neoliberalism. It is interesting to note that intra-Andean trade underwent a prolonged period of dormancy during the debt crisis of the 1980s directly "as a result of unilateral efforts by [Andean Group] members to participate in the emerging

24. Report of the Chaco Commission, *Dispute Between Bolivia and Paraguay*, LEAGUE OF NATIONS 22 (1934).

25. *See* Christian Gómez, Jr., *The Promise of Oil in Paraguay*, AMERICAS Q. (July 12, 2013), https://www.americasquarterly.org/content/promise-of-oil-in-paraguay

26. *See* YOUNG, *supra* note 20, at 21.

27. *See generally id.*

global economy."[28] The double pull of neoliberal globalization and parochial domestic policies prevented the establishment of a common external tariff, postponed liberalization for competitive goods, and limited the harmonization of industrial policies to a few sectors.[29] During the 1990s, heterodox Latin American reform and austerity policies moved again in the direction of neoliberal economic orientations, which gained support with the global financial backing of international economic organizations such as the International Monetary Fund, the Inter-American Development Bank, the World Bank, and the United States Treasury Department.[30] Codependency on extraction policies informed by oscillating waves of neoliberal engagement created a climate for regional and subcontinental integration initiatives, as recognized by the 1969 Cartagena Agreement and offshoots to establish the Latin American Free Trade Association (*Asociación Latinoamericana de Integración*), the Andean Community of Nations (*Comunidad Andina*), Mercosur (*Mercado Común del Sur*), and the Andean Integration System (*Sistema Integracion Andina*, 1996).[31] Although motivated by poverty-reduction and social-inclusion strategies, international financial institutions and regional agglomerations nevertheless encountered "a more broadly and socially contested double movement"—a kind of double movement that impedes the wider liberal project due to "the geopolitics of long-term peripheralization."[32]

The idea of remoteness in international law obscures the impetus for territorial change. Resources formerly deemed too remote or technologically unobtainable lull the international legal mind into a kind of spatial complacency. This complacency remits resolution of emergent resource disputes to territorializing principles that never perfectly sealed the gaps along the razor's edge of sovereignty[33]—*res nullius* (a thing

28. 1 "Globalization," ENCYCLOPEDIA OF TRADE, LABOR, AND POLITICS 454 (Ashish K. Vaidya ed., 2006).

29. *See id.*

30. *See* Russell Crandall, *The Pursuit of Stability in the Andes, in* THE ANDES IN FOCUS: SECURITY, DEMOCRACY & ECONOMIC REFORM 1, 5 (Russell Crandall, Guadalupe Paz, & Riordan Roett eds., 2005).

31. For background on the development of these regional and subregional organizations, see 1 "GLOBALIZATION," ENCYCLOPEDIA OF TRADE, LABOR, AND POLITICS (Ashish K. Vaidya ed., 2006).

32. Doug Porter & David Craig, *The Third Way and the Third World: Poverty Reduction and Social Inclusion in the Rise of "Inclusive" Liberalism,* 11 REV. INT'L POL. ECON. 487, 417 (2004).

33. LORD CURZON OF KEDLESTON, FRONTIERS, THE ROMANES LECTURE 7 (1907) ("Frontiers are indeed the razor's edge on which hang suspended the modern issues of war and peace.").

belonging to nobody becomes the possession of the first finder), *uti possidetis,* historical *effectivités* or factual circumstances that complement the judicial determination of title. These geospatial and temporal ordering constructs of international law formed at the center of Europe's territorializing design over the Americas. However, the forceful tug of human geography in places perceived as remote never allowed these ordering constructs to cure completely within this spatial climate of remoteness, notwithstanding the instrumentalized and politicized adaptation of cartography, languified toponomes (which serve as starting points for historical narratives of dominion), and the concentration of historiographic perspectives in self-affirming centers of information and education production and dissemination. Considerations of remoteness reframe perspectives of domination and rule-making. They uncover nuances and fissures in historical narration that help to explain anomalies and inconsistencies regarding the incorporation or receptivity of international legal norms across the hemisphere. Remoteness is a tool as much as it has been a criticism in the progressive development of international law. It is part of a process of interpretation that adds sociospatial texture to the study of international relations. It is the revenant that questions established guideposts of memory while turning international law more toward the insightful domain of spatial differentiation and equality.

Bibliography

Articles

Abrahamsson, C. "On the Genealogy of Lebensraum." 68 *Geographica Helvetica* 37–44, 2013.

Acosta, Alberto. "Extractivism and Neoextractivism: Two Sides of the Same Curse." In *Beyond Development: Alternative Visions from Latin America* 61–86. Edited by Miriam Lang and Dunia Mokrani. Quito: Fundacion Rosa Luxemburg, 2013.

Acterhuis, Hans, Rutgerd Boelens, and Margreet Zwarteveen. "Water Property Relations and Modern Policy Regimes: Neoliberal Utopia and the Disempowerment of Collective Action." In *Out of the Mainstream: Water Rights, Politics and Identity* 27–55. Edited by Rutgerd Boelens, David Getches, and Armando Guevara-Gil. Washington, DC: Earthscan, 2010.

Adams, John Q. "Special Message, March 15, 1826." In 2 *Addresses and Messages of the Presidents of the United States, Inaugural, Annual, and special, from 1789 to 1851*, 632–639. New York: Harvard University, 1853.

Aitken, Douglas, Diego Rivera, Alex Godoy-Faúndez, and Eduardo Holzapfel. "Water Scarcity and the Impact of the Mining and Agricultural Sectors in Chile." 8(2) *Sustainability* 128–146, 2016.

Akashi, Kinji. "(Re-)Examination of 'the Eurocentric Story of International Law' Through the Japanese Experience." 107 *Proceedings of the Annual Meeting (American Society of International Law)* 379–382, 2013.

Alebachew, Habtamu. "International Legal Perspectives on the Utilization of Trans-boundary Rivers: The Case of the Ethiopian Renaissance (Nile) Dam." In *Water and the Law: Towards Sustainability* 66–84. Edited by Michael Kidd, Tumai Murombo and Alejandro Iza. Cheltenham: Edward Elgar, 2014.

Allende, Juan Agustin. "Historical Constraints to Privatization: The Case of the Nationalized Chilean Copper Industry." 23(1) *Studies in Comparative International Development* 55–84, 1988.

Alvarez, Álejandro. "Latin America and International Law." 3(2) *The American Journal of International Law* 269–353, 1909.

Andreucci, Diego. "Resources, Regulation and the State: Struggles over Gas Extraction and Passive Revolution in Evo Morales's Bolivia." 61 *Political Geography* 170–180, 2017.

Andreucci, Diego, and Isabella M. Radhuber. "Limits to 'Counter-Neoliberal' Reform: Mining Expansion and the Marginalisation of Post-Extractivist Forces in Evo Morales's Bolivia." 84 *Geoforum* 280–291, 2017.

Anghie, Antony. "The Evolution of International Law: Colonial and Postcolonial Realities." 27(5) *Third World Quarterly* 739–753, 2006.

Anghie, Antony. "Legal Aspects of the New International Economic Order." 6(1) *Humanity* 145–158, 2015.

Anlauf, Axel. "¿Secar la tierra para sacar litio? Conflictos socio-ambientales en la minería del litio." In *ABC del litio sudamericano: Soberanía, ambiente, tecnología e industria* 171–186. Edited by Federico Nacif and Miguel Lacabana. Buenos Aires: Centro Cultural de la Cooperación Floreal Gorini Bernal, 2015.

Anríquez, Gustavo, and Oscar Melo. "The Socio-Economic Context of Chilean Water Consumption and Water Markets Growth: 1985–2015." In *Water Policy in Chile* 53–63. Edited by Guillermo Donoso. Cham: Springer, 2018.

Antaki, Mark. "Carl Schmitt's Nomos of the Earth." 42(2) *Osgoode Hall Law Journal* 317–334, 2004.

Archer, Christon I. "Enlightenment, Governance, and Reform in Spain and Its Empire, 1759–1808." 82(1) *Journal of Modern History* 221–223, 2008.

Arvidsson, Matilda, Leila Brännström, and Panu Minkkinen. "Editors' Introduction." In *The Contemporary Relevance of Carl Schmitt: Law, Politics, Theology* 1–16. Edited by Matilda Arvidsson, Leila Brännström, and Panu Minkkinen. New York: Routledge, 2016.

Assies, Willem. "David versus Goliath in Cochabamba: Water Rights, Neoliberalism, and the Revival of Social Protest in Bolivia." 30(3) *Latin American Perspectives* 14–36, 2003.

Ausness, Richard C. "Water Use Permits in a Riparian State: Problems and Proposals." 66(2) *Kentucky Law Journal* 191–265, 1977–1978.

Auty, R. M. "Industrial Policy, Sectoral Maturation, and Postwar Economic Growth in Brazil: The Resource Curse Thesis." 71(3) *Economic Geography* 257–272, 1995.

Axtmann, Roland. "Humanity or Enmity? Carl Schmitt on International Politics." 44(5) *International Politics* 531–551, 2007.

Azócar, Gerardo, Rodrigo Sanhueza, Mauricio Aguayo, Hugo Romero, and

María Muñoz. "Conflicts for Control of Mapuche-Pehuenche Land and Natural Resources in the Biobío Highlands, Chile." 4(2) *Journal of Latin American Geography* 57–76, 2005.

Baer, Madeline. "The Global Water Crisis, Privatization, and the Bolivian Water War." In *Water, Place, and Equity* 141–167. Edited by John M. Whiteley, Helen Ingram and Richard Warren Perry. Cambridge: MIT Press, 2008.

Baer, Madeline. "Private Water, Public Good: Water Privatization and State Capacity in Chile." 49(2) *Studies in Comparative International Development* 141–167, 2014.

Balchin, W. G. V., and Alice M. Coleman. "Graphicacy Should Be the Fourth Ace in the Pack." 3(1) *Times Educational Supplement* 23–28, 1965.

Ball, Milner S. "The Play's the Thing: An Unscientific Reflection on Courts Under the Rubric of Theater." 28(1) *Stanford Law Review* 81–115, 1975.

Barandiarán, Javiera. "Lithium and Development Imaginaries in Chile, Argentina and Bolivia." 113 *World Development* 381–391, 2018.

Barnes, Trevor J., and Claudio Minca. "Nazi Spatial Theory: The Dark Geographies of Carl Schmitt and Walter Christaller." 103(3) *Annals of the Association of American Geographers* 669–687, 2013.

Barrau, Fernando Urquidi. "Water Resources in Bolivia: A Strategic Viewpoint of the Issues Associated with Transboundary Waters." In *Diagnosis of Water in the Americas: Interamerican Network of Academies of Sciences* 91–118. Edited by Blanca Jiménez-Cisneros and José Galizia-Tundisi. Tlalpan: IANAS, 2013.

Barros, Alonso. "Water Justice, Mining, and the Fetish Form of Law in the Atacama Desert." In *A Sense of Justice: Legal Knowledge and Lived Experience in Latin America* 170–202. Edited by Sandra Brunnegger and Karen Ann Faulk. Stanford: Stanford University Press, 2016.

Bauer, Carl J. "In the Image of the Market: The Chilean Model of Water Resources Management." 3(2) *International Journal of Water* 146–165, 2005.

Bauer, Michael. "70 Years of Research and 50 Years of Lithium Clinics: From Serendipity to Gold Standard in Mood Disorders." 51(5) *Pharmacopsychiatry* 165, 2018.

Baxter, Richard. "International Law in Her Infinite Variety." 29(4) *International and Comparative Law Quarterly* 549–566, 1980.

Bederman, David J. "Constructivism, Positivism, and Empiricism in International Law." 89(2) *Georgetown Law Journal* 469–500, 2001.

Beebe, Kathryn. "Reading Mental Pilgrimage in Context: The Imaginary Pilgrims and Real Travels of Felix Fabri's 'Die Sionpilger.'" 25 *Essays in Medieval Studies* 39–70, 2008.

Benhabib, Seyla. "Carl Schmitt's Critique of Kant: Sovereignty and International Law." 40(6) *Political Theory* 688–713, 2012.

Bergoeing, Raphael, Patrick J Kehoe, Timothy J Kehoe, and Raimundo Soto. "A Decade Lost and Found: Mexico and Chile in the 1980s." 5(1) *Review of Economic Dynamics* 166–205, 2002.

Bethlehem, Daniel. "The End of Geography: The Changing Nature of the International System and the Challenge to International Law." 25(1) *European Journal of International Law* 9–24, 2014.

Biggs, Michael. "Putting the State on the Map: Cartography, Territory, and European State-Formation." 41(2) *Comparative Studies in Society and History* 374–405, 1999.

Biglaiser, Glen. "The Internationalization of Chicago's Economics in Latin America." 50(2) *Economic Development and Cultural Change* 269–286, 2002.

Bigo, Didier. "Globalized (in)Security: The Field and the Ban-Opticon." In *Terror, Insecurity and Liberty: Illiberal Practices of Liberal Regimes after 9/11* 10–48. Edited by Didier Biago and Anastassia Tsoukala. London: Routledge, 2008.

Blank, Yishai, and Issi Rosen-Zvi. "The Spatial Turn in Legal Theory." 10 *Hagar: Studies in Culture, Polity and Identities* 37–60, 2010.

Böckenförde, Ernst-Wolfgang. "Carl Schmitt Revisited." 1996(109) *Telos* 81–86, 1996.

Bodart, Adrien. "Transboundary Groundwater Management: Comparison between International Law Codification and EU Water Policy." In *Water and the Law: Towards Sustainability* 108–136. Edited by Michael Kidd, Tumai Murombo, and Alejandro Iza. Cheltenham: Edward Elgar, 2014.

Bolívar, Simón. "Letter to Sucre, Lima, February 21, 1825." In 2 *Selected Writings of Bolivar, 1823–1830*, 469–472. Edited by Harold A. Bierck Jr. Translated by Lewis Bertrand. New York: Colonial Press, 1951.

Bolívar, Simón. "Letter to Sucre, Arequipa, May 15, 1825." In 2 *Selected Writings of Bolivar, 1823–1830*, 492–497. Edited by Harold A. Bierck Jr. Translated by Lewis Bertrand. New York: Colonial Press, 1951.

Bolívar, Simón. "Letter to Sucre, Magdalena, May 12, 1826." In 2 *Selected Writings of Bolivar, 1823–1830*, 589–593. Edited by Harold A. Bierck Jr. Translated by Lewis Bertrand. New York: Colonial Press, 1951.

Boll, Alfred M. "The Asian Values Debate and Its Relevance to International Humanitarian Law." 83(841) *International Review of the Red Cross* 45–58, 2001.

Bonnefoy, Pascale. "Gas por mar." 45(174) *Estudios Internacionales* 15–25, 2013.

Bork, Robert, and Andrea Kann. "The Art, Science, and Technology of Medieval Travel." In *The Art, Science and Technology of Medieval Travel* 1–14. Edited by Robert Bork and Andrea Kann. Aldershot: Ashgate, 2008.

Boutrous-Ghali, Boutrous. "The Role of International Law in the Twenty-First Century: A Grotian Moment." 18(5) *Fordham International Law Journal* 1609–1719, 1995.

Bouzas, Roberto, and Jaime Ros. "The North-South Variety of Economic Integration: Issues and Prospects for Latin America." In *Economic Integration in the Western Hemisphere* 1–45. Edited by Roberto Bouzas and Jaime Ros. South Bend: University of Notre Dame Press, 1994.

Brender, Valerie. "Economic Transformations in Chile: The Formation of the Chicago Boys." 55(1) *The American Economist* 111–122, 2010.

Brenner, Neil, Jamie Peck, and Nik Theodore. "Variegated Neoliberalization: Geographies, Modalities, Pathways." 10(2) *Global Networks* 182–222, 2010.

Broad, Robin, and Julia Fischer-Mackey. "From Extractivism Towards Buen Vivir: Mining Policy as an Indicator of a New Development Paradigm Prioritising the Environment." 38(6) *Third World Quarterly* 1,327–1,349, 2017.

Brown, J. R. "The Frustration of Chile's Nitrate Imperialism." 32(4) *Pacific Historical Review* 383–396, 1963.

Budds, Jessica. "Water Rights, Mining and Indigenous Groups in Chile's Atacama." In *Out of the Mainstream: Water Rights, Politics and Identity* 197–211. Edited by Rutgerd Boelens. London: Earthscan, 2010.

Buisseret, David. "Spanish Colonial Cartography, 1450–1700." In *The History of Cartography Vol. 3 (Part 1), Cartography in the European Renaissance* 1,143–1,171. Edited by David Woodward. Chicago: University of Chicago Press, 2007.

Bull, Alan T., Juan A. Asenjo, Michael Goodfellow, and Benito Gómez-Silva. "The Atacama Desert: Technical Resources and the Growing Importance of Novel Microbial Diversity." 70 *Annual Review of Microbiology* 215–243, 2016.

Burgel, Gallia, Guy Burgel, and M. G. Dezes. "An Interview with Henri Lefebvre." 5 *Environment and Planning* 27–38, 1987.

Burkholder, Mark A. "Bureaucrats." In *Cities and Society in Colonial Latin America* 77–103. Edited by Louisa Schell Hoberman and Susan Migden Socolow. Albuquerque: University of New Mexico Press, 1986.

Burkholder, Mark A. "Colonies and Empire." In 1 *Oxford Companion to World Exploration* 165–166. Edited by David Buisseret. New York: Oxford University Press, 2007.

Burnett, Christina Duffy. "The Edges of Empire and the Limits of Sovereignty: American Guano Islands." 57(3) *American Quarterly* 779–803, 2005.

Burris, Matthew. "Astroimpolitic: Organizing Outer Space by the Sword." 7(3) *Strategic Studies Quarterly* 108–129, 2013.

Butler, Chris. "Critical Legal Studies and the Politics of Space." 18(3) *Social and Legal Studies* 313–332, 2009.

Butler, William Elliott. "Periodization and International Law." In *Research Handbook on the Theory and History of International Law* 379–393. Edited by Alexander Orakhelashvili. Cheltenham: Edward Elgar, 2011.

Caflisch, Lucius. "The Law of International Watercourses: Achievements and Challenges." In *International Law and Freshwater: The Multiple Challenges* 24–34. Edited by Laurence Boisson de Chazournes, Christina Leb, and Mara Tignino. Cheltenham: Edward Elgar, 2013.

Caflisch, Lucius. "Règles générales du droit des cours d'eaux internationaux." 219 *Recueil des Cours* 9–225, 1989.

Cai, Congyan. "New Great Powers and International Law in the 21st Century." 24(3) *European Journal of International Law* 755–795, 2013.

Caldwell, Bruce, and Leonidas Montes. "Friedrich Hayek and His Visits to Chile." 28(3) *Review of Austrian Economics* 261–309, 2015.

Carter, Charles. "The North-South Debate." 10(1) *Policy Studies* 51–56, 2007.

Cassese, Antonio. "The Israel-PLO Agreement and Self-Determination." 4 *European Journal of International Law* 564–571, 1993.

Castro, Leonardo Jeffs. "Las relaciones chileno-bolivianas: aproximación histórica y desafíos." 6 *Congreso de Relaciones Internacionales* 1–16, 2012.

Chafee, Zechariah. "Coming into Equity with Clean Hands." 47(7) *Michigan Law Review* 877–906, 1949.

Chimni, B. S. "Third World Approaches to International Law: A Manifesto." 8 *International Community Law Review* 3–27, 2006.

Church, Michael. "Immanuel Kant and the Emergence of Modern Geography." In *Reading Kant's Geography* 19–46. Edited by Stuart Elden and Eduardo Mendieta. Albany: State University of New York Press, 2011.

Clark, Brett, and John Bellamy Foster. "Ecological Imperialism and Global Metabolic Rift: Unequal Exchange and the Guano/Nitrates Trade." 50(3–4) *International Journal of Comparative Sociology* 311–334, 2009.

Clark, Timothy David. "Rethinking Chile's 'Chicago Boys': Neoliberal Technocrats or Revolutionary Vanguard?" 38(6) *Third World Quarterly* 1,350–1,365, 2017.

Cohen, Harlan Grant. "Fragmentation." In *Concepts for International Law: Contributions to Disciplinary Thought* 315–327. Edited by Jean d'Aspremont, Sahib Singh, and G. C. McBain. Cheltenham: Edward Elgar Publishing Limited, 2019.

Coleman, Thomas. "Who Owns the Water? An Analysis of Water Conflicts in Latin America and Modern Water Law." 12(2) *Intersections* 1–19, 2012.

Collier, J. G. "The International Court of Justice and the Peaceful Settlement of Disputes." In *Fifty Years of the International Court of Justice* 364–372. Edited by Vaughan Lowe and Malgosia Fitzmaurice. Cambridge: Cambridge University Press, 1996.

Collier, Simon. "Nationality, Nationalism, and Supranationalism in the Writings of Simón Bolívar." 63(1) *Hispanic American Historical Review* 37–64, 1983.

Cooney, Paul. "Argentina's Quarter Century Experiment with Neoliberalism: From Dictatorship to Depression." 11(1) *Revista de Economia Contemporanea* 7–37, 2007.

Correa, Sofía. "Algunos antecedents historicos del proyecto neoliberal en Chile (1955–1958)." 6 *Opciones* 106–146, 1985.

Costa, Pietro. "A 'Spatial Turn' for Legal History? A Tentative Assessment." In *Spatial and Temporal Dimensions for Legal History: Research Experiences and Itineraries* 27–62. Vol. 6. Edited by Massimo Meccarelli and María Julia Solla Sastre. Frankfurt Am Main: Max Planck Institute for European Legal History, 2016.

Cox, Kevin R. "Introduction: Globalization and Its Politics in Question." In *Spaces of Globalization: Reasserting the Power of the Local* 1–18. Edited by Kevin R. Cox. New York: Guilford Press, 1997.

Craven, Matthew. "Theorizing the Turn to History in International Law." In *The Oxford Handbook of the Theory of International Law* 21–37. Edited by Anne Orford and Florian Hoffmann. London: Oxford University Press, 2016.

Crutzen, Paul J. "The 'Anthropocene.'" In *Earth System Science in the Anthropocene: Emerging Issues and Problems* 13–18. Edited by Eckart Ehlers and Thomas Krafft. Berlin: Springer, 2000.

Cunha Filho, Clayton Mendonça, and Rodrigo Santaella Gonçalves. "The National Development Plan as a Political Economic Strategy in Evo Morales's Bolivia: Accomplishments and Limitations." 37(4) *Latin American Perspectives* 177–196, 2010.

Dalio, Danilo José. "The Vargas Administration and the Proposal of the ABC Pact: The Place of Peronist Argentina in Brazilian Foreign Policy." 38(2) *Contexto Internacional* 731–752, 2016.

D'Altroy, Terrence N. "Inca Political Organization, Economic Institutions, and Infrastructure." In *The Oxford Handbook of the Incas* 205–226. Edited by Sonia Alconini and R. Alan Covey. New York: Oxford University Press, 2018.

Darwin, Charles. "[Letter from] C. Darwin to J. D. Hooker, August 6, 1881." In *3 Life and Letters of Charles Darwin, including an autobiographical chapter* 246–249. Edited by Francis Darwin. London: John Murray, 1887.

D'Aspremont, Jean. "Critical Histories of International Law and the Repression of Disciplinary Imagination." 7 *London Review of International Law* 1–33, 2019.

Davidson, George. "Francis Drake on the Northwest Coast of America in the Year 1579." 5 *Transaction and Proceedings of the Geographical Society of the Pacific* 1–114, 1908.

Dawson, Frank Griffith. "Contributions of Lesser Developed Nations to International Law: The Latin American Experience." 13(1) *Case Western Reserve Journal of International Law* 37–81, 1981.

Dawson, Frank Griffith, and Burns H. Weston. "'Prompt, Adequate and Effective': A Universal Standard of Compensation?" 30(4) *Fordham Law Review* 723–758, 1962.

Debrix, François. "The Virtual Nomos?" In *Spatiality, Sovereignty and Carl*

Schmitt: Geographies of the Nomos 220–226. Edited by Stephen Legg. New York: Routledge, 2011.

De La Rasilla, Ignacio. "The Problem of Periodization in the History of International Law." 37(1) *Law and History Review* 275–308, 2019.

Del Castillo-Laborde, Lilian. "Case Law on International Watercourses." In *The Evolution of the Law and Politics of Water* 319–335. Edited by Joseph W. Dellapenna and Joyeeta Gupta. Dordrecht: Springer, 2009.

Dellapenna, Joseph W. "The Customary International Law of Transboundary Fresh Waters." 3/4 *International Journal of Global Environmental Issues* 264–305, 2001.

Dellapenna, Joseph W. "A Primer on Groundwater Law." 49(2) *Idaho Law Review* 265–323, 2012–2013.

Derrida, Jacques. "Plato's Pharmacy." In *Dissemination* 61–172. Translated by Barbara Johnson. Chicago: University of Chicago Press, 1981.

De Villiers, Isolde. "Leibniz, Lefebvre and the Spatial Turn in Law." 72 HTS Teologiese Studies/Theological Studies 1–6, 2016.

Diggelmann, Oliver. "The Periodization of the History of International Law." In *The Oxford Handbook of the History of International Law* 997–1011. Edited by Bardo Fassbender and Anne Peters. New York: Oxford University Press, 2012.

Domar, Evsey D. "Capital Expansion, Rate of Growth, and Employment." 14(2) *Econometrica* 137–147, 1946.

Dos Santos, Theotonio. "The Structure of Dependence." 60(2) *American Economic Review* 231–236, 1970.

Doughman, Richard Clayton. "Might the Keys to Peace Open the Doors to Extractivism? Reflections on Colombia's Post-Conflict Extractive Economy." In *Handbook on Research on Transitional Justice and Peace Building in Turbulent Regions* 444–470. Edited by Fredy Cante and Hartmut Quehl. Pennsylvania: IGI Global, 2015.

Doyle, Michael W. "Stalemate in the North-South Debate: Strategies and the New International Economic Order." 35(3) *World Politics* 426–464, 1983.

Drinot, Paulo. "Website of Memory: The War of the Pacific (1879–84) in the Global Age of YouTube." 4(4) *Memory Studies* 370–385, 2011.

Drulák, Petr. "Motion, Container and Equilibrium: Metaphors in the Discourse about European Integration." 12(4) *European Journal of International Relations* 499–531, 2006.

Duquette, Michel. "The Chilean Economic Miracle Revisited." 27(3) *Journal of Socio-Economics* 299–321, 1998.

Eckstein, Gabriel E. "Managing Buried Treasure across Frontiers: The International Law of Transboundary Aquifers." 36(5) *Water International* 573–583, 2011.

Elden, Stuart. "Reading Schmitt Geopolitically: Nomos, Territory and Großraum." 161 *Radical Philosophy* 18–26, 2010.

Epstein, Edward C. "The Piquetero Movement of Greater Buenos Aires:

Working Class Protest During the Current Argentine Crisis." 28(55) *Canadian Journal of Latin American and Caribbean Studies* 11–36, 2003.

Esquibel, José Antonio. "The People of the Camino Real: A Genealogical Appendix." In *The Royal Road: El Camino Real from Mexico City to Santa Fe* 145–176. Edited by Douglas Preston and José Antonio Esquibel. Albuquerque: University of New Mexico Press, 1998.

Falk, Richard. "Some Thoughts on the Decline of International Law and Future Prospects." 9(2) *Hofstra Law Review* 399–409, 1980.

Fang, Xin, and Huisheng Peng. "A Revolution in Electrodes: Recent Progress in Rechargeable Lithium-Sulfur Batteries." 11(13) *Small* 1,488–1,511, 2015.

Faron, Louis C. "Effects of Conquest on the Araucanian Picunche During the Spanish Colonization of Chile: 1536–1635." 7(3) *Ethnohistory* 239–307, 1960.

Fastenrath, Ulrich. "Servitudes." 10 *Encyclopedia of Public International Law* 389–392. Edited by Rudolf Bernhardt. New York: North-Holland Publishing Co., 1987.

Fernández, Julio A. "The Nationalism Syndrome in Argentina." 8(4) *Journal of Inter-American Studies* 551–564, 1966.

Fernández-Armesto, Felipe. "Maps and Exploration in Sixteenth and Early Seventeenth Centuries." In *The History of Cartography, Vol. 3 (Part 1), Cartography in the European Renaissance* 738–770. Edited by David Woodward. Chicago: University of Chicago Press, 2007.

Fernández-Armesto, Felipe. "Maritime History and World History." In *Maritime History as World History* 7–34. Edited by Daniel Finamore. Gainesville: University Press of Florida, 2004.

Ferraro, Vincent. "Dependency Theory: An Introduction." In *The Development Economics Reader* 58–64. Edited by Giorgio Secondi. New York: Routledge, 2008.

Fischer, Karin. "The Influence of Neoliberals in Chile Before, During, and After Pinochet." In *The Road from Mont Pèlerin: The Making of the Neoliberal Thought Collective* 305–346. Edited by Philip Mirowski and Dieter Plehwe. Cambridge: Harvard University Press, 2009.

Fischer-Tahir, Andreas, and Matthias Naumann. "Introduction: Peripheralization as the Social Production of Spatial Dependencies and Injustice." In *Peripheralization: The Making of Spatial Dependencies and Social Injustice* 9–26. Edited by Andrea Fischer-Tahir and Matthias Naumann. Wiesbaden: Springer VS, 2013.

Flemes, Daniel, and Michael Radsek. "Creating Multilevel Security Governance in South America." *German Institute Global and Area Studies—Working Paper No. 117*, 1–35, 2009.

Flynn, Dennis O., and Arturo Giráldez. "Born with a 'Silver Spoon': The Origin of World Trade in 1571." 6(2) *Journal of World History* 201–221, 1995.

Flynn, Dennis O., and Arturo Giraldez. "Latin American Silver and the Early

Globalization of World Trade." In *National Identities and Sociopolitical Changes in Latin America* 141–159. Edited by Mercedes F. Durán-Cogan and Antonio Gómez-Moriana. New York: Routledge, 2001.

Fontaine, Ernesto R. "Project Evaluation Training and Public Investment in Chile." 87(2) *The American Economic Review* 63–67, 1997.

Foucault, Michel *Of Other Spaces (1967), Heterotopias*, FOUCAULT.INFO, https://foucault.info/documents/heterotopia/foucault.heteroTopia.en/

Francaviglia, Richard. "Lost in the Atacama: Updates and Corrections." 50 (1) 48 (2) *Terrae Incognitae* 11–14, 2018.

Frank, Andre Gunder. "The Development of Underdevelopment." 18(4) *Monthly Review* 17–31, 1966.

Frye, Charles E. "Carl Schmitt's Concept of the Political." 28(4) *Journal of Politics* 818–830, 1966.

Garipzanov, Ildar. "The Rise of Graphicacy in Late Antiquity and the Early Middle Ages." 46(2) *Viator* 1–22, 2015.

Garrett, David T. "Inca Ancestry and Colonial Privilege." In *The Oxford Handbook of the Incas* 759–776. Edited by Sonia Alconini and R. Alan Covey. New York: Oxford University Press, 2018.

Garrett, James L. "The Beagle Channel: Confrontation and Negotiation in the Southern Cone." 27(3) *Journal of Interamerican Studies and World Affairs*. 81–109, 1985.

Gathii, James Thuo. "Africa and the History of International Law." In *The Oxford Handbook of the History of International Law* 407–428. Edited by Bardo Fassbender and Anne Peters. Oxford: Oxford University Press, 2012.

Gaudichaud, Franck, and Mariana Ortega Breña. "Popular Power, Oral History, and Collective Memory in Contemporary Chile." 36(5) *Latin American Perspectives* 58–71, 2009.

Gees, Karol N. "Permanent Sovereignty Over Natural Resources: An Analytical Review of the United Nations Declaration and its Genesis." 13(2) *International and Comparative Law Quarterly* 398–449, 1964.

Gelles, Paul H. "Cultural Identity and Indigenous Water Rights in the Andean Highlands." In *Out of the Mainstream: Water Rights, Politics and Identity* 119–129. Edited by Rutgerd Boelens, David Getches, and Armando Guevara-Gil. London: Earthscan, 2010.

Gheggi, María Soledad, and Verónica Isabel Williams. "Corrigendum to 'New Date on Food Consumption in Pre-Hispanic Population from Northwest Argentina (ca. 1000–1550 A.D.): The Contribution of Carbon and Nitrogen isotopic Composition of Human Bones.'" 2015 *Journal of Anthropology* 1–13, 2015.

Gilman, Nils. "The New International Economic Order: A Reintroduction." 6(1) *Humanity* 1–16, 2015.

Gilson, Ronald J., and Curtis J. Milhaupt. "Economically Benevolent Dictators: Lessons for Developing Democracies." 59(1) *The American Journal of Comparative Law* 227–288, 2011.

Glassner, Martin Ira. "The Río Lauca: Dispute over an International River." 60(2) *American Geographical Society* 192–207, 1970.

Glennon, Robert. "Water Scarcity, Marketing, and Privatization." 83(7) *Texas Law Review* 1,873–1,902, 2005.

Göbel, Barbara. "La minería del litio en la Puna de Atacama: interdependencies transregionales y disputas locales." 13(49) *Iberoamericana* 135–149, 2001.

Godoy, Ricardo A. "The Fiscal Role of the Andean Ayllu." 21(4) *Man* 723–741, 1986.

Goering, D. Timothy. "Concepts, History and the Game of Giving and Asking for Reasons: A Defense of Conceptual History." 7 *Journal of the Philosophy of History* 426–452, 2013.

Goldie, L. F. "Equity and the International Management of Transboundary Resources." 25(3) *Natural Resources Journal* 665–699, 1985.

Goodwin, Geoff. "Rethinking the Double Movement: Expanding the Frontiers of Polanyian Analysis in the Global South." 49(5) *Development and Change* 1,268–1,290, 2018.

Gordon, Dennis R. "The Question of the Pacific: Current Perspectives on a Long-Standing Dispute." 141(4) *World Affairs* 321–335, 1979.

Gordon, Ruth. "The Dawn of a New, New International Economic Order?" 72(4) *Law and Contemporary Problems* 131–162, 2009.

Gosovic, Branislav. "The Resurgence of South-South Cooperation." 37(4) *Third World Quarterly* 733–743, 2016.

Gould, Eliga H. "Zones of Law, Zones of Violence: The Legal Geography of the British Atlantic, circa 1772." 60(3) *William and Mary Quarterly* 417–510, 2003.

Green, William A. "Periodization in European and World History." 3(1) *Journal of World History* 13–53, 1992.

Greif, Hajo. "The Darwinian Tension: Romantic Science and the Causal Laws of Nature." 53 *Studies in History and Philosophy of Biological and Biomedical Sciences* 53–61, 2015.

Grewal, Kiran. "Can the Subaltern Speak within International Law? Women's Right Activism, International Legal Institutions and the Power of 'Strategic Misunderstanding.'" In *Negotiating Normativity* 27–44. Edited by N. Dhawan et al. Cham: Springer, 2016.

Gross, Leo. "The Peace of Westphalia 1648–1948." 42(1) *American Journal of International Law* 20–41, 1948.

Grugel, Jean, and Pía Riggirozzi. "Post-neoliberalism in Latin America: Rebuilding and Reclaiming the State after Crisis." 43(1) *Development and Change* 1–21, 2012.

Guani, Albert. "La solidarité international dans l'Amérique Latine." 8(III) *Recueil des Cours* 323–333, 1925.

Guilhot, Nicholas. "American Katechon: When Political Theology Became International Relations Theory." 17(2) *Constellations* 224–253, 2010.

Haas, Peter M. "Introduction: Epistemic Communities and International Policy Coordination." 46(1) *International Organization* 1–35, 1992.

Habermas, Jürgen. "The Horrors of Autonomy: Carl Schmitt in English." In *The New Conservatism: Cultural Criticism and the Historians' Debate* 128–139. Edited and translated by Shierry Weber Nicholsen. Cambridge: MIT Press,1989.

Haboud, Marleen. "South America: Andean Region." In *Atlas of the World's Languages in Danger* 95–102. 3d ed. Paris: UNESCO, 2010.

Hale, Charles R. "Does Multiculturalism Menace? Governance, Cultural Rights and the Politics of Identity in Guatemala." 34(3) *Journal of Latin American Studies* 485–524, 2002.

Hale, Charles R. "Neoliberal Multiculturalism: The Remaking of Cultural Rights and Racial Dominance in Central America." 28(1) *Political and Legal Anthropology Review* 10–28, 2005.

Handles, W. G. L. "Portuguese and Spanish Attempts to Measure Longitude in the 16th Century." 28 *Vistas in Astronomy* 235–241, 1985.

Handles, W. G. L. "South-East Africa as Shown on Selected Printed Maps of the Sixteenth Century." 13 *Imago Mundi* 69–88, 1956.

Hanna, Kathryn Abbey. "The Roles of the South in the French Intervention in Mexico." 20(1) *Journal of Southern History* 3–21, 1954.

Harley, J. B. "Deconstructing the Map." 26(2) *Cartographica* 1–20, 1989.

Harris, Leila M., and María Cecilia Roa-García. "Recent Waves of Water Governance: Constitutional Reform and Resistance to Neoliberalization in Latin America (1990–2012)." 50 *Geoforum* 20–30, 2013.

Harrod, R. F. "An Essay in Dynamic Theory." 49(193) *Economic Journal* 14–33, 1939.

Haslam, Paul Alexander. "Is There a Post-Neoliberal Policy Toward Foreign Direct Investment in Argentina and Chile?" In *Post-Neoliberalism in the Americas* 120–134. Edited by Laura Macdonald and Arne Ruckert. London: Palgrave Macmillan, 2009.

Hauch, Charles C. "Attitudes of Foreign Governments Towards the Spanish Reoccupation of the Dominican Republic." 27(2) *Hispanic American Historical Review* 247–268, 1947.

Hayes, Margaret Daly. "The U.S. and Latin America: A Lost Decade?" 68(1) *Foreign Affairs* 180–198, 1988/1989.

Heffernan, Michael. "Mapping Schmitt." In *Spatiality, Sovereignty and Carl Schmitt: Geographies of the Nomos* 234–243. Edited by Stephen Legg. New York: Routledge, 2011.

Heine, Jorge. "Regional Integration and Political Cooperation in Latin America." 47(3) *Latin American Research Review* 209–217, 2012.

Hell, Julia. "Katechon: Carl Schmitt's Imperial Theology and the Ruins of the Future." 84(4) *Germanic Review: Literature, Culture, Theory* 283–326, 2009.

Helmreich, Christian. "Geschichte der Natur bei Alexander von Humboldt." 10 *Internationale Zeitschrift für Humboldt Studien* 53–67, 2009.

Hessler, John W. "'An Island . . . Surrounded on All Sides by Sea': The World Map 1507." In *Seeing the World Anew: The Radical Vision of Martin Waldseemüller's 1507 and 1516 World Maps* 3–48. Edited by John W. Hessler and Chet Van Duzer. Delray Beach, FL: Levenger Press in association with the Library of Congress, 2012.

Hilton, Ronald. "The Significance of Travel Literature, with Special Reference to the Spanish- and Portuguese-Speaking World." 49(4) *Hispania* 836–845, 1966.

Hudson, Judson. "Treaty of Guadalupe Hidalgo-International Law." In 21 *Official Opinions of the Attorney-General of the United States Advising the President and Heads of Departments in relation to their Official Duties* 274–283. Edited by E. C. Brandenburg. Washington: United States Government Publishing Office, 1898.

Hudson, Manley O. "The Central American Court of Justice." 26(4) *American Journal of International Law* 759–786, 1932.

Huneeus, Carlos. "Technocrats and Politicians in an Authoritarian Regime. The 'ODEPLAN Boys' and the 'Gremialists' in Pinochet's Chile." 32(2) *Journal of Latin American Studies* 461–501, 2000.

Huntington, Samuel P. "The Clash of Civilizations?" 72 *Foreign Affairs* 22–49, 1993.

Jadresic, Esteban, and Roberto Zahler. "Chile's Rapid Growth in the 1990s: Good Policies, Good Luck, or Political Change." *IMF Working Paper WP/00/153*, 1–35, 2000.

Jain, Abhimanyu George. "The 21st Century Atlantis: The International Law of Statehood and Climate Change-Induced Loss of Territory." 50(1) *Stanford Journal of International Law* 1–52, 2014.

Janotti, Aldo. "Historigrafia Brasileira e Teoria da Fronteira Natural." 51(101) *Revista de História* 239–263, 1975.

Jones, Henry. "Lines in the Ocean: Thinking with the Sea about Territory and International Law." 4(2) *London Review of International Law* 307–343, 2016.

Jones, Henry. "Property, Territory, and Colonialism: An International Legal History of Enclosure." 39(2) *Legal Studies* 187–203, 2019.

Kapoor, Tanya. "Is Successful Water Privatization a Pipe Dream?: An Analysis of Three Global Case Studies." 40(1) *Yale Journal of International Law* 157–192, 2015.

Kaup, Brent Z. "A Neoliberal Nationalization? The Constraints on Natural-Gas-Led Development in Bolivia." 37(3) *Latin American Perspectives* 123–138, 2010.

Kelly, James. "William Dampier." In 1 *The Oxford Companion to World Exploration* 222–225. Edited by David Buisseret. New York: Oxford University Press, 2007.

Kemmerer, Alexandra. “Turning Aside: On International Law and Its History.” In *Progress in International Law* 69–93. Edited by Russell A. Miller and Rebecca M. Bratspies. Leiden: Martinus Nijhoff Publisher, 2008.

Kennedy, David. “International Law and the Nineteenth Century: History of an Illusion.” 17(1) *Quinnipiac Law Review* 99–138, 1997.

Khumprakob, Malissa. “The Vivendi-Argentina Water Dispute: ICSID Creates New Arbitration Tribunal to Hear the Longest Running Case on Its Docket.” 5(1) *Sustainable Development Law and Policy* 68–69, 2005.

Kidd, Michael, and Loretta Feris. “Introduction: Water and the Law—Towards Sustainability.” In *Water and the Law: Towards Sustainability* 1–10. Edited by Michael Kidd, Tumai Murombo, and Alejandro Iza. Cheltenham: Edward Elgar, 2014.

Kjellén, Rudolf. “Studier ofver Sveriges politiska gränser.” 19 *Ymer* 183–331, 1899.

Kohl, Benjamin, and Linda Farthing. “Material Constraints to Popular Imaginaries: The Extractive Economy and Resource Nationalism in Bolivia.” 31 *Political Geography* 225–235, 2012.

Koplow, David A. “The Fault Is Not in Our Stars: Avoiding an Arms Race in Outer Space.” 59(2) *Harvard International Law Journal* 331–388, 2018.

Koskenniemi, Martti. “Carl Schmitt and International Law.” In *The Oxford Handbook of Carl Schmitt* 592–611. Edited by Jens Meierhenrich and Oliver Simons. New York: Oxford University Press, 2017.

Koskenniemi, Martti. “International Law as Political Theology: How to Read Nomos der Erde?” 11 *Constellations* 492–511, 2004.

Kutzinsky, Vera M., and Ottmar Ette. “The Art of Science: Alexander von Humboldt’s Views of the Cultures of the World.” In *Alexander von Humboldt: Views of the Cordilleras and Monuments of the Indigenous Peoples of the Americas: A Critical Edition* xv–xxxv. Edited by Vera M. Kutzinski and Ottmar Ette. Translated by J. Ryan Poynter. Chicago: University of Chicago Press, 2012.

Laaman, John. “Viceroyalty System.” In *Conflict in the Early Americas: An Encyclopedia of the Spanish Empire’s Aztec, Incan, and Mayan Conquests* 400–402. Edited by Rebecca M. Seaman. Santa Barbara: ABC-CLIO, 2013.

Labán, Raúl, and Felipe Larraín. “Continuity, Change, and the Political Economy of Transition in Chile.” In *Reform, Recovery, and Growth: Latin America and the Middle East* 115–148. Edited by Rudiger Dornbusch and Sebastian Edwards. Chicago: University of Chicago Press, 1995.

Lapidoth, Ruth. “Dispute Settlement Under the 1997 Convention on the Law of the Non-Navigational Uses of International Watercourses.” In *International Law Across the Spectrum of Conflict: Essays in Honor of Professor L. C. Green on the Occasion of His Eightieth Birthday* 231–246. Edited by Michael N. Schmitt. Newport: Naval War College, 2000.

Larrain, Sara. “Human Rights and Market Rules in Chile’s Water Conflicts:

A Call for Structural Changes in Water Policy." 5(2) *Environmental Justice* 82–88, 2012.

Lazerwitz, David J. "The Flow of International Water Law: The International Law Commission's Law of the Non-Navigational Uses of International Watercourses." 1(1) *Indiana Journal of Global Legal Studies* 247–271, 1993.

Lee, Terence R. "The Management of Shared Water Resources in Latin America." 35 *Natural Resources Journal* 541–553, 1995.

Lehmann, Martin. "The Depiction of America on Martin Waldseemüller's World Map from 1507—Humanistic Geography in the Service of Political Propaganda." 3(1) *Cogent Arts and Humanities* 1–15, 2016.

Lesaffer, Randall. "The End of the Cold War: An Epochal Event in the History of International Law?" In *Select Proceedings of the European Society of International Law* 45–60. Edited by James Crawford and Sarah Nouwen, 2012.

Lesaffer, Randall, "International Law and Its History: The Story of an Unrequited Love." In *Time, History and International Law* 27–41. Edited by Matthew Craven, Malgosia Fitzmaurice, and Maria Vogiatzi, 2007.

Lesaffer, Randall. "The Temple of Peace: The Hague Peace Conferences, Andrew Carnegie and the Building of the Peace Palace (1898–1913)." *Tilburg Law School Legal Studies Research Paper Series No. 024/2013*, 1–38, 2013.

Letelier, Orlando. "Economic Freedom's' [sic] Awful Toll: The 'Chicago Boys' in Chile." *The Nation*, August 28, 1976.

Levy, Jack S. "Domestic Politics and War." 18(4) *Journal of Interdisciplinary History* 653–673, 1988.

Limor, Ora. "Placing an Idea: The Valley of Jehoshaphat in Religious Imagination." In *Between Jerusalem and Europe: Essays in Honour of Bianca Kühnel* 280–300. Edited by Renana Bartal and Hanna Vorholt. Leiden: Brill, 2015.

Locke, John. "The Second Treatise of Government." In *John Locke, Political Writings* 273–285. Edited with an introduction by David Wootton. Indianapolis: Hackett Publishing Company, 2003.

Macdonald, Laura, and Arne Ruckert. "Afterward: Post-Neoliberal Politics and Pathways." In *Post-Neoliberalism in the Americas* 246–249. Edited by Laura Macdonald and Arne Ruckert. London: Palgrave Macmillan, 2009.

Macdonald, Laura, and Arne Ruckert. "Post-Neoliberalism in the Americas: An Introduction." In *Post-Neoliberalism in the Americas* 1–18. Edited by Laura Macdonald and Arne Ruckert. London: Palgrave Macmillan, 2009.

Macdonald, Roderick A. "Metaphors of Multiplicity: Civil Society, Regimes and Legal Pluralism." 15(1) *Arizona Journal of International and Comparative Law* 69–91, 1988.

Mahmud, Tayyab. "Geography and International Law: Towards a Postcolonial Mapping." 5(2) *Santa Clara Journal of International Law* 525–561, 2007.

Mälksoo, Lauri. "The History of International Legal Theory in Russia: A

Civilizational Dialogue with Europe." 19(1) *European Journal of International Law* 211–232, 2008.

Mansilla, Hugo Llanos. "El Caso Del Río Silala o Siloli Diferendo Chileno-Boliviano." 21 *Ahladi* 339–365, 2013.

Marchegiani, Pia, Elisa Morgera, and Louisa Parks. "Indigenous Peoples' Rights to Natural Resources in Argentina: The Challenges of Impact Assessment, Consent and Fair and Equitable Benefit-Sharing in Cases of Lithium Mining." *Benelex Working Paper No. 19*, 1–16, 2018.

Margheritis, Ana, and Anthony W. Pereira. "The Neoliberal Turn in Latin America: The Cycle of Ideas and the Search for an Alternative." 34 *Latin American Perspectives* 25–48, 2007.

Matos, José. "L'Amérique et la Société des Nations." 28(III) *Recueil des Cours* 5–104, 1929.

Mattingly, Garrett. "No Peace Beyond What Line?" 13 *Transactions of the Royal Historical Society* 145–162, 1963.

Matua, Makau, and Antony Anghie. "What Is TWAIL?" 94 *Proceedings of the Annual Meeting (American Society of International Law)* 31–40, 2000.

Mayo, John. "Commerce, Credit and Control in Chilean Copper Mining Before 1880." In *Miners and Mining in the Americas* 33–40. Edited by Thomas Greaves and William Culver. Manchester: Manchester University Press, 1985.

Mayo, John. "A 'Company' War? The Antofagasta Nitrate Company and the Outbreak of the War of the Pacific." 28 *Boletin de Estudios Latinoamericanos y del Caribe* 3–11, 1980.

Mbembe, Achille. "At the Edge of the World: Boundaries, Territoriality, and Sovereignty in Africa." 12(1) *Public Culture* 259–284. Translated by Steven Rendall, 2000.

McCaffrey, Stephen C. "The Codification of Universal Norms: A Means to Promote Cooperation and Equity?" In *International Law and Freshwater: The Multiple Challenges* 125–139. Edited by Laurence Boisson de Chazournes, Christina Leb, and Mara Tignino. Cheltenham: Edward Elgar, 2013.

McCaffrey, Stephen C. "The Harmon Doctrine One Hundred Years Later: Buried, Not Praised." 36(4) *Natural Resources Journal* 965–1008, 1996.

McCaffrey, Stephen C. "The 1997 U.N. Watercourses Convention: Retrospect and Prospect." 21 *Pacific McGeorge Global Business and Development Law Journal* 165–174, 2008.

McConnell, Donald. "The Chilean Nitrate Industry." 43(4) *Journal of Political Economy* 506–529, 1935.

McHargue, L. R., and P. E. Damon. "The Global Beryllium 10 Cycle." 29(2) *Reviews of Geophysics* 141–158, 1991.

McKay, Christopher P., Jamie L. Molaro, and Magarita M. Marinova. "High-

Frequency Rock Temperature Data from Hyper-Arid Desert Environments in the Atacama and the Antarctic Dry Valleys and Implications for Rock Weathering." 110 *Geomorphology* 182–187, 2009.

Merrill, Thomas W. "Golden Rules for Transboundary Pollution." 46(5) *Duke Law Journal* 931–1,019, 1997.

Mesa Gisbert, Carlos D. de. "Bolivia: autonomías y pluralism politico: Un modelo condicionado por el horizonte indígena." In *Descentralización y democratización en Bolivia: La historia del Estado débil, la sociedad rebelled y el anhelo de democracia* 43–86. Edited by Moira Zuazo, Jean-Paul Faguet, and Gustavo Bonifaz. La Paz: Friedrich Ebert Stiftung, 2012.

Meza Bórquez, Gustavo. "Chile/Bolivia: ¿Es el río Silala un factor de tensión secundario?" 2 *Revismar* 152–159, 2014.

Meshram, Pratima, B. D. Pandey, and T. R. Mankhand. "Extraction of Lithium from Primary and Secondary Sources by Pre-Treatment, Leaching and Separation: A Comprehensive Review." 150 *Hydrometallury* 192–208, 2014.

Meyer, Robert, Conrad Schetter, and Janosch Prinz. "Spatial Contestation? The Theological Foundations of Carl Schmitt's Spatial Thought." 43(3) *Geoforum* 687–696, 2012.

Mignolo, Walter D. "The Making and Closing of Eurocentric International Law." 36(1) *Comparative Studies of South Asia, Africa and the Middle East* 182–195, 2016.

Minca, Claudio, and Nick Vaughan-Williams. "Carl Schmitt and the Concept of the Border." 17(4) *Geopolitics* 756–772, 2012.

Minca, Claudio, and Rory Rowan. "The Question of Space in Carl Schmitt." 39 *Progress in Human Geography* 268–289, 2014.

Miranda, Sergio González, and Cristián Ovando Santana. "'Emotivistas' bolivianos en la relación diplomática entre Bolivia y Chile en torno a la mediterraneidad." 183 *Estudios Internacionales* 39–65, 2016.

Monteagudo, Manuel. "The Debt Problem: The Baker Plan and the Brady Initiative: A Latin American Perspective." 28(1) *International Lawyer* 59–81, 1994.

Monteón, Michael. "The British in the Atacama Desert: The Cultural Bases of Economic Imperialism." 35(1) *Journal of Economic History* 117–133, 1975.

Monteón, Michael. "The Enganche in the Chilean Nitrate Sector, 1880–1930." 6(3) *Latin American Perspectives* 66–79, 1979.

Morales, Héctor M. "Construcción social de la etnicidad: Ego y alter en Atacama." 46 *Estudios Atacameños* 145–164 (2013).

Mulligan, B. M., and G. E. Eckstein. "The Silala/Siloli Watershed: Dispute over the Most Vulnerable Basin in South America." 27(3) *Water Resources Development* 595–606, 2011.

Munck, Ronaldo. "Karl Polanyi for Latin America: Markets, Society and Development." 36(4) *Canadian Journal of Development Studies* 425–441, 2015.

Murphy, Sean D. "U.S. Assistance Regarding Information on Former Chilean President Pinochet." 94(2) *American Journal of International Law* 348–381, 2000.

Murthy, Sharmila L. "The Human Right(s) to Water and Sanitation: History, Meaning, and the Controversy over Privatization." 31(1) *Berkeley Journal of International Law* 89–147, 2013.

Mutharika, A. Peter. "The Role of International Law in the Twenty-First Century: An African Perspective." 18(5) *Fordham International Law Journal* 1,706–1,719, 1994.

Mutua, Makau. "What Is TWAIL?" 94 *American Society of International Law Proceedings* 31–39, 2000.

Neocleous, Mark. "Friend or Enemy? Reading Schmitt Politically." 79 *Radical Philosophy* 13–23, 1996.

Nichols, Sandra. "Why Was Humboldt Forgotten in the United States?" 96(3) *Geographical Review* 399–415, 2006.

Nielsen, Axel E. "Pastoralism and the Non-Pastoral World in the Late Pre-Colombian History of the Southern Andes (1000–1535)." 13(2) *Nomadic Peoples* 17–35, 2009.

Nollkaemper, André. "Framing Elephant Extinction." 3(6) *ESIL Reflections* 1–4, 2014.

North, Liisa L., and Ricardo Grinspun. "Neo-extractivism and the New Latin American Developmentalism: The Missing Piece of Rural Transformation." 37 *Third World Quarterly* 1,483–1,504, 2016.

Obhof, Ute. "The Terrestrial Globe that Named America: On Historical Preservation of Martin Waldseemüller's Gores." 55/56 *Globe Studies* 13–21, 2009.

Obregón, Liliana. "Between Civilisation and Barbarism: Creole Interventions in International Law." 27(5) *Third World Quarterly* 815–832, 2006.

Obregón, Liliana. "Completing Civilization: Creole Consciousness and International Law in Nineteenth-Century Latin America." In *International Law and Its Others* 247–264. Edited by Anne Orford. Cambridge: Cambridge University Press, 2006.

Ocampo, José Antonio, and María Angela Parra. "The Commodity Terms of Trade and Their Strategic Implications for Development." In *Globalization Under Hegemony: The Changing World Economy* 164–194. Edited by Jomo Kwame Sundaram. New York: Oxford University Press, 2006.

Odysseos, Louiza, and Fabio Petito. "Carl Schmitt." In *Critical Theorists and International Relations* 305–316. Edited by Jenny Edkins and Nick Vaughan-Williams. New York: Routledge, 2009.

Ojakangas, Mika. "Carl Schmitt and the Sacred Origins of Law." 147 *Telos* 34–54, 2009.

Olmos Herrera, Christian. "Territory's Fragmentation: The Territory of Aboriginal Communities in the Process of Mining Expansion: The Case of the Atacama Desert, Chile." *Conference: 7th International Seminar on Ver-*

nacular Settlements Re-assessing Vernacular Architecture: Theories and Practices, Traditions, Identities and Globalization 1–11, 2014.

Olsen, Niklas. "Carl Schmitt, Reinhart Koselleck and the Foundations of History and Politics." 37(2) *History of European Ideas* 197–202, 2011.

Onuf, Nicholas. "Levels." 1(1) *European Journal of International Relations* 35–58, 1995.

Onuf, Nicholas. "Polemics: Fitting Metaphors—The Case of the European Union." 18(1) *Perspectives* 63–76, 2010.

Onuf, Nicholas. "Relative Strangers: Reflections on Hospitality, Social Distance and Diplomacy." In *Hospitality and World Politics* 173–196. Edited by Gideon Baker. Houndsmills: Palgrave Macmillan, 2013.

Ortega, Luis. "Nitrates, Chilean Entrepreneurs and the Origins of the War of the Pacific." 16(2) *Journal of Latin American Studies* 337–380, 1984.

Osiander, Andreas. "Sovereignty, International Relations, and the Westphalian Myth." 55(2) *International Organization* 251–287, 2001.

Otto, Dianne. "Handmaidens, Hierarchies, and Crossing the Public-Private Divide in the Teaching of International Law." 1(1) *Melbourne Journal of International Law* 35–69, 2000.

Otto, Dianne. "Subalternity and International Law: The Problem of Global Community and the Incommensurability of Difference." 5(3) *Social and Legal Studies.* 337–364, 1996.

Otto, Dianne. "'Taking a Break' from 'Normal': Thinking Queer in the Context of International Law." 101 *Proceedings of the Annual Meeting (American Society of International Law)* 119–122, 2007.

Owada, Hisashi. "Pactum de Contrahendo, Pactum de Negotiando." In *Max Planck Encyclopedia of Public International Law.* New York: Oxford University Press, 2008.

Paasi, Anssi. "Reading Stuart Elden's The Birth of Territory." 46 *Political Geography* 93–101, 2015.

Palmer, Gabrielle G. "El Camino Real de Tierra Adentro." 6(1) *Southern New Mexico Historical Review* 1–5, 1999.

Pareja, Yoer Javier Castaño. "'La Diplomacia Secreta': la participación de Colombia en el conflict entre Perú y España por las islas guaneras." 24 *Historia y sociedad* 189–214, 2013.

Parry, Benita. "Aspects of Peripheral Modernisms." 40(1) *Ariel* 27–55, 2009.

Payne, Anthony. "Samuel Purchas." In 2 *The Oxford Companion to World Exploration* 180. Edited by David Buisseret. New York: Oxford University Press, 2007.

Pearson, Alastair W., and Michael Heffernan. "The American Geographical Society's Map of Hispanic America: Million-Scale Mapping Between the Wars." 61(2) *Imago Mundi* 215–243, 2009.

Pearson, Zoe. "Spaces of International Law." 17(2) *Griffith Law Review* 489–514, 2008.

Pellegrini, Lorenzo. "Imaginaries of Development Through Extraction: The 'History of Bolivian Petroleum' and the Present View of the Future." 90 *Geoforum* 130–141, 2018.

Penrose, R. A. F. "The Nitrate Deposits of Chile." 18(1) *Journal of Geology* 1–32, 1910.

Perreault, Thomas. "Extracting Justice: Natural Gas, Indigenous Mobilization, and the Bolivian State." In *The Politics of Resource Extraction: Indigenous Peoples, Multinational Corporations, and the State* 75–101. Edited by Suzana Sawyer and Edmund Terence Gomez. New York: Palgrave Macmillan: United Nations Research Institute for Social Development, 2012.

Perreault, Thomas. "From the Guerra Del Agua to the Guerra Del Gas: Resource Governance, Neoliberalism and Popular Protest in Bolivia." 38(1) *Antipode* 150–172, 2006.

Petras, James. "Evo Morales' Pursuit of 'Normal Capitalism.'" 42(23) *Economic and Political Weekly* 2155–2158, 2007.

Petrova, Violeta. "At the Frontiers of the Rush for Blue Gold: Water Privatization and the Human Right to Water." 31(2) *Brooklyn Journal of International Law* 577–613, 2006.

Philippopoulos-Mihalopoulos, Andreas. "Law's Spatial Turn: Geography, Justice and a Certain Fear of Space." 7(2) *Law, Culture and the Humanities* 187–202, 2010.

Piccone, Paul, and G. L. Ulmen. "Introduction to Carl Schmitt." 72 *Telos* 3–14, 1987.

Piccone, Paul, and G. L. Ulmen. "Schmitt's 'Testament' and the Future of Europe." 83 *Telos* 93–148, 1990.

Piñera, José. "Latin America: A Way Out." 22(3) *Cato Journal* 409–416, 2003.

Pinkett, Harold T. "Efforts to Annex Santo Domingo to the United States, 1866–1871." 26 *Journal of Negro History* 12–45, 1941.

Plakokefalos, Ilias. "Causation in the Law of State Responsibility and the Problem of Overdetermination: In Search of Clarity." 26 *European Journal of International Law* 471–492, 2015.

Plato. "Timaeus." In *Plato: Timaeus and Critias* 1–100. Edited and translated by Robin Waterfield. New York: Oxford University Press, 2008.

Porter, Doug, and David Craig. "The Third Way and the Third World: Poverty Reduction and Social Inclusion in the Rise of 'Inclusive' Liberalism." 11(2) *Review of International Political Economy* 387–423, 2004.

Postero, Nancy. "Morales's MAS Government: Building Indigenous Popular Hegemony in Bolivia." 37(3) *Latin American Perspectives* 18–34, 2010.

Postero, Nancy, and Nicole Fabricant. "Indigenous Sovereignty and the New Developmentalism in Plurinational Bolivia." 19(1) *Anthropological Theory* 95–119, 2019.

Postero, Nancy, Helene Risør, and Manuel Prieto Montt. "Introduction: The Politics of Identity in Neoliberal Chile." 13(3) *Latin American and Caribbean Ethnic Studies* 203–213, 2018.

Potter, Pitman B. "The Doctrine of Servitudes in International Law." 9(3) *American Journal of International Law* 627–641, 1915.

Prakash, Gyan. "Colonialism, Capitalism and the Discourse of Freedom." 41(S4) *International Review of Social History* 9–25, 1996.

Praveen V., Ambesange. "Postcolonialism: Edward Said and Gayatri Spivak." 5(8) *Research Journal of Recent Sciences* 47–50, 2016.

Preston, Douglas. "The Granddaddy of the Nation's Trails Began in Mexico (El Camino Real de Tierra Adentro)." 26 *Smithsonian* 140–150, 1995.

Prieto, Manuel. "Privatizing Water in the Chilean Andes: The Case of Las Vegas de Chiu-Chiu." 35(3) *Mountain Research and Development* 220–229, 2015.

Prozorov, Sergei. "The Katechon in the Age of Biopolitical Nihilism." 45(4) *Continental Philosophy Review* 483–503, 2012.

Radhuber, Isabella M. "Indigenous Struggles for a Plurinational State: An Analysis of Indigenous Rights and Competences in Bolivia." 11(2) *Journal of Latin American Geography* 167–193, 2012.

Rajkovic, Nikolas M. "The Visual Conquest of International Law: Brute Boundaries, the Map, and the Legacy of Cartogenesis." 31(2) *Leiden Journal of International Law* 267–288, 2018.

Rajkovic, Nikolas M. "On Fragments and Geometry: The International Legal Order as Metaphor and How It Matters." 6 *Erasmus Law Review* 1–16, 2013.

Ramírez, Susan E. "Large Landowners." In *Cities and Society in Colonial Latin America* 19–45. Edited by Louisa Schell Hoberman and Susan Migden Socolow. Albuquerque: University of New Mexico Press, 1986.

Ratner, Steven R. "Drawing a Better Line: Uti Possidetis and the Borders of New States." 90(4) *American Journal of International Law* 590–624, 1996.

Ratzel, Friedrich. "Über den Lebensraum: Eine biogeographische Skizze." 21 *Die Umschau* 363–367, 1897.

Rehn, Dana. "Going to the Dogs: The Foreign and Religious Other in German Renaissance Prints." 5(2) *Otherness: Essays and Studies* 111–150, 2016.

Reich, Martin, and Huiming Gao. "Nitrate Deposits of the Atacama Desert: A Marker of Long-Term Hyperaridity." 14(4) *Elements* 251–256, 2018.

Revette, Anna C. "This Time It's Different: Lithium Extraction, Cultural Politics and Development in Bolivia." 38(1) *Third World Quarterly* 149–168, 2017.

Rieu-Clarke, Alistair, and Flavia Rocha Loures. "Still Not in Force: Should States Support the 1997 UN Watercourses Convention?" 18(2) *Review of European Community and International Environmental Law* 185–197, 2009.

Riggirozzi, Pía. "Social Policy in Post-Neo-liberal Latin America: The Cases of Argentina, Venezuela and Bolivia." 53(1) *Development* 70–76, 2010.

Ritsema Van Eck, Marianne P. "Encounters with the Levant: The Late Medieval Illustrated Jerusalem Travelogue by Paul Walter von Gugligen." 32(2) *Mediterranean Historical Review* 153–188, 2017.

Robinson, David J. "The Language and Significance of Place in Latin America." In *The Power of Place: Bringing Together Geographical and Sociological Imaginations* 157–184. Edited by John A. Agnew and James S. Duncan. Winchester: Unwin Hyman,1989.

Rosett, Claudia. "Looking Back on Chile: 1973–1984." 36 *National Review* 25–53, 1984.

Rossi, Christopher R. "A Case Ill Suited for Judgment: Constructing 'A Sovereign Access to the Sea' in the Atacama Desert." 48(2) *University of Miami–American Law Review* 28–86, 2017.

Rossi, Christopher R. "The Nomos of Climate Change and the Sociological Refugee in a Sinking Century." 50(3) *George Washington International Law Review* 613–652, 2018.

Rossi, Christopher R. "The Transboundary Dispute Over the Waters of the Silala/Siloli: Legal Vandalism and Goffmanian Metaphor." 53(1) *Stanford Journal of International Law* 55–87, 2017.

Sadoff, Claudia, and David Grey. "Beyond the River: The Benefits of Cooperation on International Rivers." 4(5) *Water Policy* 389–403, 2002.

Salman, Salman M. A. "The Nile Basin Cooperative Framework Agreement: A Peacefully Unfolding African Spring?" 38(1) *Water International* 17–29, 2013.

Salvatore, Ricardo Donato. "Local Versus Imperial Knowledge: Reflections on Hiram Bingham and the Yale Peruvian Expedition." 4(1) *Nepantla: Views from South* 67–80, 2003.

Salvatore, Ricardo Donato. "Re-discovering Spanish America: Uses of Travel Literature about South America in Britain." 8(2) *Journal of Latin American Cultural Studies* 200–217, 1999.

Scarfi, Juan Pablo. "In the Name of the Americas: The Pan-American Redefinition of the Monroe Doctrine and the Emerging Language of American International Law in the Western Hemisphere, 1898–1933." 40(2) *Diplomatic History* 189–218, 2016.

Scharf, Michael P. "Seizing the 'Grotian Moment': Accelerated Formation of Customary International Law in Times of Fundamental Change." 43(2) *Cornell International Law Journal* 439–469, 2010.

Schimmelfennig, Frank. "Goffman Meets IR: Dramaturgical Action in International Community." 12(3) *International Review of Sociology* 417–437, 2002.

Schmitt, Carl. "Großraum versus Universalism: The International Legal Struggle Over the Monroe Doctrine." In *Spatiality, Sovereignty and Carl Schmitt: Geographies of the Nomos* 46–54. Edited by Stephen Legg. Translated by Matthew Hannah. New York: Routledge, 2011.

Schröder, Stefan. "The Encounter with Islam between Doctrinal Image and Life Writing: Ambrosius Zeebout's Report of Joos van Ghistele's Travels to the East 1481–1485." In *Fear and Loathing in the North: Jews and Muslims in Medieval Scandinavia and the Baltic Region* 83–106. Edited by Cordelia Heß and Jonathan Adams. Berlin: De Gruyter, 2016.

Schwartz, Barry. "Collective Memory." In *Blackwell Encyclopedia of Sociology* 588–590. Edited by George Ritzer. New York: Wiley-Blackwell, 2007.

Schwebel, Stephen M. "The Story of the U.N.'s Declaration on Permanent Sovereignty over Natural Resources." 49(5) *American Bar Association Journal* 463–469, 1963.

Seaman, Rebecca M. "Ayllus." In *Conflict in the Early Americas: An Encyclopedia of the Spanish Empire's Aztec, Incan, and Mayan Conquests* 35–36. Edited by Rebecca M. Seaman. Santa Barbara: ABC-CLIO, 2013.

Seaman, Rebecca M. "Leyes Nuevas 1542–1543." In *Conflict in the Early Americas: An Encyclopedia of the Spanish Empire's Aztec, Incan, and Mayan Conquests* 214–216. Edited by Rebecca M. Seaman. Santa Barbara: ABC-CLIO, 2013.

Sebastián, Javiér Fernández, and Juan Francisco Fuentes. "Conceptual History, Memory, and Identity, An Interview with Reinhart Koselleck." 2(1) *Contributions to the History of Concepts* 99–127, 2006.

Seo, Ji-Hye. "Solving the Mystery of the Atacama Nitrate Deposits: The Use of Stable Oxygen Isotope Analysis and Geochemistry." 1 *Journal of Purdue Undergraduate Research* 38–45, 2011.

Sigmund, Paul E. "Revolution, Counterrevolution, and the Catholic Church in Chile." 483 *The Annals of the American Academy of Political and Social Science* 25–35, 1986.

Sikkink, Kathryn. "From Pariah State to Global Protagonist: Argentina and the Struggle for International Human Rights." 50(1) *Latin American Politics and Society* 1–29, 2008.

Silva, Eduardo. "Exchange Rising? Karl Polanyi and Contentious Politics in Contemporary Latin America." 54(3) *Latin American Politics and Society* 1–32, 2012.

Singer, J. David. "The Level-of-Analysis Problem in International Relations." 14(1) *World Politics* 77–92, 1961.

Sjaastad, Larry. "The Costs and Returns of Human Migration." 70(5) *Journal of Political Economy* 80–93, 1962.

Skouteris, Thomas. "*Engaging History in International Law*." In *New Approaches to International Law* 99–122. Edited by José María Beneyto and David Kennedy. The Hague: T. M. C. Asser Press, 2013.

Sökefeld, Martin. "Debating Self, Identity, and Culture in Anthropology." 40(4) *Current Anthropology* 417–448, 1999.

Sparke, Matthew. "Political Geography: Political Geographies of Globalization (2)—Governance." 30(3) *Progress in Human Geography* 357–372, 2006.

Spivak, Gayatri Chakravorty. "Can the Subaltern Speak?" In *Marxism and the Interpretation of Culture* 271–313. Edited by Cary Nelson and Lawrence Grossberg. London: Macmillan, 1988.

Sprecher, Christopher, and Karl DeRouen Jr. "The Domestic Determinants of Foreign Policy Behavior in Middle Eastern Enduring Rivals, 1948–1998." 1 *Foreign Policy Analysis* 121–141, 2005.

Stahler-Sholk, Richard, and Harry E. Vanden. "A Second Look at Latin American Social Movements: Globalizing Resistance to the Neoliberal Paradigm." 38(1) *Latin American Perspectives* 5–13, 2011.

Sterio, Milena. "A Grotian Moment: Changes in the Legal Theory of Statehood." 39(2) *Denver Journal of International Law and Policy* 209–237, 2011.

Street, James H. "Raúl Prebisch, 1901–1986: An Appreciation." 21(2) *Journal of Economic Issues* 649–659, 1987.

Sunkel, Osvaldo. "National Development Policy and External Dependence in Latin America." 6(1) *The Journal of Development Studies* 23–48, 1969.

Svampa, Maristella. "The 'Commodities Consensus' and Valuation Languages in Latin America." 2(1) *Alternautas* 45–59, 2015.

Tamayo, Victor Muñoz. "Chile es bandera y juventud. Efebolatría y gremialism durante la primera etapa de la dictadura de Pinochet (1973–1979)." 54 *História Crítica* 195–219, 2014.

Tarlock, A. Dan. "The Future of Prior Appropriation in the New West." 41(4) *Natural Resources Journal* 769–793, 2001.

Teichman, Judith. "Merging the Modern and the Traditional: Market Reform in Chile and Argentina." 37(1) *Comparative Politics* 23–40, 2004.

Teschke, Benno. "Decisions and Indecisions: Political and Intellectual Receptions of Carl Schmitt." 67 *New Left Review* 61–95, 2011.

Teschke, Benno. "Fatal Attraction: A Critique of Carl Schmitt's International Political and Legal Theory." 3(2) *International Theory* 179–227, 2011.

Teschke, Benno. "Geopolitics." 14(1) *Historical Materialism* 327–335, 2006.

Teubal, Miguel. "Rise and Collapse of Neoliberalism in Argentina: The Role of Economic Groups." 20(3–4) *Journal of Developing Societies* 173–188, 2004.

Thies, Cameron. "The Construction of a Latin American Interstate Culture of Rivalry." 34(3) *International Interactions* 231–257, 2008.

Thompson, Carl. "William Dampier (1651–1715): English Buccaneer, Explorer, and Travel Writer." In *Literature of Travel and Exploration: An Encyclopedia. Vol. 1: A to F* 312–314. Edited by Jennifer Speakes. New York: Fitzroy Dearborn, 2003.

Thornton, Christy. "A Mexican International Economic Order? Tracing the Hidden Roots of the Charter of Economic Rights and Duties of States." 9 *Humanity* 389–421, 2018.

Tomasek, Robert D. "The Chilean-Bolivian Lauca River Dispute and the O.A.S." 9(3) *Journal of Inter-American Studies* 351–366, 1967.

Torrico, Mario Napoleón Pacheco. "The Foundation of the Central Bank of Bolivia (1929–1932)." 2 *Revista de Humanidades y Ciencias Sociales (Santa Cruz de la Sierra)*133–184. Translated by Jeremy Jordan, 2006.

Undurraga, Tomás. "Neoliberalism in Argentina and Chile: Common Antecedents, Divergent Paths." 23 *Revista de Sociologia e Política* 11–34, 2015.

Urrutia, F. J. "La codification du droit international en Amérique." 22(II) *Recueil des Cours* 141–153, 1928.

Van Der Ree, G. "Chile's (Inter) National Identities: Framing the Relations with Bolivia and Peru." 29(2) *Bulletin of Latin American Research* 208–223, 2010.

Van Duzer, Chet. "Land of Cuba, Part of Asia: The Carta Marina 1516." In *John W. Hessler and Chet Van Duzer, Seeing the World Anew: The Radical Vision of Martin Waldseemüller's 1507 and 1516 World Maps* 49–96. Washington, DC: Levenger Press in association with the Library of Congress, 2012.

Van Duzer, Chet. "A Northern Refuge of the Monstrous Races: Asia on Waldseemüller's 1516 'Carta Marina.'" 62(2) *Imago Mundi* 221–231, 2010.

Van Schendel, Willem. "Geographies of Knowing, Geographies of Ignorance: Jumping Scale in Southeast Asia." 20(6) *Environment and Planning D: Society and Space* 647–668, 2002.

Vick, Margaret J. "The Law of International Waters: Reasonable Utilization." 12(1) *Chicago–Kent Journal of International and Comparative Law* 141–178, 2012.

Villar, Pilar Carolina. "International Cooperation on Transboundary Aquifers in South America and the Guarani Aquifer Case." 59(1) *Revista Brasileira de Politica Internacional* 1–20, 2016.

Wallerstein, Immanuel. "Semi Peripheral Countries and the Contemporary World Crisis." 3(4) *Theory and Society* 461–483, 1976.

Watts, Pauline Moffitt. "The European Religious Worldview and Its Influence on Mapping." In *History of Cartography. Vol. 3 (Part 1), Cartography in the European Renaissance* 382–400. Edited by David Woodward. Chicago: University of Chicago Press, 2007.

Wehner, Leslie. "Developing Mutual Trust: The Othering Process Between Bolivia and Chile." 36(71) *Canadian Journal of Latin American and Caribbean Studies* 109–138, 2011.

Wehner, Leslie. "From Rivalry to Mutual Trust: The Othering Process Between Bolivia and Chile." *Giga Working Paper No. 135*, 1–25, 2010.

Wernke, Steven, and Thomas Whitmore. "Agriculture and Inequality in the Colonial Andes: A Simulation of Production and Consumption Using Administrative Documents." 37 *Human Ecology* 421–440, 2009.

Weyland, Kurt. "Neoliberalism and Democracy in Latin America: A Mixed Record." 46(1) *Latin American Politics and Society* 135–157, 2004.

Whitaker, Arthur P. "Alexander von Humboldt and Spanish America." 104(3) *Proceedings of the American Philosophical Society* 317–322, 1960.

Wilgus, A. Curtis. "James G. Blaine and the Pan American Movement." 5(4) *The Hispanic American Historical Review* 662–708, 1922.

Wilkinson, Charles F. "Aldo Leopold and Western Water Law: Thinking Perpendicular to the Prior Appropriation Doctrine." 24 *Land and Water Law Review* 1–38, 1989.

Williamson, John. "What Washington Means by Policy Reform." In *Latin American Adjustment: How Much Has Happened?* 7–20. Edited by John Williamson. Washington, DC.:: Institute for International Economics, 1990.

Winkler, Inga. "The Human Right to Sanitation." 37(4) *University of Pennsylvania Journal of International Law* 1,331–1,406, 2016.

Wolf, Eric R., and Edward C. Hansen. "Caudillo Politics: A Structural Analysis." 9(2) *Comparative Studies in Society and History* 168–179, 1967.

Wolff, Hans. "The Conception of the World on the Eve of the Discovery of America—Introduction." In *America: Early Maps of the New World* 10–15. Edited by Hans Wolff. Munich: Prestel, 1992.

Wolff, Hans. "Martin Waldseemüller: The Most Important Cosmographer in a Period of Dramatic Scientific Change." In *America: Early Maps of the New World* 111–126. Edited by Hans Wolff. Munich: Prestel, 1992.

Wolff, Hans. "Sixteenth-Century Printed Maps of the World. In America: Early Maps of the New World." In *America: Early Maps of the New World* 63–89. Edited by Hans Wolff. Munich: Prestel, 1992.

Wolin, Richard. "Carl Schmitt: The Conservative Revolution and the Aesthetics of Horror." 20(3) *Political Theory* 424–447, 1993.

Wouters, Patricia. "'Dynamic Cooperation'—The Evolution of Transboundary Water Cooperation." In *Water and the Law: Towards Sustainability* 13–65. Edited by Michael Kidd, Tumai Murombo and Alejandro Iza. Cheltenham: Edward Elgar, 2014.

Wouters, Patricia. "International Law—Facilitating Transboundary Water Cooperation." *Global Water Partnership TEC Background Papers,* No. 17, 1–83, 2013.

Wouters, Patricia. "The International Law on Watercourses: New Dimensions." In *III Collected Courses of the Xiamen Academy of International Law.* Edited by Xiamen Academy of International Law. Boston: Martinus Nijhoff Publishers, 2011.

Wouters, Patricia. "The Legal Response to International Water Conflicts: The UN Watercourses Convention and Beyond." 42 *German Yearbook of International Law* 293–336, 1999.

Wright, J. Leitch. "Sixteenth Century English-Spanish Rivalry in La Florida." 38(4) *Florida Historical Quarterly* 265–279, 1960.

Xing, Li. "Understanding the Hegemony and the Dialectics of the Emerging World Order." In *The BRICS and Beyond: The International Political Economy of the Emergence of a New World Order* 1–23. Edited by Li Xing. Farnham: Ashgate, 2014.

Yamada, Chusei. "Codification of the Law of Transboundary Aquifers (Groundwaters) by the United Nations." 36(5) *Water International* 557–565, 2011.

Yepes, J. M. "La contribution de l'Amérique latine au développement du droit international public et privé." 32(II) *Recueil des Cours* 691–800, 1930.

Zalles, Alberto A. "Bolivia y Chile: los imperativos de una nueva época." 207 *Nueva Sociedad* 34–44, 2007.

Zodrow, Irina. "International Aspects of Water Law Reforms." In *Water Law for the Twenty-First Century: National and International Aspects of Water Law Reform in India* 36–58. Edited by Philippe Cullet, Alix Gowlland-Gualtieri, Roopa Madhav, and Usha Ramanathan. New York: Routledge, 2010.

Zolo, Danilo. "The Rule of Law: A Critical Reappraisal." In *The Rule of Law History, Theory and Criticism* 3–72. Edited by Pietro Costa and Danilo Zolo. Dordrecht: Springer Netherlands, 2007.

Books

Aarons, John, and Claudio Vita-Finzi. *The Useless Land: A Winter in the Atacama Desert.* London: R. Hale, 1960.

Adams, Percy G. *Travel Literature and the Evolution of the Novel.* Lexington: University Press of Kentucky, 1983.

Agamben, Giorgio. *Homo Sacer: Sovereign Power and Bare Life.* Translated by Daniel Heller-Roazen. Stanford: Stanford University Press, 1998.

Agamben, Giorgio. *State of Exception.* Translated by Kevin Attell. Chicago: University of Chicago Press, 2005.

Agnew, John A., and James S. Duncan, eds. *The Power of Place: Bringing Together Geographical and Sociological Imaginations.* Winchester: Unwin Hyman, 1989.

Ahmed, Dirdeiry M. *Boundaries and Secession in Africa and International Law: Challenging Uti Possidetis.* Cambridge: Cambridge University Press, 2015.

Akers, Charles Edmond. *A History of South America.* New York: E. P. Dutton, 1930.

Alconini, Sonia, and R. Alan Covey. *The Oxford Handbook of the Incas.* New York: Oxford University Press, 2018.

Allen, Nellie Burnham. *South America.* Boston: Ginn, 1918.

Amin, Samir. *Unequal Development: An Essay on the Social Formations of Peripheral Capitalism.* Translated by Brian Pearce. Sussex: Harvester Press, 1976.

Amunátegui, Miguel Luis. *La cuestión de límites entre Chile y Bolivia.* Santiago: Imprenta Nacional, 1987.

Anand, Ram Prakash. *Studies in International Law and History: An Asian Perspective.* Leiden: Martinus Nijhoff, 2004.

Andolina, Robert, Nina Laurie, and Sarah A. Radcliffe. *Indigenous Development in the Andes: Culture, Power, and Transnationalism.* Durham: Duke University Press, 2009.

Arditti, Rita. *Searching for Life: The Grandmothers of the Plaza de Mayo and the Disappeared Children of Argentina.* Berkeley: University of California Press, 1999.

Arechaga, Jiménez de. *Curso de Derecho Internacional Público.* Volume 2. Montevideo: Centro Estudiantes de Derecho, 1961.

Arguedas, Alcides. *Historia general de Bolivia (El proceso de la nacionalidad 1809–1921).* La Paz: Arnó hermanos,1922.

Aristotle. *On the Art of Poetry.* Translated by Ingram Bywater with a preface by Gilbert Murray. Oxford: Clarendon Press,1920.

Arvidsson, Matilda, Leila Brännström, and Panu Minkkinen. *The Contemporary Relevance of Carl Schmitt: Law, Politics, Theology.* New York: Routledge, 2016.

Arzáns de Orsúa y Vela, Bartolomé. *Tales of Potosí.* Edited and with an introduction by R. C. Padden. Translated by Frances M. López-Morillas. Providence: Brown University Press, 1975.

Auyero, Javier. *La política de los pobres: Las prácticas clientelistas del peronismo.* Buenos Aires: Editorial Manantial, 2001.

Baker, Gideon, editor. *Hospitality and World Politics.* Houndsmills: Palgrave Macmillan, 2013.

Bakewell, Peter. *A History of Latin America, c. 1450 to the Present.* 2d ed. Malden: Blackwell Publishers, 2004.

Ballesteros Gaibrois, Manuel. *Historia de America.* Madrid: Pegaso, 1946.

Barba, Alvaro Alonso. *A Collection of Scarce and Valuable Treatises upon Metals, Mines, and Minerals.* 2d ed. London: Printed for J. Hodges, 1740.

Barlow, Maude, and Tony Clarke. *Blue Gold: The Battle Against Corporate Theft of the World's Water.* New York: Routledge, 2017.

Barros, Robert. *Constitutionalism and Dictatorship: Pinochet, the Junta, and the 1980 Constitution.* New York: Cambridge University Press, 2002.

Bartal, Renana, and Hanna Vorholt, eds. *Between Jerusalem and Europe: Essays in Honour of Bianca Kühnel.* Leiden: Brill, 2015.

Bartelson, Jens. *A Genealogy of Sovereignty.* Cambridge: Cambridge University Press, 1995.

Bastien, Joseph W. *Mountain of the Condor: Metaphor and Ritual in the Andean Ayllu.* St. Paul: Waveland Press, 1978.

Batalla, Guillermo Bonfil. *México Profundo: Reclaiming a Civilization.* Mexico City: Centro de Investigaciones y Estudios Superiores en Antropología Social, 1987.

Bauer, Carl J. *Siren Song: Chilean Water Law as a Model for International Reform.* Washington, DC: Resources for the Future, 2004.

Bazoberry Quiroga, Antonio. *El Mito del Silala.* La Paz: Plural, 2003.

Beatson, Major-General Alexander. *Tracts Relative to the Island of St. Helena; written during a residence of five years.* London: W. Bulmer and Company, 1816.

Beaulac, Stéphane. *The Power of Language in the Making of International Law:*

The Word Sovereignty in Bodin and Vattel and the Myth of Westphalia. Leiden: Martinus Nijhoff Publishers, 2004.

Becker Lorca, Arnulf. *Mestizo International Law: A Global Intellectual History 1842–1933*. Cambridge: Cambridge University Press, 2014.

Beebe, Kathryne. *Pilgrim and Preacher: The Audiences and Observant Spirituality of Friar Felix Fabri (1437/8–1502)*. Oxford: Oxford University Press, 2014.

Belaunde, Victor Andrés. *Nuestra Cuestión con Chile*. Lima, Peru: Sanmarti y ca., impresores, 1919.

Bendersky, Joseph J. *Carl Schmitt: Theorist for the Reich*. Princeton: Princeton University Press, 1983.

Beneyto, José Maria, and David Kennedy, eds. *New Approaches to International Law: The European and American Experiences*. The Hague: T. M. C Asser Press, 2013.

Benton, Lauren. *A Search for Sovereignty: Law and Geography in European Empires, 1400–1900*. Cambridge: Cambridge University Press, 2010.

Bernhardt, Rudolf, ed. *Encyclopedia of Public International Law*. New York: North-Holland Pub. Co., 1987.

Berti Suman, Anna. *The Human Right to Water in Latin America: Challenges to Implementation and Contribution to the Concept*. Leiden: Brill, 2018.

Beverley, John. *Subalternity and Representation: Arguments in Cultural Theory*. London: Duke University Press, 1999.

Biago, Didier, and Anastassia Tsoukala, eds. *Terror, Insecurity and Liberty: Illiberal Practices of Liberal Regimes after 9/11*. London: Routledge, 2008.

Bianchi, Andera, ed. *International Law Theories: An Enquiry into Different Ways of Thinking*. New York: Oxford University Press, 2016.

Bierck, Harold A., Jr., ed. *Selected Writings of Bolivar, 1823–1830*. Translated by Lewis Bertrand. New York: Colonial Press, 1951.

Biersteker, Thomas J., and Cynthia Weber, eds. *State Sovereignty as Social Construct*. Cambridge: Cambridge University Press, 1996.

Bingham, Hiram. *Across South America; an account of a journey from Buenos Aires to Lima by way of Potosí, with notes on Brazil, Argentina, Bolivia, Chile, and Peru*. New York: Houghton Mifflin Company, 1911.

Bingham, Hiram. *Lost City of the Incas: The Story of Machu Picchu and Its Builders*. New York: Duell, Sloan and Pearce, 1948.

Bizzarro, Salvatore. *Historical Dictionary of Chile*. 3d ed. Lanham, MD: Scarecrow Press, 2005.

Blakemore, Harold. *From the Pacific to La Paz: The Antofagasta (Chile) and Bolivia Railway Company 1888–1988*. London: Lester Crook Academic Publishing, 1990.

Bluntschli, Johann Caspar. *Le Droit International Codifié*. Paris: Guillaumin, 1895.

Böckenförde, Ernst-Wolfgang. *State, Society and Liberty: Studies in Political The-*

ory and Constitutional Law. Translated by J. A. Underwood. New York: Berg, 1991.

Boelens, Rutgerd, David Getches, and Armando Guevara-Gil, eds. *Out of the Mainstream: Water Rights, Politics and Identity.* London: Earthscan, 2010.

Boisson de Chazournes, Laurence, Christina Leb, and Mara Tignino, eds. *International Law and Freshwater: The Multiple Challenges.* Cheltenham: Edward Elgar, 2013.

Borgoño, Luis Barros. *The Problem of the Pacific and the New Policies of Bolivia.* Baltimore: Sun Job Printing Office, 1924.

Bork, Robert, and Andrea Kann, eds. *The Art, Science and Technology of Medieval Travel.* Hampshire: Ashgate Publishing Limited, 2008.

Bornträger, Ekkehard W. *Borders, Ethnicity and National Self-Determination.* Wein: Wilhelm Braumüller, 1999.

Bosworth, Barry P., Rudiger Dornbush, and Raúl Labán, eds. *The Chilean Economy: Policy Lessons and Challenges.* Washington, DC: Brookings Institution, 1994.

Bouzas, Roberto, and Jaime Ros. *Economic Integration in the Western Hemisphere.* Notre Dame: University of Notre Dame Press, 1994.

Bowman, Isaiah. *Desert Trails of Atacama.* New York: American Geographical Society, 1924.

Bown, Stephen R. *1494: How a Family Feud in Medieval Spain Divided the World in Half.* New York: Thomas Dunne Books, 2011.

Bown, Stephen R. *A Most Damnable Invention: Dynamite, Nitrates, and the Making of the Modern World.* New York: Thomas Dunne Books, 2005.

Boxer, Charles R. *The Portuguese Seaborne Empire: 1415–1825.* New York: Alfred A. Knopf, 1969.

Brandenburg, E. C., editor. *Official Opinions of the Attorney-General of the United States Advising the President and Heads of Departments in Relation to their Official Duties.* Washington, DC: United States Government Publishing Office, 1898.

Braun, Juan, Matías Braun, Ignacio Briones, José Díaz B., Rolf Lüders S., and Gert Wagner H. *Economía Chilena 1810–1995. Estadísticas Históricas.* Santiago: Pontificia Universidad Catolica de Chile, 2000.

Breydenbach, Bernhard von. *Peregrinatio in Terram Sanctam, Eine Pilgerreise ins Heilige Land, Frühneuhochdeutscher Text und Übersetzung (Herausgegeben von Isolde Mozer).* Berlin: De Gruyter, 2010.

Brotton, Jerry. *Trading Territories: Mapping the Early Modern World.* Ithaca: Cornell University Press, 1998.

Brown, Lloyd A. *The Story of Maps.* New York: Bonanza Books, 1949.

Brunnegger, Sandra, and Karen Ann Faulk, eds. *A Sense of Justice: Legal Knowledge and Lived Experience in Latin America.* Stanford: Stanford University Press, 2016.

Brysk, Alison. *The Politics of Human Rights in Argentina: Protest, Change, and Democratization.* Stanford: Stanford University Press, 1994.

Büchi, Hernán. *The Economic Transformation of Chile: A Personal Account.* North Miami Beach: Hancer, 2010.

Buisseret, David. *The Mapmakers' Quest: Depicting New Worlds in Renaissance Europe.* Oxford: Oxford University Press, 2003.

Buisseret, David, ed. *The Oxford Companion to World Exploration.* New York: Oxford University Press, 2007.

Bull, Hedley. *The Anarchical Society: A Study of Order in World Politics.* London: Macmillan, 1977.

Butler, Judith. *Frames of War: When Is Life Grievable?* New York: Verso, 2010.

Butler, Samuel. *Erewhon and Erewhon Revisited.* New York: Modern Library, 1933.

Butterfield, Herbert. *The Whig Interpretation of History.* London: G. Bell and Sons, 1931.

Byttebier, Koen. *Towards a New International Monetary Order.* Cham: Springer, 2017.

Campo, Alicia del. *Teatralidades de la memoria: Rituales de reconciliación en el Chile de la transición.* Santiago: Mosquito Comunicaciones, 2004.

Cante, Fredy, and Hartmut Quehl, eds. *Handbook on Research on Transitional Justice and Peace Building in Turbulent Regions.* Hershey, PA: IGI Global, 2015.

Carter, Paul. *The Road to Botany Bay: An Exploration of Landscape and History.* Minneapolis, London: University of Minnesota Press, 1987.

Castells, Manuel. *The Power of Identity: The Information Age-Economy, Society, and Culture.* 2d ed. West Sussex: Wiley-Blackwell, 2010.

Cavallo, Ascanio, Manuel Salazar, and Oscar Sepúlveda. *La historia oculta del regimen military: memoria de una época 1973–1988.* Santiago: Uqbar, 2012.

Cayton, Andrew R. L., and Susan E. Gray, eds. *The American Midwest: Essays on Regional History.* Bloomington: Indiana University Press, 2001.

Cayton, Andrew R. L., and Peter S. Onuf. *The Midwest and the Nation: Rethinking the History of an American Region.* Bloomington: Indiana University Press, 1990.

Cerruti, Captain F. E. *Peru and Spain: Being A Narrative of the Events Preceding and Following the Seizure of the Chincha Islands, With an Analysis of the Despatch of Señor Salazar Y Mazarredo.* London: Williams and Norgate, 1864.

Chakrabarty, Dipesh. *Provincializing Europe: Postcolonial Thought and Historical Difference.* Princeton: Princeton University Press, 2000.

Chellaney, Brahma. *Water: Asia's New Battleground.* Washington, DC: Georgetown University Press, 2011.

Coates, Benjamin Allen. *Legalist Empire: International Law and American Foreign Relations in the Early Twentieth Century.* New York: Oxford University Press, 2016.

Collins, Joseph, and John Lear, eds. *Chile's Free-Market Miracle: A Second Look.* Oakland: Institute for Food and Development Policy, 1995.

Cooke, Captain Edward. *A voyage to the South Sea, and round the world, perform'd in the years 1708, 1709, 1710, and 1711. Containing a journal of all memorable transactions during the said Voyage; the Winds, Currents and Variation of the Compass; the taking of the Towns of Puna and Guayaquil, and several Prizes, one of which a rich Aeapulso Ship. A Description of the American Coasts, from Tierra del Fuego in the South, to California in the North, (from the Coasting-Pilot, a Spanish Manuscript.) An Historical Account of all those Countries from the best Authors. With a new map and description of the mighty River of the Amazons. Wherein an account is given of Mr. Alexander Selkirk, his Manner of living and taming some wild Beasts during the four Years and four Months he liv'd upon the uninhabited Island of Juan Fernandes. Illustrated with cuts and maps.* Vol. 2. London: printed by H.M. for B. Lintot and R. Gosling in Fleet-Street, A. Bettelsworth on London-Bridge, and W. Innys in St. Paul's Church-Yard, 1712.

Cornblit, Oscar. *Power and Violence in the Colonial City: Oruro from the Mining Renaissance to the Rebellion of Tupac Amaru (1740–1782).* Cambridge: Cambridge University Press, 1995.

Corrigan, Robert Willoughby, and James L. Rosenberg. *The Context and Craft of Drama: Critical Essays on the Nature of Drama and Theatre.* San Francisco: Chandler Publishing Company, 1964.

Cosgrove, Denis. *Apollo's Eye: A Cartographic Genealogy of the Earth in the Western Imagination.* Baltimore: Johns Hopkins University Press, 2001.

Costa, Pietro, and Danilo Zolo, eds. *The Rule of Law: History, Theory and Criticism.* Dordrecht: Springer, 2007.

Cox, Kevin R., ed. *Spaces of Globalization: Reasserting the Power of the Local.* New York: Guilford Press, 1997.

Craven, Matthew, Malgosia Fitzmaurice, and Maria Vogiatzi, eds. *Time, History and International Law.* Leiden: Martinus Nijhoff Publishers, 2007.

Crawford, James, and Sarah Nouwen, editors. *Select Proceedings of the European Society of International Law. Oxford:* Hart Publishing, 2012.

Cristi, Renato. *Carl Schmitt and Authoritarian Liberalism.* Cardiff: University of Wales Press, 1998.

Cristi, Renato. *El Pensamiento político de Jaime Guzmán: Autoridad y Libertad.* Santiago: LOM, 2000.

Cullet, Philippe, Alix Gowlland-Gualtieri, Roopa Madhav, and Usha Ramanathan, eds. *Water Law for the Twenty-First Century: National and International Aspects of Water Law Reform in India.* New York: Routledge, 2010.

Cushman, Gregory T. *Guano and the Opening of the Pacific World: A Global Ecological History.* Cambridge: Cambridge University Press, 2013.

Dahl, Edward H., and Jean-François Gauvin. *Sphæræ Mundi: Early Globes at the Stewart Museum.* Sillery, Quebec: Septentrion, 2000.

Dampier, Captain William. *A New Voyage Round the World Describing particularly, The Isthmus of America, several Coasts and Islands in the West Indies, the Isles of Cape Verd, the Passage by Terra de Fuego, the South Sea Coasts of Chile, Peru, and Mexico, the Isle of Guam one of the Ladrones, Mindanao, and other Philippine and East India Islands near Cambodia, China, Formosa, Lueoenia, Celebes, &c. New Holland, Sumatra, Nicobar Isles, the Cape of Good Hope, and Santa Hellena. Their Soil, Rivers, Harbours, Plants, Fruits, Animals, and their Inhabitants. Their Customs, Religion, Government, Trade, &c.* . . . Vol. 1. 6th ed. corrected. London: James Knapton, at the Crown in St. Paul's Church-Yard, 1717.

Darwin, Charles. *The Voyage of the Beagle.* Edited by Nora Barlow. London: Pilot Press, 1945.

Darwin, Charles. *The Voyage of the Beagle.* Annotated and with an introduction by Leonard Engle. New York: Doubleday and Company, 1962.

Darwin, Francis, ed. *Life and Letters of Charles Darwin, including an autobiographical chapter.* Vol. 3. London: John Murray, 1887.

Da Silva, Ricardo Barreto Ferreira, and Paulo Marcos Rodrigues Brancher, eds. *Foreign Investment in South America: A Comprehensive Guide to Infrastructure and the Legal Environment.* Chicago: American Bar Association, Business Law Section, 2018.

D'Aspremont, Jean, Sahib Singh, and G. C. McBains, eds. *Concepts for International Law: Contributions to Disciplinary Thought.* Cheltenham: Edward Elgar Publishing Limited, 2019.

Daugherty, William T. *German Chemical Developments in 1927.* Washington, DC: United States Department of Commerce, Bureau of Foreign and Domestic Commerce, 1928.

Dauvergne, Catherine. *Making People Illegal: What Globalization Means for Migration and Law.* Cambridge: Cambridge University Press, 2008.

Davenport, Frances Gardiner, ed. *European Treaties Bearing on the History of the United States and Its Dependencies to 1648.* Washington, DC: Carnegie Institution of Washington, 1917.

Davis, Michael. *Aristotle's Poetics: The Poetry of Philosophy.* Lanham: Rowman and Littlefield Publishers, 1992.

Davis, William Columbus. *The Last Conquistadores: The Spanish Intervention in Peru and Chile, 1863–1866.* Athens: University of Georgia Press, 1950.

Day, Alan Edwin. *Discovery and Exploration: A Reference Handbook, the Old World.* New York: K. G. Saur, 1980.

DeFries, Ruth. *The Big Ratchet: How Humanity Thrives in the Face of Natural Crisis.* Boulder: Basic Books, 2014.

Dellapenna, Joseph W., and Joyeeta Gupta. *The Evolution of the Law and Politics of Water.* Dordrecht: Springer Netherlands, 2009.

Derrida, Jacques. *Specters of Marx: The State of the Debt, the Work of Mourning, and the New International.* New York: Routledge, 1994.

Descartes, René. *Principles of Philosophy.* Translated by Valentine Rodger Miller and Reese P. Miller. Dordrecht: Kluwer Academic Publishers, 1982.

Dhawan, N., ed. *Negotiating Normativity.* Cham: Springer, 2016.

Dornbusch, Rudiger, and Sebastian Edwards, eds. *Reform, Recovery, and Growth: Latin America and the Middle East.* Chicago: University of Chicago Press, 1995.

Dosman, Edgar J. *The Life and Times of Raúl Prebisch, 1901–1986.* Montreal: McGill–Queen's University Press, 2008.

Dunkerley, James. *Bolivia: Revolution and the Power of History in the Present.* London: University of London Press, 2007.

Durán-Cogan, Mercedes F., and Antonio Gómez-Moriana, eds. *National Identities and Sociopolitical Changes in Latin America.* New York: Routledge, 2001.

Ebenstein, Alan. *Friedrich Hayek: A Biography.* New York: Palgrave, 2001.

Ebenstein, Lanny. *Chicagonomics: The Evolution of Chicago Free Market Economics.* New York: St. Martin's Press, 2015.

Edkins, Jenny, and Nick Vaughan-Williams. *Critical Theorists and International Relations.* New York: Routledge, 2009.

Edwards, John. *The Spain of The Catholic Monarchs 1474–1520.* Malden: Blackwell Publishers, 2000.

Edwards, Sebastian, and Alejandra Cox Edwards. *Monetarism and Liberalization: The Chilean Experiment.* Cambridge: Ballinger Pub., 1987.

Ehlers, Eckart, and Thomas Krafft, eds. *Earth System Science in the Anthropocene: Emerging Issues and Problems.* Berlin: Springer, 2000.

Elden, Stuart. *The Birth of Territory.* Chicago: University of Chicago Press, 2013.

Elden, Stuart, and Eduardo Mendieta, eds. *Reading Kant's Geography.* Albany: State University of New York Press, 2011.

Elias, Taslim Olawale. *Africa and the Development of International Law.* Dordrecht: M. Nijhoff, 1988.

Elizondo, José Rodríguez. *Historia de dos demandas: Perú y Bolivia contra Chile.* Santiago: Editorial El Mercurio-Aguilar, 2014.

Ericksen, George E. *Geology and Origin of the Chilean Nitrate Deposits (Geological Survey Professional Paper).* Washington, DC: United States Department of the Interior, 1988.

Evans, R. J. W., and Peter H. Wilson, eds. *The Holy Roman Empire, 1495–1806: A European Perspective.* Leiden: Brill, 2012.

Exquemelin, Alexandre Olivier. *The bucaniers of America: or, a true account of the most remarkable assaults committed of late years upon the coasts of the West-Indies, by the bucaniers of Jamaica and Tortuga, both English and French.* London: Printed for William Crooke,1684.

Eyzaguirre, Jaime. *Bolivia: An Isolated Country?* Santiago: Empresa Editora Zig-Zag, 1963.

Fabian, Johannes. *Time and the Other. How Anthropology Makes Its Object.* New York: Columbia University Press, 1983.

Fabri, Felix. *Evagatorium, or Wanderings of Brother Felix Fabri.* Vol. 2. X Palestine Pilgrims' Text Society. London: Palestine Pilgrims' Text Society, 1897.

Fagg, John Edwin. *Latin America: A General History.* 2d ed. New York: Macmillan, 1969.

Farcau, Bruce W. *The Ten Cents War: Chile, Peru, and Bolivia in the War of the Pacific, 1879–1884.* Westport: Praeger, 2000.

Fasolt, Constantine. *The Limits of History.* Chicago: University of Chicago Press, 2004.

Fassbender, Bardo, and Anne Peters, eds. *The Oxford Handbook of the History of International Law.* Oxford: Oxford University Press, 2012.

Faulk, Karen Ann. *In the Wake of Neoliberalism: Citizenship and Human Rights in Argentina.* Stanford, CA: Stanford University Press, 2013.

Feitlowitz, Marguerite. *A Lexicon of Terror: Argentina and the Legacies of Torture.* New York: Oxford University Press, 2011.

Fenwick, Charles. *International Law.* 4th ed. New York: Appleton-Century-Crofts, 1965.

Ffrench-Davis, Ricardo. *Economic Reforms in Chile: From Dictatorship to Democracy.* London: Palgrave Macmillan, 2010.

Ffrench-Davis, Ricardo, and Barbara Stallings, eds. *Reformas, crecimiento y políticas sociales en Chile desde 1973.* Santiago: LOM Ediciones, 2001.

Fifer, J. Valerie. *Bolivia: Land, Location, and Politics Since 1825.* Cambridge: University Press, 1972.

Figueroa, Uldaricio. *La demanda marítima boliviana en los foros internacionales.* Providencia, Santiago de Chile: RIL Editores, 2007.

Finamore, Daniel, ed. *Maritime History as World History.* Gainesville: University Press of Florida, 2004.

Fischer-Tahir, Andrea, and Matthias Naumann. *Peripheralization: The Making of Spatial Dependencies and Social Injustice.* Wiesbaden: Springer VS, 2013.

Foucault, Michel. *Power/Knowledge: Selected Interviews & Other Writings, 1972–1977.* Edited by Colin Gordon. Translated by Colin Gordon, Leo Marshall, John g, and Kate Soper. New York: Pantheon Books, 1980.

Foxley, Alejandro. *Latin American Experiments in Neoconservative Economics.* Berkeley: University of California Press, 1983.

Francaviglia, Richard V. *Imagining the Atacama Desert: A Five-Hundred-Year Journey of Discovery.* Salt Lake City: University of Utah Press, 2018.

Fraser, Nancy. *Scales of Justice: Reimagining Political Space in a Globalizing World.* New York: Columbia University Press, 2009.

Frazier, Lessie Jo. *Salt in the Sand: Memory, Violence, and the Nation-State in Chile, 1890 to the Present.* Durham, NC: Duke University Press, 2007.

Frézier, Amédée François. *A Voyage to the South-Sea And along the coasts of Chili and Peru in the Years 1712, 1713, and 1714, particularly describing The Genius and Constitution of the Inhabitants, as well Indians as Spaniards: Their Customs and Manners; their Natural history, Mines, Commodities, Traffick with Europe, &c.* London: Printed for J. Bowyer, 1717.

Friedman, Milton, and Rose D. Friedman. *Two Lucky People: Memoirs.* Chicago: University of Chicago Press, 1998.

Fukuyama, Francis. *The End of History and the Last Man.* New York: Free Press, 1992.

Galli, Carlo. *Janus's Gaze: Essays on Carl Schmitt.* Edited by Adam Sitze. Translated by Amanda Minervini. Durham: Duke University Press, 2015.

Gargarella, Roberto. *The Legal Foundations of Inequality: Constitutionalism in the Americas, 1776–1860.* Cambridge: Cambridge University Press, 2010.

Gibson, Charles. *Spain in America.* New York: Harper Colophon Books, 1966.

Goffman, Erving. *Encounters.* Indianapolis: Bobbs-Merrill, 1961.

Goffman, Erving. *Frame Analysis: An Essay on the Organization of Experience.* Boston: Northeastern University Press, 1986.

Goffman, Erving. *Interaction Rituals.* Garden City, NY: Anchor Books, 1967.

Goffman, Erving. *Strategic Interaction.* Philadelphia: University of Pennsylvania Press, 1969.

Goffman, Erving. *The Presentation of Self in Everyday Life.* Garden City, NY: Doubleday, 1959.

Gose, Peter. *Invaders as Ancestors: On the Intercultural Making and Unmaking of Spanish Colonialism in the Andes.* Toronto: University of Toronto Press, 2008.

Gottfried, Paul Edward. *Carl Schmitt: Politics and Theory.* New York: Greenwood Press, 1990.

Gould, Peter, and Rodney White. *Mental Maps.* Harmondsworth: Penguin, 1974.

Greaves, Thomas, and William Culver, eds. *Miners and Mining in the Americas.* Manchester: Manchester University Press, 1985.

Greenwood, Ned H. *The Sinai: A Physical Geography.* Austin: University of Texas Press, 1997.

Grewe, Wilhelm G. *Epochen der Völkerrechtsgeschichte.* Baden-Baden: Nomos Verlagsgesellschaft, 1984.

Grimson, Alejandro, and Gabriel Kessler. *On Argentina and the Southern Cone: Neoliberalism and National Imaginations.* New York: Routledge, 2005.

Gross, Raphael. *Carl Schmitt and the Jews: The "Jewish Question," the Holocaust, and German Legal Theory.* Translated by Joel Golb. Madison: University of Wisconsin Press, 2007.

Grotius, Hugo. *Mare Liberum 1609–2009.* Edited by Robert Feenstra, introduction by Jeroen Vervliet. Leiden: Brill, 2009.

Grovogui, Siba N. *Beyond Eurocentrism and Anarchy: Memories of International Order and Institutions.* New York: Palgrave Macmillan, 2006.

Grovogui, Siba N'Zatioula. *Sovereigns, Quasi Sovereigns, and Africans: Race and Self-Determination in Law.* Minneapolis: University of Minnesota Press, 1996.

Hachette, Dominique, and Rolf Lüders. *Privatization in Chile: An Economic Appraisal.* San Francisco: ICS Press, 1993.

Hanke, Lewis. *The Imperial City of Potosí: An Unwritten Chapter in the History of Spanish America.* The Hague: Nijhoff, 1956.

Hansen, Roger D. *Beyond the North-South Stalemate.* New York: McGraw-Hill, 1979.

Haring, C. H. *The Spanish Empire in America.* New York: Oxford University Press, 1947.

Harvey, David. *Neoliberalism.* Oxford: Oxford University Press, 2005.

Harvey, David. *Social Justice and the City.* Athens: University of Georgia Press, 1973.

Hathaway, Oona A., and Scott J. Shapiro. *The Internationalists: How a Radical Plan to Outlaw War Remade the World.* New York: Simon & Schuster, 2017.

Haughney, Diane. *Neoliberal Economics, Democratic Transition, and Mapuche Demands for Rights in Chile.* Gainesville: University Press of Florida, 2006.

Haushofer, Karl, Erich Obst, Hermann Lautensach, and Otto Maull. *Bausteine zur Geopolitik.* Berlin: Kurt Vowinckel, 1928.

Hayek, F. A. *Law, Legislation and Liberty.* Chicago: University of Chicago Press, 1976.

Heß, Cordelia, and Jonathan Adams, eds. *Fear and Loathing in the North: Jews and Muslims in Medieval Scandinavia and the Baltic Region.* Berlin: De Gruyter, 2016.

Healy, David. *James G. Blaine and Latin America.* Columbia: University of Missouri Press, 2001.

Heaney, Christopher. *Cradle of Gold: The Story of Hiram Bingham, a Real-Life Indiana Jones, and the Search for Machu Picchu.* New York: Palgrave Macmillan, 2010.

Heffter, A. G. *Le Droit International Public de L'Europe.* Translated by J. Bergson. Paris: Cotillon, 1857.

Hemming, John. *Oxford Atlas of Exploration.* New York: Oxford University Press, 1997.

Herf, Jeffrey. *Reactionary Modernism: Technology, Culture, and Politics in Weimar and the Third Reich.* Cambridge: Cambridge University Press, 1984.

Herrera, Antonio de. *Descripcion de las Islas, y tierra firme del mar oceano, que llaman Indias Ocidentales.* Colección de historiadores de Chile y documentos relativos a la historia nacional, 1601.

Herrera, Antonio de. *Historia general de los hechos de los Castellanos en las Islas y tierra firme de Mar Oceanos.* Madrid: En la Emplenta Real, 1601.

Herrero, Montserrat. *The Political Discourse of Carl Schmitt: A Mystic of Order.* London: Rowman & Littlefield International, 2015.

Hesiod. *Theogony and Works and Days: A New Bilingual Edition.* Translated by Kimberly Johnson. Chicago: Northwestern University Press, 2017.

Hessler, John W., and Chet Van Duzer. *Seeing the World Anew: The Radical Vi-*

sion of Martin Waldseemüller's 1507 & 1516 World Maps. Delray Beach: Levenger Press in association with the Library of Congress, 2012.

Hill, Norman. *Claims to Territory in International Law and Relations.* New York: Oxford University Press, 1945.

Hobbes, Thomas. *Leviathan or the Matter, Forme and Power of a Commonwealth Ecclesiasticall and Civill.* London: Printed for Andrew Crooke, 1651.

Hoberman, Louisa Schell, and Susan Migden Socolow, eds. *Cities and Society in Colonial Latin America.* Albuquerque: University of New Mexico Press, 1986.

Hobson, John A. *The Evolution of Modern Capitalism: A Study of Machine Production.* New York: W. Scott, 1894.

Hollender, Rebecca, and Jim Shultz. *Bolivia and Its Lithium: Can the "Gold of the 21st Century" Help Lift a Nation Out of Poverty?* Cochabamba, Bolivia: The Democracy Center, 2010.

Holsti, Ole R. *Public Opinion and American Foreign Policy.* Ann Arbor: University of Michigan Press, 1996.

Hooker, William. *Carl Schmitt's International Thought: Order and Orientation.* Cambridge: Cambridge University Press, 2009.

Hormazábal Díaz, Fernando. *El libro blanco de Chile: El problema marítimo boliviano.* Santiago: Centro de Estudios Bicentenario, 2005.

Howard, Donald R. *Writers and Pilgrims: Medieval Pilgrimage Narratives and Their Posterity.* Berkeley: University of California Press, 1980.

Howgego, Raymond John. *Encyclopedia of Exploration to 1800.* Potts Point, N.S.W.: Hordern House, 2003.

Humboldt, Alexander Von, and Aimé Bonpland. *Personal Narrative of Travels to the Equinoctial Regions of the New Continent, During the Years 1799–1804.* 7 vols. London: Longman, 1819–1829.

Hussain, Safqat. *Remoteness and Modernity: Transformation and Continuity in Northern Pakistan.* New Haven: Yale University Press, 2015.

Hutchings, Paul, Richard Franceys, Stef Smits, and Snehalatha Mekala. *Community Management of Rural Water Supply: Case Studies of Success from India.* New York: Routledge, 2017.

Isbell, William H. *Mummies and Mortuary Monuments: A Postprocessual Prehistory of Central Andean Social Organization.* Austin: University of Texas Press, 1997.

Islam, Nahid. *The Law of Non-Navigational Uses of International Watercourses: Options for Regional Regime-Building in Asia.* Alphen aan den Rijn, The Netherlands: Kluwer Law International, 2010.

Jacob, Christian. *The Sovereign Map: Theoretical Approaches in Cartography Throughout History.* Chicago: University of Chicago Press, 2006.

Jacobs, Michael. *Andes.* Berkeley: Counterpoint, 2011.

Jiménez-Cisneros, Blanca, and José Galizia-Tundisi. *Diagnosis of Water in the Americas: Interamerican Network of Academies of Sciences.* Tlalpan, Mexico: IANAS, 2013.

Johnson, Allen W., and Timothy Earle. *The Evolution of Human Societies: From Foraging Group to Agrarian State.* 2d ed. Stanford: Stanford University Press, 2000.

Kant, Immanuel. *Perpetual Peace: A Philosophical Essay.* Translated with introduction and notes by M. Campbell Smith. 3d ed. London: George Allen & Unwin Ltd., 1917.

Katzenstein, Peter, ed. *Civilizations in World Politics: Plural and Pluralist Perspectives.*
New York: Routledge, 2009.

Kaup, Brent Z. *Market Justice: Political Economic Struggle in Bolivia.* Cambridge: Cambridge University Press, 2013.

Kennedy, Paul. *The Rise and Fall of the Great Powers: Economic Change and Military Conflict from 1500 to 2000.* New York: Random House, 1987.

Kent, James. *Commentaries on American Law.* Vol. 3. 3d ed. New York: E. B. Clayton and James Van Norden, 1836.

Kidd, Michael, Tumai Murombo, and Alejandro Iza, eds. *Water and the Law: Towards Sustainability.* Cheltenham, UK: Edward Elgar, 2014.

Kjellén, Rudolf. *Der Staat als Lebensform.* Leipzig: S. Hirzel, 1917.

Kläger, Roland. *'Fair and Equitable Treatment' in International Investment Law.* New York: Cambridge University Press, 2011.

Klein, Herbert S. *A Concise History of Bolivia.* 2d ed. New York: Cambridge University Press, 2011.

Klinghoffer, Arthur Jay. *The Power of Projections: How Maps Reflect Global Politics and History.* Westport: Praeger Publishers, 2006.

Kluber, J. L. *Droit des Gens Moderne de L'Eruope.* Vol. 1. Stuttgart: J. G. Cotta, 1819.

Kohanski, Tamarah. *The Book of John Mandeville.* Tempe: Arizona Center for Medieval and Renaissance Studies, 2001.

Kolata, Alan L. *Ancient Inca: Case Studies in Early Societies.* New York: Cambridge University Press, 2013.

Koskenniemi, Martti. *Fragmentation of International Law: Difficulties Arising from the Diversification and Expansion of International Law.* Helsinki: Erik Castrén Institute of International Law, 2007.

Koskenniemi, Martti. *The Gentle Civilizer of Nations: The Rise and Fall of International Law 1870–1960.* Cambridge: Cambridge University Press, 2002.

Kosseleck, Reinhart. *Begriffsgeschichten.* Frankfurt am Main: Suhrkamp Verlag, 2006.

Kutzinski, Vera M., and Ottmar Ette, eds. *Alexander von Humboldt: Views of the Cordilleras and Monuments of the Indigenous Peoples of the Americas: A Critical Edition.* Translated by J. Ryan Poynter. Chicago: University of Chicago Press, 2012.

Lagos, Ricardo. *The Southern Tiger: Chile's Fight for a Democratic and Prosperous Future.* New York: Palgrave Macmillan, 2012.

Laity, Julie. *Deserts and Desert Environments.* Chichester: Wiley-Blackwell, 2008.

Lammers, J. G. *Pollution of International Watercourses: A Search for Substantive Rules and Principles of Law.* Boston: M. Nijhoff, 1984.

Lane, Kris. *Potosí: The Silver City that Changed the World.* Oakland: University of California Press, 2019.

Lang, Miriam, and Dunia Mokrani, eds. *Beyond Development: Alternative Visions from Latin America.* Quito, Ecuador: Fundacion Rosa Luxemburg, 2013.

Larrain Valdés, Gerardo. *Dios, Sol y Oro: Diego de Almagro y el descubrimiento de Chile.* Santiago de Chile: Editorial Andres Bello, 1987.

Latour, Bruno. *Facing Gaia: Eight Lectures on the New Climatic Regime.* Translated by Catherine Porter. Cambridge: Polity Press, 2017.

Leb, Christina. *Cooperation in the Law of Transboundary Water Resources.* Cambridge: Cambridge University Press, 2013.

Lefebvre, Henri. *The Production of Space.* Translated by Donald Nicholson-Smith. Cambridge: Blackwell, 1991.

Legg, Stephen, ed. *Spatiality, Sovereignty and Carl Schmitt: Geographies of the Nomos.* New York: Routledge, 2011.

Le Goff, Jacques. *Must We Divide History Into Periods?* Translated by M. B. DeBevoise. New York: Columbia University Press, 2015.

Leibnitz, Gottfried Wilhelm Freiherr von. *Discourse on Metaphysics and the Monadology.* Translated by George R. Montgomery. Mineola: Dover Publications, 2005.

Lenin, V. I. *Imperialism, the Highest Stage of Capitalism: A Popular Outline.* New York: International Publishers, 1939.

Letelier, Orlando. *Chile: Economic "Freedom" and Political Repression.* Washington, DC: Institute for Policy Studies, 1976.

Lister, Raymond. *Antique Maps and Their Cartographers.* Hamden: Archon Books, 1970.

Lloyd, Robert. *Spatial Cognition: Geographic Environments.* Boston: Kluwer Academic, 1997.

Lorenz, Chris, and Berber Bevernage, editors. *Breaking Up Time: Negotiating the Borders Between Present, Past and Future.* Göttingen, Germany: Vandenhoeck & Ruprecht, 2013.

Lovejoy, Arthur O. *The Great Chain of Being: A Study of the History of an Idea.* Cambridge: Harvard University Press, 1936

Lowe, Vaughan, and Malgosia Fitzmaurice, eds. *Fifty Years of the International Court of Justice.* Cambridge: Cambridge University Press, 1996.

Lucretius, *De Rerum Natura.* Translated by William Ellery Leonard. London: J. M. Dent, 1921.

Macdonald, Laura, and Arne Ruckert. *Post-Neoliberalism in the Americas.* London: Palgrave Macmillan, 2009.

Magsig, Bjørn-Oliver. *International Water Law and the Quest for Common Security*. New York: Routledge, Taylor & Francis Group, 2015.

Malanczuk, Peter. *Akehurst's Modern Introduction to International Law*. 7th rev. ed. New York: Routledge, 1997.

Mani, Kristina. *Democratization and Military Transformation in Argentina and Chile: Rethinking Rivaly*. Boulder, CO: First Forum Press, 2011.

Mares, David R. *Violent Peace: Militarized Interstate Bargaining in Latin America*. New York: Columbia University Press, 2001.

Mares, Michael A., ed. *Encyclopedia of Deserts*. Norman: University of Oklahoma Press, 1999.

Markham, Clements R. *The War Between Peru and Chile: 1879–1882*. London: Sampson Low. Marston, Searle & Rivington, 1882.

Marks, Michael P. *Metaphors in International Relations Theory*. New York: Palgrave Macmillan, 2011.

Marks, Michael P. *The Prison as Metaphor: Re-imagining International Relations*. New York: Peter Lang Publishing, 2004.

Martínez, Tomás, Enrique Lamadrid, and Jack Loeffler. *El Camino Real De Tierra Adentro*. Cuauhtémoc: Mundi-Prensa México, 2009.

Massey, Doreen. *For Space*. London: Sage Publications, 2005.

Masur, Gerhard. *Simon Bolivar*. Albuquerque: University of New Mexico Press, 1948.

Maus, Ingeborg. *Bürgerliche Rechtstheorie und Faschismus: Zur sozialen Funktion und aktuellen Wirkung der Theorie Carl Schmitt's*. Munich: Wilhelm Fink, 1980.

Mayo, John. *British Merchants and Chilean Development, 1851–1886*. Boulder: Westview, 1987.

Mayo, John, and Simon Collier. *Mining in Chile's Norte Chico: Journals of Charles Lambert, 1825–1830*. Oxford: Westview Press, 1998.

Mbembe, Achille. *On the Postcolony*. Berkeley: University of California Press, 2001.

McAlister, Lyle N. *Spain and Portugal in the New World: 1492–1700*. Minneapolis: University of Minnesota Press, 1984.

McCaffrey, Stephen C. *The Law of International Watercourses: Non-Navigational Uses*. New York: Oxford University Press, 2001.

Meagher, Arnold J. *The Coolie Trade: The Traffic in Chinese Laborers to Latin America 1847–1874*. Philadelphia: Xlibris, 2008.

Meccarelli, Massimo, and María Julia Solla Sastre, eds. *Spatial and Temporal Dimensions for Legal History: Research Experiences and Itineraries*. Vol. 6. Frankfurt Am Main: Max Planck Institute for European Legal History, 2016.

Mehring, Reinhard. *Carl Schmitt: A Biography*. Translated by Daniel Steuer. Cambridge: Polity Press, 2014.

Meierhenrich, Jens, and Oliver Simons, eds. *The Oxford Handbook of Carl Schmitt*. New York: Oxford University Press, 2017.

Meller, Patricio. *The Unidad Popular and the Pinochet Dictatorship: A Political Economy Analysis.* Translated by Tim Ennis. New York: St. Martin's Press, 2000.

Mellor, Roy E. H. *Nation, State, and Territory.* New York: Routledge, 1989.

Michaels, Walter Benn. *The Trouble with Diversity: How We Learned to Love Identity and Ignore Inequality.* New York: Metropolitan Books, 2006.

Mignolo, Walter D. *Local Histories/Global Designs: Coloniality, Subaltern Knowledges, and Border Thinking.* Princeton: Princeton University Press, 2000.

Miller, Russell A., and Rebecca M. Bratspies, eds. *Progress in International Law.* Leiden: Martinus Nijhoff Publishers, 2008.

Mirowski, Philip, and Dieter Plehwe. *The Road from Mont Pèlerin: The Making of the Neoliberal Thought Collective.* Cambridge: Harvard University Press, 2009.

Moll, Herman. *A System of Geography: or, a New Accurate Description of the Earth In all its Empires, Kingdoms and States.* London: Timothy Childe at the White Hart at the West-end of St. Paul's Church-yard, 1701.

Moll, Herman. *A view of the Coasts, Countries and Islands Within the Limits of the South-Sea-Company. Containing An Account of the Discoveries, Settlements, Progress and Present State; together with the Bays, Ports, Harbours, Rivers, &c. The Various Winds and Soundings; the Products, People, Manufacturers, Trade and Riches of the several Places: viz. From the River Aranoca to Terra del Fuego, and from thence through the South Sea to the farthest Bounds of the late Act of Parliament. To which is added, An Account of Former Projects in England for a Settlement, and the Accomplishment of the Last in the Establishing the New Company; with a List of the Commissioners Names appointed by Her Majesty to take the Subscriptions. As also some Useful Observations on the several Voyages that have been hitherto Publish'd. The Whole Collected from the best Authors, as well.* London: Printed for J. Morphew, 1711.

Morales, Waltraud Q. *Bolivia: Land of Struggle.* Boulder: Westview Press, 1992.

Morales, Waltraud Q. *A Brief History of Bolivia.* 2d ed. New York: Facts on File, 2010.

Morgenthau, Hans. *Politics among Nations: The Struggle for Power and Peace.* 6th rev. ed. New York: Knopf, 1985.

Müller, Jan-Werner. *A Dangerous Mind: Carl Schmitt in Post-War European Thought.* London: Yale University Press, 2003.

Mussey, Orville D. *Water Requirements of the Copper Industry.* Washington, DC: United States Government Printing Office, 1961.

Nacif, Federico, and Miguel Lacabana. *ABC del litio sudamericano: Soberanía, ambiente, tecnología e industria.* Buenos Aires: Centro Cultural de la Cooperación Floreal Gorini Bernal, 2015.

Nelson, Cary, and Lawrence Grossberg, eds. *Marxism and the Interpretation of Culture.* London: Macmillan, 1988.

Neumann, Iver B. *Concepts of International Relations, for Students and Other Smarties.* Ann Arbor: University of Michigan Press, 2019.

Newton, Isaac. *Principia: The Mathematical Principles of Natural Philosophy.* Translated by Andrew Motte. New York: Daniel Adee, 1846.

Nicholsen, Shierry Weber, ed. *The New Conservatism: Cultural Criticism and the Historians' Debate.* Cambridge: MIT Press,1989.

Northcott, Michael S. *A Political Theology of Climate Change.* Grand Rapids: William B. Eerdmans Publishing Company, 2013.

O'Brien, Philip, and Jacqueline Roddick. *Chile: The Pinochet Decade: The Rise and Fall of the Chicago Boys.* London: Latin America Bureau, 1983.

Ocampo, José Antonio, and Juan Martin, eds. *A Decade of Light and Shadow: Latin America and the Caribbean in the 1990s.* Santiago: Economic Commission for Latin America and the Caribbean, 2003.

Olson, James S. *The Indians of Central and South America: An Ethnohistorical Dictionary.* New York: Greenwood Press, 1991.

Onuf, Nicholas. *The Mightie Frame: Epochal Change and the Modern World. Oxford:* Oxford University Press, 2018.

Orakhelashvili, Alexander, ed. *Research Handbook on the Theory and History of International Law.* Cheltenham: Edward Elgar, 2011.

Orford, Anne, ed. *International Law and Its Others.* Cambridge: Cambridge University Press, 2006.

Orford, Anne, and Florian Hoffmann (with Martin Clark). *The Oxford Handbook of the Theory of International Law.* Oxford: Oxford University Press, 2016.

Osgood, Robert E., and Robert W. Tucker. *Force, Order, and Justice.* Baltimore: Johns Hopkins Press, 1967.

Otto, Dianne, ed. *Queering International Law: Possibilities, Alliances, Complicities, Risks.* Basingstoke: Taylor & Francis, 2017.

Oviedo, José Miguel. *La Edad del Oro.* Barcelona: Tusquets, 1986.

Pahuja, Sundhya. *Decolonising International Law: Development, Economic Growth and the Politics of Universality.* Cambridge: Cambridge University Press, 2011.

Paredes, Julian de. *Recopilación de leyes de los reynos de las indias.* Libro II. Título 15. Madrid: Julian de Paredes, 1681.

Parodi, Carlos A. *The Politics of South American Boundaries.* Westport: Praeger, 2002.

Pereira, Anthony W. *Political (In)Justice, Authoritarianism and the Rule of Law in Brazil, Chile, and Argentina.* Pittsburgh: University of Pittsburgh Press, 2005.

Peuquet, Donna J. *Representations of Time and Space.* New York: Guilford Press, 2002.

Phillimore, Robert. *Commentaries Upon International Law.* 3d edition. London: Butterworths, 1879.

Phillips, Mark Salber. *On Historical Distance.* New Haven: Yale University Press, 2013.

Pochat, Victor. *Water Agenda for South America: Challenges, Vision and Strategy.* Caracas: CAF, 2015.

Pocock, J. G. A. *The Machiavellian Moment: Florentine Political Thought and the Atlantic Republican Tradition.* Princeton: Princeton University Press, 1975.

Polanyi, Karl. *The Great Transformation.* New York: Farrar & Rinehart, 1944.

Pollock, Sir Frederick. *Torts.* 11th ed. London: Stevens and Sons, 1920.

Portugali, Juval, ed. *The Construction of Cognitive Maps.* Boston: Kluwer Academic Publishers, 1996.

Prescott, H. F. M. *Once to Sinai: The Further Pilgrimage of Friar Felix Fabri.* London: Eyre & Spottiswood, 1957.

Prescott, Victor, and Gillian D. Triggs. *International Frontiers and Boundaries: Law, Politics and Geography.* Leiden: Martinus Nijhoff Publishers, 2008.

Preston, Douglas, and José Antonio Esquibel, eds. *The Royal Road: El Camino Real from Mexico City to Santa Fe.* Albuquerque: University of New Mexico Press, 1998.

Purchas, Samuel. *Hakluytus Posthumus, or Purchas his Pilgrimes, Contayning a History of the World, in Sea Voyages & Lande Travels, by Englishmen and others.* London: by W. Stansby for H. Fetherstone, 1625.

Radding, Cynthia. *Wandering Peoples: Colonialism, Ethnic Spaces, and Ecological Frontiers in Northwestern Mexico, 1700–1850.* Durham: Duke University Press, 1997.

Rasilla del Moral, Ignacio de la, and Ayesha Shahid, eds. *International Law and Islam: Historical Explorations.* Leiden: Brill Nijhoff, 2018.

Ratzel, Friedrich. *Politische Geographie.* Munich: R. Oldenbourg, 1897.

Reid, Michael. *Forgotten Continent: A History of the New Latin America.* New Haven: Yale University Press, 2017.

Remini, Robert V. *Henry Clay: Stateman for the Union.* New York: W. W. Norton, 1991.

Retamal Salazar, Jaime. *Nos siguen pegando abajo: Jaime Guzmán, dictadura, concertación y alianza: 40 años de educación de Mercado.* Santiago: Ceibo, 2013.

Rippy, J. Fred. *British Investments in Latin America, 1822–1949: A Case Study in Operations of Private Enterprise in Retarded Regions.* Hamden: Archon Books, 1966.

Ritter, Carl. *Die Erdkunde im Verhältnis zur Natur und zur Geschichte des Menschen.* Berlin: G. Reimer, 1817.

Ritzer, George, ed. *Blackwell Encyclopedia of Sociology.* New York: Wiley-Blackwell, 2007.

Rivero, Mariano Edward, and John James von Tschudi. *Peruvian Antiquities.* Translated by Francis L. Hawks. New York: Putnam, 1853.

Roberts, Anthea. *Is International Law International?* New York: Oxford University Press, 2017.

Rodríguez, Jeanette, and Ted Fortier. *Cultural Memory: Resistance, Faith, and Identity.* Austin: University of Texas Press, 2007.

Rogers, Captain Woodes. *A cruising voyage round the world: first to the South-Sea, thence to the East-Indies, and homewards by the Cape of Good Hope. Begun in 1708, and finish'd in 1711. Containing a journal of all the remarkable Transactions; particularly of the taking of Puna and Guiaquil, of the Acapulca Ship, and other Prizes: An Account of Alexander Selkirk's living alone four Years and four Months in an Island: and a brief Description of several Countries in our Course noted for Trade, especially in the South-Sea. With Maps of all the Coast, from the best Spanish Manuscript Draughts.* 2d ed. corrected. London: Bernard Lintot and Edward Symon, 1726.

Roniger, Luis, and Mario Sznajder. *The Legacy of Human-Rights Violations in the Southern Cone: Argentina, Chile, and Uruguay.* Oxford: Oxford University Press, 1999.

Rosenmüller, Christoph. *Corruption and Justice in Colonial Mexico, 1650–1755.* Cambridge: Cambridge University Press, 2019.

Ross, Elizabeth. *Picturing Experience in the Early Printed Book: Breydenbach's Peregrinatio from Venice to Jerusalem.* University Park: Pennsylvania State University Press, 2014.

Rossi, Christopher R. *Equity and International Law: A Legal Realist Approach to International Decisionmaking.* Irvington: Transnational Publishers, 1993.

Rossi, Christopher R. *Sovereignty and Territorial Temptation: The Grotian Tendency.* Cambridge: Cambridge University Press, 2017.

Rossi, Christopher R. *Whiggish International Law: Elihu Root, The Monroe Doctrine, and International Law in the Americas.* Boston: Brill Nijhoff, 2019.

Ruschenberger, W. S. W. *Three Years in the Pacific: including Notices of Brazil, Chile, Bolivia, and Peru.* Philadelphia: Carey, Lea & Blanchard, 1834.

Saavedra, Bautista. *El Ayllu. La Paz:* Imp. artística, Velarde, Aldazosa y ca., 1903.

Sánchez, Gervasio. *La caravan de la muerte: Las vítimas de Pinochet.* Barcelona: Barcelona Press, 2001.

Sánchez, Marco A. Flores. *Crónica: El Incidente de Talambo.* Chepén: Perú, 2006.

Sardar, Zain. "The Horizon of International Law: Earth-Thinking, Ordering and Disciplinary International Law in the Colonial/Modern World-System" PhD dissertation, Birkbeck: University of London, 2018.

Sassen, Saskia. *Losing Control? Sovereignty in the Age of Globalization.* New York: Columbia University Press, 1996.

Sater, William F. *Andean Tragedy: Fighting the War of the Pacific, 1879–1884.* Lincoln: University of Nebraska Press, 2007.

Sater, William F. *Chile and the War of the Pacific.* Lincoln: University of Nebraska Press, 1986.

Saunders, Stephen. *IHS Jane's Fighting Ships 2014–2015.* 116th rev. ed. London: Jane's Information Group, 2014.

Sawyer, Suzana, and Edmund Terence Gomez, eds. *The Politics of Resource Extraction: Indigenous Peoples, Multinational Corporations, and the State.* New

York: Palgrave Macmillan: United Nations Research Institute for Social Development, 2012.

Scarfi, Juan Pablo. *The Hidden History of International Law in the Americas: Empire and Legal Networks.* Oxford: Oxford University Press, 2017.

Scheuerman, William E. *Carl Schmitt: The End of Law.* Lanham: Rowman & Littlefield, 1999.

Schmitt, Carl. *The Concept of the Political.* Chicago: University of Chicago Press, 2007.

Schmitt, Carl. *Constitutional Theory.* Translated by Jeffrey Seitzer. Durham: Duke University Press, 2008.

Schmitt, Carl. *The Leviathan in the State Theory of Thomas Hobbes: Meaning and Failure of a Political Symbol,* 1938. Translated by George Schwab and Erna Hilfstein. Chicago: University of Chicago Press, 2008.

Schmitt, Carl. *Nomos of the Earth and the International Law of the Jus Publicum Europaeum.* Translated by G. L. Ulman. New York: Telos Press, 2006.

Schmitt, Carl. *Political Theology: Four Chapters on the Concept of Sovereignty.* Translated by George Schwab. Chicago: University of Chicago Press, 2005.

Schmitt, Carl. Völkerrechtlische Grossraumordnung mit Interventionsverbot für Raumfremde Mächte: ein Beitrag zum Reichsbegriff im Völkerrecht. Berlin: Duncker & Humblot, 1939.

Schmitt, Michael N., editor. *International Law Across the Spectrum of Conflict: Essays in Honor of Professor L. C. Green on the Occasion of His Eightieth Birthday.* Newport: Naval War College, 2000.

Schrijver, Nico. *Sovereignty Over Natural Resources: Balancing Rights and Duties.* New York: Cambridge University Press, 1997.

Scott, James C. *The Art of Not Being Governed: An Anarchist History of Upland Southeast Asia.* New Haven: Yale University Press 2009.

Scott, James. *Seeing Like a State: How Certain Schemes to Improve the Human Condition Have Failed.* New Haven: Yale University Press, 1998.

Seaman, Rebecca M., ed. *Conflict in the Early Americas: An Encyclopedia of the Spanish Empire's Aztec, Incan, and Mayan Conquests.* Santa Barbara: ABC-CLIO, 2013.

Secondi, Giorgio. *The Development Economics Reader.* New York: Routledge, 2008.

Sexton, Jay. *The Monroe Doctrine: Empire and Nation in Nineteenth-Century America.* New York: Hill and Wang, 2011.

Seymour, Michael, ed. *Mandeville's Travels.* Oxford: Clarendon Press, 1967.

Short, John Rennie. *The World Through Maps: A History of Cartography.* Toronto: Firefly Books, 2003.

Singh, Prabhakar, and Benoît Mayer. *Critical International Law: Postrealism, Postcolonialism, and Transnationalism.* New Delhi: Oxford University Press, 2014.

Skuban, William E. *Lines in the Sand: Nationalism and Identity on the Peruvian-Chilean Frontier.* Albuquerque: University of New Mexico Press, 2007.

Sobel, Dava. *Longitude: The True Story of a Lone Genius Who Solved the Greatest Scientific Problem of His Time.* New York: Walker, 1995.

Sokolow, Jayme A. *The Great Encounter: Native Peoples and European Settlers in the Americas, 1492–1800.* Armonk: M. E. Sharpe, 2003.

Solimano, Andrés. *Chile and the Neoliberal Trap: The Post-Pinochet Era.* New York: Cambridge University Press, 2012.

Speakes, Jennifer, ed. *Literature of Travel and Exploration: An Encyclopedia. Vol. 1, A to F.* New York: Fitzroy Dearborn, 2003.

Spero, Joan Edelman, and Jeffrey A. Hart. *The Politics of International Economic Relations.* 5th ed. New York: St. Martin's Press, 2013.

Stirling, Stuart. *Pizarro, Conqueror of the Inca.* Stroud: Sutton Pub., 2005.

St. John, Ronald Bruce. *The Bolivia-Chile-Peru Dispute in the Atacama Desert.* International Boundaries Research Unit. Durham: United Kingdom, 1994.

St. John, Ronald Bruce. *Boundaries, Trade, and Seaports: Power Politics in the Atacama Desert.* Amherst: Latin American Studies Program, University of Massachusetts at Amherst, 1992.

Stoddart, David Ross. *On Geography and Its History.* New York: B. Blackwell, 1986.

Sumption, Jonathan. *The Age of Pilgrimage: The Medieval Journey to God.* Mahwah: HiddenSpring, 2003.

Sundaram, Jomo Kwame, editor. *Globalization Under Hegemony: The Changing World Economy.* New York: Oxford University Press, 2006.

Talbott, Robert D. *A History of the Chilean Boundaries.* Ames: Iowa State University Press, 1974.

Tanzi, Attila, and Maurizio Arcari. *The United Nations Convention on the Law of International Watercourses: A Framework for Sharing.* Boston: Kluwer Law International, 2001.

Tauber, Alfred I., ed. *The Elusive Synthesis: Aesthetics and Science.* Boston: Kluwer, 1996.

Taylor, Diana, and Sarah J. Townsend, eds. *Stages of Conflict: A Critical Anthology of Latin American Theater and Performance.* Ann Arbor: University of Michigan Press, 2008.

Taylor, Marcus. *From Pinochet to the "Third Way": Neoliberalism and Social Transformation in Chile.* London: Pluto Press, 2006.

Telles, Edward. *Pigmentocracies: Ethnicity, Race, and Color in Latin America.* Chapel Hill: University of North Carolina Press, 2014.

Teschke, Benno. *The Myth of 1648: Class, Geopolitics and the Making of Modern International Relations.* New York: Verso, 2003.

Townsend, Camilla. *Fifth Sun: A New History of the Aztecs.* New York: Oxford University Press, 2019.

Tschudi, Johann Jakob von. *Travels in Peru, During the Years 1838–1842, on the coast, in the sierra, across the cordilleras and the Andes, into the primeval forests.* New York: Wiley & Putnam, 1847.

Tuan, Yi-Fu. *Space and Place: The Perspective of Experience.* Minneapolis: University of Minnesota Press, 1977.

Tuan, Yi-Fu. *Topophilia: A Study of Environmental Perception, Attitudes and Values.* New York: Columbia University Press, 1990.

Ulloa, Antonio de. *A Voyage to South America. Describing at large, the Spanish cities, towns, provinces, &c. on that extensive Continent. Interspersed throughout . . .* Vol. 2. London: L. Davis and C. Reymers, 1760.

United Nations Trade and Development. Bilateral Investment Treaties 1995–2006: Trends in Investment Rulemaking. Switzerland: United Nations, 2007.

Urteaga, Patricia, and Rutgerd Boelens, eds. *Derechos colectivos y políticas hídricas en la region andina.* Lima: Walir/IEP, 2006.

Valdés, Juan Gabriel. *Pinochet's Economists: The Chicago School in Chile.* Cambridge: Cambridge University Press, 1995.

Vale, Brian. *A War Betwixt Englishmen: Brazil Against Argentina on the River Plate 1825–1830.* London: I. B. Tauris, 2000.

Van Cott, Donna Lee. *From Movements to Parties in Latin America: The Evolution of Ethnic Politics.* New York: Cambridge University Press, 2005.

Van Duzer, Chet. *Sea Monsters on Medieval and Renaissance Maps.* London: British Library, 2013.

Van Duzer, Chet, and Ilya Dines. *Apocalyptic Cartography: Thematic Maps and the End of the World in a Fifteenth-Century Manuscript.* Boston: Brill/Hes & De Graaf, 2015.

Van Overtveldt, Johan. *The Chicago School: How the University of Chicago Assembled the Thinkers Who Revolutionized Economics and Business.* Chicago: Agate Publishing, 2008.

Varela Marcos, Jesús. *El Tratado de Tordesillas en la política atlántica castellana.* Valladolid: Universidad de Valladolid, 1997.

Vega, Garcilaso de la. *El Inca, Royal Commentaries of the Incas and General History of Peru. Part* 2. Translated by Harold V. Livermore. Austin: University of Texas Press, 1966.

Verdugo, Patricia. *Chile, Pinochet, and the Caravan of Death.* Coral Gables: North-South Center Press, 2001.

Vespucci, Amerigo. *Mundus Novus: Letter to Lorenzo Pietro di Medici.* Translated by George Tyler Northrup. Princeton: Princeton University Press, 1916.

Vespucci, Giocondo. *Mundus Novus: Ein Bericht Amerigo Vespucci's an Lorenzo de Medici über seine Reise nach Brasilien in den Jahren 1501/1502.* Strassburg: J. H. E. Heitz (Heitz & Mündel), 1903.

Vitányi, Bela. *The International Regime of River Navigation.* Alphen aan den Rijn: Sijthoff & Noordhoff, 1980.

Waldseemüller, Martin. *Universalis cosmographia secundum Ptholomaei traditionem et Americi Vespucii alioru[m]que lustrationes*, Strasbourg, France [?] 1507.

Walker, R. B. J. *Inside/Outside: International Relations as Political Theory*. New York: Cambridge University Press, 1993.

Wallerstein, Immanuel. *The Modern World-System. Vol. Capitalist Agriculture and the Origins of the European World-Economy in the Sixteenth Century*. New York: Academic Press, 1974.

Walther, Paulus. *Fratris Pauli Waltheri von Guglingen Guglingensis Itinerarium in Terram Sanctam et ad Sanctam Catharinam (Herausgegeben und mit erläuterungen versehen von Matthias Sollweck)*. Tübingen: Litterarischer verein in Stuttgart, 1892.

Waltz, Kenneth. *Man, the State, and War*. New York: Columbia University Press, 1959.

Washburn, Emory. *A Treatise on the American Law of Easements and Servitudes*. 3d ed. Boston: Little Brown, 1873.

Waterfield, Robin, ed. *Plato: Timaeus and Critias*. New York: Oxford University Press, 2008.

Watson, Robert Grant. *Spanish and Portuguese South America During the Colonial Period*. Vol. 1. London: Trübner & Co, 1884.

Weber, Cynthia. *Queer International Relations: Sovereignty, Sexuality, and the Will to Knowledge*. New York: Oxford University Press, 2016.

Werlich, David P. *Peru: A Short History*. Carbondale: Southern Illinois University Press, 1978.

Wertheim, Eric. *The Naval Institute Guide to Combat Fleets of the World, Their Ships, Aircraft, and Systems*.16th ed. Annapolis: Naval Institute Press, 2013.

Wheaton, Henry. *Elements of International Law: With A Sketch of the History of the Science*. Philadelphia: Carey, Lea & Blanchard, 1836.

Whiteley, John M., Helen Ingram, and Richard Warren Perry. *Water, Place, & Equity*. Cambridge: MIT Press, 2008.

Williamson, John, ed. *Latin American Adjustment: How Much Has Happened?* Washington, DC: Institute for International Economics, 1990.

Wittgenstein, Ludwig. *Tractatus Logico-Philosophicus*. With an introduction by Bertrand Russell. London: Kegal Paul, Trench, Trubner & Co., 1922.

Wolff, Hans, ed. *America: Early Maps of the New World*. Munich: Prestel, 1992.

Wood, Denis, and John Fels. *The Power of Maps*. New York: Guilford Press, 1992.

Woodward, David, ed. *History of Cartography. Vol. 3 (Part 1), Cartography in the European Renaissance*. Chicago: University of Chicago Press, 2007.

Wootton, David, ed. *John Locke, Political Writings*. Indianapolis, Cambridge: Hackett Publishing Company, 1993.

Wytfliet, Cornelius. *Ptolemaicae Augmentum*. Lovenii, 1597.

Xiamen Academy of International Law. *Collected Courses of the Xiamen Academy of International Law*. Vol. III. Boston: Martinus Nijhoff Publishers, 2011.

Xing, Li, ed. *The BRICS and Beyond: The International Political Economy of the Emergence of a New World Order*. Farnham: Ashgate, 2014.

Yergin, Daniel, and Joseph Stanislaw. *The Commanding Heights: The Battle Between Government and the Marketplace That Is Remaking the Modern World.* New York: Simon & Schuster, 1998.

Zeebout, Ambrosius. *Tvoyage van Mher Joos van Ghistele.* Edited by R. J. G. A. A. Gaspar. Verloren: Hilversum, 1998.

Zerubavel, Eviatar. *Terra Cognita: The Mental Discovery of America.* New Brunswick: Rutgers University Press: 1992.

Zuazo, Moira, Jean-Paul Faguet, and Gustavo Bonifaz. *Descentralización y democratización en Bolivia: La historia del Estado débil, la sociedad rebelled y el anhelo de democracia.* La Paz, Bolivia: Friedrich Ebert Stiftung, 2012.

Name Index

Subject Index

Printed and bound by CPI Group (UK) Ltd, Croydon, CR0 4YY
20/08/2025
14722214-0002